Besant's History of London

The Tudors

Titles available from The Village Press are:-

The London Library:

Hardback
Village London Volume I
Village London Volume II
London Recollected Volume I
London Recollected Volume II
London Recollected Volume III
London Recollected Volume IV
London Recollected Volume V
London Recollected Volume VI
Village London Atlas
Besant's History of London - The Tudors

Paperback
Village London Pt. 1 West and North
Village London Pt. 2 North and East
Village London Pt. 3 South-East
Village London Pt. 4 South-West
Village London Atlas
Old Fleet Street
Cheapside and St. Paul's
The Tower and East End
Shoreditch to Smithfield
Charterhouse to Holborn
Strand to Soho
Covent Garden and the Thames to Whitehall
Westminster to St. James's
Haymarket to Mayfair
Hyde Park to Bloomsbury
Belgravia, Chelsea and Kensington
Paddington Green to Seven Sisters
Highgate & Hampstead to the Lea
(The above thirteen titles are extracts from the hardback edition of London Recollected.)

Other titles published are:

The Village Atlas - Birmingham and The West Midlands
The Village Atlas - Manchester, Lancashire & North Cheshire

QUEEN ELIZABETH (1533-1603)

From the painting by Gerard at Burleigh House.

Besant's History of London

The Tudors

The Village Press

First published in 1904 by Adam & Charles Black
under the title *London in the Time of the Tudors*.

This edition published November 1989
by The Village Press Limited,
7d, Keats Parade, Church Street, London N9 9DP.

British Library Cataloguing in Publication Data
Besant, Walter, *1836-1901*
  Besant's history of London, the Tudors.
  I. Title   II. Besant, Walter, *1836-1901* : Survey of London

ISBN 1-85540-001-4

Printed and bound in Great Britain by
Redwood Burn Ltd, Trowbridge, Wiltshire.

CONTENTS

TUDOR SOVEREIGNS

LONDON IN THE TIME OF THE TUDORS

ILLUSTRATIONS

LONDON IN THE TIME OF THE TUDORS

ILLUSTRATIONS

LONDON IN THE TIME OF THE TUDORS

TUDOR SOVEREIGNS

CHAPTER I

HENRY VII

On stepping out of the fifteenth into the sixteenth century one becomes conscious of a change; no such change was felt in passing from the twelfth to the thirteenth century, or from the fourteenth to the fifteenth. The world of Henry the Sixth was

HENRY VII. (1457-1509)
From the painting in the National Portrait Gallery, London.

the same world as that of Edward the First; it was also the same as that of Henry the Second. For four hundred years no sudden, perceptible, or radical change took place either in manners and customs, language, arts, or ideas. There had, of course, been outbreaks; there had been passionate longings for change; men before their

3

time, like Wyclyf, had advanced new ideas which sprang up like grass and presently withered away; there had been changes in religious thought, but there was no change, so far, in religious institutions. At the beginning of the sixteenth century, however, we who know the coming events can see the change impending, change already begun. Whether the Bishops and Clergy, the Monks and Friars, were also conscious of impending change, I know not. It seems as if they must have been uneasy, as in France men were uneasy long before the Revolution. On the other hand, Rome still loomed large in the imagination of the world: the Rock on which the Church was established; the Throne from which there was no appeal; the hand that held the Keys. We have now, however, to chronicle the part, the large part, played by London in this great century of Revolution.

After forty years of Civil War,—with murders, exactions, executions, treacheries, and perjuries innumerable, with the ruin of trade, with the extinction of ancient families, with the loss of all the French conquests,—the City, no less than the country at large, welcomed the accession of a Prince who promised order and tranquillity at least. Of all the numerous descendants of Edward the Third who might once have called themselves heirs to the Crown before the Duke of Richmond, there remained but two or three. Of the Lancastrians Henry alone was left, and his title was derived from a branch legitimised. The two brothers of Henry V. had no children; the only son of Henry VI. was dead. On the Yorkist side Edward's two sons were dead; Richard's only son was dead; there remained the young Earl of Warwick, son of Clarence. He was the one dangerous person at the time of Henry's accession. Edward Plantagenet, Earl of Warwick, was not the heir to the Yorkist claims—this was certainly the eldest daughter of Edward the Fourth; but he was the son of George, Duke of Clarence, and the last male descendant of the York line. He was now fifteen years of age, and had been kept in some kind of confinement at a place called Sheriff Hutton Castle, in the County of York. Considering the practice of the time, and the reputation of Richard III., one wonders at his forbearance in not murdering the boy. Henry sent him—it was his first act after his victory –to the Tower for better safety. Grafton[1] calls this unfortunate Prince "the yongling borne to perpetual captivitie." He is said to have been a simple youth, wholly ignorant of the world. Though, as we shall see later on, Henry found it expedient to treat this young Prince after the manner of his time. A dead Prince can never become a Pretender.

And no other fate was possible in the long-run for one whom conspirators might put up at any moment as the rightful claimant of the Crown. The unfortunate youth was only one of a long chain of possible claimants, all of whom paid the penalty of their inheritance by death. Among them were Edward's infant Princes; his own

---

[1] Richard Grafton, Chronicler, born *circa* 1572.

father; Henry's son, Edward, Prince of Wales; and later on Lady Jane Grey, and Mary Queen of Scots.

In the same castle of Sheriff Hutton, in similar confinement, was the Lady Elizabeth, Edward the Fourth's elder daughter, whom Richard proposed to marry with the sanction of the Pope, his own wife, Anne, having strangely and mysteriously come to her death. Bosworth Field put a stop to that monstrous design. According to Grafton, the purpose of Richard was well known to the world, and was everywhere detested and condemned.

Henry rode to London immediately after his victory. At Shoreditch he was received by the Mayor, Sheriffs, and Aldermen, clothed in violet and bearing a gift of a thousand marks. He then went on to St. Paul's and there deposited three standards—on one was the image of St. George, on another a "red fierie dragon beaten upon white and greene sarcenet," and on the third was painted "a dun cow upon yellow *tarterne*." He also heard a Te Deum.

Four weeks after Henry's entrance into the City there broke out, quite suddenly, with no previous warning, a most deadly pestilence known as the sweating sickness. This dreadful epidemic began with a "burning sweat that invaded the body and vexed the blood, and with a most ardent heat infested the stomach and the head grievously." If any person could bear the heat and pain for twenty-four hours, he recovered, but might have a relapse; not one in a hundred, however, of those that took the infection survived. Within a few days it killed two Mayors, namely, Sir Thomas Hill and Sir William Stocker; and six Aldermen. The sickness seems to have been swifter, and more deadly while it lasted, than even the Plague or the Epidemic of 1349. But it went away after a time as quickly as it had appeared.

Henry's coronation was celebrated on the 13th of October. His predecessor had disguised the weakness of his title by the splendour of his coronation. Henry, on the other hand, made but a mean display—perhaps to show that he was not dependent on show or magnificence. Stanley perceives in this absence of ostentation a kind of acknowledgment that his title to the Crown rested more upon his victory than his descent. This opinion seems to me wholly fanciful; Henry would never at any moment acknowledge that his title was weak. On the other hand, he stoutly claimed, through his mother, to be the nearest heir in the Lancastrian line. His known dislike to ostentation is quite a sufficient reason to account for the comparative poverty of the Coronation show—at which, however, one new feature was introduced, namely, the bodyguard of the King's person, known as the Yeomen of the Guard. The King's belief in the strength of his own title was shown in his treatment of the Lady Elizabeth. He had solemnly promised to marry her; he did so in January 1486, five months after his victory; but he was extremely loth to crown her, lest some should say that the Queen was Queen by right, and not merely the Queen consort. The coronation of the Queen was postponed for two years.   The celebration, however, when it did take place, was accompanied by a great deal of splendour.

The business of Lambert Simnel shows the real peril of the King's position. The experience of the last forty years had taught the people a most dangerous habit. They were ready to fly to arms on the smallest provocation.   Who was Henry, " the unknown Welshman," as Richard called him, that he should be allowed to sit in peace upon a throne from which three occupants had been dragged down, two by murder and one by battle?   But the occasion of the rising was ridiculous.   The young Earl of Warwick was in the Tower; it was possible to see him—Henry, in fact, made him ride through the City for all the world to see.   Yet the followers of Lambert Simnel proclaimed that he was Edward Plantagenet, Earl of Warwick. Lambert's father was a joiner of Oxford; Sir Richard Symon, a priest, was his tutor.   The boy, who in 1486 was about eleven years of age, was of handsome appearance and of naturally good manners.

After the defeat of his cause, Lambert and the priest who had done the mischief were taken.   The priest was consigned to an ecclesiastical prison for the rest of his natural life; the boy was pardoned—they could not execute a child—and contemptuously thrust into the King's kitchen as a little scullion.   He afterwards rose to be one of the King's falconers—the only example in history of a Pretender turning out an honest man in the end.   Can we not see the people about the Court gazing curiously upon the handsome scullion in his white jacket, white cap, and white shoes, going to and fro upon his duties, washing pans with zeal and scraping trenchers? The boy had a lovely face, and manners very far beyond his station.   Can we not hear them whispering that this young man had once been as good as King, and knew what it was to exercise royal authority?

The Earl of Warwick was still, however, allowed to live.

The King, who was magnanimous when it was politic, could also exhibit the opposite quality on occasion.   He had never found it easy to forgive Edward's Queen for submitting herself and her daughters to Richard after she had consented to Henry's attempt upon the Crown, on the condition of his marrying the eldest. He laid the matter before his Council, who determined that Elizabeth, late Queen, should forfeit all her lands and possessions, and should continue for the rest of her life in honourable confinement in the Abbey of Bermondsey.   Here, in fact, she died, not long afterwards, the second Queen who breathed her last in that House.

One Pretender removed, another arose.   Perkin Warbeck professed, as we know, to be the younger son of Edward IV., namely, Richard, Duke of York, who, it was pretended, had escaped from the Tower.   The strange adventures of Perkin are told in every history of England.   He is connected with that of London on three occasions. The first was after his abortive attempt to land in Kent.   The Kentish men, refusing to join him, attacked his followers, drove some of them back to their ships, and took prisoners a hundred and sixty men with four Captains. These prisoners were all brought to London roped together, a curious sight to see. Those who lived on London Bridge saw many strange sights, but seldom anything more strange than these poor prisoners, who were not Englishmen but aliens, thus tied together. They were all hanged, every one : some on the seashore, where their bodies might warn other aliens not to come filibustering into England ; and the rest at Tyburn.

The Cornish Rebellion was an episode in the history of the Perkin Warbeck

PERKIN WARBECK (1474-1499)
From a drawing in the Municipal Library, Arras.

business. The men of Cornwall refused to pay taxes and resolved to march upon London. Led by Lord Audley they advanced through Salisbury and Winchester into Kent : they were there opposed, and moved towards London, finally lying at Blackheath. The battle that followed was chiefly fought at the bridge at Deptford Strand. Two thousand of the rebels were killed ; fifteen hundred were taken ; Lord Audley was beheaded ; two demagogues who had instigated the rising, namely, Flammock an attorney, and Joseph a farrier, were hanged ; the rest were not pursued or punished.

The City, meantime, showed its loyalty by a loan of £4000 to the King and

by putting London into a state of defence.   Six Aldermen and a number of repre-
sentatives from the Livery Companies were deputed to attend to the City ordnance ;
houses built close to the wall were taken down ; the Mayor was allowed an additional
twelve men, and the Sheriffs forty serjeants and forty valets to keep the peace.

Among those appointed to guard the City gates was Alderman Fabyan the
Chronicler.

The next episode in Perkin's career which touches London is that ride which he
undertook, very much against his will, from Westminster to the Tower.   Everybody
knows how he gave himself up to the Prior of Shene.   The King granted him his
life, but he imposed certain conditions.   He was placed in the stocks opposite the
entrance to Westminster Hall, where he sat the whole day long, receiving "innumerable reproaches, mocks and scornings."   The day after he was carried through
London on horseback, in sham triumph.   They were ingenious in those days in their
methods of putting offenders to open shame.   At an earlier date the traitor Turberville had to ride in shameful guise ; and when Lord Audley, Captain of the Cornish
Rebels, was led out to execution, he was attired in a paper robe painted with his arms,
the robe being slashed and torn.   No doubt Perkin was handsomely attired in
coloured paper, with a tinsel crown upon his head ; no doubt, too, he bestrode a
villainous hack, while all the 'prentices of London ran after him, laughing and
mocking.   They placed him on a scaffold by the Standard in Chepe and kept him
there all day long.   In the course of the day he read aloud his own confession,
which is a very curious document.

" First it is to be knowne, that I was borne in the towne of Turneie in Flanders, and my father's name
is John Osbecke, which said John Osbecke was controller of the said towne of Turneie, and my moother's
name is Katherine de Faro . . . againste my will they made me to learn Englishe and taught me what I
shoulde do or say.   And after this they called me Duke of Yorke. . . . And upon this the said Water,
Stephen Poitron, John Tiler, Hubert Burgh, with manie others, as the aforesaid earles, entered into this
false quarrell.   And within short time after the French king sent an ambassador into Ireland, whose
name was Loit Lucas, and maister Stephen Friham, to advertise me to come into France.   And thense
I went into France, and from thense into Flanders, and from Flanders into Ireland, and from Ireland into
Scotland and so into England."   (Grafton.)

The last occasion of his public appearance was on the day when he was hanged.
After his two days' enjoyment of pillory he was taken to the Tower and was contemptuously told that he would have to end his days there in confinement.   Here
he soon brought an end upon himself.   He found in the Tower the young Earl of
Warwick, who, as we have seen, was a very simple young man.   Perhaps Perkin
understood very well that, even if his own pretensions were hopelessly discredited,
with the real Earl of Warwick, Clarence's undoubted son, grandson of the great
Earl, the last male representative of the House of York, there would be the chance
of a far greater rising than either Simnel's or his own.   He was already sick of

prison ; the chances of a rising seemed worth taking, with all its perils and dangers ; he was probably desperate and reckless. He accordingly bribed his keepers with promises to connive at the escape of the Earl and himself. One has an instinctive feeling that they only pretended to connive ; that the course of the plot was daily communicated to the Governor of the Tower, and by him to the King ; that the wretched man was encouraged and urged on in order to give an opening for the greatly desired destruction of the Earl as well as his own. However that may be, in the end Perkin and a fellow-conspirator, one John Atwater, were placed on hurdles and drawn to Tyburn, where they received the attentions reserved for traitors. Perkin died, it is said, confessing his guilt. Guilty or not guilty, it was a convenient way of ridding the King not only of an impudent pretender, but also of a dangerous rival. Edward Plantagenet was beheaded on Tower Hill : his end is said to have been suggested by the King of Spain before the betrothal of Prince Arthur to Katherine of Aragon. It was sixteen years after his accession that Henry caused the unlucky youth to be beheaded ; and now no rival was left to disturb the security of Henry's crown.

There was, however, still a third personation, passed over by most historians, this time by a native of London. The new Pretender was named Ralph Wilford, the son of a shoemaker. He fell into the hands of a scoundrel named Patrick, an Augustine friar, who taught him what to say and how to say it. The two began to go about the country in Kent, and to whisper among the simple country folk the same story that Lambert Simnel had told. This lad was none other than the Earl of Warwick. When the friar found that the thing was receiving, here and there, a little credence, he began to back up the boy, and even went into the pulpit and preached on the subject. But this time the matter was not allowed to get to a head. There was no rebellion : both the rebels were arrested, the young man was hanged at St. Thomas Waterings, and the friar was put into prison for the rest of his natural life.

In the year 1500 was a "great death" in London and in other parts. The "great death" was due to an outbreak of plague ; not the sweating sickness, which also returned later, but apparently some form of the old plague, the "Black Death.' It is one of the many visitations which fell upon the City, afflicted it for a time, filled the churchyards with dead bodies, then passed away and was forgotten. Twenty thousand persons, according to Fabyan, were carried off in London alone. The King retired to Calais till the worst was over.

On the 14th November 1501, Prince Arthur, then a little over fifteen years of age, was married to Katherine of Aragon, who was then three years older. They were married in St. Paul's Cathedral. Holinshed says that a long stage was erected, 6 feet high, leading from the west doors to the Choir ; that at the end was raised a Mount on which there was room for eight persons, with steps to go up and down ;

and that on this platform stood the King and Queen and the bridegroom, and on it also the Mayor and Aldermen were allowed a place.

After the ceremony a splendid feast was held, with dancing and disguisings. Holinshed concludes his account of the wedding by an anecdote which, if true, proves that the Princess was truly the wife of Arthur.   The day after, the Royal party went to Westminster, where there were tournaments and great rejoicings.   The Prince died five months afterwards.   Another royal wedding, held on the 25th January 1502, caused even greater rejoicing.   It was that of the Princess Margaret with the King of Scotland ; a marriage which promised peace and goodwill between the two

KATHERINE OF ARAGON AND ARTHUR, PRINCE OF WALES
C. Butler's Collection.

nations ; a promise which has been fulfilled in a manner unexpected, by the failure of the male line of Tudors.   One observes how strong the desire of Henry VII. was to conciliate the goodwill of London.   He borrowed money from the City over and over again, but he always repaid these loans.   The exactions that we find recorded are chiefly those of his old age—when he was fifty-two years of age, which was old for that time, when he had grown covetous.   He could be ostentatious when show was wanted, witness the marriage of Prince Arthur with Katherine.   He could also entertain with regal splendour, witness the Christmas cheer he offered to the Mayor and Aldermen.

"Henry VII., in the ninth Year of his Reign, holding his Feast of Christmas at Westminster, on the twelfth Day, feasted Ralph Anstry, then Mayor of London, and his Brethren the Aldermen, with other

Commoners in great number; and, after Dinner, dubbing the Mayor Knight, caused him with his Brethren to stay and behold the Disguisings and other Disports in the Night following, shewed in the great Hall, which was richly hanged with Arras, and staged about on both sides; which Disports being ended, in the Morning, the King, the Queen, the Embassadors, and other Estates, being set at a Table of Stone, sixty knights and esquires served sixty Dishes to the King's Mess, and as many to the Queen's (neither Flesh nor Fish), and served the Mayor with twenty-four Dishes to his Mess, of the same manner, with sundry

THE EXCHEQUER IN THE TIME OF HENRY VII.
From a print in the British Museum.

Wines in most plenteous wise. And, finally, the King and Queen being conveyed, with great Lights, into the Palace, the Mayor, with his Company, in Barges, returned and came to London by Break of the next day." (Maitland, vol. i. p. 218.)

Henry VII. was respected and feared, rather than loved. He kept his word; if he borrowed he paid back; he was not savage or murderous; and he was a great lover of the fine arts. But the chief glory of his reign is that he enforced order throughout the realm : it is his chief glory, because order is a most difficult thing to enforce at a time when the people have been flying to arms on every possible occasion for forty years. In the rising of Lambert Simnel ; in that of Perkin Warbeck ; in the strange determination of the Cornishmen to march upon London,—one can see the natural result of a long civil war. Men become, very easily, ready to refer everything to the arbitration of battle ; in such arbitration anything may happen. It was such arbitration that set Edward up and pulled Henry down, and then reversed the arrangement. It was such arbitration that placed the crown on Henry Tudor's head. Why should not young Perkin step into a throne as Richard, Duke of York ? Henry accepted the arbitrament of battle, defeated his rival, and dispersed the rebel armies one after the other. One would think that the spirit of rebellion would be quickly daunted by so many reverses. It was not so ; for nearly a hundred years later there were rebellions. They broke out again and again : the people could not lose that trick of flying to arms ; the barons could not understand that their power was gone ; the memory still survived of princes dragged down, and princes set up, as Fortune turned the way of Victory.

Henry, like all the Tudors, was arbitrary : he had no intention of being ruled by the City ; by his agents Empson and Dudley he levied fines right and left upon the wealthier merchants ; he put the Mayor and the Sheriffs in the Marshalsea on a trumped-up charge, and they had to pay a fine of £1400 before he would let them out. He seized Christopher Hawes, Alderman, and put him also in prison, but the poor man died of terror and grief. He imprisoned William Capel, Alderman, who refused to pay a fine of £2000 for his liberty, and remained in prison till the King died. Lawrence Aylmer, ex-Mayor, was also imprisoned in the Compter, where he remained till the King's death. Henry understood very clearly that with a full Treasury many things are possible that are impossible with empty coffers. He accumulated, therefore, a tremendous hoard : it is said to have amounted to one million eight hundred thousand pounds in money, plate, and jewels.

The events which belong especially to London in this reign, as we have seen, were not numerous, nor were they of enduring importance. As regards building, the King pulled down a chapel and a house—the house where Chaucer once lived—at the west end of Westminster Abbey, and built the Chapel called after his name ; the Cross of Westchepe was finished and put up ; Baynard's Castle was rebuilt, " not after the former manner with embellishments and Towers," but more convenient. It was the time when the castle was passing into the country house ; it became now a large and handsome palace, built round two courts facing the river, much like those palaces built along the Strand, but without any garden except the courts.

The City showed more than its usual jealousy of strangers when in 1486 it passed an Ordinance that " no apprentice should be taken nor Freedom given, but to such as were gentlemen born, agreeable to the clause in the oath given to every

The Children of K. HENRY VII and ELIZABETH his Queen.

I. Prince ARTHUR.   II. Pᵉ HENRY.   III. Pˢˢ MARGARET.

From the Royal Collection at Kensington Palace.

To his GRACE the most Noble THOMAS Duke of LEEDS, this is most humbly inscrib'd &c.

From E. Gardner's Collection.

Freeman at the time he was made Free." . . . "You shall take no Apprentice but if he be free born." These are Maitland's words. The statement is surely absurd. For suppose such a regulation to hold good for the wholesale distributing Companies, how could it be sustained in the case of the Craft Companies? Did a gentleman's son ever become a working blacksmith or a journeyman saddler? Another kind of jealousy was shown by the City when they passed an Act which prohibited any citizen under penalty of £100 (one-third to be given the Informer) for taking any goods or merchandise to any Fair or Market within the Kingdom, for the term of seven years. What did it mean? That the country merchants should come to London for their wares? Parliament set aside this Regulation the following year.

A sanitary edict was passed to the effect that no animals should be killed within the City. There is no information as to the length of time that this edict was obeyed, if it were ever obeyed at all.

In 1503 the King showed his opinion of the authority of the City when he granted a Charter to the Company of Merchant Taylors which practically placed them outside the jurisdiction of the Mayor. Some of the other Companies, perceiving that, if this new independence were granted everywhere, there would be an end of the City, joined in a petition to Parliament for placing them formally under the authority of the Mayor and Aldermen. The City got a Charter from the King in 1505. The Charter, which cost 5000 marks, was especially levelled against recent encroachments of foreigners in buying and selling, and was drawn up to the same effect, and partly in the same words, as the Fifth and last Charter of King Edward the Third. Thus the conclusion of Edward's Charter was as follows :—

"We . . . have granted to the said Mayor, etc., that no strangers shall from henceforth sell any Wares in the same City or Suburbs thereof by Retail, nor shall keep any House, nor be any Broker in the said City or Suburbs thereof, saving always the merchants of High Almaine, etc."

Henry's Charter was as follows :—

"That of all Time, of which the Memory of Man is not to the contrary, for the Commonweal of the Realm and City aforesaid, it hath been used, and by Authority of Parliament approved and confirmed, that no Stranger from the Liberty of the City may buy or sell, from any Stranger from the Liberties of the same City, any Merchandize or Wares within the Liberties of the same City, upon Forfeiture of the same."

A curious story of this reign relates how the King, to use a homely proverb, cut off his nose to spite his face. For the conduct of Margaret, Duchess of Burgundy, in acknowledging the Pretender, so incensed him against the Flemings that he banished them all. No doubt he inflicted hardship upon the Flemings, but he also—which he had not intended—deprived the Merchant Adventurers of London of their principal trade. The Hanseatic Merchants, perceiving the possible advantage to themselves, imported vast quantities of Flemish produce. Then the 'prentices rose and broke into the *Gildhalla Teutonicorum*—the Steelyard—pillaging the rooms and warehouses. There was a free fight in Thames Street, and after a time the rioters were dispersed. Some were taken prisoners and a few hanged. As nothing more is said about the Flemings, one supposes that they all came back again.

There had been grave complaints about the perjuries of Juries in the City. The Jurymen took bribes to favour one cause or the other. It was therefore enacted:—

"That, for the future, no Person or Persons be impannelled or sworn into any jury or Inquest in any of the City Courts, unless he be worth forty Marks; and if the Cause to be tried amount to that Sum, then no

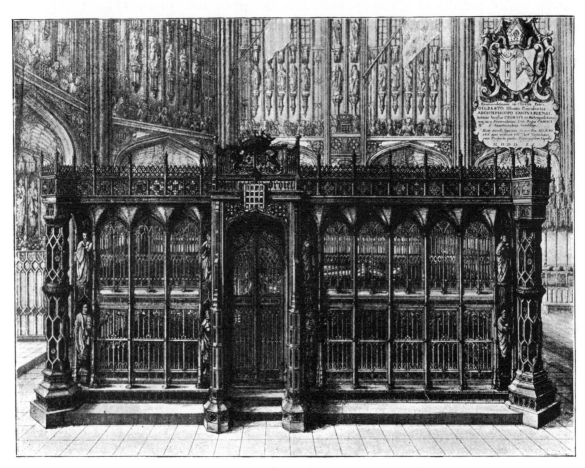

SCREEN IN HENRY VII.'S CHAPEL, WESTMINSTER ABBEY
E. Gardner's Collection.

Person shall be admitted as a Juror worth less than one hundred Marks; and every Person so qualified, refusing to serve as a Juryman, for the first Default to forfeit one Shilling, the second two, and every one after to double the Sum, for the Use of the City.

And when upon Trial it shall be found, that a Petty Jury have brought in an unjust Verdict, then every Member of the same to Forfeit twenty pounds, or more, according to the Discretion of the Court of Lord-Mayor and Aldermen; and also each Person so offending to suffer six Months' imprisonment, or less, at the Discretion of the said Mayor and Aldermen, without Bail or Mainprize, and for ever after to be rendered incapable of serving in any jury.

And if upon Enquiry it be found, that any Juror has taken Money as a Bribe, or other Reward, or Promise of Reward, to favour either Plaintiff or Defendant in the Cause to be tried by him then, and in every such case, the Person so offending to forfeit and pay to the Party by him thus injured ten times the

Value of such Sum or Reward by him taken, and also to suffer imprisonment as already mentioned, and besides, to be disabled from ever serving in that Capacity; and that every Person or Persons guilty of bribing any Juror, shall likewise forfeit ten times the value given, and suffer imprisonment as aforesaid." (Maitland, vol. i. p. 219.)

INTERIOR OF HENRY VII.'S CHAPEL, WESTMINSTER ABBEY
E. Gardner's Collection.

Fortifications commanding roads and approaches to the City were erected in the year 1496, especially on the south side, in order to defend the City against the Cornish rebels. It is quite possible that some of them remained, and that some of the supposed works of 1642 were only a restoration or a rebuilding of forts and bastions on the same places.

In the year 1498 many gardens in Finsbury Fields were thrown into a spacious Field for the use of the London Archers or Trained bands. This field is now the Artillery Ground with Bunhill Fields Cemetery. In 1501 the Lord Mayor erected Kitchens and Offices in the Guildhall, by means of which he entertained the Aldermen and the principal citizens.

Towards the end of his reign, the King, finding himself afflicted with an incurable disease, took steps in the nature of atonement for his sins. He issued a general pardon to all men for offences committed against his laws—thieves, murderers, and certain others excepted. He paid the fees of prisoners who were kept in gaol for want of money to discharge their fees ; he also paid the debts of all those who were confined in the "counters" of Ludgate, *i.e.* the free men of the City, for sums of forty shillings and under ; and some he relieved that were confined for as much as ten pounds. "Hereupon," says Holinshed, "there were processions daily in every City and parish to pray to Almighty God for his restoring to health and long continuance in the same." But in vain ; for the disease continued and the King died.

Here is a note on the first visit of Henry the Eighth to the City :—

"Prince Henry, who afterwards succeeded his father on the throne as King Henry VIII., but was at the time a child of seven years, paid a visit to the City (30 Oct. 1498), where he received a hearty welcome, and was presented by the Recorder, on behalf of the citizens, with a pair of gilt goblets. In reply to the Recorder, who in presenting this 'litell and powre ' gift, promised to remember his grace with a better at some future time, the prince made the following short speech :—

'Fader Maire, I thank you and your Brethren here present of this greate and kynd remembraunce which I trist in tyme comyng to deserve. And for asmoche as I can not give unto you according thankes, I shall pray the Kynges Grace to thank you, and for my partye I shall not forget yor kyndnesse.'" (Sharpe, *London and the Kingdom*, vol. i. p. 334.)

The funeral of the King was most sumptuous.

"His corpse was conveyed from Richmond to St. Paul's on the 9th May, being met on its way at St. George's Bar, in Southwark, by the mayor, aldermen, and a suite of 104 commoners, all in black clothing and all on horseback. The streets were lined with other members of the companies bearing torches, the lowest craft occupying the first place. Next after the freemen of the city came the 'strangers'—Easterlings, Frenchmen, Spaniards, Venetians, Genoese, Florentines and 'Lukeners'—on horseback and on foot, also bearing torches. These took up their position in Gracechurch Street. Cornhill was occupied by the lower crafts, ordered in such a way that 'the most worshipful crafts' stood next unto 'Paules.' A similar order was preserved the next day, when the corpse was removed from Saint Paul's to Westminster. The lowest crafts were placed nearest to the Cathedral, and the most worshipful next to Temple Bar, where the civic escort terminated. The mayor and aldermen proceeded to Westminster by water, to attend the 'masse and offering.' The mayor, with his mace in his hand, made his offering next after the Lord Chamberlain ; those aldermen who had passed the chair offered next after the Knights of the Garter, and before all 'knights for the body' ; whilst the aldermen who had not yet served as mayor made their offering after the knights." (*Ibid.* p. 341.)

CHAPTER II

HENRY VIII

LONDON has now changed its character: the old quarrels and rivalries of Baron, Alderman, or Lord of the Manor with merchant, of merchant with craftsman, of

Spooner & Co.

HENRY VIII. WHEN YOUNG (1491-1547)
From a portrait by Holbein.

master with servant, have ceased. The Lord of the Manor has disappeared in the City; the craft companies have at last gained their share in the government of the City, but, so far to their own advantage, they are entirely ruled by the employers and

2

masters who belong to them, so that the craftsmen themselves are no better off than before.   The authority of the King over the City is greater now than at any preceding time, but it will be restrained in the future not so much by charters, by bribes and gifts, as by the power of the Commons.   The trade of the City, which had so grievously suffered by the Civil wars, is reviving again under the peace and order of the Tudor Princes, though it will be once more injured by the religious dissensions. Lastly, the City, like the rest of the country, is already feeling the restlessness that belongs to a period of change.   At Henry's accession, men were beginning to be

HENRY VIII. (1491-1547)
From the portrait by Holbein in Windsor Castle.

conscious of a larger world: wider thoughts possessed them; the old learning, the old Arts, were rising again from the grave; the crystallised institutions, hitherto fondly thought to be an essential part of religion, were ready to be broken up.   Even the most narrow City merchant, whose heart was in his money-bags, whose soul was to be saved by a trental of masses, an anniversary, or a chantry, felt the uneasiness of the time, and yearned for a simpler Faith as well as for wider markets across the newly-traversed seas.   I propose to consider the events of this reign, which were of such vast importance to London as well as the country at large, by subjects instead of in chronological order as hitherto.

And I will first take the relations of the City and the King.

They began with a manifest desire of the young King to conciliate the City. Evidently in answer to some petition or representation, he banished all "foreign" beggars, *i.e.* those who were not natives of London; and ordered them to return to their own parishes. It is easy to understand what happened: the "foreign" beggars, in obedience to the proclamation, retired to their holes and corners; the streets were free from them for some days; the Mayor and Sheriffs congratulated themselves; then after a decent interval, and gradually, the beggars ventured out again. The

KATHERINE OF ARAGON (1485-1536)
From the painting in the National Portrait Gallery, London.

difficulty, in a word, of dealing with rogues and vagrants and masterless men was already overwhelming. In the time of Elizabeth it became a real, a threatening, danger to the town. We must remember that one effect of a long war, especially a civil war, which calls out a much larger proportion of the people than a foreign war, is to throw upon the roads, at the close of it, a vast number of those who have tasted the joys of idleness and henceforth will not work. They would rather be flogged and hanged than work. They cannot work. They have forgotten how to work. They rob on the high road; they murder in the remote farm-houses; in the winter, and when they grow old, they make for the towns, and they beg in the streets. However, Henry greatly pleased the City by his order, and for a time there was improvement. He then took a much more important step towards winning the affection of the City. He committed Empson and Dudley to the Tower. They were accused of a conspiracy against the Government—in reality they had been the approved agents of the late King; but this it would have been inconvenient to confess. They were therefore found guilty and executed—these unfortunately too willing tools of a rapacious sovereign. Henry offered restitution to all who had suffered at their hands. It was found on subsequent inquiry that six men, all of whom had been struck off the lists for perjury, had managed to get replaced, and had been busy at work for Empson and Dudley in raking up false charges against Aldermen or in taking bribes for concealing offences. These persons, as being servants and not principals, were treated leniently. They were set in pillory, and then driven out of the City.

The loyalty of the City showed itself on the day of the Coronation when the King, with his newly married Queen, rode in magnificent procession from the Tower to Westminster, where the Crowning was performed with a splendour which surpassed that of all previous occasions.

On St. John's Eve 1510 the King, disguised as one of his own yeomen, went into the City in order to witness the finest show of the year, the procession of the City Watch. He was so well pleased with the sight that on St. Peter's Eve following he brought his Queen and Court to Cheapside to see the procession again :—

"The March was begun by the City musick, followed by the Lord-Mayor's officers in Party-coloured Liveries; then the Sword-Bearer on Horseback, in beautiful Armour, preceded the Lord-Mayor, mounted on a stately Horse richly trapped, attended by a Giant, and two Pages on Horseback, three Pageants, Morrice-dancers, and Footmen; next came the Sheriffs, preceded by their Officers, and attended by their Giants, Pages, Pageants, and Morrice-Dancers. Then marched a great body of Demi-Lancers, in bright Armour, on stately Horses; next followed a Body of Carabineers, in white Fustian Coats, with a symbol of the City Arms on their Backs and Breasts; then marched a Division of Archers, with their Bows bent, and Shafts of Arrows by their Side; next followed a Party of Pikemen in their Corslets and Helmets; after them a Body of Halberdeers in Corslets and Helmets; and the March was closed by a great Party of Billmen, with Helmets and Aprons of Mail; and the whole Body, consisting of about two thousand Men, had between every Division a certain Number of Musicians, who were answered in their proper Places by the like Number of Drums, with Standards and Ensigns as veteran troops. This nocturnal March was illuminated by Nine hundred and forty Cressets; two hundred whereof were defrayed at the City Expence, five hundred at that of the Companies, and two hundred and forty by the City Constables. The March began at the Conduit at the west end of Cheapside, and passed through Cheapside, Cornhill, and Leadenhall Street, to Aldgate; whence it returned by Fenchurch Street, Gracechurch Street, Cornhill, and so back to the Conduit. During this March, the Houses on each side the said streets were decorated with Greens and Flowers, wrought into Garlands, and intermixed with a great number of Lamps." (Maitland, vol. i. p. 222.)

There is no more pleasant page in the whole of history than that which relates the first years of King Henry's reign. He was young; he was strong; he was married to a woman whom he loved ; he was tall, like his grandfather King Edward, and of goodly countenance, like his grandmother Elizabeth Woodville ; he was a lover of arts, like his father ; and of learning, like his grandmother Margaret, Countess of Richmond ; he was brave, like all his race ; he was masterful, as became a king as well as a Tudor ; he was skilful in all manly exercises. Add to all this that at the time of his accession he was the richest man in Europe. This accomplished Prince, according to Holinshed, used, even in his progresses, to exercise himself every day in shooting, singing, dancing, wrestling, casting the bar, playing on the recorders, the flute, the virginals, or writing songs and ballads and setting them to music. His songs are principally amorous. He wrote anthems, one of which is extant. The words are taken from the Song of Solomon (Vulgate). His verse is melodious and pretty :—

> " O my hart and O my hart
>   My hart it is so sore !
> Since I must nedys from my love depart
>   And know no cause wherfore."

Or a song of constancy :—

> " Grene grouth the holy, so doth the ivie
> Thow winter's blastys blow never so hye.
> As the holy growith grene and never chaungyth hew
> So I am—ever hath bene—unto my lady trew.
>   Grene grouth, etc.
>
> As the holy grouth grene with ivie all alone
> Whose flowerys cannot be seen and grene wode levys
>   be gone,
> Now unto my lady, promyse to her I make
> From all other only to her I me betake.
> Adew myne owne lady, adew my specyall
> Who hath my hart trewly, be sure, and ever shall.
>   Grene grouth, etc."

And the song which became so popular, " Pastyme with good Company." This song was actually taken by Latimer as a text for a sermon before Edward the Sixth :—

> " Pastyme with good companye
> I love and shall untyll I dye ;
> Gruche who list—but none denye,
> So God be plesyd thus leve wyll I ;
>   For my Pastance
>   Hunt, syng, and dance,
>   My hart is sette ;
>   All goodly sport for my comfort
>   Who shall be let ?
>
> Youth must have some dalliance,
> Of good or yll sum pastance ;
> Companye me thynkes then best
> All thoughts and fansys to dejest ;
>   For idleness
>   Is chief mistress
>   Of vices all ;
>   Then who can say
>   But myrth and play
>   Is best of all ?

Company with honeste
Is vertu—vices to flee ;
Company is good and ill,
But every man hath hys fre wyll ;
    The best ensew,
    The worst eschew,
    My Mynde shall be
    Vertu to use,
    Vice to refuse,
       Thus shall I use me."

At the outset there was nothing but feasting, jousts, feats of arms, masques, devices, pageants, and mummeries. At the feasts the King was lavish and free of hand ; at the tilting the King challenged all and won the prize ; at the masques and mummeries he was the best of all the actors ; at the dance he was the most graceful

HENRY VIII. AS A MUSICIAN
From a Royal MS. in British Museum.

and the most unwearied. There are long pages in contemporary history on this festive and splendid life at the Court, when as yet all the world was young to Henry, and no one had been executed except Empson and Dudley. The following extract from Holinshed shows the things in which he gloried, and the nature of a Court Pageant :—

"Then there was a device or a pageant upon wheels brought in, out of the which pageant issued out a gentleman richlie apparelled, that shewed how in a garden of pleasure there was an arbor of gold wherein were lords and ladies, much desirous to shew pastime to the queene and ladies, if they might be licenced so to doo ; who was answered by the queene, how she and all other there were verie desirous to see them and their pastime. Then a great cloth of arras that did hang before the same pageant was taken away, and the pageant brought more neere. It was curiouslie made and pleasant to beholde, it was solemne and rich : for every post or piller thereof was covered with frised gold, therein were trees of hawthorne, eglantine, rosiers, vines, and other pleasant floures of diverse colours, with gillofers, and other hearbs, all made of sattin, damaske, silver and gold, accordinglie as the naturall trees, hearbs, or floures ought to be. In this arbor were six ladies, all apparelled in white satin and greene, set and embroidered full of H. & K. of Gold, knit together with laces of gold of damaske, and all their garments were replenished with glittering spangels gilt over, on their heads are bonets all opened at the foure quarters overfrised with flat gold of damaske, and orrellets were of rolles, wreathed on lampas doucke holow, so that the gold shewed through the lampas doucke : the fassis of their head set full of new devised fashions. In this garden also was the king and five with him apparelled in garments of purple sattin, all of cuts with H. & K. everie edge garnished with frised gold, and everie garment full of posies, made of letters of fine gold in bullion as thicke as they might be, and everie person had his name in like letters of massie gold. The first Cureloial, the second Bon Voloire, the third Bon Espoir, the fourth Valiant Desire, the fifth Bon Foy, the sixt Amour Loial, their hosen, cape, and coats were full of posies, with H. & K. of fine gold in bullion, so that the ground could scarse appeere, and yet was in everie void place spangles of gold. When time was come, the said pageant was brought foorth into presence, and then descended a lord and a ladie by couples, and then the minstrels which were disguised also dansed, and the lords and ladies dansed, that it was a pleasure to behold. In the meane season the pageant was conveyed to the end of the palace, there to tarie till the danses were finished, and so to have received the lords and ladies againe : but suddenlie the rude people ran to the pageant, and rent, tare, and spoiled the pageant so that the lord steward nor the head officers could not cause them to absteine, except that they should have foughten and drawen blood and so was this pageant broken. Then the king with the queene and the ladies returned to his chamber, where they had a great banket, and so this triumph ended with mirth and gladnes." (Holinshed, vol. iii. p. 560.)

On the proclamation of war against France, the City was ordered to furnish a contingent of 300 men fully armed and equipped. There seems to have been no difficulty in getting the men. The money for their outfit was subscribed by the Companies, who raised £405, and so the men were despatched, clad in white with St. George's Cross and Sword, and a rose in front and back.

In June 1516 Cardinal Wolsey addressed an admonition to the City : they must look to the maintenance of order ; there was sedition among them ; the statute of apparel was neglected ; vagabonds and masterless men made the City their resort— an instructive commentary on the King's ordinances of seven years before. The sedition of which Wolsey complained was due to the intense jealousy with which the people of London always regarded the immigration of aliens. They were always coming in, and the freemen—the old City families—were always dying out or going away. In 1500, and again in 1516, orders were issued for all freemen to return with their families to the City on pain of losing their freedom. Had they, then, already begun the custom of living in the suburbs and going into town every morning? The case against the foreigners is strongly put by Grafton :—

"In this season the Genowayes, Frenchmen and other straungers, sayd and boasted themselves to be in suche favor with the king and hys counsayle, that they set naught by the rulers of the city : and the multitude of straungers was so great about London, that the poore English artificers could scarce get any lyvyng : and most of al the straungers were so prowde, that they disdayned, mocked, and oppressed the Englishmen, which was the beginning of the grudge. For among all other thinges there was a carpenter in London called Wylliamson which boughte two stocke Doves in Chepe, and as he was about to pay for them, a Frenchman tooke them out of his hande, and sayde they were not meat for a Carpenter : well sayde the Englisheman I have bought them, and now payde for them, and therefore I will have them ; nay sayde the Frencheman I will have them for my Lorde the Ambassador, and so for better or worse, the Frenchman called the Englishman knave and went away with the stock Doves. The straungers came to the French Ambassador, and surmised a complaint against the poore Carpenter, and the Ambassador came to my

Lord Maior, and sayde so much, that the Carpenter was sent to prison : and yet not contented with this so complayned to the king's counsayle, that the king's commaundement was layde on him. And when syr John Baker and other worshipfull persons sued to the Ambassador for him, he aunswered by the body of God that the Englishe knave should loose his lyfe, for he sayde no Englisheman should denie what the Frenchmen requyred, and other aunswere had they none. Also a Frenchman that had slayne a man, should abjure the realme and had a crosse in his hande, and then sodainely came a great sort of Frenchman about him, and one of them sayde to the Constable that led him, syr is thys crosse the price to kill an Englisheman. The Constable was somewhat astonied and aunswered not. Then sayde another Frenchman, on that price we would be banished all by the masse, this saiyng was noted to be spoken spitefully. Howbeit the Frenchmen were not alonly oppressors of the Englishemen, for a Lombard called Frances de Bard, entised a man's wyfe in Lombarde Streete to come to his Chamber with her husband's plate, which thing she did. After when her husband knew it, he demanded hys wife, but answere was made he should not have her ; then he demanded his plate, and in like manner answere was made that he should neyther have plate nor wife. And when he had sued an action against the straunger in the Guyldehall, the stranger so faced the Englishman that he faynted in his sute. And then the Lombard arrested the poore man for his wyfes boord, while he kept her from her husband in his chamber. This mocke was much noted, and for these and many other oppressions done by them, there encreased such a malice in the Englishmen's hartes : that at the last it brast out." (Grafton's *Chronicles*, vol. ii. p. 289.)

He goes on to relate that a certain John Lincoln, a broker, desired a priest named Dr. Standish to move the Mayor and Aldermen at his Spital sermon on Easter Monday to take part with the Commonalty against the aliens. Standish refused. John Lincoln then went to a certain Dr. Bele, Canon in St. Mary Spital, and represented the grievous case of the people.

. . . "lamentably declared to him, how miserably the common artificers lyved, and scarce could get any worke to find them, their wives and children, for there were such a number of artificers straungers, that toke away all their living in manner."

Then followed the tumult known as Evil May Day. Dr. Bele preached the Spital Sermon of Easter Tuesday. He first read Lincoln's letter representing the condition of the craftsmen thus oppressed by the aliens, and then taking for his text the words, "Caelum caeli Domino Terram autem dedit Filiis hominum"—the Heavens to the Lord of Heaven, but the Earth hath he given to the Sons of Men— he plainly told the people that England was their own, and that Englishmen ought to keep their country for themselves, as birds defend their nests. Thus encouraged, the people began to assault and molest the foreigners in the City. Some of them were sent to Newgate for the offence ; but they continued. Then there ran about the City a rumour that on May Day all the foreigners would be murdered, and many of them, hearing this rumour, fled. The rumour reached the King, who ordered Cardinal Wolsey to inquire into it. Thereupon the Mayor called together the Council. Some were of opinion that a strong watch should be set and kept up all night ; others thought that it would be better to order every one to be indoors from nine in the evening till nine in the morning. Both opinions were sent to the Cardinal, who chose the latter. Accordingly the order was proclaimed. But it was not obeyed. Some time after nine, Alderman Sir John Mundy found a company of young men in Cheapside playing at Bucklers. He ordered them to desist and to go home. One of them asked why? For answer the Alderman seized him and ordered him to be taken to the Compter. Then the tumult began. The 'prentices raised the cry of "Clubs! Clubs!" and flocked together; the man was rescued; the people crowded in from every quarter; they marched, a thousand strong, to Newgate, where they took out the Lord Mayor's prisoners, and to the Compter, where they did the

CARDINAL WOLSEY (1471-1530)
From the painting in the National Portrait Gallery, London.

same; at St. Martin's they broke open doors and windows and "spoiled everything." And they spent the rest of the night in pulling down the houses of foreigners. When they grew tired of this sport, they gradually broke up and went home, but on the way the Mayor's men arrested some three hundred of them and sent them to the Tower. Another hundred rioters were arrested next day. Dr. Bele was also sent to the Tower. Then began the trials. Lincoln and some twenty or thirty others were found guilty and sentenced to be hanged, drawn, and quartered. Ten pairs of gallows were set up in different parts of the City for their execution. Lincoln, however, was the only one who suffered. For the rest a reprieve was granted. Then the affair was concluded in a becoming and solemn manner :—

"Thursday the xxij day of May, the king came into Westminster Hall, for whome at the upper ende was set a cloth of estate, and the place hanged with arras. With him was the Cardinall, the Dukes of Norfolke and Suffolke, the Earles of Shrewsbury, of Essex, Wilshire and of Surrey, with manye Lordes and other of the kinges Counsale. The Maior and Aldermen, and all the chief of the City, were there in their best livery (according as the Cardinall had them appoynted) by ix of the clocke. Then the king commaunded that all the prisoners should be brought forth. Then came in the poore yonglings and olde false knaves bound in ropes all along, one after another in their shirtes, and every one a Halter about his necke, to the number of foure hundred men and xj women. And when all were come before the kinges presence, the Cardinall sore layd to the Maior and commonaltie their negligence, and to the prisoners he declared that they had deserved death for their offence : then all the prisoners together cryed mercy gracious Lorde, mercy. Then the Lordes altogether besought his grace ot mercy, at whose request the king pardoned them all. And then the Cardinall gave unto them a good exhortation to the great gladnesse of the heerers. And when the generall pardon was pronounced, all the prisoners showted at once, and altogether cast up their Halters unto the Hall rooffe, so that the king might perceyve they were none of the discretest sort. Here is to be noted that dyvers offenders which were not taken, heeryng that the king was inclined to mercys, came well apparayled to Westminster, and sodainlye stryped them into their shirtes with halters, and came in among the prisoners willingly, to be partakers of the kinges pardon, by the which doyng, it was well knowen that one John Gelson yoman of the Crowne was the first that beganne to spoyle, and exhorted other to do the same, and because he fled and was not taken, he came in the rope with the other prisoners, and so had his pardon. This companie was after called the blacke Wagon. Then were all the Galowes within the Citie taken downe, and many a good prayer sayde for the king, and the Citizens tooke more heede to their servants." (Grafton's *Chronicles*, vol. ii. p. 294.)

A singular story belongs to the arrival of the French embassy charged with negotiating the marriage of the King's infant daughter and the Dauphin. The ambassadors were escorted by a company of their own King's bodyguard and another of the English King's bodyguard. They were met at Blackheath by the Earl of Surrey, richly apparelled, and a hundred and sixty gentlemen ; four hundred archers followed ; they were lodged in the merchants' houses and banqueted at Taylors' Hall. And then, says the historian, "the French hardermen opened their wares and made Taylors' Hall like to the paunde of a mart. At this doing many an Englishman grudged but it avayled not." In other words, a lot of French hucksters, under cover of the embassy, brought over smuggled goods and sold them in the Taylors' Hall at a lower price than the English makers could afford.

The reception of the Emperor Charles by Henry in this year was as royally magnificent as even Henry himself could desire. The procession was like others of the same period and may be omitted.

In 1524 a curious proclamation was made by the Mayor. Evidently papers or letters of importance had been lost.

"My lorde the maire streihtly chargith and commaundith on the king or soveraigne lordis behalf that if any maner of person or persons that have founde a hat with certeyn lettres and other billes and writinges therin enclosed, which lettres been directed to our said sovereign from the parties of beyond the see, let hym or theym bryng the said hat, lettres, and writinges unto my saide lorde the maire in all the hast possible and they shalbe well rewarded for their labour, and that no maner of person kepe the said hat, lettres, and writinges nor noon of them after this proclamacioun made, uppon payn of deth, and God save the king." (Sharpe, *London and the Kingdom*, vol. i. p. 373.)

Two cases, that of Sir George Monoux and that of Paul Wythypol, prove that the City offices were not at this time always regarded as desirable. In the former case, Sir George Monoux, Alderman and Draper, was elected (1523) Mayor for the second time, and refused to serve. He was fined £1000, and it was ordained by the Court of Aldermen that any one in future who should refuse to serve as Mayor should be fined that amount. In this case Monoux was permitted to retire, probably

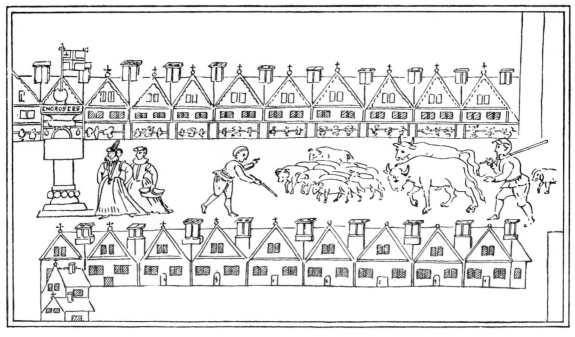

EASTCHEAP MARKET
From an old drawing in British Museum.

on account of ill-health. The second case, which happened in 1537, was that of Paul Wythypol, merchant-taylor. He was a man of some position in the City: he had been one of the Commoners sent to confer with Wolsey on the "amicable" loan (Sharpe, *London and the Kingdom*, vol. i. p. 377); he attended the Coronation banquet of Anne Boleyn; he was afterwards M.P. for the City, 1529-1536. They elected him Alderman for Farringdon Within. For some reason he was anxious not to serve; rather than pay the fine he got the King to interfere on his behalf. Such interference was clearly an infringement of the City liberties; the Mayor and Aldermen consulted Wolsey, who advised them to seek an interview with the King, then at Greenwich. This they did, and went down to Greenwich. When they arrived they were taken into the King's great chamber, where they waited till evening, when the King received them privately. What passed is not known, but in the end Wythypol remained out of office for a year afterwards. At the end of that time he was again elected Alderman, and was ordered to take office or to swear that his property did not amount to £1000. He refused and was committed to Newgate, the King no longer offering to help him. Three weeks later he appeared before the Court and offered to pay a fine of £40 for three years' exemption from office. The Court refused this offer and sent him back to prison. Three months later—Wythypol must have been a very stubborn person—he again appeared before the Court, and was ordered to take up office at once or else swear that his property was not worth £1000. If he did not, he was to be fined in a sum to be assessed by the Mayor, Aldermen, and Common Council. He did not take office, and it is therefore tolerably certain that he paid a heavy fine.

In the year 1529 sat the memorable Court presided over by Cardinals Campeggio and Wolsey, which was to try the validity of Henry's marriage with his brother's widow. It was held in the great hall of the Dominican Friars. No more important case was ever tried in an English Court of Law, nor one which had wider or deeper consequences. Upon this case depended the national Faith; the nation's fidelity to the Pope; its continued adhesion to the ecclesiastical order as it had developed during fifteen hundred years. This trial belongs to the national history.

In October of that year (1529) the King, enraged by the Legate's delay in the marriage business, deprived Wolsey of the Seals, seized his furniture and plate, and ordered him to leave London. In November of the same year, at a Parliament held in the Palace of Bridewell, a Bill was passed by the Lords disabling the Cardinal from being restored to his dignities. In February 1530 Wolsey was restored to his Archbishopric but without his palace, which the King kept for himself; he was summoned to London on a charge of treason, but he fell ill and died on the way.

No Englishman before or after Wolsey has ever maintained so much state and splendour; no Englishman has ever affected the popular imagination so much as Cardinal Wolsey. Contemporary writers exhaust themselves in dwelling upon the more than regal Court kept up by this priest. It is like reading of the Court of a great king. We must, however, remember, that all this state was not the ostentation of the man so much as, first, the glorification of the Church and of the ecclesiastical dignities, and next, a visible proof of the greatness of the King in having so rich a subject.

Between 1527 and 1534 there were disputes on the subject of tithes and offerings to the clergy. At this time began the dissolution of the Monasteries, to which we will return presently.

So far as regards the relations between the King and the City. Let us now return to the City itself. We have already seen that the intervals of freedom from

plague were growing shorter. In this reign of thirty-eight years there was a
return of the sweating sickness in 1518; a return of the plague, which lasted from
1519 to 1522; another appearance of the sweating sickness in 1528; and another

THE KING IN PARLIAMENT
From a print in the British Museum.

attack of the plague in 1543. It seems strange that no physician should have
connected the frequency and violence of the disease with the foulness and narrowness of the streets. From the beginning of the sixteenth century to the Great Fire
of 1666, London, crowded and confined, abounded with courts and slums of the
worst possible kind; it swarmed with rogues and tramps and masterless men who

lived as they could, like swine.   There were no great fires to cleanse the City.
The condition of the ground, with its numberless cesspools, its narrow lanes into
which, despite laws, everything was thrown; its frequent laystalls; the refuse and
remains of all the workshops; the putrefying blood of the slaughtered beasts
sinking into the earth,—must have been truly terrible had the people realised it;
but they did not.   Fluid matter sank into the earth and worked its wicked will
unseen and unsuspected; the rains washed the surface; no man saw farther than
the front of his own house; therefore when pestilence appeared among them it
did not creep, according to its ancient wont, from house to house, but it flew swiftly
with wings outspread over street and lane and court.

Steps were taken to protect and to improve the medical profession.   It was
ordained in 1512 that no one should practise medicine or surgery within the City or
for seven miles outside the City walls without a license from the Bishop of London
or the Dean of St. Paul's; the said license only to be obtained by examination
before the Bishop or the Dean by four of the Faculty.   Two years later surgeons
were exempted from serving on juries, bearing arms, or serving as constables.   In
1519 the Physicians obtained a Charter of Incorporation, by which they were
allowed a common seal; to elect a President annually; to purchase and hold land;
and to govern all persons practising physic within seven miles of London.   The
College of Physicians, observe, was at first only considered as one of the City
Companies: it had jurisdiction over London and over seven miles round London,
but no more.   The positions of both Physicians and Surgeons were enormously
improved by these Acts of Parliament.

There were in this reign, for the admiration of the people, an extraordinary
number of executions, both of noble lords and hapless ladies, as well as of divines,
monks, friars, gentlemen, gentlewomen, and the common sort, for treason, heresy,
and the crimes which are the most commonly brought before the attention of
justice.   What reign before this would exhibit such a list as the following?   Two
Queens, Anne Boleyn and Katherine Howard; of others, the Marquis of Exeter, the
Earl of Surrey, the Earl of Kildare, the Duke of Buckingham, Lord Rochford,
Lady Rochford, Lady Salisbury, Fisher, More, Empson, Dudley, Cromwell.
Of abbots, priors, monks, friars, doctors, priests, for refusing the oath of the
King's supremacy a great number; of lesser persons for heresy or treason
another goodly company.   Some were beheaded—those were fortunate; others
were burned, not being so fortunate; the rest were drawn on hurdles, and treated
in the manner we have already seen.

The dissolution of the Religious Houses, the changes in the Articles of
Religion, and their effect upon the City of London, will be found in another place
(see p. 109).   In this chapter a few cases are given to illustrate the changes of
thought and the general excitement in the minds of men.

There is, first, the case of Lambert. He was a learned man and a schoolmaster who denied the Real Presence in the Sacrament. The case had been already brought before the Archbishop, who had given a sentence against Lambert. The King, who ardently believed in the Real Presence, announced his intention of arguing publicly with this heretic. The argument was actually held in Westminster Hall in the presence of a great number of people. In the end the King, apparently, got the worst of it, for we find him becoming judge as well as disputant, and ordering the unfortunate man to recant or burn. Lambert would not recant—the pride and stubbornness of these heretics were wonderful; in some cases, perhaps in

HENRY VIII. GRANTING THE BARBER-SURGEONS' CHARTER
After the picture by Holbein in Barber-Surgeons' Hall, London.

this, the man stood for a party: he would not recant for the sake of his friends as well as himself. He was burned.

The case of Anne Askew is remarkable for the introduction of torture, which was then unusual either with criminals or heretics. She was so miserably tortured— yet perhaps the torture was intended as a merciful act, in the hope of rescuing her from worse than earthly flames—that she could not stand or walk. She, like Lambert, suffered for denying the Real Presence. She was a gentlewoman of very good understanding.

The Holy Maid of Kent, Elizabeth Barton, was a woman of a much lower order. She was hysterical and weak-minded. At the present day she would be looked after and gently cared for. She had fits and convulsions, during which her face and her body were drawn, and she talked rambling nonsense. That she was unintelligible was quite enough to make the ignorant country folk flock about her, listening for inspired words in her hysterical ejaculations. She passed among them for one to whom God had sent a new revelation of His Will and Intentions. She was taken to see Bishops Fisher and More, who do not seem to have regarded her as a person of the slightest importance. But certain priests—it is said so ; one may believe it or not—obtained influence over her and persuaded her to prophesy—no doubt she believed what they told her—that if the King took another wife he would not remain King for another year. Henry was not the man to be turned aside from his fixed purpose by such a gross cheat. He arrested the Maid and her accomplices. They were all brought to the Star Chamber and examined ; they all confessed. They were then exposed on a scaffold at St. Paul's and publicly confirmed their confessions. Her confederates included six ecclesiastics, of whom two were monks of Canterbury and one a Friar Observaunt ; two were private gentlemen ; one was a serving-man. Confession made, they were taken back to the Tower and their case laid before Parliament, which met after Christmas. They were all sentenced to the same traitor's death and, after being kept in prison for three months, were carried out to Tyburn. The last words of the girl if they are correctly reported are very pathetic and to the purpose. But they look as if they had been written for her.

"Hether am I come to die, and I have not beene the onele cause of mine owne death, which most justly I have deserved, but also I am the cause of the death of all these persons which at thys time here suffer : and yet to saye the truth I am not so much to be blamed, consydering it was well known unto these learned men that I was a poore wenche, without learnyng, and therefore they might have easily perceyved that the thinges that were done by me could not proceede in no suche sort, but their capacities and learning coulde right well judge from whence they were proceeded, and that they were altogether fayned : but because the things which I fayned was profitable unto them, and therefore they much praised mee and bare me in hande that it was the holy ghost, and not that I did them, and then being puffed up with their prayses, fell into a certaine pride and foolish phantasie with my self, and thought I might fayne what I would, which thing hath brought me to this case, and for the which now I crye God and the King's highnesse most hartely mercie, and desire all you good people to pray to God to have mercie on me, and all them that here suffer with me."

One cannot refrain in this place from remarking on the change which has come over the temper of the people as regards the sacred person of the priest. Henry the Seventh would not send to execution even those mischievous priests who invented and carried out the impudent personations. Yet his son, thirty years later, sends to block, stake or gallows, bishops, abbots, priors, priests, monks, and friars, by the dozen.

The story of Richard Hun illustrates the condition of popular feeling which made these executions of ecclesiastics possible. He was a citizen of good position and considerable wealth, a merchant-taylor by calling ; he was greatly respected by the poorer sort on account of his charitable disposition. "He was a good almesman and relieved the needy." It happened that one of his children, an infant, died and was buried. The curate asked for the "bearing sheet" as a "mortuary."[1] Richard Hun replied that the child had no property in the sheet. The reply shows either bad feeling towards the curate or bad feeling towards the clergy generally. Most likely it was the latter, as the sequel shows.

The order and manner of the burning of *Anne Askew, John Lacels, John Adams, Nicholas Belenian,* with certaine of the Councell sitting in Smithfield.

The priest cited him before the spiritual court. He replied by counsel, suing the curate in a praemunire. In return Hun was arrested on a charge of Lollardry and put into Lambeth Palace. And here shortly afterwards he was found dead. He had hanged himself, said the Bishop and Chancellor. The people began to murmur. Hanged himself? Why should so good a man hang himself? A coroner's inquest was held upon the body. The jury indicted the Chancellor and

---

[1] "Mortuary = a gift left by a man at his death to his parish church for the recompence of his personal tythes and offerings not duly paid in his lifetime" (*Johnson's Dictionary*).

two men, the bell-ringer and the summoner, for murdering Richard Hun. The King's attorney, however, would go no further in the matter. By the Bishop's orders the body was burned at Smithfield. But the murder—if it was a murder—of Richard Hun was not forgotten. Nor was it forgotten that without a trial his body was burned as a heretic's. These things lay in the minds of the people. And they rankled.

In the reign of Henry VI. (1447), four new grammar schools had been established in the City : viz. in the parishes of All Hallows the Great ; St. Andrew's

DEAN COLET (1467-1519)
From an engraved portrait in Holland's *Heroologia*.

Holborn ; St. Peter's Cornhill ; and in St. Thomas Acons' Hospital. Nine years later, five other parish schools had been founded or restored, namely, that of St. Paul's ; of St. Martin's ; of St. Mary le Bow ; of St. Dunstan's in the East ; and of St. Anthony's Hospital. All these schools seem to have fallen more or less into decay during the next hundred years. But very little indeed is known as to the condition of education during this period. There is, however, no doubt that in the year 1509 the Dean of St. Paul's, John Colet, found the condition of St. Paul's School very much decayed. He was himself a man of large means, being the son of a rich merchant who had been Sheriff in 1477, Mayor in 1486, and

Alderman, first of Farringdon Ward Without, and afterwards of Castle Baynard and Cornhill successively. The Dean resolved upon building a new school and endowing it. He therefore bought a piece of land on the east side of the Cathedral; there placed a school and entrusted the revenues with which he endowed it to the Mercers' Company, saying, that though there was nothing sacred in human affairs, he yet found the "least corruption" among them. Later on, the Merchant Taylors founded a school; the Mercers founded another school; and

THOMAS CROMWELL, EARL OF ESSEX (1485(?)-1540)

John Carpenter, Clerk, founded the City of London School. The educational endowments founded by London citizens amount to nearly a hundred.

The enclosure of common lands has always been a temptation to those who live in the neighbourhood and a grievance to those who are thus robbed of their common property. Both in the north and south of London there stretched wide common lands in which the people possessed rights of pasture, cutting wood, and other things. Many of these common lands still remain, though greatly shorn of their former proportions. On the north Hampstead Heath is all that is left of land which began at

Moorfields and stretched northwards as far as Muswell Hill and Highgate and eastward to include the Forests of Epping and Hainault. In a map of London of the
sixteenth century these common lands must be laid down as a special and very
fortunate possession of the City, where people could in a few minutes find themselves in pure country air. Early in the century, however, there were murmurings
on account of the enclosure of the fields north of London. "Before this time,"
says Grafton, "the townes about London, as Islington, Hoxton, Shordyche, and
other, had enclosed the common fields with hedges and ditches that neyther the
yonge men of the City might shoote, nor the auncient persons might walk for their
pleasure in the fields, except eyther their bowes and arrows were broken or taken
away, or the honest and substantiall persons arrested or indicted, saiving that no
Londoner should goe oute of the City but in the high wayes." It is not stated

DEAN COLET'S HOUSE, STEPNEY

how long this grievance lasted; probably it grew gradually: field after field was
cut off; one enclosure after another was made; until the Londoners rubbed their
eyes and asked each other what had become of their ancient grounds—especially
the delightful fields called the Moor, on whose shallow ponds they skated and slid
in winter, and where they practised the long bow, while the elders looked on, in the
summer. They were gone: in their place were fields hedged and ditched, with
narrow lanes in which two people might walk abreast. How long they looked on
considering this phenomenon we know not. At length, however, the pent-up waters
overflowed. "Suddenly this yere" (1514) a great number of people assembled in
the City, and a "Turner" attired in a fool's coat ran about among them crying,
"Shovels and Spades." Everybody knew what was meant. In an incredibly
short time the whole population of the City were outside the walls, armed with

shovels and spades.   Then the ditches were filled in, and hedges cut down, and
the fields laid open again.   The King's Council, hearing of the tumult, came to
the Grey Friars and sent for the Mayor to ascertain the meaning, for a tumult in
the City might become a very serious thing indeed.   When, however, they heard
the cause and meaning of it they "dissimuled" the matter with a reasonable
admonition to attempt no more violence, and went home again.   But the fields
were not hedged in or ditched round any more.

In 1532 there was held a general Muster of all the citizens aged from sixteen to
sixty.   The City, never slow to display its strength and wealth, turned out in great
force.   The men mustered at Mile End, probably because it was the nearest place

PROCESSION.   TIME OF HENRY VIII.
E. Gardner's Collection.

which afforded a broad space for marshalling the troops.   They were dressed in
white uniforms with white caps and white feathers ; the Mayor, Sheriffs, Aldermen,
and Recorder wore white armour, having black velvet jackets with the City arms
embroidered on them, and gold chains.   Before each Alderman marched four halberdiers, each with a gilt halberd.   Before the Lord Mayor marched sixteen men in
white satin jackets, with chains of gold and long gilt halberds ; four footmen in white
satin ; and two pages in crimson velvet, with gold brocade waistcoats ; two stately
horses carrying, the one the Mayor's helmet, the other the Mayor's pole-axe.

All citizens of distinction on such occasions wore white satin jackets and gold
chains.   The vast expenditure of money on a single day's pageant such as this, was
quite common at this time and in the preceding age.   It may perhaps be explained
by certain considerations.   Thus : it was an age of great show and external

splendour; the magnificence of dress, festivals, masques, ridings, and pageants, is difficult to realise in this sober time. Wealth, rank, position, privileges, were in fact marked by display. We have seen the splendour of the Baron who rode to his town house with an army of 500 followers all richly dressed. And it has been observed that it was not wholly the mere love of magnificence that caused a nobleman or an ecclesiastic to keep up this great state. So, in preparing this martial show, with 15,000 men of arms all fully and richly equipped, the Mayor and Aldermen intended to illustrate to the King and his Ministers the power of the City, the wealth of the City, and the resolution of the City to defend their liberties. And I have no doubt that this intention was thoroughly understood by Henry and taken to heart. The March began at nine in the morning. The troops marched through Aldgate, through the City, and so to Westminster by Fleet Street and the Strand—a little over four miles. At five in the evening the last company marched past the King. That part of the business therefore must have lasted about six hours.

In the matter of the King's divorce the City, or the populace, had taken a very strong side in favour of Queen Katherine. It may indeed be true that the King's conscience was awakened after all these years of marriage as to the legality of marrying his brother's widow: he saw perhaps in the failure of male heirs a sign of the Divine displeasure; that may be: it is not possible to understand all the motives which guide a man. To the outside world the simplest motive seems always the certain motive. Katherine was no longer young, no longer beautiful. Anne Boleyn was both. When the second marriage was announced, the citizens were greatly displeased: partly on account of their sympathy with Katherine, partly because they remembered that Anne was the grand-daughter of a mayor, one of themselves. No honour is ever felt to be conferred upon the people by the marriage of a Prince with one of themselves, but quite the reverse. Edward IV. and James II. are examples, as well as Henry VIII. So much did the citizens show their disgust, that at an Easter sermon some of them went out of the church before the prayers for the Queen were read. The King sent word to the Mayor about it. He called the guilds together and bade them cease murmuring against the King's marriage, and cause their journeymen and apprentices and even their wives to offend no more.

On the 29th of May the Queen passed from Greenwich to the Tower, and on the 31st from the Tower to Westminster. The City hastened on this occasion to show their loyalty by preparing a splendid reception for the Queen. The Pageant is described below.

The Princess Elizabeth was born in September of the same year (1533). In the spring of the following year Parliament passed an Act of Succession declaring that she, and not Mary, was heir to the Crown; the whole of the citizens took the oath in acknowledgment of this Act. If any were so hardy as to refuse, they were executed.

HENRY VIII., PRINCESS MARY, AND WILL SOMERS

From Earl Spencer's Collection.

Of Pageants and Ridings no reign ever saw so many, nor was the City ever more honoured in the part which it was invited to take in them. Here, for instance, is a list of the more important: the Coronation in 1509; the reception of the French Ambassadors in 1518; that of the Legate Cardinal Campeggio; that of the Emperor Charles in 1522; the Coronation of Anne Boleyn;—every one an occasion for the display of sumptuous raiment, tapestry, gold chains and allegorical groups. Two of these functions stand out above all others: the Coronation of Anne and the Christening of her child. Let us take the account of the Water Pageant as furnished by Grafton:—

"The xix day of May the Maior and his brethren all in Scarlet, and such as were knightes had collers of Esses and the remnaunt havyng good chaynes, and the counsayle of the Citie with them assembled at saint Marie Hyll, and at one of the clocke dissended to the Newstayre to their Barge, which was garnished with many goodly Banners and instruments, which continually made goodly armony. After that the Maior and his brethren were in their Barge seing that al the companies to the number of fiftie Barges were readie to wayte upon them. They gave commaundement to the companies that no Barge should rowe neerer to another then twise the length of the Barge upon a great paine. And to see the order kept, there were three light Wheryes prepared, and in every one of them two officers to call on them to keepe their order, after which commaundement given they set foorth in order as hereafter is described. First before the Maior's Barge was a Foyst or Wafter full of ordynaunce, in which Foyst was a great Dragon contynually moovyng, and casting wilde fyre: and round about the sayde Foyst stood terrible monsters and wilde men casting fire, and making hideous noyses: next after the Foyst a good distaunce came the Maior's Barge, on whose right hand was the Batchelers' Barge, in the which were Trumpets and divers other melodious Instruments. The deckes of the sayde Barge and the sailyardes and the top Castels were hanged with riche cloth of Golde and silke. At the foreship and the sterne were two great banners riche beaten with the armes of the King and the Quene, and on the top Castell also was a long streamer newely beaten with the sayde armes.

At three of the clock the Queene appered in riche clothe of Gold and entered into her Barge accompanied with divers Ladies and gentlewomen, and incontinent the Citizens set forwardes in their order, their Musicians continually plaiyng, and the Batchelers' Barge goyng on the Queenes right hande, which she toke great pleasure to behold. About the Queenes Barge were many Noblemen, as the Duke of Suffolke, the Marques Dorset, the Erle of Wilshire her father, the Erles of Arrondell, Darby, Rutland, Worcester, Huntyngton, Sussex, Oxford, and many Bishoppes and noblemen, every one in his Barge which was a goodly sight to behold. Shee thus being accompanied rowed toward the Tower, and in the meane waye the shippes which were commaunded to lye on the shore for lettyng of the Barges shot divers peales of Gonnes, and or shee landed there was a marvailous shot out of the Tower as ever was harde there. And at her landing there met with her the Lorde Chamberlaine with the officers of armes and brought her to the king, which received her with lovyng countenance at the posterne by the waterside, and kyssed her, and then she turned back againe and thanked the Maior and the citizens with many goodly words and so entered the Tower." (Grafton's *Chronicles*, vol. ii. p. 448.)

The Insurrection in the North, called the Pilgrimage of Grace, the most dangerous rising in this reign, caused the King to look to the City for assistance. The Mayor sent him 300 men fully armed and equipped.

The Mayor took another step in the interests of the Crown and of order. Although the suppression of the Houses was only begun, the intention of the King was manifest, and the rising in the North showed the temper of some part of the people. It is probable that in the City the popular voice was with the

King. But there was a minority consisting of some of the monks and friars ejected, some of the people who had lost their occupation and their service, some partisans of the old order; and these were dangerous. The Court of Aldermen, therefore, deprived every priest, monk, friar, and religious person of every kind, of all weapons except their meat knives. A rising of the Religious, maddened with rage and fear, joined by one knows not how many of lay partisans, hotheads and ribalds always anxious for a row, might have been a very serious thing indeed. We may be quite sure that there were many within and without the walls who would have desired nothing so much as the sack and pillage of the rich merchants' houses in the sacred name of the Holy Church. Perhaps one of the reasons of the City's acquiescence in the destruction of the Religious Houses was the knowledge that such a rebellion would have produced some kind of alliance with the rogues and vagabonds of their lanes and slums.

The execution of Anne Boleyn and the succession of Henry's queens may be passed over here as belonging to the national history.

In June and July 1536 a Convocation was held at St. Paul's, presided over by Cromwell, the King's Vicar-General. A more important assembly was never held in this country. For this Convocation separated the Church of England altogether from Rome: it held that the King, as Supreme Head of the Church, ought to disregard all citations from the Pope. Once before the Pope's citations had been disregarded and scoffed at, viz. by John; but that was on his own authority, apart from his Clergy and his people. In this case Henry kept up the show of consultation with his Clergy. Not he, but Convocation, decided that he was wholly independent of the Pope.

In the year 1543 the plague appeared and carried off a great many. The City Authorities ordered all infected houses to be marked with a cross; all infected persons who recovered were to remain in quarantine for a month; all straw and rushes from infected houses were to be carried away and burned; and infected clothes were to be carried out of the City. Dogs, except watch-dogs, were to be killed. It proved, happily, to be a short though sharp visitation.

In 1544 the City sent 1000 men to aid Henry in his war with France, in two contingents of 500 each; and in the following year a third contingent of 2000 men was sent to France. In 1545 a tax for two-fifteenths was imposed for the purpose of bringing water from Hackney, Muswell Hill, and Hoxton, into the City. The conclusion of the war with France in 1546 was celebrated by a Procession which was solemn and magnificent. It marched from St. Paul's to Leadenhall Chapel and back again. First came men carrying the silver crosses of the Parish Churches; then all the Parish Clerks, Choristers and Priests in London; then the Choir of St. Paul's, in their school caps: they were followed by the City Companies in their liveries. Last of all marched the Lord Mayor and Aldermen in scarlet robes.

Peace, however, brought with it an invasion of disbanded soldiers, riotous, and given to acts of robbery and violence. They were accompanied by their camp-followers, whose character may be guessed. The Mayor gave orders that the old soldiers should be allowed to beg for a certain number of days, but that the vagabond followers should be driven out of the City. So I suppose they got rid of a few while

EMBARKATION OF HENRY VIII. AT DOVER

the greater number remained behind—an addition to the rogues and beggars of the City, who had already become a most dangerous element. (See p. 366.)

In the last year of Henry's reign (1546) he bestowed an endowment of 500 marks a year on the City Poorhouses on condition that the City itself raised as much. He also gave the City, only a few days before his death, the Hospital of St. Bartholomew, to be called the House of the Poor; the House of the Grey Friars, and the House or Hospital of Bethlehem. Henry died on the 28th of January 1547 at his Palace of Whitehall.

I will now discuss a few more incidents in the history of this reign.

In 1511 Roger Acheley, Mayor, caused the City Granary of Leadenhall to be stored with grain for prevention in time of scarcity. This Mayor also caused Moor fields to be levelled, and bridges and causeways to be erected thereon.

In 1512 the Sheriffs were, by Act of Parliament, empowered to empanel Juries for the City Courts. Every Juryman was to be a citizen worth 100 marks. If he failed to appear upon the first summons he was to forfeit one shilling and eight-pence; for the second, three shillings and fourpence—and so on, the penalty being doubled for each occasion.

In 1517 the Court of Conscience was first established. Two Aldermen and four "discreet" Commoners were appointed every month to sit at the Guildhall twice a week, on Wednesday and Saturday, to hear causes between citizens and freemen of debts not exceeding forty shillings. The Act was passed for two years only; but as it proved highly serviceable it was continued by repeated Acts of Council until the Court was confirmed by James I.

In 1519 the King by Charter removed the Sessions of Peace from St. Martin's le Grand to the Guildhall, to the great contentment of the citizens.

In 1519 the Tower Ditch, between Aldgate and the Tower Postern, was scoured and cleansed—the work cost £95 : 3 : 4. The Chief Ditcher was paid 7d. a day; the second Ditcher 6d.; the rest 5d.; the "Vagabonds," i.e. men pressed into the work, got a penny and their food. It follows from this that the wage of a working man was then 5d. or 6d. a day. The pay of a chantry priest was in most cases £6 a year, or about 4d. a day. So that the craftsman received, to support himself and his family, very little more than the priest for the support of himself. This fact shows that even the despised chantry priest occupied a much higher social position than the craftsman.

In 1525 Wolsey proposed to levy a tax of one-sixth of all the goods and chattels of the laity, and a fourth of those of the clergy. There was so much indignation at this tax that the King gave way, sending a letter to the Mayor in which he stated that he would never exact anything of his people by compulsion, but would rely on their benevolence. It appeared, however, when Wolsey sent for the Mayor and Aldermen to confer with them upon the subject, that the City was not disposed to grant any benevolence at all, relying on a statute of Richard III. abolishing such benevolences. It was in vain that Wolsey pointed out to them the facts that Richard was a murderer and a tyrant: the City stood by the Law, and the benevolence was dropped.

In 1526 occurs an early example of the boycott. The City found that certain foreign merchants had purchased license to import woad contrary to law. It was therefore resolved that no London citizen should have any dealings with any foreign merchant who should import woad.

About the year 1527 there was an attempt made by Wolsey to pass laws in the teeth of the simple rule of supply and demand. The war with Spain caused great losses to the manufacturers of cloth, who were obliged to dismiss their servants and to stop the production. Wolsey thereupon sent for the principal merchants of the City and ordered them to go on buying from the manufacturers as usual; in other words, to ruin themselves and their own servants in order to prevent the dismissal of the factory hands. Should they disobey, the great Cardinal threatened to remove the cloth market from Blackwell Hall to Westminster. "However," Maitland remarks quietly, "it was neither in the power of the King, nor in that of his Minister, to execute the aforesaid injunction: wherefore commerce continued on the same footing as before, till the conclusion of a Peace."

In 1529, after the meeting of Convocation already mentioned, a Proclamation was passed in London prohibiting all commercial intercourse with Rome.

In the same year the City recovered the right of the Great Beam. The King had taken over this important right with all the profits belonging to it and had conveyed it to Sir William Sidney. For ten years the City had been endeavouring to recover their rights even by bribing, but without success. In 1531 a compromise was arrived at, by which Sir William Sidney continued to hold the Beam at an annual rent, and by Royal Charter the right was once more conveyed to the Mayor and Corporation, the Grocers' Company having the privilege of appointing the weighers.

Another attempt was made to regulate the price of food. It was complained that butchers who were not freemen had put up stalls along Leadenhall Street where they sold their meat before the doors of the houses. The Mayor made them all go into Leadenhall Market, where they had to pay rent to the Corporation. He also fixed the price of beef at a half-penny a pound, and of mutton at three-farthings. As a whole sheep could be bought for 2s. 10d., it would seem as if the whole sheep weighed only 45 lbs. It was discovered, however, that the regulation only made meat dearer. Therefore it was not enforced. At this time French wine was sold at 8d. a gallon; Malmsey and other sweet wines at a shilling.

In 1542 occurred the business of George Ferrers. He was M.P. for Plymouth, and he was arrested for debt in the City and lodged in the Compter, a manifest infringement of the privileges of the House. The Serjeant-at-Arms was therefore ordered by the House to proceed to the City and to demand the release of the prisoner. The Sheriffs—Rowland Hill and Henry Suckley—in their zeal for the privileges of Parliament, not only refused to obey, but abused the serjeant and maltreated him. Upon which he returned to Westminster and informed the House of what had been done. The House therefore ordered the serjeant to return and to demand the prisoner without writ or warrant. Meanwhile the Sheriffs had learned the meaning of their action and were beginning to feel uncomfortable. They released the prisoner and, accompanied by the creditor, one White, they attended at the Bar of the House. The Sheriffs and the creditor and one of their clerks were sent to the Tower; the arresting clerk and four others to Newgate. And in this melancholy plight they continued for some days, until they were released by the intercession of the Mayor. This was an example to all future Sheriffs not to take too much upon themselves.

About this time also the principal streets of the suburbs were first completely paved: viz. Holborn, High Street, Aldgate as far as Whitechapel Church, Chancery Lane, Gray's Inn Lane, Shoe Lane, Fetter Lane, White Cross Street, Chiswell Street, Grub Street, Shoreditch, Goswell Street, St. John's Street, Cannon Street, Wych Street, Holy Well Street (by Clement Danes), the Strand; Petty France in Westminster; Water Lane in Fleet Street; Long Lane in Smithfield; and Butcher Row without Temple Bar. The paving was not yet the flat slab of stone introduced later, but the round cobble stone, with a channel or gutter running down the middle.

In 1543 an Act was passed empowering the City to bring water from Hampstead and Muswell Hill, and two years later a conduit was set up in Lothbury with water from Hoxton Fields. (Appendix I.)

The death of Henry left the City in a condition of the greatest confusion and disorder. The streets were full of returned soldiers, and of the idle vagabonds who follow the army: in holes and corners there were lurking unfrocked friars and people turned out of their work in the Religious Houses; there were no hospitals for the sick; none for the blind; none for the insane. If these were the fruits of the King's supremacy, then, men whispered to each other, it were better to return to the old superstitions.

CHAPTER III

EDWARD VI

THE City presents few points of interest during this reign which do not belong to the national history. The Progress of the Reformation is the subject which more especially belongs to and interests the world in this young King's short reign.

EDWARD VI. (1537-1553)
From a portrait by Holbein at Windsor Castle.

There can be no doubt whatever that just as in the reign of Richard II. the City was saturated with Lollardry, so in the last years of Henry VIII. it was filled with the new ideas. The connection with the Pope severed; the religious Orders clean swept away; the reading of the Bible rapidly spreading; the teaching and example of men like Cranmer, Latimer, Rogers, Ridley, Hooper, and others; the derision poured upon the old things such as pilgrimages, image worship, repeated services and monasticism; the popular attack on the Religious by such writers as Fish in the *Supplicacyon of Beggars* and Barnabe Googe in his *Popish Kingdom;* the lectures and sermons carefully composed with the design of overthrowing and casting contempt upon the old Faith; the natural instinct of men to see in new ideas a certain remedy for old ills;—these things made it inevitable that the new thoughts should spread and take root.　We hear no more, for instance, of the Mayor disarming men who had been monks and friars.

The new ideas, again, appealed to the nobler and more generous part of humanity.　To stand erect before the Creator without the intervention of a priest; no longer to be called upon to believe that which the Bible would not allow to be believed; the introduction of Reason into the domain of Doctrine; the abandonment of childish pilgrimages to the tombs of fallible and sinful mortals; the abolition of the doctrine that pardons, indulgences, Heaven itself, can be bought with money; no longer to believe that fasting and the observance of days may avail to salvation; —these things caught hold of men's minds and ran rapidly from class to class.　And then there was the reading of the Bible for themselves by the folk who could do no more than read.　There are no means of deciding how far the old English Version had been read and passed from hand to hand.

In the reign of Edward VI. we see the first-fruits of the new ideas.　Already, however, there were signs of change other than those ordered and authorised by the most autocratic of sovereigns.　The Mayor abolished the service of the Boy Bishop at St. Paul's; sober citizens were haled before the courts charged with blaspheming the mass; men rose in their places and made a noise in church during celebration; one, a boy, threw his cap at the Host during the time of elevation: "at this tyme" (*Grey Friars Chron.*) "was moche spekyng agayn the Sacrament of the Auter, that some called it Jack of the boxe, with divers other shameful names."

Thus the new reign began.

It was a time of great uncertainty and trouble in religious matters.　We see the citizens, ignorant of Greek, disputing over the interpretation of a text; over the conditions of salvation; over matters too high for them—one grows hot and says things that ought not to be said.　The informer in the crowd—there is always an informer—steals away and lays information.　Then the hasty citizen is lucky if he gets off with a fine.　They whisper thus and thus concerning the intentions of the Protector and the opinions of the Archbishop.　It is rumoured that the new Bishop of this or that will not be consecrated in his robes; it is rumoured that there will be more changes in the Articles of Religion; it is rumoured that there will be a vast rising of the ejected priests and the starving friars; it is rumoured that they have already risen in the East and in the West.　The air is full of rumours.　Trade is very bad. There is no money anywhere; the coinage is debased : a shilling is worth no more than sixpence ; a groat is twopence ; a penny is a half-penny ; and the price of provisions is certainly double what it was! It is a strange, perplexed time.

There were other events connected with the City besides these constant alarms about the change of Faith. Traitors were executed, notably the two Seymours ; rebels were drawn, hanged and quartered, notably the four Captains of the Cornish

EDWARD VI. (1537-1553)
From a portrait by Holbein at Windsor Castle.

Rising; the sweating sickness appeared again in 1550 and lasted for six months, carrying off men only and sparing women and children. The cloister of St. Paul's, commonly called the Dance of Death, and the Charnel House of St. Paul's, were destroyed and carried away ; there were risings in Cornwall, Norfolk, and Yorkshire ; a woman named Joan of Kent was burned at Smithfield for heresy ; then happened the famous murder of Arden of Faversham, for which his wife, his maid, and one of the murderers were all burned ; three men and one woman hanged ; a Dutchman named George of Paris was burned for heresy in Smithfield.

An important acquisition, however, was gained by the City in 1550. The Borough of Southwark consisted of three manors, the Guildable Manor, the King's Manor, and the Great Liberty Manor. Edward III. had granted the first of these to the City. Edward IV. had confirmed and amplified this grant, giving the City the right of holding a yearly Fair in the month of September together with a Court of Pie Powder. The City next claimed the right of holding a market twice a week in Southwark. On this claim there were disputes. Finally the City bought all the rights of the Crown in Southwark for the sum of £647 : 2 : 1. They thus obtained a recognised right to hold four weekly markets, and to administer the whole borough excepting the two prisons of the Marshalsea and the King's Bench, and the Duke of Suffolk's House.

A very curious difference was made between the new Ward of Bridge Without, then founded, and the other wards. It is this : that in the election of Aldermen the people of the Ward have never had any voice and have never taken any part. And they are not represented in the Common Council.

In one respect the civic history of this reign is very fine—the citizens grappled manfully with the question of the poor and the sick. We have seen how Henry gave them Grey Friars, Bartholomew's, and Bethlehem. In aid of the former they levied on the City a tax of one-half of a fifteenth, i.e. a thirtieth. And the memory of the old Religious Fraternities lingered still, for we find them founding a Brotherhood for the Relief of the Poor, to which Sir John Gresham, then Mayor, and most of the Aldermen belonged. Nor was this all. They obtained by purchase, at the cost of £2500, the Hospital of St. Thomas in Southwark.

After the poor, the children. Grey Friars House was taken in hand and altered to convert it into a school. In a few months 400 children were admitted. This was the work of Sir Richard Dobbs as Mayor. When Ridley was lying in prison, shortly before his death he wrote to Dobbs in these words :—" Oh Dobbs, Dobbs, Alderman and Knight, thou in thy year didst win my heart for evermore, for that honourable act, that most blessed work of God, of the erection and setting up of Christ's Holy Hospitals and truly Religious Houses which by thee and through thee were begun."

After the sick and the children come those who cannot work and those who will not work. In 1553 the young King consented to give his disused Palace of Bride-well for the purpose of turning it into a Work-house or hospital for those who could work no longer, and for a House of Correction to those who would not work (see also p. 368). The King gave also 700 marks and all the beds and bedding of the Palace of the Savoy. The very last act of Edward VI. was a Charter of Incorporation, appointing the Mayor, Aldermen, and Commonalty, Governors of these Royal Hospitals in the City.

In the first year of Edward the House of Commons passed an Act which

EDWARD VI. GRANTING CHARTER TO BRIDEWELL

From E. Gardner's Collection.

showed that the old spirit of independence and the desire to form Unions were not dead among the craftsmen of London. They enacted :—

"That if any Artificers, Workmen, or Labourers do conspire, covenant, or promise together, that they shall not make or do their work but at a certain Price or Rate, or shall not enterprize nor take upon them to finish that work which another hath begun, or shall do but a certain work in a day, or shall not work but at certain Hours or Times; that then every Person so conspiring, covenanting, or offending, being thereof convicted by Witnesses, Confession, or otherwise, shall forfeit for the first offence £10 or twenty days' Imprisonment; for the second offence £20 or Pillory; and for a third offence £40 or to sit on the Pillory, and to have one Ear cut off, besides being rendered infamous and incapable of ever giving Evidence upon Oath."   (Maitland, vol. i. p. 239.)

The Act is explained to apply especially to butchers, bakers, brewers, poulterers, cooks, etc.—in a word, to those who provided the daily necessaries of life.

In 1548 the Marching Watch was revived by Sir John Gresham, after being in abeyance for many years. It was London's finest show. (See p. 362.)

The Deposition and trial of the Protector are matters of national history. The part taken by the City is not generally recorded by the historian. It is told by Maitland :—

"The Earl of *Warwick*, and divers Lords of the Privy-Council, being highly dissatisfied with the Administration of *Edward Seymer*, Duke of *Somerset*, the Protector, withdrew from Court, associated, and armed themselves and Domesticks, and secured the Tower of *London* by a Stratagem of the Lord Treasurer's, without the Effusion of Blood; and, having removed the Governor, substituted one of their Friends to succeed him.   Having luckily succeeded in their first Attempt, *Warwick* removed into the City, and lodged at the House of *John York*, one of the Sheriffs of *London*.

Upon advice of these proceedings at *London*, the Protector was so greatly intimidated, that he instantly removed with the King from *Hampton-Court* to *Windsor*, and began strongly to fortify the Castle. In the Interim the Lords at *London* had a Conference with the Lord-Mayor and Aldermen, whom they earnestly importuned to provide a Power sufficient for Defence of the City: Which being assented to, the several Companies were ordered alternately to mount Guard, to be ready to oppose all Attempts that might be made against them.   They likewise desired a Supply of five hundred Men, to enable them to bring the Protector to Justice.   To which Answer was returned, That nothing could be done in that Affair without consulting the Common-Council; to which End, the Lord-Mayor summoned all the Members thereof to assemble the next Day in *Guildhall*.

In the mean time the Lords convened in the Mayor's House; where after having drawn up a trifling charge against the Protector, they caused it to be proclaimed in divers parts of the City.   After which they conferred with the Mayor and Aldermen in the Council-Chamber (before they met the Commons) and, having come to several Resolutions, the Mayor and Aldermen repaired to the Common-Council; where, in a full Assembly, they produced a Letter from the King, commanding them immediately to send him five hundred Men completely armed to *Windsor*.   However, *Robert Brook*, the Recorder, earnestly exhorted them rather to supply the Lords with that Number, by whose assistance they would be enabled to call the Protector to an Account, and thereby redress the Grievances of an injured Nation; without which the City was not only in Danger of being ruined, but likewise the whole Kingdom to become a Prey to his insatiable Avarice.   This Speech, instead of having the desired Effect, occasioned a profound Silence : which greatly amazing the Orator, he reassumed his Discourse, and seriously pressed them for an Answer : Whereupon *George Stadlow*, a prudent and judicious Citizen, rose up, and spoke as followeth :—

'I remember,' sayth he, 'in a Story written in Fabian's Chronicle, of the Warre betweene the King and his Barons, which was in the time of King *Henry* III. and the same Time the Barons, as our Lordes do now, demaunded Ayde of the Maior and Citie of *London*, and that in a rightful Cause for the Commonweale, which was for the Execution of divers good Lawes, whereunto the King before had geven his Consent, and after would not suffer them to take Place; and the Citie did ayde the Lords, and it came to an open Battayl, wherein the Lordes prevayled, and toke the King and his sonne Prisoners, and upon certaine Condycions the Lordes restored againe the King and his Sonne to their Liberties; and, amonge

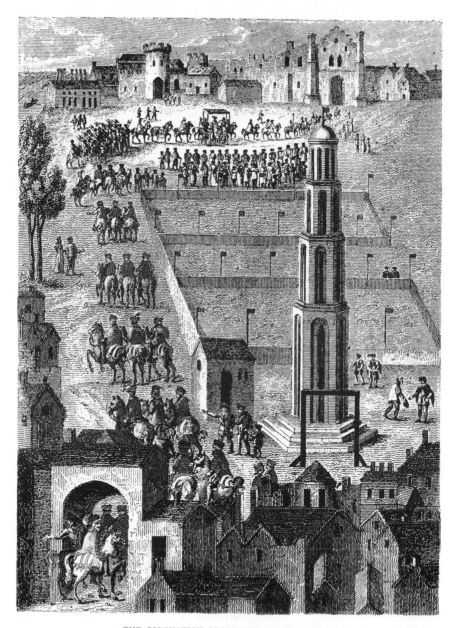

THE CORONATION PROCESSION OF EDWARD VI.

other Condycions, this was one, That the King should not only graunt his Pardon to the Lordes, but also to the Citezens of *London*; which was graunted, yea, and the same was ratified by Act of Parliament: But what followed of it? Was it forgotten? No, surely, nor forgiven during the King's life; the Lyberties of the City were taken away, Straungers appointed to be our Heades and Gouvernors, the Citezens geven away

Bodye and Goodes, and from one Persecution to another were most miserably afflicted. Such it is to enter into the Wrath of a Prince, as *Solomon* sayth, *The Wrath and Indignation of a Prince is Death.* Wherefore, forasmuch as this Ayd is requyred of the King's Majestie, whose Voyce we ought to hearken unto, for he is our high Shepherd, rather than unto the Lords; and yet I would not with the Lords to be clearly shaken off, but that they with us, and we with them, may joyne in Sute, and make our most humble Petition to the King's Majestie, that it would please his Highness to heere suche Complaynt against the Government of the Lorde Protector, as maye be justly alleged and proved; and, I doubt not, but this Matter will be pacefied, that neither shall the King, nor yet the Lordes, have Cause to seeke for further Ayde, neyther we to offend any of them bothe.'" (Maitland, vol. i. p. 240.)

It would seem that the nobles had resumed the old custom of having a great train of followers. For at the departure of Mary Queen of Scots from London, where she had been entertained for four days, the Duke of Northumberland attended her with a hundred mounted men, of whom forty were dressed in black velvet, with velvet hats and feathers, and had gold chains about their necks. The Earl of Pembroke was there with a hundred and twenty men, also in hats and feathers; and the Lord Treasurer had a hundred gentlemen and yeomen. The last glimpse which London had of the young King was when Sir Hugh Willoughby sailed down the river on that voyage which was to discover a N.E. passage through the ice and snow of North Siberia. The ships were dressed with streamers; trumpeters stood in the bows; guns were fired for a farewell salute as they passed Greenwich Palace, and the dying Prince was brought out for one more look upon the glory of his realm in the courage and enterprise of his subjects.

CHAPTER IV

MARY

THE proclamation of Lady Jane Grey as Queen, the short-lived and ill-fated period of that usurpation, belong to the history of the country, not to that of London.

It was on the evening of the 3rd of August that Mary made her entry into the

MARY TUDOR (1516-1558)
From a woodcut of the portrait by Antonio Moro, in Prado, Madrid.

City accompanied by her half-sister Elizabeth. She came from Newhall in Essex where, a few days before, she had received a deputation from the City with a present of £500 in gold. At the Bars of Aldgate she was met by the Mayor, who gave her the City Sword. The order of the procession is related by a contemporary as follows :—

" First, the citizens' children walked before her magnificently dressed; after followed gentlemen habited in velvets of all sorts, some black, others in white, yellow, violet and carnation; others wore satins or taffety, and some damasks of all colours, having plenty of gold buttons; afterwards followed the Mayor, with the City Companies, and the chiefs or masters of the several trades; after them, the Lords, richly habited, and the most considerable knights; next came the ladies, married and single, in the midst of whom was the Queen herself, mounted on a small white ambling nag, the housings of which were fringed with gold thread; about her were six lacqueys, habited in vests of cloth of gold. The Queen herself was dressed in violet velvet, and was then about forty years of age, and 'rather fresh-coloured.' Before her were six lords bareheaded, each carrying in his hand a golden mace, and some others bearing the arms and crown. Behind her followed the archers, as well of the first as the second guard. . . . She was followed by her sister, named Madame Elizabeth, in truth a beautiful princess, who was also accompanied by ladies both married and single. Then might you hear the firing of divers pieces of artillery, bombards and canons, and many rejoicings made in the City of London; and afterwards the Queen, being in triumph and royal magnificence in her palace and castle of Oycemestre [Westminster], took it into her head to go and hear mass at Paules, that is to say, at the church of St. Paul, and she was attended by six hundred guards, besides the cere, that is to say the servants of lords and nobles." (*Antiquarian Repertory.*)

On the 10th of August the remains of the late King were buried according to the forms of the Book of Common Prayer. It was not long, however, before every one understood clearly the mind of the Queen.

On the 1st of October Mary rode through the City to Westminster for her Coronation. Sharpe notes the significant fact that the daily service at St. Paul's was not held because all the priests not suspended for Protestantism were wanted at Westminster Abbey.

Queen Mary was crowned with every possible care to return to the old ritual. Fresh oil, blessed by the Bishop of Arras, had been brought over; she was afraid that St. Edward's Chair had been polluted by her brother, the Protestant, sitting in it; she had therefore another chair sent by the Pope. The death of Edward took place on the 6th of July 1553, the Coronation of Mary on the 1st of October. The Queen must have requested the Pope to send her the chair immediately on her accession if that chair had arrived within eighty-five days.

In November Lady Jane Grey, her husband, two of his brothers, and Cranmer, were tried at the Guildhall and sentenced to death; but execution was delayed. Probably in the case of Lady Jane Grey the sentence would never have been carried out had it not been for Wyatt's Rebellion in January 1554. The ostensible cause was the Spanish match, which was regarded with the greatest dislike and suspicion by the whole people—" Yea, and thereat allmost eche man was abashed, looking daylie for worse matters to grow shortly after." When the Rebellion broke out the City stood loyally by the Queen: the Companies set watch; no munitions of war were allowed to go out of the City; chains were set up at the Bridge foot; and 500 men were hurriedly raised and equipped. Mary herself showed the courage of her race. She rode into the City and met the citizens at the Guild-hall, making them a very spirited speech. She spoke in a loud voice so that everyone should hear. No action in her reign shows her nearly so well as this natural and courageous speech.

The following is Mary's speech as given by Maitland :—

"In my owne Person I am come unto you, to tell you that which yourselves already doe see and know; I mean, the traiterous and seditious Number of the *Kentish Rebels*, that are assembled against Us and You: Their Pretence, as they say, is to resist a Marriage between Us and the Prince of *Spain.* Of all their Plots, pretended Quarrels and evil-contrived Articles, you have been made privy. . . . What I am, loving Subjects, you right well know, your Queene, to whom at my Coronation, when I was wedded to the Realme, and to the Lawes of the same (the Spousal Ring whereof I have on my Finger, which never hitherto was, nor hereafter shall be left off), ye promised your Allegeance and Obedience unto me; and that I am the right and true Inheritor to the *English* Crown, I not only take all *Christendome* to Witness, but also your Acts of Parliaments confirming the same.

And this I say further unto you in the Word of a Prince, I cannot tell how naturally a Mother loveth her Children, for I was never the Mother of any; but certainly, if a Prince and Governour may as naturally love their Subjects, as the Mother doth her Child, then assure yourselves, that I, being your Soveraigne Lady and Queene, doe as earnestly and tenderly love and favour you; and I, thus loving you, cannot but thinke, that you as heartily and faithfully love me againe; and so, this Love bound together in the Knot of Concord, we shall be able, I doubt not, to give these Rebels a short and speedy Overthrow. . . .

But if, as my Progenitors have done before, it might please God that I might leave some Fruit of my Body to be your Governour, I trust you would not only rejoice thereat, but also I know it would be to your great Comfort; and certainly if I either did know or thinke that this Marriage should either turne to the Danger or Loss of any of you, my loving Subjects, or to the Detriment of any Part of the Royal Estate of this *English* Realme, I would never consent thereunto, neither would I ever marry, whilst I lived.

Wherefore, good Subjects, plucke up your Hearts, and, like true Men, stand fast with your lawful Prince against these Rebels, both ours and yours, and fear them not, for I assure you, I do not, and will leave with you my Lord *Howard* and my Lord Treasurer, to be assistant with my Lord-Maior, for the Safe-guard of the City from Spoile and Sackage, which is the onely Scope of this rebellious Company." (Maitland, vol. i. p. 249.)

The failure of the revolt was due to the spirited and prompt action of the City.

All this belongs to the history of the country. Yet we cannot pass over the execution of Lady Jane Grey. It is the most melancholy of all the many tragedies which belong to the Tower during the fifteenth and sixteenth centuries. Perhaps it seemed necessary at the time, in order to prevent other risings like that of Wyatt, in the same way that it had seemed necessary to Henry VII. that the young Earl of Warwick should be removed; and later to Elizabeth that Mary Queen of Scots should no longer be an occasion of conspiracy. At the same time it is wonderful that it should have been thought even possible to bring to the scaffold this girl of sixteen who had been made to play a part. The story of her execution and of her noble words, told with simple directness by Holinshed, cannot be read without tears :—

"By this time was there a scaffold made upon the greene over against the White Tower, for the ladie Jane to die upon, who being nothing at all abashed, neither with feare of hir owne death, which then approched, neither with the sight of the dead carcasse of hir husband when he was brought into the chapell, came forth, the lieutenant leading hir, with countenance nothing abashed, nor hir eies anything moistened with teares, with a booke in hir hand, wherein she praied untill she came to the said scaffold. Whereon when she was mounted, this noble yoong lady as she was indued with singular gifts both of learning and knowledge so was she as patient and mild as anie lambe at hir execution, and a little before hir death uttered these words :—

'Good people I am come hither to die, and by a law I am condemned to the same. My offence against the queenes highness was onelie in consent to the device of other, which now is deemed treason : but it was never of my seeking, but by counsell of those who should seem to have further understanding of

LADY JANE GREY (1537-1554)
After the portrait in the Collection of the Earl of Stamford and Warrington

things than I, which knew little of the law and much lesse of the titles to the crowne. But touching the procurement and desire thereof by me, or on my behalfe, I doo wash my hands in innocencie thereof before God, and the face of all you (good Christian people) this daie.' And therewith she wroong her hands wherein she had hir booke. Then (said she) 'I praie you all good Christian people, to beare me witnesse that I die a true Christian woman and that I looke to be saved by none other meanes, but onlie by the mercie of God, in the bloud of his onlie sonne Jesus Christ : and I confesse that when I did know the word of God, I neglected the same, and loved myselfe and the world, and therefore this plague and punishment is justlie and worthlie happened unto me for my sins, and yet I thanke God of his goodnesse, that he hath given me a time and respit to repent. And now, good people, while I am alive I praie you assist me with your praiers.' Then kneeling downe she said the psalme of *Miserere mei Deus* in English, and then stood up and gave hir maid (called mistress Ellin) hir gloves and handkercher, and hir booke she also gave to maister Bridges the lieutenant of the Tower, and so untied her gowne : and the executioner pressed to helpe her off with it, but she desired him to let hir alone, and turned hir toward hir two gentle-women, who helped hir off therewith, and with hir other attires, and they gave hir a faire handkercher to put about hir eies. Then the executioner kneeled downe and asked her forgiveness, whom she forgave most willinglie. Then he willed her to stand upon the straw, which doone, she saw the blocke and then she said, I praie you dispatch me quickly. Then she kneeled down saieng, Will you take it off before I laie me downe? Whereunto the executioner answered, No, Madame. Then tied she the handkercher about her eies and feeling for the blocke she said, Where is it? Where is it? One of the standers by guided her thereunto and she laid downe hir head upon the blocke and then stretched forth her bodie and said, Lord, into thy hands I commend my spirit ; and so finished hir life." (Holinshed, vol. iv. p. 22.)

Mary's first Parliament met with the celebration of mass, which was ominous ; but it was not too compliant : it was ready to restore the situation as it was in the last years of Henry VIII. ; it was unwilling to submit to Rome ; and it refused absolutely to restore the Church property. Further, it presented a petition against the proposed foreign marriage. Mary's second Parliament, more obedient to the will of the Queen, gave its consent to the proposed marriage, but refused to re-enact the statute for the burning of heretics. Her third Parliament went a step farther : it re-enacted the statute for the burning of heretics ; it agreed to reconciliation with Rome ; but it refused, like its predecessors, to sanction the surrender of Church lands. They were ready to obey their sovereign in matters of faith : the soul may always be left to the care of the Church ; but property—property—that, if you please, belongs to the Lay mind. Convocation, on the other hand, was very thorough : it denounced the Book of Common Prayer ; it demanded the suppression of the Catechism ; it recommended violent measures against the clergy who should deny the Real Presence and against those who should not put away their wives. This meant Revolution. Hosts of priests, and those who still survived from the monasteries, rejoiced to say mass once more, even in the ruined and desecrated churches that were left to them. It meant Restoration. Priests sprang up everywhere from the ground—how had they lived for ten years ? Priests in the villages and the parish churches put on their old robes ; dragged out the censing vessels ; replaced the Host. Ex-monks who had been pensioned from the monasteries ; ex-friars who had received no pensions but had been simply turned into the street ; ecclesiastics from abroad ;— all came, eager to revive the forbidden worship. They looked around them ruefully at the dishonoured shrines and the ruined chapels : it would take centuries to make everything as it had been ; but still—one must try.

Meantime, think, if you can, of the deadly hatred which these priests must have felt towards those who had done these mischiefs ; think of the silent satisfaction with which even the best of them would witness the execution of one who had been a leader—a Hooper or a Latimer—in bringing about this destruction. But the destruction was stayed. Holy Church was back again, and of course for ever. The

Great Rebellion, they thought, was ended. As for the beneficed clergy in possession, many conformed for fear and for safety; very few indeed gave up their wives;
happy were the contumacious if their contumacy brought no worse consequence than
to beg their bread on the road; happy if it did not lead to a speedy trial, conviction,
and the certainty of becoming a fiery example. They might have made up their
minds at the outset that Mercy was not a quality for which Mary would be con-
spicuous. Before the Fires of Smithfield began there were the executions for the
Rebellion of Wyatt. It was an excellent opportunity for winning the hearts of the

ST. PETER AD VINCULA, OVERLOOKING TOWER GREEN
E. Gardner's Collection.

people; Lady Jane Grey's party never had the smallest chance: she herself might
have been allowed to be at liberty with no danger to the Queen, while to execute
her boy-husband was as barbarous and useless as to execute herself. Fifty persons,
however, officers, knights, and gentlemen, were put to death in consequence of the
Rebellion. Four hundred common men were hanged about London. Fifty were
hanged on gibbets, and there left to hang a great part of the summer.

Meantime, the people of London—partly exasperated by the sight of these
gibbets; partly hating the Spanish marriage; partly hating the break-up of the
Reformation—showed their minds in every possible way. They shot at preachers
of Papistry; they dressed up a cat like a Roman Priest, and hanged it on a gallows

in Cheapside ; they found a girl who pretended to receive messages from a spirit. It was called the Spirit in the Wall. When the Eucharist was carried through Smithfield a man tried to knock the holy elements out of the priest's hands. And on Easter Day a priest saying mass in St. Margaret's, Westminster, was attacked by a man with a knife.

The Marian Persecution began in January 1555. The Queen issued a proclamation that bonfires should be lit in various places in the City to show the people's joy and gladness for the abolition of heresies. This was the signal for the martyrdoms. John Rogers, Prebendary of St. Paul's, was burned, to begin with, at Smithfield ; Hooper, at Gloucester ; Ferrar at St. David's ; Rowland Taylor at Hadleigh ; Lawrence Saunders at Coventry ; William Flower at Westminster ; John Cardmaker at Smithfield ; John Bradford at Smithfield. It is enough to state that the martyrs of this Persecution were two hundred and eighty-eight in number : including five Bishops, twenty - one clergy, fifty-five women, four children, and two hundred and three laymen. Of the laymen, only eight were gentlemen. I will invite consideration of this fact later on.

The flames of martyrdom lasted till within a month of Mary's end. It is difficult to understand how the Bishops could believe that the burning of this kind of heretic stamped out heresy. Hundreds, nay, thousands, of families went in perpetual mourning for the death of brother or cousin, a martyr faithful to the end. The Bishops might have understood the signs of the times : they might have seen the Mayor and Aldermen trying vainly to show conviction rather than obedience in attending all the processions and functions of the Church at which the people looked on sullenly and with murmurs ; they might have listened to the wisdom of Cardinal Pole, who pointed out to the Queen and the Council that these severities were destructive to the Catholic Faith in the country. The Persecution reads like the revenge of a revengeful woman. " Burn ! Burn ! Burn ! " she cries. " To avenge the tears of my mother ; to avenge the unhappiness of my childhood ; to avenge the act that made me illegitimate ; to avenge the marriage of Anne Boleyn. Burn ! Burn ! Burn ! "

Everybody knows the eager hopes and expectation with which Mary looked forward to the birth of a child. The tales of the common people about the Queen's supposed pregnancy are illustrated by a story in Holinshed.

"There came to see me, whome I did both heare and see, one Isabel Malt, a woman dwelling in Aldersgate Street in Horne allie, not farre from the house where this present book was printed, who before witnesse made this declaration unto us, that she being delivered of a man-child upon Whitsuntide in the morning, which was the eleventh daie of June Anno 1555, there came to hir the Lord North, and another lord to her unknowne, dwelling then about old Fish Street, demanding of hir if she would part with hir child, and would swear that she never knew nor had no such child. Which if she would, hir sonne (they said) should be well provided for, she should take no care for it, with manie faire offers if she would part with the child. After that came other women also, of whome one (she said) should have been the rocker :

EXECUTION OF LADY JANE GREY

From the painting by Paul Delaroche in the Tate Gallery, London.

p. 58.

but she in no wise would let go hir sonne, who at the writing hereof, being alive and called Timothie Malt, was of the age of thirteene yeares and upward. Thus much (I saie) I heard of the woman hirself. What credit is to be given to hir relation, I deale not withall, but leave it to the libertie of the reader to believe it they that list : to them that list not, I have no further warrant to assure them." (Vol. iv. p. 83.)

The same Chronicler gives us a glimpse of the divided state of the popular mind on the occasion of the removal of Dr. Sands, Vice-Chancellor of Cambridge, to London, to be tried for heresy. As he left Cambridge the Papists came out to jeer at him, and his friends to mourn for him. When he got to London, one like a milk-wife hurled a stone at him, which struck him in the breast. When he came to Tower Hill a woman cried out, " Fie on thee, thou knave, thou traitor, thou heretic!" For which she was upbraided by another woman who called out, " Good gentleman : God be thy comfort and give thee strength to stand in God's cause even to the end!" When, after some weeks, they brought him from the Tower to the Marshalsea the people had gone round already, and " poperie was unsaverie." Everywhere they prayed to God to comfort him and to strengthen him in the truth. In the Marshalsea, Sands fell into the hands of a Protestant keeper, who gave him all the indulgence he could. And in the end he escaped into Holland, and there stayed till the death of Mary.

The examples of Henry the Seventh's reign were not likely to be lost so soon. A lad of eighteen named William Fetherstone, a miller's son, was reported to be at Eltham in Kent giving himself out for King Edward, who, he declared, was not dead at all. Was the boy mad? It is not known. He himself declared that he had been made to say this : it is quite possible that certain hot-headed Protestants thought to set up King Edward again, and so to get back the new religion. Such a thing can never be attempted without encouragement—perhaps the lad was soft and easily moulded. Being brought before the Council he rambled in his talk ; wherefore he was committed to the Marshalsea as a lunatic. That conclusion did not prevent them from whipping the boy all round the Palace at Westminster and all the way from Westminster to Smithfield. They then packed him off to his birthplace in the North, where he might have rested in peace ; but the unlucky wretch began to talk again about Edward VI., who, he said, was still alive. Therefore they brought him up to London and hanged him at Tyburn.

To return to the other points connected with London during this reign. They are not many. One of the difficulties was the rush into London of Spaniards who came over after the marriage of Philip and Mary. It is interesting to note how with every consort of foreign origin the people of the country to which he or she belonged flocked over to London in multitudes. After the Norman Conquest came troops of Normans ; after the accession of Henry II. came Angevins ; after the arrival of Eleanor of Provence came men of Provence ; and now came Spaniards. Was

Certaine Bishops talking with Maister Bradford in prison.

Iesus receiue vs.

Repent England.

The description of the burning of Maſter Iohn Bradford
Preacher, and Iohn Leafe a Prentice.

London, then, always considered a Promised Land to those who lived outside? It was but a poor Land of Promise in these years, when all the world was torn by civil and religious wars. However, the Spaniards were everywhere: "a man should have mete in the streets for one Englishman above iiij Spanyardes"; the Court was crammed with Spaniards; and Philip, so far from attempting to win the hearts of the English nobles, held himself aloof with Castilian ceremony. We hear little more of the Spaniards after Philip's departure: probably they found London an unfavourable soil for a permanent settlement and withdrew; the Spanish

INTERIOR OF THE BELL TOWER, WHERE PRINCESS ELIZABETH WAS IMPRISONED BY HER SISTER QUEEN MARY
E. Gardner's Collection.

element as shown in the names of the Londoners at the present day, or in the Parish Registers, is small indeed.

The jealousy of foreigners, especially of Spaniards, caused trouble in the City throughout this reign. There were rumours that thousands of Spaniards were coming over; the old jealousy of the Hanseatic League was renewed: the Mayor gave orders that work should not be given to foreigners; they were forbidden to open shops in the City; they were not allowed to keep school; their shutters were forcibly closed. One feels that the situation of the foreigner in the City was anything but pleasant, especially if he were a Spaniard.

The submission of Juries to the Judges was expected in matters of treason, if not in other things. The case of Nicholas Throgmorton, charged with high treason and complicity in the Rebellion of Wyatt, proves this. Doubtless it was in opposition to the Judge's charge that the Jury brought in a verdict of Not Guilty. For this they were summoned before the Star Chamber, where four of the twelve made submission; the remaining eight were sent to prison, where they remained for six months. They were then brought before the Star Chamber again, where they defended their finding as being in accordance with their own consciences. As if Juries in matters of treason could have consciences! So they were sent back to prison, and only got out by paying a fine—some of £44, some of £60 apiece.

In 1556 the City gave Mary a loan of £6000.

War with France was declared in June 1557. The City was instructed to put its munitions of war on a sound and serviceable footing. It complied, and raised a force of 500 men, which joined the army commanded by Lord Pembroke. In less than a month the Queen sent a letter to the Mayor informing him of the departure of Philip and commanding him to raise another force of 1000 men. After a good deal of protest and grumbling, and after vain appeals to the liberties and franchises of the City respecting the sending of men on active service, submission was made and the men were got together. This was early in August. But it does not seem that they were sent. On 27th August the French were defeated at St. Quentin. Towards the end of the year it was known that Calais was in a dangerous position. On 2nd January a message arrived from the Queen, ordering the despatch of 500 men at once. They were wanted for the relief of Calais. But Calais fell on the 7th. Then the City was called upon to furnish another 2000 men. On the 13th the Queen wrote to say that a violent storm had crippled her fleet—the men were to be kept back, but in readiness. Then it was heard that Philip's forces were on their way to Flanders, under the Duke of Savoy, and that the Channel was kept open by a Spanish fleet. A regiment of 500 was therefore sent off to Dover in order to be shipped for Dunkirk.

In March 1558 Mary raised a loan of £20,000 on the security of the Crown lands, from the City Companies. The greater Companies contributed £16,983:6:3, the rest being made up by the smaller Companies. The Mercers gave £3275; the smaller Companies sums varying from £50 to £300.

For the better regulation of trade an Act of Parliament was passed in 1554 by which non-residents were not allowed to sell their wares in any town.

"Whereas the Cities, Boroughs, Towns Corporate and Market Towns, did heretofore flourish, where Youth were well educated, and civilly brought up, and were highly serviceable to the Government; but were brought to great Decay, and were like to come to utter Ruin and Destruction, by Reason that Persons dwelling out of the said Cities and Towns came and took away the Relief and Subsistence of the said Cities and Towns by selling their Wares there: For Remedy whereof, be it enacted, That no Person or Persons dwelling any where out of the said Cities or Towns (the Liberties of the two Universities only excepted) shall hereafter sell, or cause to be sold, by Retail, any Woollen and Linnen Cloth (except of their

PHILIP II. OF SPAIN (1527-1598)

From the painting by Alonso Sanchez Coello in the Berlin Museum.

own making), or any Haberdashery, Grocery, or Mercery Ware, at or within any of the said Cities, Boroughs, Towns Corporate, or Market Towns within this Realm (except in open Fairs), on Pain to forfeit and lose, for every Time so offending, six shillings and eight Pence, and the whole Wares so sold, offered or profered to be sold." (Maitland, vol. i. p. 251.)

An attempt was made to reduce the number of Taverns in London and Westminster. There were to be no more than forty in the City and three in Westminster. But the law was not enforced nor obeyed.

In this reign we first hear of the abuse of prisons. One of the two Compters then stood in Bread Street. The warden or keeper, one Richard Husbands, was accused of maltreating his prisoners barbarously; also of receiving men and women of criminal and disreputable character, and giving them lodging within the prison for fourpence a night. The Corporation therefore built a larger and more convenient compter in Wood Street, to which they removed the prisoners, appointing a new keeper in place of Husbands.

In January 1557 one Christopher Draper, Alderman of Cordwainer Street Ward, employed a man to walk nightly about the streets of the Ward, ringing a bell and calling on the people to take care of their fires and lights; to help the poor; and to pray for the dead. This was the origin of the office of Bellman.

In this year arrived the first Ambassador from Russia. He was wrecked on the coast of Scotland. The Russia Company sent officers into Holland with money and necessaries, and with orders to bring him to London. On his arrival he was met by eighty merchants on horseback, richly accoutred and with gold chains round their necks, and was taken to a house in Highgate, where he was royally entertained for the night. Next day he rode into the City and was received by the Mayor and Lord Montague, who escorted him to his quarters in Fenchurch Street. During the whole of his stay his charges were defrayed by the Russia Company.

The profuse expenditure expected of the Mayor and Sheriffs during their year of office, made many citizens who ought to have filled these posts, retire into the country rather than put themselves to such great expense.

The Common Council took up the matter: in a very curious array of ordinances it was provided among other things

"That thenceforth the Mayor should have no more than one course either at Dinner or Supper; and that on a Festival, being a Flesh Day, to consist of no more than seven Dishes, whether hot or cold; and on every Festival, being a Fish Day, eight Dishes; and on every common Flesh Day, six Dishes; and on every common Fish Day, seven Dishes, exclusive of Brawn, Collops with Eggs, Sallads, Pottage, Butter, Cheese, Eggs, Herrings, Sprats and Shrimps, together with all sorts of Shell-fish and Fruits: That the Aldermen and Sheriffs should have one Dish less than the above-mentioned; and all the City Companies at their several Entertainments the same number of Dishes as the Aldermen and Sheriffs; but with this Restriction, to have neither Swan, Crane, nor Bustard, upon the Penalty of forty Shillings; etc. etc. etc."

On the 17th of November 1558 Mary died. The bonfires which hailed the accession of her sister were fires of rejoicing over the death of the unhappy Queen. The whole City was united in joy, with the exception of the Bishops and the Priests. Not only was religion concerned, but the domination of Spain; the immigration of Spaniards; the humiliation of the country. The general rejoicing was marked by the keeping the day of Elizabeth's accession as a holiday for a hundred and fifty years to come.

CHAPTER V

ELIZABETH

"My Lady Elizabeth," the Venetian Ambassador writes in the lifetime of Queen Mary, "the daughter of Henry VIII. and Anne Boleyn, was born in 1533 (in the

Walker & Cockerell.

QUEEN ELIZABETH (1533-1603)
From a painting, attributed to Zuccaro, in the National Portrait Gallery, London.

month of September—so that she is at present twenty-three years of age). She is a lady of great elegance both of body and mind, although her face may be called rather pleasing than beautiful; she is tall and well made; her complexion fine though rather sallow; her eyes, but, above all, her hands, which she takes care not to conceal, are of superior beauty. In her knowledge of the Greek and Italian languages she surpasses the Queen. She excels the Queen in the knowledge of languages; for, in addition to Latin, she has acquired no small acquaintance with Greek. She speaks Italian, which the Queen does not. In this language she takes such delight, that in the presence of Italians it is her ambition not to converse in any other. Her spirits and understanding are admirable, as she has proved by her conduct in the midst of suspicion and danger, when she concealed her religion and comported herself like a good Catholic. She is proud and dignified in her manners; for, though her mother's condition is well-known to her, she is also aware that this mother of hers was united to the King in wedlock, with the sanction of the Holy Church and the concurrence of the Primate of the realm; and though misled with regard to her religion, she is conscious of having acted with good faith; nor can this latter circumstance reflect upon her birth, since she was born in the same faith as that professed by the Queen. Her father's affection she shared at least in equal measure with her sister; it is said that she resembles her father more than the Queen does, and the King considered them equally in his will, settling on both of them 10,000 *scudi* per annum. Yet with this allowance she is always in debt. And she would be much more so if she did not studiously abstain from enlarging her establishment, and so giving greater offence to the Queen. For indeed there is not a knight or a gentleman in the kingdom who has not sought her service, either for himself or for some son or brother; such is the affection and love that she commands. This is one reason why her expenses are increased. She always alleges her poverty as an excuse to those who wish to enter her service, and by this means she has cleverly contrived to excite compassion, and at the same time a greater affection; because there is no one to whom it does not appear strange that she—the daughter of a king —should be treated in so miserable a manner. She is allowed to live in one of her houses about twelve miles distant from London, but she is surrounded by a number of guards and spies, who watch her narrowly and report every movement to the Queen. Moreover, the Queen, though she hates her most sincerely, yet treats her in public with every outward sign of affection and regard, and never converses with her but on pleasing and agreeable subjects. She has also contrived to ingratiate herself with the King of Spain, through whose influence the Queen is prevented from bastardising her, as she certainly has it in her power to do by means of an Act of Parliament, which would exclude her from the throne. It is believed that but for this interference of the King, the Queen would without more remorse chastise her in the severest manner; for whatever plots against the Queen are discovered, my Lady Elizabeth or some of her people may always be sure to be mentioned among the persons concerned in them."

Attention has already been called to the rejoicings of the people on the death of Mary and the uplifting of that long-continued cloud. The bells of the City were rung; bonfires were lit; loaded tables open for all comers were spread in the streets—yea, even in that dark night of November. A week later the new Queen rode from Hatfield to the Charter House, where she stayed for five days; on the 28th she rode in state to the Tower; here she remained till the 5th of December, when she went by water to Somerset House. On the 17th of December, the body of Mary was laid in West-

Walker & Cockerell.

QUEEN ELIZABETH (1533-1603)
From a painting in the National Portrait Gallery, London. Painter unknown.

minster Abbey, with the Roman Catholic Service; on the 12th of January, the Queen returned to the Tower, and thence on the following day she rode to Westminster. The reader has probably remarked, in the course of this history, that neither King nor Queen, nor Mayor nor people, ever paid the slightest regard for weather or for season. A Royal Riding with Pageants and red cloth and tapestry, and a procession in boats, was undertaken as readily in January, when there is generally hard frost; in April, when there is generally east wind; in July, when there is generally the heat of summer; or in October, when there is generally fine weather with the repose of autumn. Season and weather, sunshine or frost, made no difference. In her desire to win the hearts of the people, Elizabeth probably paid no heed to the weather, whether it was cold or not.

We have remarked a great change in the temper and attitude of the City towards the Sovereign. We hear from time to time murmurings about the City liberties; but nothing of importance. The reasons are several: the Tudor sovereigns carefully respected those liberties which, so to speak, made the most show; they abstained from interference with the City elections; they would not interfere with the City Courts. As regards the point of real importance to themselves—the raising of money and men—their demands were generally arbitrary; witness the calls of Mary for men and still more men. Another cause for cheerful loyalty was that when the religious discussions were at length appeased, it was incumbent on everybody to do his utmost for the Protestant Cause, which became the National Cause. For these reasons we find the City cheerfully giving to Elizabeth what it reluctantly gave, or refused to give, to Henry the Third or Richard the Second.

It was understood by those who welcomed the Queen so joyously that her first care must be the restoration of the Reformed Faith. Every craftsman who threw up his cap expected so much. Fortunately, the events of the last reign had turned the hearts of most people wholly away from the mass. Elizabeth was fully informed as to the opinion of the majority of her subjects; as for her own opinion, it is said that she favoured the old Church. Perhaps so; that is to say, she would rather, as a matter of choice, listen to the Roman Mass than to the English Litany—it is certainly more beautiful; at the same time, one cannot but believe that she was sincere in making her choice and in keeping steadfast to it. Her kindness to the Catholic Faith was shown in the relaxation of persecution. She would not at first persecute any for believing what she herself publicly professed not to believe. Her first step, however, clearly showed the direction of future law. She put forth a royal proclamation ordering the cessation of disputations and sermons, and ordered in their place the reading of the Epistle and Gospel for the Day, with the Ten Commandments, in the vulgar tongue. She also appointed, in the first year of her reign, certain Commissioners, whose duty it was to visit every diocese, for the establishment of religion according to the new Act of Parliament. Those for London were Sir Richard Sackville, knight; Robert Horne, Doctor of Divinity; Doctor Huicke; and Master Savage. The Commissioners visited every parish, calling before them persons of every sort, whom they instructed and admonished. They suppressed all the Religious Houses that Mary had established—the Abbey of Westminster, Syon House, the House of Shene, the Black Friars of Smithfield and those of Greenwich. They further pulled down all the new roods and images, and burned all the vestments, altar cloths, banners, mass books, and rood lofts. In

REPRESENTATION DES FEVS DE IOYE QVI FVRENT FAICTS SVR
LEAV DANS LONDRES A L'HONNEVR DE LA REYNE LA NVICT
DV IOVR DE SON ENTREE

E. Gardner's Collection.

fact, the people showed very plainly that their minds were all for the Protestant religion.

An Act of Uniformity followed, which forbade the use of any form of public prayer other than that of the Prayer Book of Edward VI. with one or two slight alterations. This book was replaced in the churches, and service was conducted in accordance with it on Whit Sunday 1559. What happened immediately after? A pulling out of Bibles from hiding-places; a return to the old talk, restrained for five years for fear of informers; an enjoyable plunge into the anti-Scriptural aspects of the Roman Creed; and a rush for the ornaments, roods, tombs, the vestments and the incense vessels and the candles in all the City churches. In some cases the wafers, vestments, and altar cloths, books, banners, and other ornaments of the churches were burned—things which had cost thousands when they were renewed under Queen Mary. All this happened, and an incredible amount of mischief was done before the destruction was stopped.

There appears to have been little strength of feeling or spirit of martyrdom among the Roman Catholics in London. They submitted; more than this, they made no attempt to maintain their religion; their children, if not themselves, became wholly Anglican; such Roman Catholic worship as survived lurked in holes and corners, or was maintained secretly by a few nobles and gentlemen. Before long, however, the Government had to deal with that advanced form of Protestantism which had been brought over from the Continent. In 1565 an order was issued that all the clergy were to wear the surplice. A good number of them refused, and left their churches, with their congregations. This was the beginning of Nonconformity. But Elizabeth made no attempt to enforce obedience or to persecute those who dissented.

On the 25th of May 1570, the temper of the people was plainly indicated by their reception of a Bull from the Pope, which was actually found nailed to the door of the Bishop of London's Palace in Paul's Churchyard. It was in Latin. Holinshed gives both text and translation.

"Pius, Bishop, servant of God's servants, etc. Queene Elizabeth hath cleane put awaie the sacrifice of the masse, praiers, fastings, choise or difference of meats and single life. She invaded the kingdome, and by usurping monstrouslie the place of the supreme head of the Church in all England, and the cheefe authoritie and jurisdiction of the same, hath againe brought the said realme into miserable destruction. Shee hath remooved the noble men of England from the king's councell. Shee hath made hir councell of poore, darke, beggerlie fellows, and hath placed them over the people. These councellors are not onlie poore and beggerlie, but also heretikes. Unto hir all such as are the woorst of the people resort, and are by hir received into safe protection, etc. We make it knowne that Elizabeth aforesaid, and as manie as stand on hir side in the matters abovenamed, have run into the danger of our cursse. We make it also knowen that we have deprived hir from that right shee pretended to have in the kingdome aforesaid, and also from all and every hir authoritie, dignity, and privilege. We charge and forbid all and every the nobles and subjects, and people, and others aforesaid, that they be not so hardie as to obey hir or hir will, or commandements or laws, upon paine of the like accursse upon them. We pronounce that all whosoever by anie occasion have taken their oth unto hir, are for ever discharged of such their oth, and also from all fealtie and service, which was due to hir by reason of hir government, etc." (vol. iv. p. 253).

The crime was brought home to one John Felton, who on 4th August, three months later, was arraigned at the Guildhall on the charge of affixing the said Bull. Four days later he was drawn from Newgate to St. Paul's Churchyard and there duly hanged, cut down alive, bowelled, and quartered. On the same day—which shows that their office was not an easy one—the Sheriffs of London, after seeing the

Walker & Cockerell.

QUEEN ELIZABETH (1533-1603)
From a painting in the National Portrait Gallery, London. Painter unknown.

end of Felton, had to accompany two young men, who had been found guilty of coining, to Tyburn, where they suffered the same horrible punishment.

Meantime the Catholic enemy never relaxed his attempt to effect the reconversion, or, failing that, the subjugation, of this country. Not by Bulls alone did he work. Seminary priests were sent over to work secretly upon the people and so, it was hoped, gradually to make them ready for conversion. After the tender mercies of the last reign one would believe that the task was hopeless : one is persuaded that even if the secret missionaries had been allowed to put an advertisement in the windows openly proclaiming their object they could have done no harm. But the Queen's Council, whether wisely or not, were extremely jealous of these priests. They charged the City Authorities to try every means of laying hands on them : they were to arrest all persons who did not attend church ; and to banish all strangers who did not go to church ; they were to make every stranger subscribe the Articles. A proclamation was issued ordering English parents to remove their children from foreign colleges ; declaring that to harbour Jesuit priests was to harbour rebels ; imposing a fine upon those who did not attend church ; which

QUEEN ELIZABETH (1533-1603)
From the " Ermine " portrait in the possession of the Marquis of Salisbury.

involved a strict watch upon all the parishes to find out what persons kept away. The two chief conspirators moving about England were two priests, named Campion and Parsons. Campion was presently arrested and, after undergoing torture, was executed in the usual manner. Parsons got back to the Continent, where he continued in his machinations. Catholic historians are eloquent on the sufferings of the Catholics during this reign ; we must, however, acknowledge that the conspiracies and intrigues of such men as Campion, Allen, and Parsons went far to explain the persecution to which they were liable.

The failure of the Armada : the failure of Philip's second attempt, destroyed by tempest; the fact that the Catholic cause was now in the minds of the people the Spanish cause, and therefore execrable; the manifest proofs that the heart of the nation was sound for the Queen and the Protestant religion;—did not put a stop

QUEEN ELIZABETH (1533-1603)
From the engraving by Isaac Oliver. A. Rischgitz' Collection.

to Catholic spies and Catholic conspirators. The emissaries are always called "Spanish," though they were generally English by birth; it is probable that Cardinal Allen found the emissaries, whose work Philip certainly did not discourage. These emissaries were ecclesiastics, who came over disguised in every possible way. Those who were young called themselves, or became, students at Oxford and

Cambridge; those who were older rode about the country disguised as simple gentlemen, merchants, physicians; they worked secretly, everywhere with the design of sapping the loyalty of the people towards the Queen and the Protestant Faith. They did so at great peril, with the certainty of tortures if they were caught; and their courage in facing the dangers was so great that it elevates their conspiracies into the propaganda of a sacred cause. The greatest exertions were made for their detection, and chief among these was the means already mentioned of noting those who did not go to church. However, it does not appear that many were caught, and perhaps the numbers were exaggerated. Sharpe has found a description of one whom they desired to arrest in 1596 (i. 550) :—

"A yonge man of meane and slender stature, aged about xxvj, with a high collored face, red nose, a warte over his left eye, havinge two greate teeth before, standinge out very apparant, he nameth himselffe Edward Harrison, borne in Westmerland; apparelled in a crane collored fustian dublet, rounde hose, after the frenche facion, an olde paire of yollowe knit neather stockes, he escaped without either cloake, girdle, garters or shoes."

The constant discussion of religious matters and agitation on points of Faith produced the natural phenomenon of religious enthusiasts, strange sects, and mad beliefs.

The growth of the Puritan spirit is shown by a letter written by the Lord Mayor on the 14th of January 1583. A large number of people were assembled one Sunday for Sport, *i.e.* Bear-baiting, in Paris Gardens; they were standing round the pit on twelve scaffolds, when the scaffolds all fell down at once, so that many were killed and wounded. The Mayor wrote as follows to the Lord Treasurer :—

"That it gave great occasion to acknowledge the hand of God, for such abuse of his Sabbath-day; and moved him in Conscience to beseech his Lordship to give Order for Redress of such Contempt of God's service. And that he had for that end treated with some Justices of Peace of that County, who shewed themselves to have very good Zeal, but alledged Want of Commission; which they humbly referred to his honourable Wisdom." (Maitland, vol. i. p. 267.)

After Religion, Charity. The bequests to religious purposes had become fewer and of smaller importance during the fifteenth century: they were almost discontinued in the reign of Henry VII.; they ceased under Henry VIII. and his son; and they hardly revived during the reign of Mary. There can be no surer indication of the change of thought. Under Elizabeth we have not only a complete change of thought but the commencement of a new era in Charity. We now enter upon the period of Endowed Charities. Not that they were before unknown, but that they were grafted upon and formed part of Religious Endowments, as St. Anthony's School, which belonged to the Religious House of that name, and Whittington's Bedesmen, who formed part of Whittington's College. The Religious element now disappears except for the erection of a chapel for the Bedesmen. The list of Charitable Endowments founded in this century is large and very laudable. They consist of colleges, schools, and almshouses, not in London only, but by London citizens for their native places, for Oxford, and for Cambridge.

Of London as a City of Soldiers we hear much less under Elizabeth, despite

SIR PHILIP SIDNEY AND HIS BROTHER LORD LISLE
From the picture in the possession of Lord De L'Isle and Dudley, Penshurst Place, Kent.

the contingent sent to fight the Spanish invader, than under any king. London no longer sallies forth ten thousand strong for this claimant or that. She finds, however, the money for ships, and on occasion she raises and equips for foreign service, 400 men, 600 men, 1000 men, at the order of the Queen.

The first appearance of Londoners under arms was a mere parade, to which the

City sent 1400 men. They were equipped by the twelve principal Companies, who also supplied officers from their own body. In 1562 the Queen asked the City for a force of 600 men. These were raised. Next year she applied again for 1000 men for the holding of Havre; only 400, however, were wanted. These sailed for Havre, but the garrison being attacked by the plague there was no fighting, and the town surrendered.

In 1572 the Queen in a letter to the Mayor commanded him to raise a large body of men, young and strong, for instruction in the Military Arts. Accordingly the Companies chose young men to the number of 3000; armed them; placed officers of experience over them, and instructed them. This appears to have been the beginning of the London Trained Bands. In May of the same year they were reviewed by the Queen. In 1574 the City was called upon to furnish 400 soldiers for the Queen's service.

In 1578 the City was ordered to provide 2000 arquebusiers. Scarcely had the order been received when there came another for 2000 men to be raised and kept in readiness.

On the 8th March 1587, the Queen sent a letter, followed by one from the Privy Council, to the same effect, informing the Mayor that certain intelligence had been received of warlike preparations being made in foreign parts, and calling upon the City to provide a force of 10,000 men fully armed and equipped, of whom 6000 were to be enrolled under Captains and Ensigns and to be trained at times convenient.

The men were raised in the following numbers from each ward :—

Farringdon Ward Within .	807	Broad Street.		373
Bassishaw .	177	Bridge Ward Within		383
Bread Street .	386	Castle Baynard		551
Dowgate .	384	Queenhithe .		404
Lime Street .	99	Tower Street		444
Farringdon Without	1264	Walbrook .		290
Aldgate Ward .	347	Vintry .		364
Billingsgate .	365	Portsoken .		243
Aldersgate .	232	Candlewick .		215
Cornhill .	191	Cripplegate .		925
Cheap .	358	Bishopsgate .		326
Cordwainer .	301			
Langbourne .	349	Total .		10,007
Coleman Street Ward	229			

We may apply this total in order to make a guess at the population of London in 1587. Thus supposing x to be the percentage of the population taken from each ward to fill the ranks, since the population of each ward = the number taken, multiplied by 100, and divided by x,

p. 76.

THE SPANISH ARMADA (THE FIRST ENGAGEMENT)

From Pine's engravings of the House of Lords tapestry hangings.

Therefore the whole population of the City

     = whole number taken, multiplied by 100, and divided by x

     = $1,000,700 \div x$.

If 10 per cent of the population were taken we should have a total of 100,070 or roughly 100,000.

The City also supplied a fleet of sixteen ships, the largest in the river, fully found, with four light pinnaces, and paid the men during their services. It was with these ships that Drake ran into Cadiz and Lisbon, destroyed a great quantity of shipping, and threw into the sea the military materials that had been accumulated there.

The Earl of Leicester, who was in command at Tilbury, received 1000 of the London force only, and that on condition that they brought their own provisions.

The London men wore a uniform of white with white caps, and the City arms in scarlet on back and front. Some carried arquebuses; some were halberdiers; some were pikemen. They marched in companies according to their arms. Their officers rode beside the men dressed in black velvet. They were preceded by billmen, corresponding to the modern pioneers; by a company of whifflers, *i.e.* trumpeters; and in the midst marched six Ensigns in white satin faced with black sarsenet, and rich scarves. The dress of officers and men was just as useless and unfit for continued work as could well be devised. It is melancholy to find that the Earl of Leicester, who was in command at Tilbury, held a very poor opinion of the London contingent. " I see," he writes to Walsingham, "that their service will be little, except they have their own captains, and having them I look for none at all by them when we shall meet the enemy." Most fortunately there was no enemy to meet, and the heroism of the Londoners remains unchallenged. The Captain of the London Trained Bands was Martin Bond, citizen, whose tomb remains at St. Helen's Church.

When the danger was over, the Aldermen looked to it that the price of provisions should not be raised when the sick and wounded were brought home. But it was some time before the welcome news was received of the final dispersion of the invading fleet. The first public notification was made in a sermon preached at Paul's Cross by the Dean of St. Paul's, in the presence of the Mayor and Aldermen and the Livery Companies in their best gowns.

On the 18th November the Queen rode into the City in state and attended a Thanksgiving Service.

Sharpe calls attention to the fact that two at least of the great naval commanders were well-known in the City :—

"Both Frobisher and Hawkins owned property in the City, and in all probability resided there, like their fellow-seaman and explorer, Sir Humphrey Gilbert, who was living in Red Cross Street, in the parish of St. Giles, Cripplegate, in 1583, the year that he met his death at sea. The same parish claims

Frobisher, whose remains (excepting his entrails, which were interred at Plymouth, where he died) lie buried in St. Giles's Church, and to whom a mural monument was erected by the Vestry in 1888, just three centuries after the defeat of the Armada, to which he had contributed so much. If Hawkins himself did not reside in the City, his widow had a mansion house in Mincing Lane. He, too, had probably lived there; for although he died and was buried at sea, a monument was erected to his memory and to that of Katherine, his first wife, in the church of St. Dunstan-in-the-East. There is one other—a citizen of London and son of an alderman—whose name has been handed down as having taken an active part in the defence of the kingdom at this time, not at sea, but on land. A monument in the recently restored church of St. Helen, Bishopsgate, tells us that Martin Bond, son of Alderman William Bond, 'was captaine in ye yeare 1588 at ye campe at Tilbury, and after remained chief captaine of ye trained bands of this Citty until his death.' The monument represents him as sitting in a tent guarded by two sentinels, with a page holding a horse." (Sharpe, vol. i. pp. 544-545.)

In 1591 a further contingent of 400 men was ordered. In 1594 the City was called upon to raise 450 men. In 1596 a message came to the Mayor and Aldermen from the Queen. They were listening to a sermon at Paul's Cross. The letter commanded them to raise a thousand men immediately. They rose and left the sermon, and instantly set to work. Before eight of the clock they had raised their men. But the order was countermanded, and the men were disbanded. On Easter Day in the morning another message came to the same effect, and then—it is a curious story—the Mayor and Aldermen went round to the churches in the respective wards. Remember that on such a day every man in the City would be in church. The Mayor shut the doors, picked his men, and before noon had raised his thousand men. This order also was countermanded, and the men returned home. A strange interruption of an Easter morning's service!

In the same year the Queen asked for more men. Then the City Common Council expostulated. On the sea service alone, they pointed out, the City had spent 10,000 marks within the last few years. In 1597 they raised first 500 men, then 300 more, and sent the Queen £60,000 on mortgage. In 1598, on a new alarm of another Spanish invasion, the City found sixteen ships and a force of 6000 men.

It will thus be seen that during this reign the City furnished over 6000 fully equipped soldiers for active service; that it raised at an hour's notice, on two separate occasions, 1000 men ready for immediate service; that it raised a force of Trained Bands 3000 strong; that on occasion it could increase this number to 10,000; that it could fit out for sea a fleet of twenty or thirty ships. I do not think that the expenditure of the City on these military services has ever been published, but it must have been very great. A corresponding expenditure at the present time would be enormous; it would be expressed in many millions. This simple fact both proves and illustrates the tried loyalty of the City. The time, however, had gone by when the Londoners could, and did, send out an army capable of deposing one king and setting up another. That power and that spirit died with

A View of the House of Peers, Queen Elizabeth on the Throne, the Commons attending.
Taken from a Painted Print in the Cottonian Library.

Cancellary sedes

Prolocutor

Milites Provinciarum et Burgeses (quos vocant) utrinq: qui Cameram Parlamenti inferiorem constituunt Prolocutorem conducentes.

The Knights of Shires & Burgesses (as they call them) which constitute ÿ lower house of Parliament, presenting their Speaker.

the accession of the Tudors. In the beginning of Elizabeth's reign the citizens even prayed to be excused the practice of arms even as a volunteer force, seeing that "the most parte of those our apprentices and handy craftesmen who continually are kept at work; who also, if they should have that libertie to be trayned and drawn from their workes in these matters, wolde thereby fall into such idleness and insolency that many would never be reduced agayne into any good order or service."

We have seen repeated proofs that the City was never friendly towards foreigners. At this time there were many causes beside the old trade jealousy why the people should view strangers with an unfriendly eye. During the last reign the City swarmed with Spaniards; from the very first day of this long reign until the very last, Spain never ceased plotting, conspiring, and carrying on war with the Queen and the new Religion. In the foreign merchants' houses the conspirators found a refuge. There were, again, thousands of immigrants from Flanders or Spain, flying from religious persecution; and though many of the people settled down to steady industry, there were many who were by no means the virtuous, law-abiding persons, such as the present age would expect of Huguenots.

From time to time, partly in order to allay the jealousy and terror of the people, partly for the sake of getting at the facts, there was a numbering of the strangers. Thus, in 1567, such a numbering showed 45 Scots; 428 French; 45 Spaniards and Portuguese; 140 Italians; 2030 Dutch; 44 Burgundians; two Danes; and one Liégeois: in all 2735 persons. In 1580 another census of aliens was taken; wherein it was shown that there were 2302 Dutch; 1838 French; 116 Italians; 1542 English born of foreign parents; of other nations not specified 447; and of persons not certified 217: in all 6462. In 1593 a third census showed 5259 strangers in London. These figures are not without interest. In the first year we find a large number of Dutch; they are fugitives. In the next we find that the whole number of strangers has more than doubled: there has been a large accession of Huguenots; in the third census the numbers have gone down a little. In our time a great outcry has been raised over the invasion of the Town by 50,000 Polish Jews; that means a proportion of one in a hundred. In 1560 there were 6500 for a population of, say, 120,000, which means one in twenty (approximately). Now, one in twenty is a large fraction out of the general population.

At one time the hatred of the Apprentices grew so irrepressible that a conspiracy like that of Evil May Day was formed among the Apprentices, with the design of murdering all the foreigners. The conspiracy was happily discovered, and the conspirators laid by the heels in Newgate. A Petition to the Queen against the grievous encroachments of aliens will be found in Appendix III.

The domestic history of Elizabeth's reign is crammed full of hangings, burnings, and the executions of traitors, with all the barbarity of that punishment. There are so many, that in order to make this remarkable shedding of blood intelligible, I have compiled a list of the executions mentioned by Holinshed and Stow during one part of her reign. The list will be found in Appendix X., (Executions, 1563-1586). This list, which principally concerns London and is apparently incomplete, even within its narrow limits shows that between the years 1563 and 1586, there were in all 64 executions at which 228 persons suffered. Of these, seventy-one were rebels hanged on two occasions; seventeen were executed for murder; three for military offences; twelve for counterfeiting, clipping, or

WILLIAM CECIL, FIRST BARON BURGHLEY (1520-1598)
From the painting by Marc Gheeraedts (?) in the National Portrait Gallery, London.

debasing the coinage; two for counterfeiting the Queen's signature; twenty-nine were pirates; two were executed for witchcraft or conjuring; twelve for robbery; one for adultery; three for heresy, and seventy-six for high treason. Among the traitors were Dr. John Storey; Edmund Campion; William Parry; the Babington conspirators; the Charnock conspirators; and many Roman Catholic priests. There can be no doubt that the priests who came over with secret designs for the conversion of the country constituted a real and ever-present danger; if anything could justify the barbarities committed upon them when they were caught these conspiracies were enough. That the people at large did not condemn these

6

barbarities is proved by the fact that there was no feeling of sympathy for the sufferers; that the common opinion was that for treason no punishment could be too severe; and that the country after Elizabeth's reign was concluded was far more Protestant than at the beginning. The conspiracies and secret goings in and out of Catholic priests came to an end in the reign of James, for the best of all reasons, viz. that there was no one left with whom a priest could conspire or whom he could convert. Two women were burned for poisoning their husbands—a most dreadful offence, and one which called for the direst terrors of the law; one woman was burned for witchcraft; another was only hanged for the same offence—but such differences in sentences are not unknown at the present day. One more point occurs. Were the last dying speeches correctly reported? If so, since they are always so moving, and sometimes so eloquent, why did they elicit no response of sympathy or indignation among the bystanders? When Thomas Appletree was to be hanged for firing a gun accidentally into the Queen's barge (see p. 389), the people wept, and the culprit wept, but the justice of the sentence was not questioned. Now in the Marian Persecution the people looked on indignant and sympathetic, being restrained from demonstrations by force and fear. Whether the dying speeches are correctly reported or invented, matters very little. They show one thing, that there was no unmanly terror observed at the last moment: every one, guilty or innocent, mounted the ladder with an intrepid countenance. Death has no terrors either for the arch-conspirator Storey, or for the pirate hanged at Execution Dock.

The privileges granted to the foreign merchants of the Steelyard and the Hanseatic League were finally withdrawn by Queen Elizabeth.

This withdrawal had been in preparation for nearly two hundred years. In the time of Henry IV. English merchants began to trade in the Baltic and with Norway and other parts. This aroused the jealousy of the Hanseatic League, which seized upon several of the English ships. Complaints were laid before the King, who withdrew such of the privileges enjoyed by the League as interfered with the carrying on of trade by his own merchants. He also granted a charter to the merchants trading to the Eastlands. This charter was renewed and enlarged by Edward IV. In the first and second of Philip and Mary a charter was granted to the Russia Company—we have seen how the first Russian Ambassador came to England in the reign of Mary. This Company obtained a confirmation of their charter under Queen Elizabeth. Now, although our people enjoyed many more privileges than of old, yet the Hanseatic League still had the advantage over them by means of their well-regulated Societies and their privileges, insomuch that when the Queen wanted hemp, pitch, tar, powder, and other munitions of war, she had to buy them of the foreign merchants at their own price. The Queen, therefore, began to encourage her own people to become merchants: she assisted them to form companies; she gave them Charters; she withdrew all the privileges from the Hansa. Not the least of the debt which England owes to this great Queen is her wisdom in the encouragement of foreign trade.

The strange and foolish rising of the Earl of Essex belongs to national history. It was, however, met and repressed in the first outbreak by the City. Not one person offered to join the Earl; he was proclaimed traitor in Cheapside; the Bishop of London raised, in all haste, the force which stopped him on Ludgate Hill.

Towards the end of Queen Elizabeth's reign there were great complaints of hawkers and pedlars—in fact we begin to hear of the London Cries. These street cries did great harm to London tradesmen. We have seen that there were no shops at all originally, except in the appointed markets; these hawkers, with their itinerant barrows and baskets, brought the market into every part of London. Steps were taken to prevent this nuisance; but they were unavailing.

In 1580 the Queen issued a Proclamation against the building of new houses and the further increase of London :—

"To the preservation of her People in Health, which may seem impossible to continue, though presently, by God's Goodness, the same is perceived to be in better Estate universally than hath beene in Man's Memorie; yet where there are such great Multitudes of People brought to inhabite in small Roomes, whereof a great Part are seene very poore, yea, such as must live of begging, or by worse Means, and they heaped up together, and in a sort smothered with many families of Children and Servants in one House or small Tenement; it must needes followe, if any Plague or popular Sicknes should, by God's Permission, enter amongst those Multitudes, that the same would not only spread itself and invade the whole Citie and Confines, but that a great Mortalitie would ensue the same, where her Majesties personal Presence is many times required.

For Remedie whereof, as Time may now serve, until by some further good Order be had in Parliament or otherwise, the same may be remedied; her Majestie, by good and deliberate advice of her Counsell, and being also thereto moved by the considerate opinions of the Lord-Mayor, Aldermen, and other the grave wise men in and about the Citie, doth charge and straightly command all manner of Persons, of what Qualitie soever they be, to desist and forbeare from any new Buildings of any House or Tenement within three miles from any of the Gates of the sayde Citie of *London*, to serve for Habitation or Lodging for any Person, where no former House hath bene knowen to have bene in the Memorie of such as are now living; and also to forbeare from letting or setting, or suffering any more Families than one onely to be placed, or to inhabite from henceforth in any one House that heretofore hath bene inhabited."

On the 6th of December 1586, a very solemn and tragic ceremony was performed, first in Cheapside; then in Leadenhall; then at the end of London Bridge, and lastly at the south end of Chancery Lane; where the Mayor with the Aldermen, and attended by many of the Nobility and eighty of the principal citizens in chains of gold, proclaimed the sentence of death passed upon the unfortunate Mary Queen of Scots.

The importance of the act; the publicity given to it; the formalities attending the Proclamation,—show the desire of the Queen and her Council that the people should understand the dreadful necessity of removing this cause of endless intrigue and conspiracy.

One more trade regulation closes the history of London in the reign of Elizabeth. A practice had grown up among hucksters and others of setting up stalls in the streets in front of the shops, in consequence of which the trade of the shopkeepers was greatly injured, insomuch that many of them were obliged to employ these very people to sell their wares for them. It was therefore ordered that no one should erect any stall, or stand, before any house under a penalty of twenty shillings.

One of the last things done in the name of the Queen was the offer to all Debtors in prison of freedom if they would volunteer to serve on board the fleet newly raised for the suppression of Spanish pirates.

On the death of the Queen, the City, which was always most truly loyal and faithful to her, put up in most churches a tablet or a statue to her memory.

This brief and bald account of the relations between the Crown and the City is not proffered as a history of London during the Tudor period. This history will, it is hoped, be found in the following pages. I have only hinted at the creation of the Trading Companies and the connection of the great Sea Captains with London. The Poor Law of 1572 ; the granting of monopolies ; the wonderful outburst of Literature ; the troubles caused by the substitution of pasture for agriculture ; the growth of Puritanism and the beginnings of the High Church,—all these things belong to the history of London. The diplomacy ; the Court intrigues ; the rise and fall of Ministers ; the anxieties concerning the Succession,—these things do not belong to the history of London.

CHAPTER VI

THE QUEEN IN SPLENDOUR

THE Court of Queen Elizabeth was almost as itinerant as that of Henry the Second. The Queen understood thoroughly that for a sovereign to be at once loyally served and wholesomely feared it is not enough to sit still in one place. She must be seen by her people: they must realise by ocular demonstration how great is her power and authority; they must learn it by the sight of her person glittering with jewels

HAMPTON COURT
From a print in the British Museum.

and all glorious with silk and velvet; by the splendour of her train; by the noble lords who attend her; by the magnificence of the entertainment she receives. Nearly every year of her long reign was marked by one or more Progresses; some of her nobles she visited more than once: she was the guest of Cecil at Theobalds on twelve different occasions, each visit costing the host two or three thousand pounds; three times she visited Leicester at Kenilworth. These Progresses, though they belong not to the history of London, must be borne in mind in thinking of this long and glorious reign.

When Elizabeth was not travelling she resided at Whitehall, at St. James's, at Greenwich, at Hampton Court, Windsor, Richmond, Nonsuch, Chelsea, Hunsdon. In moving from one palace to another a huge quantity of plate and furniture had to be carried about. And during the change of residence the City bells were set ringing. If the Queen went by river, or from Westminster to Greenwich, she was attended by the barges of the Mayor and the Companies, all newly painted and beautified : they had artillery on board, and there was a great shooting of guns; also there was "great and pleasant melodie of instruments which plaed in most sweet and heavenly manner."

On the day before her coronation the Queen received the Pageant devised in her honour by the City of London.

A full account of this Pageant is preserved in a tract first printed in 1604, and reproduced in Nichols's *Progresses of Queen Elizabeth*. It is too long to quote in full. The following, therefore, is greatly abridged from the original :—

"Entryng the Citie was of the People received marveylous entirely, as appeared by the assemblie, prayers, wishes, welcomminges, cryes, tender woordes, and all other signs, which argue a wonderfull earnest love of most obedient subjectes towarde theyr soveraigne. And on thother side, her Grace, by holding up her hand and merie countenance to such as stode farre of, and most tender and gentle language to those that stode nigh to her Grace, did declare herselfe no leswe thankefully to receive her Peoples good wyll than they lovingly offered it unto her. To all that wyshed her Grace well, she gave heartie thankes, and to such as bade God save her Grace, she sayde agayne God save them all, and thanked them with all her heart : so that on eyther syde there was nothing but gladnes, nothing but prayer, nothing but comfort. The Quenes Majestie rejoysed marveilously to see that so exceadingly shewed towarde her Grace, which all good Princes have ever desyred. I meane so earnest love of subjectes, so evidently declared even to her Grace's owne person, being carried in the middest of them." . . . "Thus therefore the Quenes Majestie passed from the Towre till she came to Fanchurche, the people on eche side joyously beholdyng the viewe of so gracious a Ladye theyr Quene, and her Grace no lesse gladly notyng and observing the same. Nere unto Fanchurch was erected a scaffolde richely furnished, whereon stode a noyes of instrumentes and a chylde in costly apparell, which was appoynted to welcome the Quenes Majestie in the hole Cities behalfe. Against which place when her Grace came, of her owne wyll she commaunded the chariot to be stayde, and that the noyes might be appeased tyll the chylde had uttered his welcome oration, which he spake in English meter as here followeth :—

'O pereles Soveraygne Quene, behold what this thy Town
Hath thee presented with at thy fyrst entraunce here :
Behold with how riche hope she ledeth thee to thy Crown,
Beholde with what two gyftes she comforteth thy chere.

The first is blessing tonges which many a welcome say,
Which pray thou mayst do wel, which praise thee to the sky,
Which wish to thee long lyfe, which blesse this happy day
Which to thy kingdomes heapes, all that in tonges can lye.

The second is true hertes which love thee from their roote,
Whose sute is tryumphe now, and ruleth all the game.
Which faithfulness have wone, and all untruthe driven out,
Which skip for joy when as they heare thy happy name.

Welcome therefore, O Quene, as much as herte can thinke ;
Welcome agayn, O Quene, as much as tong can tell ;
Welcome to joyous tonges, and hartes that will not shrink.
God thee preserve we praye and wishe thee ever well.'

At which wordes of the last line the hole People gave a great shout, wishing with one assent, as the chylde had said. And the Quenes Majestie thanked most heartely both the Citie for this her gentle receiving at the first, and also the People for confirming the same."

In Gracious (Gracechurch Street) was erected a "gorgeous and sumptuous Arke":—

"A stage was made whiche extended from th'one syde of the streate to th'other, richely vawted with battlementes conteining three portes, and over the middlemost was avaunced three severall stages in degrees. Upon the lowest stage was made one seate Royall, wherein were placed two personages representyng Kyng Henrie the Seventh, and Elyzabeth his wyfe, doughter of Kyng Edward the Fourth, eyther of these two Princes sitting under one cloth of estate in their seates, no otherwyse divided, but that th'one of them, whiche was King Henrie the Seventh, proceeding out of the House of Lancastre, was enclosed in a Redde Rose, and th'other, which was Quene Elizabeth, being heire to the House of Yorke, enclosed with a Whyte Rose, eche of them Royally crowned, and decently apparailled as apperteinted to Princes, with Sceptours in their hands, and one vawt surmounting their heades, wherein aptly were placed two tables, eche conteining the title of those two Princes. And these personages were so set, that the one of them joined handes with th'other, with the ring of matrimonie perceived on the finger. Out of the which two Roses sprang two branches gathered into one, which were directed upward to the second stage or degree, wherein was placed one, representing the valiant and noble Prynce, King Henry the Eight, which sprong out of the former stock, crowned with a Crown Imperial, and by him sate one representing the right worthy Ladie Quene Ann, wife to the said King Henry the Eight, and Mother to our most soveraign Ladie Quene Elizabeth that now is, both apparelled with Sceptours and Diademes, and other furniture due to the state of a King and Queene, and two tables surmounting their heades, wherein were written their names and titles. From their seate also proceaded upwardes one braunche directed to the thirde and uppermost stage or degree, wherein lykewyse was planted a seate Royall, in the whiche was sette one representyng the Queenes most excellent Majestie Elizabeth nowe our moste dradde Soveraigne Ladie, crowned and apparalled as th'other Prynces were.   Out of the forepart of this Pageaunt was made a standyng for a chylde, whiche at the Quenes Majesties comeing declared unto her the hole meaning of the said Pageaunt.   The two sides of the same were filled with loud noyses of musicke.   And all emptie places thereof were furnished with sentences concerning unitie.   And the hole Pageant garnished with Redde Roses and White, and in the forefront of the same Pageant in a faire Wreathe, was written the name and title of the same, which was, ' The uniting of the two Howses of Lancastre and Yorke.' Thys Pageant was grounded upon the Quenes Majesties name.   For like as the long warre between the two Houses of Yorke and Lancastre then ended, when Elizabeth doughter to Edward the Fourth matched in marriage with Henry the Seventhe, heyre to the Howse of Lancastre: so since that the Quenes Majesties name was Elizabeth, and forsomuch as she is the onelye heire of Henrye the Eighth, which came of bowthe the howses, as the knitting up of concorde, it was devised, that like as Elizabeth was the first occasion of concorde, so she, another Elizabeth, myght maintaine the same among her subjectes, so that unitie was the ende whereat the whole devise shotte as the Quenes Majesties name moved the first grounde.

The childe appoynted in the standing above named to open the meaning of the said Pageant, spake these wordes unto her Grace :—

' The two Princes that sit under one cloth of state,
    The Man in the Redde Rose, the Whoman in the White,
Henry the VII. and Quene Elizabeth his Mate,
    By ring of marriage as Man and Wife unite.

Both heires to both their bloodes, to Lancastre the Kyng,
    The Queene to Yorke, in one the two Howses did knit :
Of whom as heire to both, Henry the Eighth did spring,
    In whose seat, his true heire, thou, Quene Elizabeth doth sit.

Therefore as civill warre, and fuede of blood did cease
    When these two Houses were united into one,
So now that jarrs shall stint, and quietnes encrease,
    We trust, O noble Quene, thou wilt be cause alone.'

The which also were written in Latin verse, and both drawn in two tables upon the forefront of the saide Pageant.

These verses and other pretie sentences were drawn in voide places of thys Pageant, all tending to one ende, that quietness might be mainteyned, and all dissention displaced, and that by the Quenes Majestie, heire to agrement and agreing in name with her, which tofore had joyned those Houses, which had been th'occasion of much debate and civill warre within thys Realme, as may appeare to such as will searche Cronicles, but be not to be touched in thys treatise, openly declaring her Graces passage through the Citie, and what provisyon the Citie made therfore. And ere the Quenes Majestie came wythin hearing of thys Pageaunt, she sent certaine, as also at all other Pageauntes, to require the People to be silent. For her Majestie was disposed to heare all that shoulde be sayde unto her. When the Quenes Majestie had hearde the chylde's oration, and understoode the meanyng of the Pageant at large, she marched forward toward Cornehill, alway received with lyke rejoysing of the People: and there, as her Grace passed by the Conduit, which wes curiously trimmed agaynst that tyme with riche banners adourned, and a noyse

NONSUCH HOUSE
From an old print.

of loude instrumentes upon the top thereof, she espyed the seconde Pageant: and because she feared for the People's noyse that she shoulde not heare the child which dyd expound the same, she enquired what that Pageant was ere that she came to it: and there understoode that there was a chylde representing her Majesties person, placed in a seate of Government, supported by certayn vertues, which suppressed their contrarie vyces under their feete, and so forthe.". . . "Against Soper Lane ende was extended from th'one side of the streate to th'other a Pageant, which had three gates, all open. Over the middlemost whereof wer erected three severall stages, whereon sate eight children, as hereafter followeth: On the uppermost one childe, on the middle three, on the lowest foure, eche having the proper name of the blessing that they did represent written in a table, and placed above their heades. In the forefront of this Pageant, before the children which did represent the blessings, was a convenient standing, cast out for a chylde to stand, which did expownd the sayd Pageant unto the Quenes Majestie as was done in th'other tofore. Everie of these children wer appointed and apparelled according unto the blessing which he did represent. And on the forepart of the sayde Pageant was written, in fayre letters, the name of the said Pageant, in this maner following :—

'The eight Beatitudes expressed in the V chapter of the Gospel of St. Matthew applyed to our Soveraigne Lady Quene Elizabeth.'

Over the two syde portes was placed a noyse of instrumentes. And all voyde places in the Pageant were furnished with pretty sayinges, commending and touching the meaning of the said Pageant, which was the promises and blessinges of Almightie God to his People." . . . "At the Standard in Cheape, which was dressed fayre agaynste the tyme, was placed a noyse of trumpettes, with banners and other furniture. The Crosse lykewyse was also made fayre and well trimmed. And neare unto the same, uppon the porche of Saint Peter's church dore, stode the waites of the Citie, which did geve a pleasant noyse with their instrumentes as the Quenes Majestie did passe by, whiche on every saide cast her countenance and wished well to all her most loving people. Sone after that her Grace passed the Crosse, she had espyed the Pageant erected at the Little Conduit in Cheape, and incontinent required to know what it might signifye. And it was tolde her Grace, that there was placed Tyme. 'Tyme?' quoth she, 'and Tyme hath brought me hether.' And so forth the hole matter was opened to her Grace : as hereafter shalbe declared in the description of the Pageant. But in the opening when her Grace understode that the Byble in Englyse shoulde be delivered unto her by Trueth which was therin represented by a chylde : she thanked the Citie for that gyft, and sayde that she would oftentymes reade over that booke, commaunding Sir John Parrat, one of the Knightes which helde up her canapy, to goe before, and to receive the booke. But learning that it shoulde be delivered unto her Grace downe by a silken lace, she caused him to staye, and so passed forward till she came agaynste the Aldermen in the hyghe ende of Cheape tofore the Little Conduite, where the companies of the Citie ended, whiche beganne at Fanchurche and stoode along the streates, one by another enclosed with rayles, hanged with clothes, and themselves well apparelled with many riche furres, and their livery whodes uppon their shoulders, in comely and semely maner, having before them sondry persones well apparelled in silkes and chaines of golde, as wyflers and garders of the sayd companies, beside a number of riche hangings, as well of tapistrie, arras, clothes of golde, silver, velvet, damaske, sattin, and other silkes, plentifullye hanged all the way as the Quenes Highnes passed from the Towre through the Citie. Out at the windowes and penthouses of every house did hang a number of ryche and costlye banners and streamers, tyll her Grace came to the upper ende of Cheape. And there, by appoyntment, the Right Worshipfull Maister Ranulph Cholmeley, Recorder of the Citie, presented to the Quenes Majestie a purse of crimeson sattin richely wrought with gold, wherin the Citie gave unto the Quenes Majestie a thousand markes in gold, as maister Recorder did declare brieflie unto the Quenes Majestie: whose woordes tended to this ende, that the Lorde Maior, his brethren, and Comminaltie of the Citie, to declare their gladnes and good wille towardes the Quenes Majestie dyd present her Grace with that golde, desyering her Grace to continue theyr good and gracious Queen, and not to esteme the value of the gift, but the mynd of the gevers. The Quenes Majestie, with both her handes, tooke the purse, and

COACHES OF QUEEN ELIZABETH
From *Archæologia.*

answered to hym againe mervelous pithilie: and so pithilie, that the standers by, as they embraced entirely her gracious answer, so they mervailed at the cowching thereof: which was in wordes truely reported these: 'I thanke my Lorde Maior, his Brethren and you all. And wheras your request is that I shoulde continue your good Ladie and Quene, be ye ensured, that I will be as good unto you as ever Quene was to her People. No wille in me can lacke, neither doe I trust shall ther lacke any power. And perswade your selves, that for the safetie and quietnes of you all I will not spare, if need be, to spend my blood. God thanke you all.' Which answere of so noble an hearted Pryncesse, if it moved a mervaylous showte and rejoysing, it is nothyng to be mervayled at, since both the heartines thereof was so wonderfull and the woordes so joyntly knytte. When her Grace hadde thus answered the Recorder, she marched toward the Little Conduit, where was erected a Pageant with square proporcion standynge directly before the same Conduite, with battlementes accordyngelye. And in the same Pageant was advaunced two hylles or mountaynes of convenient heyghte. The one of them beyng on the North syde of the same Pageaunt, was made cragged, barreyn, and stonye : in the whiche was erected one tree, artificiallye made, all withered and deade, with braunches accordinglye. And under the same tree, at the foote thereof, sate one in homely and rude apparell, crokedlye, and in mourning maner, havynge over hys headde, in a table, written in Laten and Englyshe, hys name, whiche was, 'Ruinosa Respublica,' 'A Decayed Commonweale.' And upon the same withered tree were fixed certayne tables, wherein were written proper sentences, expressing the causes of the decaye of a Commonweale. The other hylle, on the South syde, was made fayre, fresh grene, and beawtifull, the grounde thereof full of flowers and beawtie : and on the same was erected also one tree very fresh and fayre, under the whiche stoode uprighte one freshe personage, well apparayled and appoynted, whose name also was written bothe in Englyshe and Latin, whiche was, 'Respublica bene instituta,' 'A florishyng Commonweale.' And uppon the same tree also were fixed certayne tables, conteyning sentences which expressed the causes of a flourishing Common-weale. In the middle, between the sayde hylles, was made artificially one hollow place or cave, with doore and locke enclosed : oute of the whiche, a lyttle before the Quenes Highness commynge thither, issued one personage, whose name was Tyme, apparaylled as an olde man, with a sythe in his hande, havynge wynges artificiallye made, leadinge a personage of lesser stature than himselfe, whiche was fynely and well apparaylled, all cladde in whyte silke, and directlye over her head was set her name and tytle, in Latin and Englyshe, 'Temporis filia,' 'The Daughter of Tyme.' Which two so appoynted, went forwarde toward the South syde of the Pageant. And on her brest was written her propre name, whiche was 'Veritas,' 'Trueth,' who helde a booke in her hande, upon the whiche was written, 'Verbum Veritatis,' 'The Woorde of Trueth.' And out of the South syde of the Pageaunt was cast a standynge for a childe, which shoulde enterprete the same Pageant. Against whom when the Quenes Majestie came, he spake unto her Grace these woordes :—

> 'This olde man with the sythe olde Father Tyme they call,
>   And her his daughter Truth, which holdeth yonder boke :
> Whom he out of his rocke hath brought forth to us all,
>   From hence for many yeres she durst not once out loke.
>
> The ruthful wight that sitteth ynder the barren tree,
>   Resembleth to us the fourme when Commonweales decay :
> But when they be in state tryumphant, you may see
>   By him in freshe attyre that sitteth under the baye.
>
> Now since that Time again his daughter Truth hath brought
>   We trust, O worthy Quene, thou wilt this Truth embrace :
> And since thou understandst the good estate and nought,
>   We trust wealth thou wilt plant, and barrenness displace.
>
> But for to heale the sore, and cure that is not seene,
>   Which thing the boke of Truth doth teache in writing playn,
> She doth present to thee the same, O worthy Quene,
>   For that, that wordes do flye, but wryting doth remayn.'

When the childe had thus ended his speache, he reached his booke towardes the Quenes Majestie, whiche, a little before, Trueth had let downe unto him from the hill: whiche Sir John Parrat was received, and delivered unto the Quene. But she, as soone as she had receyved the booke, kissed it, and with both her handes helde up the same, and so laid it upon her breast, with great thankes to the Citie thereof. And so went forward towardes Paules Churchyarde. . . . When she was come over against Paules Scole, a childe appointed by the scolemaster thereof pronounced a certein oration in Latin, and certein verses, which also wer there written." . . . "In this maner, the people on either side rejoysing, her Grace went

ROYAL PROCESSION TO ST. PAUL'S
From a picture painted in 1616, in the possession of the Society of Antiquaries. E. Gardner's Collection.

forwarde, towarde the Conduite in Flete-street, where was the fifte and last Pageaunt erected, in forme following: From the Conduite, which was bewtified with painting, unto the North side of the strete, was erected a stage, embattelled with foure towres, and in the same a square platte rising with degrees, and uppon the uppermost degree was placed a chaire, or seate royall, and behynde the same seate, in curious and artificiall maner, was erected a tree of reasonable height, and so farre advaunced above the seate as it did well and semelye shadow the same, without endomaging the syght of any part of the Pageant: and the same tree was bewtified with leaves as greene as arte could devise, being of a convenient greatnes, and conteining therupon the fruite of the date, and on the toppe of the same tree, in a table, was set the name thereof, which was 'A palme tree': and in the aforesaide seate, or chaire, was placed a semelie and mete personage, richlie apparelled in Parliament robes, with a sceptre in her hand, as a Quene crowned with an open crowne, whose name and title was in a table fixed over her head, in this sort: 'Debora the judge and restorer of the House of Israel, Judic. iv.' And the other degrees, on either side, were furnished with vi personages: two representing the Nobilitie, two the Clergie, and two the Comminaltye. And before these personages was written, in a table, 'Debora with her estates, consulting for the good Government of Israel.' At the feete of these, and the lowest part of the Pageant, was ordeined a convenient rome for a childe to open the meaning of the Pageant. When the Quenes Majestie drew nere unto this Pageant, and perceived, as in the other, the childe readie to speake, her Grace required silence, and commaunded her chariot to be removed nigher, that she myght plainlie heare the childe speake, whych said as hereafter foloweth :—

'Jaben of Canaan King had long by force of armes
Opprest the Israleites which for God's People went:
But God minding at last for to redresse their harmes,
The worthy Deborah as judge among them sent.

In war she, through God's aide, did put her foes to fright,
And with the dint of sworde the hande of bondage brast ;
In peace she, through God's aide, did alway mainteine right,
And judges Israell till fourty yeres were past.

A worthie President, O worthie Queen, thou hast,
A worthie woman judge, a woman sent for staie.
And that the like to us endure alway thou maist,
Thy loving subjectes will with true hearts and tonges prai.'

Which verses were written upon the Pageant: and the same in Latin also. The voide places of the Pageant were filled with pretie sentences concerning the same matter. Thys ground of this last Pageant was, that forsomuch as the next Pageant before had set before her Grace's eyes the florishing and desolate states of a Commonweale, she might by this be put in remembrance to consult for the worthy Government of her People: considering God oftimes sent women nobly to rule among men: as Debora, whych governed Israell in peas the space of xl years: and that it behoved both men and women so ruling to use advise of good counsell. When the Quenes Majestie had passed this Pageant, she marched toward Templebarre: but at St Dunstones church, where the children of thospitall wer appointed to stand with their governours, her Grace perceiving a childe offred to make an oration unto her, stayed her chariot and did cast up her eyes to heaven, as who should saye: 'I here see thys mercyfull worke towarde the poore, whom I muste in the middest of my royaltie nedes remembre!' And so turned her face towarde the childe, which, in Latin, pronounced an oracion. The childe, after he had ended his oracion, kissed the paper wherein the same was written, and

QUEEN ELIZABETH GOING IN PROCESSION FROM SOMERSET HOUSE TO ST. PAUL'S CHURCH, TO RETURN
THANKS FOR THE DEFEAT OF THE SPANISH ARMADA, NOVEMBER 24, 1588

From an engraving in British Museum.

reached it to the Quenes Majestie, whych received it graciouslye both with woordes and countenance, declaring her gracious mynde towarde theyr reliefe. From thence her Grace came to Temple Barre, which was dressed fynelye with the two ymages of Gotmagot the Albione, and Corineus the Briton, two gyantes bigge in stature, furnished accordingly : which held in their handes, even above the gate, a table, wherin was writen, in Latin verses, the effect of all the Pageantes which the Citie before had erected. Which versis wer also written in Englishe meter, in a lesse table, as hereafter foloweth :—

'Behold here in one view thou mayst see all that payne,
O Princesse, to this thy people the onely stay :
What echewhere thou hast seen in this wide town again
This one arche whatsoever the rest conteynd doth say.

The first arche, as true heyre unto thy father dere,
Did set thee in the throne where thy graundfather satte :
The second did confirme thy seate as Princesse here.
Vertues now bearing swaye, and Vyces bet down flatte.

The third, if that thou wouldst goe on as thou began,
Declared thee to be blessed on every syde ;
The fourth did open Trueth and also taught thee whan
The Commonweale stoode well, and when it did thence slide.

The fifth as Debora, declared thee to be sent,
From Heaven, a long comfort to us thy subjectes all :
Therefore goe on, O Quene, on whom our hope is bent,
And take with thee this wishe of thy town as finall :

Live long, and as long raygne, adourning thy countrie
With Vertues, and mayntayne thy people's hope of thee :
For thus, thus Heaven is won : thus must you pearce the sky.
This is by Vertue wrought, all other must nedes dye.'

On the South side was appoynted by the Citie a noyse of singing children : and one childe richely attyred as a poet, which gave the Quenes Majestie her farewell, in the name of the hole Citie, by these wordes :—

'As at thyne entraunce first, O Prince of high renown,
Thou wast presented with tonges and heartes for thy fayre ;
So now, sith thou must nedes depart out of this towne,
This citie sendeth thee firme hope and earnest prayer.

For all men hope in thee, that all vertues shall reygne,
For all men hope that thou none errour wilt support,
For all men hope that thou wilt trueth restore agayne,
And mend that is amisse, to all good mennes comfort.

And for this hope they pray thou mayst continue long
Our Quene amongst us here, all vyce for to supplant :
And for this hope they pray, that God may make thee strong
As by His grace puissant so in his trueth constant.

Farewell, O worthy Quene, and as our hope is sure
That into Errour's place thou wilt now Truth restore :
So trust we that thou wilt our Soveraigne Quene endure,
And loving Lady stand, from henceforth evermore.'

Whyle these woordes were in saying, and certeine wishes therein repeted for maintenaunce of Trueth and rooting out of Errour, she now and then helde up her handes to heavenwarde, and willed the people to say Amen. When the child had ended she said, 'Be ye well assured I will stande your good Quene.' At whiche saying her Grace departed forth through Temple Barre towarde Westminster with no lesse shoutyng and crying of the People, then she entred the Citie, with a noyse of ordinance, whiche the Towre shot of at her Grace's entraunce first into Towre-streate. The childes saying was also in Latin verses, wrytten in a table which was hanged up there. Thus the Quenes Hyghnesse passed through the Citie, whiche, without any forreyne persone, of itselfe beawtifyed itself, and receyved her Grace at all places, as hath been before mentioned, with most tender obedience and love, due to so gracious a Quene and Soveraigne Ladie. And her Grace lykewise of her side, in all her Grace's passage, shewed herselfe generally an ymage of a woorthye Ladie and Governour: but privately these especiall poyntes wer noted in her Grace as synges of a most princelyke courage, wherby her loving subjectes maye ground a sure hope for the rest of her gracious doinges hereafter."

The most beautiful thing about the accession and coronation of Elizabeth was the moment when she passed out of the gates of the Tower, where once before she had lain in daily expectation of death. Her carriage waited for her. She stood looking round her; in the clear, cold, winter light she saw the City rising before her with its spires and gables—her City—filled with hearts that longed above all things for the restoration of the new Faith. And she raised her eyes to heaven and cried:—

"O Lord, Almighty and Everlasting God, I give Thee most humble thanks, that Thou hast been so merciful unto me as to spare me to behold this joyful day; and I acknowledge that Thou hast dealt wonderfully and mercifully with me. As Thou didst with thy servant Daniel the prophet, whom Thou deliveredst out of the den from the cruelty of the raging lions, even so was I overwhelmed, and only by Thee delivered. To Thee, therefore, only be thanks, honour, and praise for ever. Amen."

The Service in the Abbey was the Coronation Mass; but the Litany was read in English, and the Gospel and Epistle both in Latin and in English. All the Bench of Bishops were absent except one; and the Abbot of Westminster took his part in the Service for the last time. Yet a few weeks and all England knew that the Reformation had come back to them. For this gift the people never ceased to love and venerate Queen Elizabeth. There has been no English sovereign save Queen Victoria who was so wholly and unfeignedly loved by the English people as she. This is a commonplace, but it is well, in such a work as this, to remind ourselves how the citizens of London, one and all, and throughout her long reign, were ready to fight and to die for their beloved Queen. She was sometimes hard; she was always inflexible; she was sometimes vindictive; but above all things people delight in a strong king. Henry the First; Henry the

Second ; Edward the First ; Henry the Fifth ; Henry the Eighth ; Elizabeth ; William the Third,—have been the best loved of all the English sovereigns, because of their strength and courage. In the woman's heart of the Maiden Queen lay all the courage and all the strength of her masterful father.

The new opinions made rapid and, for the most part, unchecked advance. It was observed how, at the burial of a certain gentlewoman in St. Thomas Acons, no priests or singing clerks were present, but in their stead the new preachers in their gowns, who neither spoke nor sang until they came to the church, and when the

THE TOWER
From Visscher's *Panorama of London*.

body was lowered into the grave, a Collect was read in English, instead of Latin, and a chapter of St. Paul was read—probably the same chapter which is now read at funerals. The spirit of the time was also marked by a Proclamation forbidding the players of whatever Company to play any more for a certain time.

It has been observed that there were few noblemen left in the City : we observe, however, that Lord Wentworth when he was acquitted for the loss of Calais, went to live at Whittington College. At the funeral service held for the death of King Henry II. of France the sermon, preached by the Bishop-elect of Hereford, turned upon Funeral Ceremonies, pointing out the simplicity of the

7

Primitive Church—a sermon pointing to change; after the sermon the Communion was administered both of wine and of bread.

In August, on St. Bartholomew's Day, there was a great burning of roods, copes, crosses, altar cloths, rood cloths, books, banners, and other church gear, in London. In May, six months after the Queen's accession, the English service was ordered to be held in all the churches. And the Mayor and Aldermen who had been accustomed to go in procession to St. Paul's, there to pray at the tomb of Bishop William, with other ceremonies, changed this practice into hearing a sermon. Early in 1560 we find the people all together singing a Psalm in metre, the custom having been brought from abroad by the Protestant refugees. By

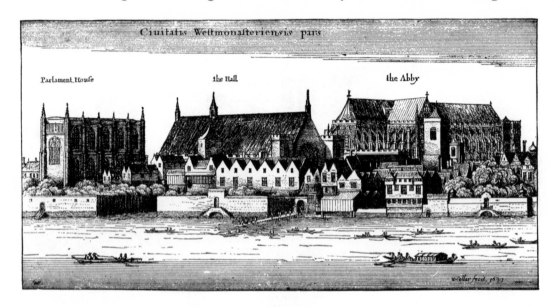

WESTMINSTER
From an engraving by Hollar.

this time the Protestant form of worship seems to have been firmly established, though it wanted the Spanish Armada and the risings and conspiracies in favour of the old Faith to make it impossible that the great mass of the people should desire a return.

Meantime not only by her Progresses, but by her evenings on the river, her presence at jousts and tilts, her personal reviewing of troops and trained-bands, Queen Elizabeth kept herself continually in evidence. (*See* Appendix IV.) The people crowded after her, especially on the river, where in her honour they fired off guns and blew trumpets, beat drums, played lutes, and threw squibs into the air. The Queen even took part in the rough national sports, sitting for whole afternoons with the Foreign Ambassadors, looking on at the baiting of bears and bulls, and hawking was a favourite amusement of hers. A description of Whitehall Palace and its treasures is given by the German traveller Hentzner.

"In Whitehall are the following things worthy of observation :—

I. The Royal Library, well stored with Greek, Latin, Italian, and French books : amongst the rest, a little one in French, upon parchment, in the handwriting of the present reigning Queen Elizabeth, thus inscribed : 'To the most High, Puissant, and Redoubted Prince, Henry VIII. of the Name, King of England, France, and Ireland, Defender of the Faith : Elizabeth his most humble daughter, Health & Obedience.' All these books are bound in velvet of different colours, though chiefly red, with clasps of gold and silver : some of pearls and precious stones set in their bindings.

II. Two little silver cabinets of exquisite work, in which the Queen keeps her paper, and which she uses for writing-boxes.

III. The Queen's bed, ingeniously composed of woods of different colours, with quilts of silk, velvet, gold, silver, and embroidery.

IV. A little chest, ornamented all over with pearls, in which the Queen keeps her bracelets, ear-rings, and other things of extraordinary value.

V. Christ's Passion in painted glass.

VI. Portraits : among which are Queen Elizabeth at sixteen years old ; Henry, Richard, Edward, Kings of England ; Rosamond ; Lucrece ; a Grecian Bride, in her nuptial habit ; the Genealogy of the Kings of England ; a picture of King Edward VI. representing at first sight something quite deformed, till, by looking through a small hole in the cover, which is put over it, you see it in its true proportions ; Charles V., Emperor ; Charles Emanuel Duke of Savoy, and Catherine of Spain his wife ; Ferdinand Duke of Florence, with his Daughters ; one of Philip King of Spain when he came into England and married Mary ; Henry VII., Henry VIII. and his Mother ; besides many more of illustrious men and women, and a picture of the Siege of Malta.

VII. A small hermitage, half hid in rock, finely carved in wood.

VIII. Variety of emblems, on paper, cut in the shape of shields, with mottoes, used by the nobility at tilts and tournaments, hung up here for a memorial.

IX. Different instruments of music, upon one of which two persons may perform at the same time.

X. A piece of clock-work, an Aethiop riding upon a rhinoceros, with four attendants, who all make their obeisance when it strikes the hour : these are all put into motion, by winding up the machine. At the entrance into the park from Whitehall is this inscription :—

> The Fisherman who has been wounded learns though late to beware
> But the unfortunate Actaeon always presses on.
> The chaste Virgin naturally pitied :
> But the powerful Goddess revenged the wrong.
> Let Actaeon fall a prey to his dogs
> An example to Youth
> A disgrace to those that belong to him.
> May Diana live the care of Heaven
> The delight of mortals
> The security of those that belong to her.

In a garden joining to this Palace, there is a Jet d'eau with a sun-dial, which, while strangers are looking at, a quantity of water, forced by a wheel, which the gardiner turns at a distance, through a number of little pipes, plentifully sprinkles those that are standing round."

The entertainment of a noble visitor was hospitable and generous. This is shown in the case of John Casimir, Count Palatine of the Rhine and Duke of Bavaria. He arrived about seven of the clock on the evening of 22nd January 1579. He landed at the Tower, and was there received by divers noblemen and others, who conveyed him by cresset and torchlight to the house of Sir Thomas Gresham in Bishopsgate Street, where he was received with the sounding of trumpets, drums, fifes, and other instruments, and a great concourse of people; here he rested for some days. He was then taken by some of the nobility to the Queen at Westminster, and lodged at Somerset House. The week after he hunted at Hampton Court. On Sunday the first of February he was entertained with a great tilting at Westminster; on Monday with a sword-fight at barriers. On Tuesday he dined with the Mayor; on Wednesday with the Duchess of Suffolk at the Barbican; on Thursday at the Steelyard. On February the 8th he was made a Knight of the Garter. And when he went away he took with him presents worth 3000 crowns.

The tiltings at Westminster attracted an immense number of spectators: in the year 1581 so great was the concourse and so crowded were the scaffolds that they broke down, and many persons were injured or killed.

April the 4th, 1581, was a day to be remembered. On that day the Queen came from Greenwich by water to Deptford, where there was moored a certain ship newly returned from a voyage round the world, the first made by an Englishman. The ship was called *The Golden Hind*, the Captain, Francis Drake. The Queen examined the ship, questioned the Captain, looked at the charts, and saw the things collected and brought home. Then she graciously dined on board, and after dinner conferred the honour of knighthood upon the Captain. An immense number of persons were gathered to see the Queen, and to gaze upon the ship which had been all round the world. A wooden bridge on which one hundred persons were standing broke, but happily none were killed. The ship was laid up in Deptford Dockyard, till she was cut to pieces by visitors taking each a piece of her timbers away. When she was at length broken up, a chair was made out of the wood, and given by a Mr. John Davis to the University of Oxford.

The observance of the Maundy was held in great state :—

First, the Hall was prepared with a long table on each side, and forms set by them; on the edges of which tables and under those forms were laid carpets and cushions for her Majesty to kneel, when she washed the poor. There was also another table laid across the upper end of the Hall, where the Chaplain stood. A little beneath the middle of the Hall a stool and "cushion of estate" were placed for her Majesty to kneel at during service time. This done, the holy-water basons, alms, and other things, being brought into the Hall, and the Chaplain and the poor women, the recipients of the Queen's bounty, having taken their places, the Yeoman of the Laundry, armed with a fair towel, and taking a silver bason filled with warm water and flowers, washed their feet, all, one after another, wiped the same with his towel, and so, making a cross a little above the toes, kissed them. After them followed the Sub-Almoner, doing likewise, and after him the Almoner himself also; so that the feet of the poor folk were three times washed before the Queen appeared. When she came into the Hall, they sang certain psalms and read certain prayers, together with the Gospel of Christ's washing His disciples' feet; then thirty-nine gentlewomen [in accordance with the Queen's age —this account refers to the year 1572] presented themselves with aprons and towels to wait upon her Majesty; and she, kneeling down upon the cushions and carpets under the feet of the poor women, first washed one foot of every one of them in

"HOW TO FLEE THE HEARON"
From Turberville's *Booke of Falconrie*, 1575.

so many several basons of warm water, and sweet flowers, brought to her severally by the said ladies and gentlewomen, then wiped, crossed, and kissed them, as the Almoner and others had done before. When her Majesty had thus gone through the whole number of thirty-nine (of which twenty sat on the one side of the Hall and nineteen on the other) she began again with the first, and gave to each one certain yards of broad cloth. This done, she again began with the first, giving to each in turn a pair of shoes. Fourthly, to each of them she gave a wooden platter, wherein were laid a side of salmon, with an equal weight of ling, six red herring, and two loaves of bread. Fifthly, she began with the first again, and gave to each of them a white wooden bason filled with wine. Sixthly, she received of each Waiting Gentlewoman her towel and apron, and gave one towel and apron to each poor woman. After this the Treasurer of the Chamber came to her Majesty with thirty-nine small white purses wherein were also thirty-nine pence according to the number of the years of her Majesty's age; and of him she received and distributed them severally; which done, she received of him the same number of red leather purses, each containing twenty shillings, for the redemption of her Majesty's gown, which, by ancient custom, should have been given to some one of them at her pleasure; the Queen, however, had changed that reward into money, to be equally divided amongst them all, namely, twenty shillings apiece; and those she also delivered particularly to each one of the whole company; and "so, taking her ease upon the cushion of state, and hearing the choir a little while, her Majesty withdrew herself and the company departed; for it was by that time the sun-setting." This account is taken from that of William Lambarde an Antiquary, who is quoted by John Nichols in his *Progresses of Queen Elizabeth* (vol. i.).

The custom of making New Year's gifts to the Queen was duly honoured every year. The list of the gifts for 1562 as presented by Nichols contains the names of all the noble lords and great ladies in the kingdom, the Bishops, and the Court: nearly two hundred in number. These gifts are of all kinds: gold boxes; purses of money; embroidered sleeves; sugar loaves; ginger; sweetmeats; a smock of silk; handkerchiefs "garnished with gold, silver, and silk"; carved coffers; sleeves embroidered with gold; silk hose—two such gifts; fine glass; gilt cups; tankards, bowls, spoons, and salts; and so on. On the other hand, the gifts which the Queen had to make constantly to Ambassadors, to her officers, to the christening and marriage feasts of the people about the Court, would seem to run away with most of these presents. It is worthy of note that in all the long list of gifts of 1562 there is not one single picture or statue.

The following is Hentzner's account of the Queen's Court at Greenwich (Nichols vol. ii.):—

"We next arrived at the Royal Palace of Greenwich, reported to have been originally built by Humphrey, Duke of Gloucester, and to have received very magnificent additions from Henry VII. It was here Elizabeth, the present Queen, was born, and here she generally resides, particularly in Summer, for the delightfulness of its situation. We were admitted, by an order Mr. Rogers procured from the Lord Chamberlain, into the Presence Chamber, hung with rich tapestry, and the floor after the English fashion strewed with hay, through which the Queen commonly passes on her way to Chapel; at the door stood a Gentleman

The Chariot drawne by fowre Horses upon which Chariot stood the Coffin covered with purple Velvett and upon that the representation. The Conopy borne by fox Knights.

QUEEN ELIZABETH'S FUNERAL

A section from a contemporary MS. scroll in British Museum.

dressed in velvet, with a gold chain, whose office was to introduce to the Queen any person of distinction that came to wait on her; it was Sunday, when there is usually the greatest attendance of Nobility. In the same Hall were the Archbishop of Canterbury, the Bishop of London, a great number of Counselors of State, Officers of the Crown, and Gentlemen, who waited the Queen's coming out: which she did from her own apartment when it was time to go to prayers, attended in the following manner: First went Gentlemen, Barons, Earls, Knights of the Garter, all richly dressed and bareheaded; next came the Chancellor, bearing the seals in a red silke purse, between two; one of which carried the Royal Sceptre, the other the Sword of State, in a red scabbard, studded with golden fleurs-de-lis, the point upwards; next came the Queen, in the sixty-fifth year of her age, as we are told, very majestic: her face oblong, fair, but wrinkled; her eyes small, yet black and pleasant; her nose a little hooked; her lips narrow and her teeth black (defect the English seem subject to from their too great use of sugar); she had in her ears two pearls, with very rich drops; she wore false hair and that red; upon her head she had a small crown, reported to be made of some of the gold of the celebrated Lunebourg Table. Her bosom was uncovered, as all the English Ladies have it till they marry; and she had on a necklace of exceeding fine jewels; her hands were small, her fingers long, and her stature neither tall nor low; her air was stately, her manner of speaking mild and obliging. That day she was dressed in white silk, bordered with pearls of the size of beans, and over it a mantle of black silk, shot with silver threads; her train was very long, the end of it borne by a Marchioness; instead of a chain, she had an oblong collar of gold and jewels. As she went along in all this state and magnificence, she spoke very graciously, first to one, then to another, whether foreign ministers or those who attended for different reasons, in English, French, and Italian; for, besides being well skilled in Greek, Latin, and the languages I have mentioned, she is mistress of Spanish, Scotch, and Dutch; whoever speaks to her, it is kneeling; now and then she raises some with her hand. While we were there, W. Slawata, a Bohemian Baron, had letters to present to her; and she, after pulling off her glove, gave him her right hand to kiss, sparkling with rings and jewels, a mark of particular favour; wherever she turned her face as she was going along, everybody fell down on their knees. The ladies of the Court followed next to her, very handsome and well-shaped, and for the most part dressed in white; she was guarded on each side by the Gentlemen Pensioners, fifty in number, with gilt battle-axes. In the anti-chapel next the Hall, where we were, petitions were presented to her, and she received them most graciously, which occasioned the acclamation of 'Long live Queen Elizabeth!' She answered it with, 'I thank you, my good people.' In the Chapel was excellent music; as soon as it and the service was over, which scarce exceeded half an hour, the Queen returned in the same state and order, and prepared to go to dinner. But while she was still at prayers, we saw her table set out with the following solemnity : A Gentleman entred the room bearing a rod, and along with him another who had a table-cloth, which, after they had both kneeled three times with the utmost veneration, he spread upon the table, and after kneeling again they both retired. Then came two others, one with the rod again, the other with a salt-cellar, a plate, and bread ; when they had both kneeled, as the others had done, and placed what was brought upon the table, they too retired with the same ceremonies performed by the first. At last came an unmarried

THE PALACE OF GREENWICH (PLACENTIA)

lady (we were told she was a Countess) and along with her a married one, bearing a tasting knife ; the former was dressed in white silk, who, when she had prostrated herself three times in the most graceful manner, approached the table, and rubbed the plates with bread and salt, with as much awe as if the Queen had been present ; when they had waited there a little while, the Yeomen of the Guard entered, bare-headed, cloathed in scarlet, with a golden rose upon their backs, bringing in at each turn a course of twenty-four dishes, served in plate, most of it gilt ; these dishes were received by a gentleman in the same order they were brought, and placed upon the table, while the lady-taster gave to each of the guards a mouthful to eat, of the particular dish he had brought, for fear of any poison. During the time that this guard, which consists of the tallest and stoutest men that can be found in all England, being carefully selected for the service, were bringing dinner, twelve trumpets and two kettle-drums made the hall ring for half an hour together. At the end of this ceremonial, a number of unmarried ladies appeared, who, with particular solemnity, lifted the meat off the table, and conveyed it into the Queen's inner and more private chamber, where, after she has chosen for herself, the rest goes to the Ladies of the Court. The Queen dines and sups alone, with very few attendants; and it is very seldom

Walker & Cockerell.

QUEEN ELIZABETH (1533-1603)
From a painting in the National Portrait Gallery. Painter unknown, but probably Marc Gheeraedts.

that anybody, foreigner or native, is admitted at that time, and then only at the intercession of somebody in power."

The great popularity of the Queen, and the affection with which she was regarded by all classes, is shown by the following Proclamation issued in the year 1563, relating to persons making portraits of Queen Elizabeth :—

"Forasmuch as thrugh the natural desire that all sorts of subjects and peple, both noble and mean, have to procure the portrait and picture of the Queen's Majestie, great number of Paynters, and some Printers and gravers, have alredy and doe dayly attempt to make in divers manners portraietures of hir Majestie in paynting, graving, and prynting, wherein is evidently shewn that hytherto none hath sufficiently expressed the naturall representation of hir Majesties person, favor, or grace, but for the most part have also erred therein, as thereof dayly complaints are made amongst hir Majesties loving subjectes, in so much that for redres hereof hir Majestie hath lately bene so instantly and so importunately sued unto by the Lords of hir Consell and others of hir nobility, in respect of the great disorder herein used, not only to be content that some speciall conning payntor might be permitted by access to hir Majestie to take the natural representation of hir Majestie, whereof she hath bene allwise of her own right disposition very unwillyng, but also to prohibit all manner of other persons to draw, paynt, grave, or pourtrayet hir Majesties personage or visage for a time, untill by some perfect patron and example the same may be by others followed. Therfor hir Majestie, being herein as it were overcome with the contynuall requests of so many of hir Nobility and Lords, whom she cannot well deny, is pleased that for their contentations, some coning person mete therefor shall shortly make a pourtrait of hir person or visage to be participated to others for satisfaction of hir loving subjects, and furthermore commandeth all manner of persons in the mean tyme to forbear from payntyng, graving, printing, or making of any pourtraits of hir Majestie, until some speciall person that shall be by hir allowed shall have first finished a pourtraiture thereof, after which fynished, hir Majestie will be content that all other painters, printers, or gravers, that shall be known men of understanding, and so thereto licensed by the hed officers of the plaices where they shall dwell (as reason it is that every person should not without consideration attempt the same) shall and maye at their pleasures follow the sayd patron or first portraiture. And for that hir Majestie perceiveth that a grete nomber of hir loving subjects are much greved and take great offence with the errors and deformities allredy committed by sondry persons in this behalf, she straitly chargeth all hir officers and ministers to see to the due observation hereof, and as soon as may be to reform the errors already committed, and in the meantime to forbid and prohibit the shewing or publication of such as are apparently deformed, until they may be reformed which are reformable."

RELIGION

CHAPTER I

THE DISSOLUTION AND THE MARTYRS

In speaking of the Dissolution of the Religious Houses it must be understood that I am considering this momentous step with reference to London only. The influences of the Continental movement; the lessons of history; the turn taken by theological controversy; the unedifying spectacle of Rome in the fourteenth and fifteenth centuries; the talk of scholars; the strength of the conservatism which rallied about the Church at first; the apparent power of the Church, which seemed, indeed, able to crush every opponent, whatever his rank and station ;—these things moved not, consciously at least, the man of London. He became acquiescent in the changes imposed upon him by other considerations. And I believe that had not his acquiescence been understood as certain to follow, these changes would not have been attempted. Henry VIII. was the most masterful sovereign of his time; but a king cannot outrage and trample upon the settled religious faith of his subjects. The Old Faith had gone to pieces when Constantine proclaimed the New. The New, in its turn, now grown old and incrustated, and hidden by a thousand additions, superstitions, and superfluities, was in its turn ready for departure, in Northern Europe at least, when Henry effected the separation from Rome which began the Reformation in England.

Among an ignorant and an uncritical people the ancient Faith passed unquestioned—was it not the Faith of all those in authority? Its doctrines were supported less by teaching than by outward forms, ceremonies, pageants, splendours and traditional conventions. In every church the story of the Gospels was partly represented, but overlaid with stories of the Saints; the Christian virtues were never, even at the lowest point of Church History, forgotten, yet their practice had become crystallised; almsgiving was part of the Rule of every Religious Order, but it was indiscriminate; mercy towards the criminal had become a refuge for those who continued in their evil practices under cover of Sanctuary; the tradition of austerity no longer brought respect to the Benedictine; the tradition of self-sacrifice no longer brought love to the Franciscan : to the former, as to the College of All Souls, Oxford, the members were *bene nati*, and, I believe, for the

most part *bene morati* and *moderate docti;* in the more secluded religious
communities discipline was relaxed and scandals had crept in; for a hundred years
and more the people had been gradually ceasing to endow the Religious Houses
with bequests. At the commencement of the sixteenth century they had wholly
ceased the practice, formerly universal. Monk and Nun; Friar and Sister; Hermit,
Anchorite, Anchress, now received no more bequests; of all the Religious Orders
none had fallen into disrepute so hopelessly as the Franciscans: they were selling
the lead off the roofs of their stately churches; they were selling their sacred vessels
of silver gilt; their boxes, hung up in the shops—if the shopkeepers admitted
them—received no more offerings; they were insulted in the streets; their numbers
were dwindling daily. Now all these things were like an open book in which
those who passed along the way might read daily, and did read unconsciously, so
that their minds were moulded and directed, they could not tell why or how.

As for the spread of the ideas called Lollardry, one knows not how far they
survived the persecution under Henry V. and the disturbances of the Civil Wars.
But such ideas, whose strength lies in the exercise of reason, so far as men can
reason, do not easily die; the case of Richard Hun (p. 32) shows that they
were still alive. The socialistic side of Lollardry had vanished, but some, at
least, of the religious side survived.

Yet the old things went on apparently undisturbed. Nothing could surpass
the external splendour of a Cardinal Archbishop: no authority was greater in
appearance than his. The rich endowments of the greater Abbeys made the
Houses magnificent and the Brethren proud, generous, and profuse in hospitality
and in alms. Who could be more dignified than the Abbot of St. Peter's,
Westminster? Still the Church seemed to rule in everything: the Fraternities
continued; they still attracted members; they still marched in procession, each
with its chaplain and its singing men, its banners and its brethren, through the
streets on its appointed day; the City Companies were incorporated as Religious
as well as Trade Societies; the Manger and the Holy Tomb still adorned the
churches on the great Festivals; the Angel still flew over the people from the
roof on the Day of Pentecost; the pictures on the wall in every church recorded
the martyrdom of the Saint of Dedication and the miracles which commanded his
canonisation. No one could have dreamed, no one could have prophesied, when
the scholarly young King thundered against Luther that the old order was drawing
to its allotted end, and that for Rome, as well as Northern Europe, Reform was
at hand.

In many ways the Church had long lost its former hold. No longer were
the architects Churchmen; no longer were the bridge builders a distinct fraternity;
the lawyers were clerks, indeed, but not in Holy Orders; the King's Ministers
were no longer necessarily of the Clergy; scholars were no longer of necessity

ordained priests or deacons; physicians were laymen; the clergy were allowed to practise surgery, provided that they did not use fire or steel—in other words, did not conduct operations; in trade the lending of money—formerly in the hands of the Jews and afterwards in those of the so-called "Caursini," Italians licensed by the Popes—was now recognised as necessary, and was carried on more or less openly by merchants; in a word, the daily life of the world, which had been shot through and through, like a piece of silk with its coloured threads, by Religion, had long been emancipating itself, by slow and gradual steps, from the control of the Church and the interference of the priest.

How much these things were understood at the time it is not necessary to inquire. Probably the people, who knew no history, had been unconsciously moulded and changed, and were far from realising the great gulf which now divided them from their ancestors.

Yet there were other signs of change, could they have been rightly interpreted. Scholars, like Erasmus, openly derided the adoration of relics; some of them, under new Pagan influence, denied the Christian faith itself; the scholars of France, like Rabelais and Étienne Dolet, scoffed at the Pope and the Papal pretensions; yet Rabelais did not dare to publish in his lifetime the most daring and the most deadly part of his work.

Add to these things the long-standing disaffection towards the Roman authority. For centuries the Pope had been attempting fresh encroachments, claiming new powers, demanding more contributions. All travellers to Rome brought back the same story of corruption and laxity; men asked themselves why they should submit to the oppression of an Italian prince. In 1529 the House of Commons drew up a petition in which, while they did not ask for a change of doctrine, they complained of the independent legislation claimed by Convocation, the number of officers, the exorbitant fees of ecclesiastical courts, the granting of benefices to children, pluralities, non-residence and other grievances. Surely such a man as Wolsey must have discerned in all these symptoms a warning, clear and loud, that their house must be set in order. Perhaps not, however: nothing is more difficult than for the ecclesiastical mind to see, outside its fences of doctrine and usage, the questioning people, and to hear and understand the awakened mind.

The action of Henry, which, on the face of it, seems the most masterful thing ever attempted by a king, was, on the contrary, approved and accepted by the great mass of the people; especially by the people of London, by the scholars, and by the clergy. There were few who emulated the constancy of the unfortunate Carthusians or the martyrdom of More and Fisher; the old order crumbled and fell to pieces at a touch; out of the débris, among the fallen monarchs of the forest, rose up a tangled mass of vegetation, from which the nobler kinds had to be separated by trial and proof, by persecution and by cultivation.

The first direct step towards the Reformation was, assuredly, not considered as such. It was the suppression by Cardinal Wolsey of certain small houses with whose revenues he endowed his Colleges.

The second direct step was the Petition of the House of Commons, which also passed the Upper House, in 1529.

In January 1531 the House of Commons, in demanding of the clergy the payment of £118,000—an enormous sum, representing more than a million of our money—gave Henry the title of Head of the Church. This was before the break with Rome; so far it meant only that the civil power should be superior to the ecclesiastical.

Then followed the Bill for the abolition of *annales* or payment to the Pope of the first year's income of benefice or see. This was at first held *in terrorem* over the head of the Pope.

The divorce of Katherine and the King's marriage with Anne Boleyn in spite of the opposition of the Pope completed the separation. Henceforth the King was Head of the Church within his own realm.

It was to show to the whole world that he was in earnest and that he meant indeed to be Head of the Church, that Henry caused the execution of the Carthusian monks, of Bishop Fisher, and Sir Thomas More. All Christendom shuddered when those holy men were dragged forth to suffer the degrading and horrible death of traitors; yet all Christendom recognised that there was a King in England who would brook no interference, who knew his own mind, and would work his own will.

I need not follow the course and the development of the Reformation, for its history belongs to the whole country. As regards London, two or three points present themselves for consideration: as, for instance, the condition of the Houses; the manners and morality of the Religious; and the mind of the people.

Let us consider these points from the position of a contemporary Londoner, so far as is possible. First, as to the condition of the Houses.

The enormous wealth of the Church could not fail to impress every one with the incongruity of ecclesiastical professions and practices. The sight of those scores of able-bodied men, most of them with no pretensions to be considered scholars, or divines, or even gentlemen—a qualification which, at the time, might have been sufficient justification for living on the work of others—but men of low origin and of narrow attainments, lounging about the streets and in the taverns—some, as the friars, with no apparent duties at all; some, like the chantry priests, with half an hour's work every day; many of them without the least pretence to piety or virtue—could not but become a powerful aid in the popular approval of the Dissolution. In London alone, a very large part of the City belonged to the Church. The streets swarmed with ecclesiastics who, in the midst of a busy and industrial population, seemed idle and useless.

In the Italian *Relations of England* the writer speaks of the vast wealth of the Church and the power of the ecclesiastics. "I for my part," he says, "believe that the English priests would desire nothing better than what they

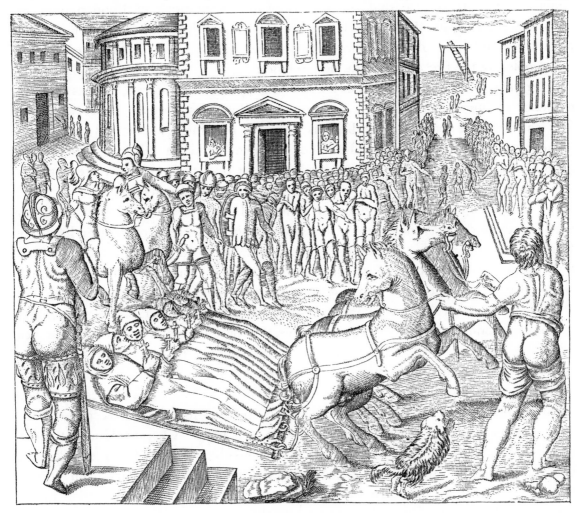

CARTHUSIAN MARTYRS
From a historical print in the British Museum.

have got, were it not they are obliged to assist the Crown in time of war, and also to keep many poor gentlemen, who are left beggars in consequence of the inheritance devolving to the eldest son. And if the Bishops were to decline this expense they would be considered infamous, nor do I believe that they would be safe in their own churches."

There is surely some confusion here. It is true that younger sons attached themselves to the following of the great Lords Spiritual as well as Temporal, but I have nowhere else found it stated that it was the duty of the Church to keep them.   Also many of them, as we have seen, had City connections and embarked in trade.   For "Church" we should perhaps read "the Monastic Houses."

If we come to consider the condition of the Religious on the score of morality, all that can be said concerning those of London is that we hear nothing against them.   It is true that the details of the Visitations of London have not been revealed.   But there could not have been anything very bad, or it would have been laid hold of and enlarged upon, and pointed out for the execration of the people, by the preachers of the new religion.

Froude, in his paper on the Dissolution of the Monasteries, argues that the evidence of immorality on the part of certain Religious Houses is overwhelming. His case against that of St. Albans is certainly convincing, so far as that House alone is concerned.   And it is difficult not to believe that in other cases about the country the evidence of the visitors, even granting that their own private character left a good deal to be desired, is much too detailed for pure invention.

But, as regards the Religious of London, I am not aware that there is any evidence to prove that they were either notoriously or secretly corrupt or luxurious. Considering the pristine standard of the Rule, they were doubtless degenerate, just as in a College of Oxford or Cambridge fifty years ago, the Fellows who should have carried on the lamp of learning spent their time in the study of Port and the practice of Whist.   Father Gasquet argues in favour of the whole body of nuns—London or country—when he cites the case of Sister Joan.   In the year 1535 the Archbishop of York visited a certain convent in his diocese and learned that one of the nuns had been guilty of unchastity.   He inflicted upon her a sentence of great severity : she was to be kept in prison for two years, without speaking to any one but the Prioress ; she was to fast altogether on Wednesday and Friday ; and on every Friday she was to be taken to the Chapter House, there to receive discipline—i.e. to be whipped.   Is it possible, Father Gasquet asks, that the nunneries of England could be grossly and openly immoral—even secretly immoral—when such a severe punishment was meted out to an offender by the visiting archbishop ?   One might point out that a severe punishment may tell of two things : either of horror at a rare and heinous offence, or of a determination, by severe measures, to put down a too frequent breaking of the vows of chastity.

Concerning, therefore, the morals of the London Religious, there has been no special charge, so far as I know, brought against the whole body.   We may remember, however, that the number of persons bound by vows of celibacy was very large ; that even at the present time, when there is certainly more self-restraint, it would be impossible for these vows to be kept by so large a proportion of the people; and that the clergy, in morals and in practice, have never been more than a little in advance of the laity.

The many acts of unchastity of which one reads in the books were perhaps scattered and solitary instances. I refer, however, to certain documents which prove, not the common prevalence of vice, but relaxation of the Rule. They are a collection of papers, the charges of Langland, Bishop of Lincoln, early in the sixteenth century, published in *Archæologia* (vol. xlvii.). They point to laxity, not to vice.

SIR THOMAS MORE (1478-1535)
From the painting by Holbein in the National Portrait Gallery, London.

The first is a charge to the Abbess and Convent of Elstow, near Bedford. In this House the Sisters, instead of assembling in the Fratry for their meals, were accustomed to gather together in what they called their "Households"; apparently messes of two or more, at which secular men, women, and children were allowed to be present. This has to be amended. Henceforth they may repair to the Misericorde, but only one or two at a time, and then under charge of an elderly sister. Their attendance at the services in the "Quire" has become irregular, henceforth they are all to attend every service; they are not to look about the church upon the people during service, for which purpose a door is to be constructed shutting off the choir. They had become irregular about their dress, henceforth they are not to wear their dresses cut low. As for the Lady Abbess, she herself is ordered to get up and attend matins with the rest, and not to break her fast nor to sup with the steward or any secular man.

Clearly, a House requiring reformation, yet not blameworthy of the grosser sins.

There was the Priory of Studley, a Benedictine Nunnery in the Parish of Beckley, Oxfordshire, the burial-place of the British Saint Donanverdh, and one of the residences of Richard of Almayn, brother of Henry. The Prioress is warned to dismiss a certain steward, named Marten Whighill; she is not to suffer her ladies to become godmothers, nor to go out on visits to their kinsfolk "onles it be for their comforte in tyme of ther syknesse, and yett nott then onlesse it shal seme to you, ladye priores, to be behoveful and necessarye, seeing that undre such pretence muche insolency have bene used in religion." Considering, further, that the House is in great debt, the Prioress is to grant no more corrodies, *i.e.* right of board and lodging in the House; to have fewer servants; and to live "in a scarcer manour." She is to look more carefully after the food of the Sisters; she is to see that they wear their robes; and she is to admit more ladies.

The Prioress of Cotham, in Lincolnshire, is to see that there is more order in the singing of the novices. This House has grown very lax. The kinsfolk of the Sisters were no longer to be admitted; the Chaplain was not to be allowed the key of the church; the Lord of Misrule was not to be admitted at Christmas. Then, some of the Sisters had been allowed to go out into the world under pretence of pilgrimage, which license had caused great scandals. Henceforth they were not to be allowed out of the House for the night, nor out of the House at all unless accompanied by a devout Sister. Again, the Sisters had been allowed to go on visits to Thornton, Newsome, Hull (where there were other nunneries), and the Bishop speaks strongly of the reproach, rebuke, and shame which the rumours of their conduct had brought upon them. This House is the worst case of the four. Certain persons named are absolutely forbidden within the walls. Sir John Warde, Sir Richard Calverley, Sir William Johnson, the Parson of Skotton, and Sir William Sele, are those who have brought upon themselves by their misconduct this prohibition. Lastly, since the House had been reduced to miserable poverty, the Prioress must diminish her servants, grant no more corrodies, sell no more plate, and get the necessary repairs effected as speedily as possible.

The last of the charges is one to the Abbot of Missenden, in Buckinghamshire. This House, also, has fallen into poverty; there must be a diminished number of servants and a simpler table; there must be no more granting of corrodies; the House must be put into repair. There was no school for the novices; a man learned in grammar must be appointed at once; the boys must be kept apart; in future the monks must not be allowed to wander about outside, day and night, as had been the case. And no women were to be admitted either by day or by night. John Compton was to be turned out of the monastery at once—he was probably the steward; and Dom John Slithurst was to be put in prison and kept there.

These accounts indicate very clearly the decay of discipline in the Houses. The Prioress eats and drinks with her steward; the Sisters entertain their kinsfolk within the walls; the church plate is sold to pay debts; the Sisters get outside on any pretext—then come scandals. Certain persons are so much mixed up with these scandals that they must never be allowed within the House at all; the Sisters adopt as much of the fashions of the world as they can; they shirk the services; they relieve the monotony of their lives by going on pilgrimages. As to the monks they get out alone, all night long. What scandals made the Bishop so determined upon keeping women out of the House altogether? And what had Dom Slithurst done, more than his fellows, that he was to be clapped into prison and kept there?

It will be replied that these are all Houses in the country. That is quite true; yet I think that, considering the attacks on the Religious; the decay of the Friars; the withdrawal of bequests from monks and friars alike,—the London Houses must have been open at least to charges of laxity; and I would not press against them anything more severe. In the admonition of the Dean of St. Paul's to the Nuns of St. Helen's, laxity, not vice, was the principal complaint. Those who believe that graver charges might be brought may read the famous accusation against the Abbot of St. Albans—a thing, to my mind, impossible to get over. True, St. Albans is not London, which is a saving clause.

Enough about the condition of the Houses and the morality of the Religious. I hear certain whispers where men congregate: they murmur—*tacenda*. I have no proof that they are true; but I understand that the holiness of the Religious is no longer accepted as a matter of course; it is enough for one that this is so. The work of the Houses is done when the people no longer desire the prayers of brethren *inclusi*, and sisters immured; and no longer expect the pristine devotion of the Friars.

The suppression of the Religious Houses and its immediate effects in London are passed over by Stow, in his *Survey*, with great brevity. It is a pity; we should like so much to have a clear understanding of how the people at large received these measures. Now this historian was born in 1525; he could remember, therefore, not only the Dissolution, but also the condition of the City under the old *régime*. It is much to be lamented, further, that though he could find time and space to give whole pages to the Coronation of Anne Boleyn, he could not give more than a brief note on the suppression of one House after another.   He remembered the Franciscans going in and about everywhere in their grey gowns; the Dominicans in black; the Carmelites in white; he remembered the riding apparel of the monks; he remembered—he notices, in fact —the hospitality of the richer houses; he remembered the stately churches towering above the humble parish churches, as Westminster above St. Margaret's; St. Augustine's over Peter le Poor; the Holy Trinity over St. Catherine Cree; their peals of bells; their organs; their treasures of gold and silver plate; their church furniture, sumptuous with cloth of gold and velvet.   He remembered the splendour, wealth, authority, and power of the old ecclesiastics.   Their authority seemed rooted in the solid rock, never to be destroyed; and he remembered how this substantial ecclesiastical structure vanished at a word, at a touch, leaving behind it nothing but ruined cloisters; churches desecrated; carvings and marbles broken up.   In his old age he sat alone and marvelled over these things.   But he spoke not.   Perhaps it was dangerous, even for a historian, to speak—Stow had already been accused of being a favourer, at least, of the old Order; regrets were accounted traitorous; sympathy with the outcast monk was heresy—or, which was as dangerous, was *lèse Majesté*.   Not every one desired the crown of martyrdom: to most people it was disagreeable to be burned—one would avoid this method of extinction if possible; almost as disagreeable was it to be dragged on a hurdle, half hanged, cut down, and then quartered.   So Stow wrote nothing about the old time as compared with that which followed.

In a single passage, however, Stow does allow us to understand something of his opinion as to the whole business.   No doubt many people looked about for some mark of the Divine displeasure upon those who took an active part in the Dissolution.   To this day, certain persons whisper about the families which succeeded to the monastic houses; if anything happens to them it is put down to the vengeance which must be expected to follow upon the sacrilegious occupation of monastic property; nothing is said, of course, as to the long prosperity which has attended most of the families which still occupy the old monastic lands.

"About such time as Cardinall Wolsey was determined to erect his new Colledges in Oxford and Ipswich, he obtayned licence and authoritie of Pope Clement the Seventh to suppresse about the number of fortie Monasteries of good fame, and bountifull hospitalitie, wherin the King bearing with all his doings, neyther Bishop nor temporall Lorde in this Realme durst saye any worde to the contrarie.

In the executing of this business, five persons were his chiefe instruments, who on a time made a demaunde to the Prior and Convent of the Monasterie of Daintrie, for occupying of certayne of theyr groundes, but the Monkes refusing to satisfie their requests, streightway they picked a quarrel agaynst the house, and gave information to the Cardinall agaynste them, who taking a small occasion, commaunded the house to bee dissolved, and to bee converted to hys new Colledge, but of thys irreligious robberie, done of no conscience, but to patch up pride, whiche private wealth coulde not furnishe, what punishmente hath since ensued at God's hande (sayeth myne Author) partly ourselves have seene, for of those fyve persons, two fell at discorde betweene themselves, and the one slewe the other, for the which the survivor was hanged; the thirde drowned himselfe in a well; the fourth beeing well knowne, and valued worth two hundred pounde, became in three yeares so poore, that hee begged to hys dying day; and the fifth called Doctor Allane, beeyng chiefe executor of these doyngs, was cruelly maymed in Irelande, even at suche tyme as hee was a Bishop; the Cardinall falling after into the King's greevous displeasure, was deposed, and dyed miserably; the Colledges whiche hee meante to have made so glorious a building, came never to good effect; and Pope Clement himselve, by whose authoritie these houses were throwne downe to the ground was after enclosed in a dangerous siege within the Castell of Saint Angell in Rome by the Emperialles; the Citie of Rome was pitifully sacked; and himselfe narrowly escaped with his life."

I have repeatedly spoken of the falling off in bequests to the various Religious Orders during the hundred years preceding the Reformation. The fact, indeed, seems to be most important in considering the attitude of the citizens. That it is a fact may be proved by the following table, compiled from the *Calendar of Wills*. I have already made some extracts from the Wills in proof of the change of popular opinion in this respect; this table considers the fact from another point of view.

Of course we have not, in these pages, all the Wills, nor anything more than a small fraction of the Wills made by the Citizens during the centuries covered by the contents of these two volumes. But they may be taken as representative wills, in whatever manner they present contemporary opinion. Now, as regards bequests to Religious Houses, I have made the following analysis. I take three periods. (1) from 1250 to 1350; (2) from 1350 to 1450; (3) from 1450 to the Dissolution, say 1538; covering nearly three centuries. During these three periods the following is the number of bequests :—

1. To the various Orders of Friars for 1250-1350 20
                          1350-1450 12
                          1450-1540 4
2. To the Charter House for the 1st period, not founded.
                     2nd ,, ... 31
                     3rd ,, ... 14
3. To the Grey Friars for the 1st period, bequests included among the various Orders.
                     2nd ,, ... 20
                     3rd ,, ... none
4. To the Black Friars 1st period, included among various Orders.
                     2nd ,, ... 10
                     3rd ,, ... 1
5. To the Holy Trinity Priory for the 1st period 17
                     2nd ,, ... 46 (?)
6. To Eastminster for the 1st period, not yet founded.
                     2nd ,, ... 7
                     3rd ,, ... 2
7. To St. Helen's for the 1st period 18
                     2nd ,, ... 12
                     3rd ,, ... none
8. Crutched Friars for the 1st period 13
                     2nd ,, ... 10
                     3rd ,, ... 1

9. Carmelite or White Friars, 1st period	15
2nd ,, ...	11
3rd ,, ...	1
10. Austin Friars for 1st period	13
2nd ,, ...	13
3rd ,, for masses	2
11. St. Bartholomew's for 1st period	14
2nd ,, ...	13
3rd ,, ...	2
12. Haliwell for 1st period	12
2nd ,, ...	20
3rd ,, ...	2
13. Minoresses for 1st period	9
2nd ,, ...	18
3rd ,, ...	3

These figures show most unmistakably that the monastic life was no longer regarded as it had been by the people of London. By the friars especially, *i.e.* by those who could read the signs of the time, it must have been understood that the end was very near. Not the alleged immorality of the Religious, but the decay of their numbers, the wasting of their property, the withdrawal of support by the laity, might have warned those under vows that a change was nigh at hand. I do not suppose that many of them heard this warning. Who could believe, standing in the great church, glittering with lights, with gold and silver, rich with colour, splendid with carved work, that the axe was already laid to the root?

The people of London were not, it is true, consulted. Henry was not the kind of man to consult the illiterate on points of Theology or Spiritual Government. They were, however, filled with a vague unrest of new ideas; we know not what survivals of the old Lollardry lingered and were whispered about, or spoken openly; we know not how widely the ballads and satirical verses against monks and friars were repeated and sung and made the subject of merriment in the taverns. We do know, however, that the King ordered and that the people of London obeyed. I think it incredible that even the most masterful of English kings should have dared to force changes so radical upon an unwilling city. London was never remarkable for meekness, and in matters religious was never uncertain. The King must have known that the people of London, at least, would be with him. London, therefore, obeyed; the people looked on while the Pope of Rome vanished; they made no protest when they saw Monks, Nuns, and Friars turned out of doors and their Houses closed; they looked on without a murmur even when the Carthusians were dragged to a horrible doom. Was this callousness? Was it fear? Was it acquiescence in the Revolution, with the hope of larger things to follow? For my own part, looking at the attitude of the citizens during the successive reigns of Henry, Edward, Mary, and Elizabeth, I think there can be no doubt as to the general opinion at the time, and that it was from the outset in favour of the Dissolution of the Houses and the Dispersion of the Religious; in favour of denying the authority of the Pope; eager for the free readings of the Holy Scriptures in the vulgar tongue and for the right of that private interpretation which seems so easy to the illiterate. As regards ritual, the changes, as will be explained later, were gradual; the introduction of distinctive Protestant doctrine was not brought

MARTYRS AT SMITHFIELD
E. Gardner's Collection.

about in a day; the genesis of the Puritanic spirit does not belong to the Revolution under Henry.

Let us endeavour to realise something of the extraordinary change which the Suppression of the Houses brought about in London. Fortunately the work was carried on by successive Acts, covering a period of fifteen years or so; it was not until 1548, for instance, that the whole of the chantries, colleges, etc., were suppressed.

The point of departure is, naturally, the expulsion and the dispersion of the Religious of all Orders. At this point most historians stop. Yet this was only the beginning.

Consider, then, the number of those turned out of the London Houses. We may arrive at an approximation of the number by the following considerations. There were 202 Houses, not counting Friaries, dissolved in 1538-1540.

They contained, in all, 3221 Monks and Canons. This gives an average of 16 Brethren to each House. Now there were in London some twenty Houses great and small—say from St. Peter's, Westminster, to Jesus Commons. In the same proportion there would thus be 300 Monks and Canons. In the same proportion, also, there would be about a fourth of that number of Nuns. Now, these monks and nuns were not sent out into a cold world empty-handed. Not at all. They received pensions. The nuns of St. Helen's, for instance, received pensions of £2 : 14 : 4 each. The chantry priests of the same place, whose stipends had been £6 : 13 : 4 and £7 respectively, obtained pensions of £5 each. We must, in fact, put aside altogether the generally received notion of the Dissolution as an Act which drove thousands of holy men and women out of their homes—abodes of piety and virtue—to starve. There was no starvation at all : the pensions though small were intended to be sufficient ; we have therefore the fact that some 400 Religious of London were made to lay down the habit of their Profession and to go forth into the world on pensions large enough to maintain them. What became of them ? Many of the older monks and nuns doubtless felt acutely the change of habit ; the loss of the former life—its quiet, its self-centred interests, its community ; some of the younger men, we cannot doubt, willingly turned themselves to secular pursuits ; some lived quietly, keeping up privately, two or three together, some manner of religious life ; some were concealed in the country and a few, perhaps, in town, and led the life of the Rule in a clandestine manner ; some, again, the restraint of their vows being withdrawn, ran into excesses and fell into the mire ; some haunted taverns, to the disgrace of their former calling. But of suffering or privation I cannot discover that there was much, if any, either for monks or nuns. It is pretended that the pensions were irregularly paid. The evidence seems to me insufficient ; in regard to the nuns of St. Helen's, we have positive evidence pointing in the opposite direction.

The greatest sufferers were, as we have seen, the friars. For them there was no pity ; for them there were no pensions ; no one believed in them any longer ; their day was done. There appeared, a short time ago, a book written by one who had been for twelve years a friar : he came out of the House ; he laid down his frock and renounced his vows ; and he wrote a book in which he described the life of his late brethren. It is not an exaggerated or an ill-natured book ; it is simply a plain statement of the manner of life led by the friars of these days. Looking through its pages one begins unconsciously to consider the friars of the early sixteenth century—the friars in their last days—by the light of this revelation. Now the modern friar is a man of some education and some culture. Take away his education and his culture in order to get at the friar of the Tudor time. Place him in a time much rougher and coarser in manners; give him nothing to do: no work either of mental or physical kind; and to the general futility and unreality of life in a modern friary add the temptations, almost irresistible to the uneducated mind of the ordinary friar, of the world around him. In this way one may succeed, perhaps, in understanding the reasons for the unpopularity of the friars.

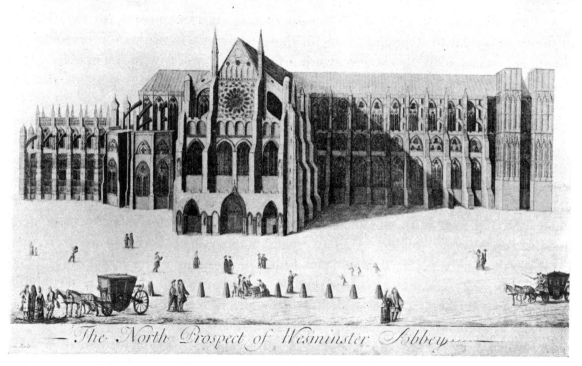

The North Prospect of Wesminster Abbey

From an engraving by G. Collins. A. Rischgitz' Collection.

It is generally stated that riches flowed in upon the friars as a consequence of the respect in which they were held. That is not the case: they were never rich. They owned a few houses built within the limits of their own precinct, the rent of which went to maintain the fabric of the church, and the service. For themselves the friars possessed no great buildings, except the Church, the Library, and the Hall: and they lived on charity at the end of their time as at the beginning. Wyclyf makes much of their churches. "Freres bylden mony grete churches and costily houses, and cloystris as hit were castels and that withoute nede. Grete houses make not men holy, and onely by holiness is God wel served."

The friars were not rich, but they were proud : they arrogated power and sanctity for their very robe.   Those who died in the Franciscan habit could never, they said, be carried away by the devil.   Walsingham, who had, perhaps, the jealousy of a monk, thus wrote of them :—

"The friars, unmindful of their profession, have even forgotten to what end their Orders were instituted ; for the holy men their lawgivers desired them to be poor and free of all kind of temporal possessions, that they should not have anything which they might fear to lose on account of saying the truth.   But now they are envious of possessors, approve the crimes of the great, induce the commonalty into error, and praise the sins of both ; and with the intent of acquiring possessions, they who had renounced possessions, with the intent of gathering money, they who had sworn to persevere in poverty, call good evil and evil good, leading astray princes by adulation, the people by lies, and drawing both with themselves out of the straight path."

They disappeared.   What became of them?   It is impossible to say.   Some of the Sisters went to Flanders ; some of those who were in priests' orders obtained benefices ; some took up honest work ; for many, work was impossible.   If a man gets to thirty or so without doing any work, it becomes impossible that he should ever do any work.

The Brethren, however, were not the only people who lived upon the revenues of the House.   Every Monastic Foundation had its own establishment and was complete in itself.   Of course, the superfluity of officers and the general waste of work were, from a modern point of view, deplorable.   Every House had its mill, its brewery, its bakery, its still-rooms, its gardens, orchards, fish-ponds, vineyards ; its servants of all kinds, including bailiffs, serjeants, scriveners, illuminators, carvers, gilders, singing men, singing schools, huntsmen, farmers, carpenters, plumbers, gardeners, agriculturists, sextons, gate-porters, rent-collectors, lawyers, stewards, and one knows not what besides.   When the House was closed all these people were turned adrift, certainly, without pensions. Thousands of families, for these people were not under vows and were married, were suddenly deprived of their means of livelihood.   What could they do? The ordinary craftsmen would make shift : their Companies helped them ; but the better sort, the scriveners, limners, illuminators, painters, carvers, gilders ; the bailiffs, lawyers, stewards,—what could they do?   For fifteen years London was flooded with the people of the monasteries turned adrift to find a means of living ; they were not people who swelled the ranks of the vagabond and the masterless ; they were respectable and honest folk.   Their struggles and their sufferings, if we could get at them, must have been very real and, in many cases, very terrible.

There were, next, the people who lived by the making and selling of things no longer wanted under the new order.   There were the makers of ecclesiastical vestments and robes ; altar cloths ; wax tapers ; instruments required in the celebration of Mass ; crosses and crucifixes ; beads, reliquaries, images, and all the "properties" required for the old Faith. Also all those who sold tapers, beads, crosses, images, relics, books of hours, mass books, censers and every kind of church vessel. One has only to look at the shops in the vicinity of a French cathedral to understand the extent of the business when not a single cathedral, but a hundred and fifty parish churches, and monastic chapels, had

STEPHEN GARDINER, BISHOP OF WINCHESTER (1483(?)-1555)
From an engraving of the portrait in Trinity Hall, Cambridge.

to be provided for, and when all the people, with one consent, acquiesced in the doctrines, and practised the ritual of the Church.

All these people, thus deprived of their livelihood, were skilled craftsmen. When their occupation was gone, when embroidered altar-cloths, copes and vestments stiff with cloth of gold, carven images, sacred pictures, beads and crosses and crucifixes, were no longer wanted, what could they do? If, at the present day, any single branch of industry is suddenly destroyed, what happens? It is too late for the people concerned to learn another trade. What happened to these unfortunates it is impossible to guess. One thing we know, namely, in general terms, that London was in a miserable condition for a quarter of a century after the Dissolution of the Houses; and we may fairly conclude that not bad trade alone, but also the great number of poor and forlorn creatures who had been hurled by the Reformation from comfort to penury, was one cause of the depression.

Or, if we consider the immediate external effects of the Suppression; think of the unwonted silence, when all the bells of all the Monastic Houses were taken down: instead of the melodious pealing from forty chapels, there was left only the sorry tinkle of the parish bell.

From the streets disappeared all the friars: those of St. Francis, of St. Dominic, of St. Augustine, the Carmelites, and those with the Iron Cross. The old familiar figures had been diminishing in numbers, but they were still visible when the end came: still they went about, opening their money-boxes in the shops, and finding nothing. Afterwards one met, flitting along the streets, stray and forlorn figures clad like craftsmen, but knowing no craft; sturdy beggars who would not work; men and women turned out into the stony-hearted streets, filled with rage and bitterness; looking always for the restoration of the old Order and their own return to the quiet house of ease and comfort. Gone, too, were the servants of the Houses; they had been known by the badge upon their shoulders; gone was the vast army of chantry priests, subdeacons, and ecclesiastics, with all the minor Orders. When Queen Mary restored the ancient Faith the priests appeared again, leaping out from unknown dens and secret places, ready to resume suddenly the restored service before the newly adorned altar. And as London always attracted the masterless and the vagabond and the criminal, so from all parts of England flocked to the City those whom the Reformation had sent out homeless and penniless. The clergy, for their part, lost the greater part of their fees. The baptisms, marriages, and funerals, it is true, continued, but the fees for masses to be said for the dead—the most important part of the fees—the endowments of chantries, post obits, and memorial days, were all swept away. There were many chantry priests in every parish church. Why, only a few years before the Reformation, on the death of Lady Jane Seymour, Sir Richard Gresham ordered 1200 masses to be sung in the City churches for the repose of her soul. And when prayers for the dead were forbidden, and what had been an aristocratic Heaven, open especially to the rich because they could buy their entrance by masses, became a democratic Heaven, open to the poor and lowly as much as to the high and mighty, the loss to the clergy from this source was very great. There was also another loss in the abolition of pilgrimage, and another in the abolition of confession, penance, and extreme unction.

As for the people, they had their losses to deplore as well as their gains to rejoice over. They were deprived, for instance, of the most splendid and gorgeous spectacle open to them, the services of the Church with the rolling music of the organ, the singing of the choir, the chanting of the priests; with the illumination of the altar; the fragrance of the incense; the pictures on the wall; the brilliant side chapels; the many votive candles; the sculptured saints; and all that appealed to the eye and to the ear. That service had been performed by moving figures, they seemed not men, in wondrous robes set off by the bright lights. It was a service at which the hearts of men and women with imagination were daily, keenly, sincerely moved and led heavenward. All this they had to give up. In its place they were offered a cold and quiet service with a sermon an hour long, appealing to their reason and bidding them base their faith on logic and argument instead of the authority and the Voice of the Church, inviting them to trust in right doctrine rather than in the Fold of Christ. The service had been the chief instructor in art, music, and æsthetics. When it was gone what had they left? There were no more pictures for the people; there was no more grand and solemn music for them; only the tinkling of the mandoline in the tavern, or the "noise" of the whifflers who marched before a prisoner; there was nothing else for them. Mary's martyrs made them hate the name of Catholic; they pelted her chaplains in the street; they hung up a dog, head shorn, to mock the tonsure; they hung up a cat with a wafer in its paws to mock the Elevation of the Host. Yet though they were no longer Catholics it cannot be maintained that they had got very far in Protestantism.

Some of the ancient forms remained: it still continued the duty of every Christian, as it has always been the duty of every follower of the Roman Church, to attend service on Sunday morning, and to communicate on the great festivals of Easter, Christmas, Trinity, and Whit Sunday. The fast days remained: no flesh could be sold; the butchers' shops were closed; none could be eaten on Fridays or in Lent; there were some who followed the ancient austerities so far as to fast on Wednesday as well. All classes, high and low, rich and poor, were constantly engaged in reading the New Testament for proofs of new doctrine, and the Old Testament for examples and for warnings. In every ale-house the men wrangled on points of doctrine over their pots; the women in the doorways discussed obscure points in the teaching of St. Paul; there were none so ignorant as not to be able to formulate a whole body of doctrines; in every barber's shop there was a Bible; already men had begun to set up strange and absurd teachings, in their ignorant and fond attempts to discern the Truth in a weak translation; already some had begun to go about in sad-coloured garments, without ornament, colour, or decoration, even with texts ostentatiously bound round their hats or their sleeves, like the phylacteries of the Pharisees.

In London the better sort of people towards the end of the century became infected with Puritanism. Puritans were known by their outward and visible signs: they wore texts on their arms; they hated starch and had limp cuffs; they wore no hatbands; they would not curl their hair, but carried it lank; those who were shopkeepers always had a Bible open on the counter; they hated the theatre and all other amusements; in church they would have no organ; they used strange words, calling, for instance, godfather and godmother "witnesses"; they spoke of Christ-tide instead of Christmas; whole trades in London went "solid" for Puritanism, *e.g.* the feathermen of Blackfriars; they were intolerant and fanatic; they desired above all things to abolish Episcopacy. They showed their opinions by their manner of singing, which was without the accompaniment of organs, and by slowly drawling their words.   The Puritans would not greatly care for irreverence in St. Paul's: they gave no reverence to a consecrated place; yet they went to church in order to worship and to hear godly sermons.   Therefore they could not look on unmoved when they saw St. Paul's crowded with people who went there in order to transact business, to buy and sell, to talk, to quarrel, to fight, to make assignations or to keep them, to display fine dress, to be hired in service.

To a certain class, the larger class, otherwise the thing would have been impossible; these changes were welcomed with the greatest joy because they declared and emphasised the revolution of religious thought.   For the majority the pendulum had swung round from the faith and trust in the Fold of the Church, to the sense of individual responsibility.   The pendulum is always swinging backwards and forwards.   In our own time we have witnessed a partial return to the belief in a Fold.   The cold service with its long sermon of doctrine; the private study of the Scriptures; the exercise of individual judgment, free though unlettered, upon points of doubt and apparent contradiction;—all formed part of the same movement and appealed to the majority.

At the same time there was another section to whom these things were hateful and horrible and blasphemous.   This was the class which was ready to forget the old grievances, the intolerable burden of Church property; the multitudes who lived in sloth, as it appeared; the wide difference between practice and profession; and thought only, as so many at the present day think, of the haven of safety promised to the faithful; the beauty, splendour, and stateliness of the service; the ecstasy of the believer; the yielding of spirit before the Ineffable Presence; the visible power and authority of the Roman Catholic Church.   These people looked and prayed daily for a return of the old Faith; they were recusants under Elizabeth; they concealed the priests who came over to concoct their conspiracies; they were Romanists first and Englishmen next, until the horrors of the persecution in Flanders, of the massacres in France, and the designs of the Spaniards upon England, made them Englishmen first and Catholics next.

An irreparable loss to the world was the wholesale destruction of the libraries. Printing, an invention of no longer standing than fifty years, had as yet produced comparatively few books. When, for instance, the learned Anthony Brockby had written his book *Ad Fratres* against the King's Supremacy, he did not get it printed, but had a duplicate copy made, which he presented to the Franciscans, his brothers. By far the greater part of theology, philosophy, science, and literature remained in MS., and these MSS. formed the Monastic

A. Rischgitz.

QUEEN ELIZABETH AT PRAYER

Frontispiece to *Christian Prayers*, 1569. From a copy in the Lambeth Palace Library, which probably belonged to the Queen herself.

Libraries. When the Houses were suppressed, those who obtained them as a gift from the King for the most part cared nothing about the books: they were dispersed without any consideration for their use or value; if they were well bound, the covers were pulled off and the books thrown away, or turned into waste paper. Thus John Bale writes (*Antiq. English Franciscans*):—

"Covetousness was at that time so busy about private interest, that public wealth was not anywhere regarded. A number of them which purchased those superstitious Mansions reserved of those Library Books some to serve their Jakes, some to scowr their candlesticks, and some to rub their Boots, and some they sold the Grocers and Soap sellers, and some they sent over sea to the Bookbinders: not in small number, but, at times, whole ships full. Yea, the Universities of this Realm are not all clear in this Fact; but cursed is the belly which seeks to be fed with so ungodly gains, and so deeply shameth his natural country. I know a Merchant man (which shall at this time be nameless) that bought the Contents of two noble Libraries for forty shillings price; a shame it is to be spoken. This stuff hath he occupied, instead of grey paper, by the space of more than these ten years, and yet he hath store enough for as many years to come. A prodigious example is this, and to be abhorred of all men which love their nation as they should do. Yea, what may bring our realm to more shame and rebuke than to have it noised abroad that we are despisers of learning? I judge this to be true, and utter it with heaviness, that neither the Britons under the Romans and Saxons, nor yet the English people under the Danes and Normans had ever such damage of their learned Monuments as we have seen in our time. Our posterity may well curse this wicked fact of our age, this unreasonable spoil of England's most noble Antiquities." . . . "How many admirable manuscripts of the Fathers, Schoolmen, and Commentators were destroyed by this means? What number of historians of all ages and Countries? The Holy Scriptures themselves, as much as these Gospellers pretended to regard them, underwent the fate of the rest. If a Book had a cross on it it was condemned for Popery, and those with lines and circles were interpreted the Black Art and destroyed for Conjuring. And thus, as Fuller goes on, Divinity was profaned, Mathematicks suffered for Corespondence with Evil Spirits, Physick was maimed, and a Riot committed on the Law itself."

One change, one result, of the Suppression, everybody can understand. This was the closing of the Hospitals. London was full of Hospitals, but they were Religious Houses. St. Bartholomew's, attached to the Priory; St. Thomas', Southwark; St. Mary Spital; Elsing Spital for the blind; St. Mary of Bethlehem for the insane; the House on Tower Hill also for the insane; the House of St. Augustine Papey for old priests; the Infirmary in every Monastic House;—all these provided for the sick poor. I have no doubt, though on the subject I have no information, that the Companies, which certainly took care of their sick and their infirm, must have done so through the existing Hospitals. When the Houses were closed, what became of the sick? It is commonly believed that they were turned into the street, no one caring for them. This was certainly not the case. The Companies cared for their own; the City cared for its freemen and their families; would the City, which maintained a debtors' prison for its freemen, so that they should not be confined with the general herd, suffer its sick and poor to starve? There was a residuum of those who were not free, namely, the vagabonds and masterless men and women. For them there was a time of great misery; when they were ill there was no one to visit them; no hospital where they might be taken; no hands to minister and alleviate; no voice to console and to fortify. And we know nothing, and cannot estimate the suffering because there were no journalists to publish the things they saw; and the sick and poor lay unheeded and starved, and died unknown and uncared for in the dirt and misery of the Tudor slum.

There is no doubt, also, that the open house kept by such a monastery as the Holy Trinity, where the poor received every day the broken meat and a great deal more, was greatly missed and deplored by the whole company of the masterless. What with daily open house at the greater monasteries, the broken meats of the smaller, the doles and charities of the parish, the "mind days" with their loaves and gifts to the poor, bequeathed by rich citizens, a family which objected to work might rub along in solid and well-fed comfort all the year round. And this resource, looked upon as certain and unfailing like a perennial spring, was suddenly stopped. Then all these people had to work, or to beg, or to rob. The streets became pestered with sturdy beggars : the by-places of Elizabethan Literature present most vivid pictures of the companies of beggars, impostors, rogues and vagabonds. They were the people whom the monks and nuns had fed without asking questions ; the folk who would not work ; the people turned out of the monasteries ; ex-friars ; ex-chantry priests ; former makers of images, crucifixes, beads, candlesticks and the rest : these were the people who felt most bitterly the abolition of indiscriminate charity and the cruel choice offered them under the new order of work ; mendicancy with the whip, or crime with the gallows.

Out of all these evils and sufferings was born, like a sweet flower on a heap of rubbish, the Spirit of modern Charity.

The Church had taken over to herself the whole of Mediæval charity. Did a citizen desire to help the poor, he gave money for the purpose to the Church. If a poor man wanted help, it was not to a merchant that he went, but to a monastery.

For charity, that is, for pity, for almsgiving, the world has always felt the most profound respect. The most popular of mediæval saints was the hard and austere Bishop of whom the world remembered that he had once divided his cloak with a beggar. There were six churches dedicated to St. Martin in the City of London alone.

And when the friars first came over, and men, wondering, saw that they did not lock themselves up in their cloister to pray for the world like the other Religious, but that they went about among the people ministering, comforting, preaching, consoling ; that they found no den too revolting, no disease too loathsome, no criminal too base, for their ministrations ; then, indeed, there was an outburst of gratitude, of joy, of respect, of awe for men so saintly. They were considered the veritable children of God.

But it was not to be thought that the poor sinners outside the monastery should imitate their example. Nay, St. Francis, their founder, had himself separated his Order from the world, they were called out from the rest of humanity, they were kept separate by vows of celibacy, poverty, obedience. Modern charity as yet did not exist, as we now understand it, only the respect for charity as an ecclesiastical institution.

I believe that the early followers of St. Francis perceived the weak point of this separation from the world. We can hear one wiser than the rest saying, " There is danger that the early zeal may decline. All things human have in them the germs of decay ; if there comes a time when our brethren shrink from the task they have undertaken, if their vows become a sham, their prayers a form, their work a pretence and a profession, then it would have been better for the world had St. Francis never existed, because we shall have taken from the layman the duty of personal service and killed it by our own neglect."

To meet this danger, not to take renunciation and self-sacrifice wholly out of the world, they created another Order, that called the *Fratres de Saccâ*. This Order contained men and women of the world, married men and married women; they were allowed to go about their daily work; those who were single were not forbidden to marry; they took vows, but not those of celibacy nor of poverty.

When the Houses were suppressed, all the institutions which they had supported were suppressed as well. Yet it did not immediately occur to the people that the burden of the poor, which they had long since willingly laid upon the Church, was now laid upon themselves. When the City took over the House of the Grey Friars; the House of St. Bartholomew; the House of St. Mary Bethlehem; the Palace of Bridewell; the House of St. Thomas,—it seemed to take the place of the Church and to attempt, by way of taxation, all that the Monastic Houses had tried, or professed, to do from their own resources. We hear of sundry collections for the poor; we do not hear of work among the poor, or of responsibility for the poor, for a hundred years and more after the Reformation.

I am not, happily, called upon in this place to attack, or to defend, the Dissolution. I have only to consider its effect upon London. And as regards the London Houses, I repeat, I can find no scandals. The judgment of the people, though that was not asked or regarded, seems to have arrived at a very clear understanding as to the actual spiritual value, apart from any pretension or profession, of the life of seclusion and celibacy. It was a very low estimate. On the other hand, the City does not seem to have been openly hostile to the Religious. They were an institution; these holy men were their own kin; the Monastic Houses were a part of the daily life.

There were violent things published against monks and friars at this time, but they were written by vehement partisans and were forced upon the people. For example, the work of Barnabe Googe with his *Popish Kingdom.* Had there been any active hatred against them it would have shown itself by the acts and deeds of the 'prentices, who always reflected, roughly but surely, the direction of the current of contemporary opinion. Such slight indications of feeling on the subject as are afforded by the literature in the next generation point to reverence as regards the nuns; while as regards monks and friars they are clean forgotten—a sure sign that they were not very actively hated. At the same time it does seem most remarkable that the treatment of the Carthusians, who must have been regarded as innocent victims and martyrs, unless they were represented as political traitors, should not have excited any popular indignation.

One can only suppose that the spectacle of a prisoner drawn on a hurdle, hanged, and quartered, was so familiar, that people hardly troubled to ask who the sufferer was, or for what crime he suffered.

Let us now pass on to speak of certain Martyrs and Confessors. It is by this time needless to point out that the constancy shown by a Ridley and a Latimer for the Protestant form of doctrine was fully equalled by that of those who passed through the way of fire for the ancient faith. There was, however, this difference, that the Catholic martyrs were monks, priests, and men of mark like Fisher and More, while the Protestants included a vast number of men and women from the lower ranks—from the uneducated, who yet dared to hold a

Twenty two PROTESTANTS taken into Custody on account of their Religion, and brought in one Band with Cords round their Arms, from Colchester to London, by order of Bloody Queen Mary.

belief of their own based, as they thought, on private judgment,—really on the training of the sermons that they had heard.

The case of Dr. Forest, Confessor to Queen Katherine, must not be forgotten when one speaks of the martyrs of this time. Forest, an old man, was committed to gaol, where he lay for two years among the common malefactors, because he refused to acknowledge the supremacy of the King. After two years of Newgate, two years in a close, stifling, and noisome prison, the venerable priest was informed that he was to be hanged over a fire and so slowly done to death. No more terrible form of death was known in England, where the horrors of the French and German capital punishments were never practised. It was the same punishment as had been meted out to Oldcastle, and it was inflicted on

Forest for the same reason: to show the hatred and abhorrence of the judges for the doctrines he taught. When the unfortunate Katherine heard of the sentence she wrote to him. The letter, too long for reproduction in these pages, together with Forest's reply, may be found in *The Antiquities of the English Franciscans*: they are probably genuine and are very pitiful. The Queen, however, was spared the misery of hearing of her Confessor's torturing death: he was respited and continued to lie in prison. Two years after the Queen's

HUGH LATIMER (1485 (?)-1555)
From the painting in the National Portrait Gallery, London.

death, and when he had been confined in Newgate for four years, Forest was brought out for execution.

On the 22nd of May 1518 they placed the old man on a sledge and dragged him from Newgate to Smithfield, where he was hung in chains from a gallows over a fire. This was the most terrible of all deaths. In ordinary cases, the sufferer, bound to a thick stake with iron chains, was enclosed up to the middle, and perhaps higher, with dry faggots: it would seem that the fierce flames enveloping the victim caused death by suffocation in a very few moments. Latimer, for instance, died in this manner almost immediately; if, however, the flames were blown away, the lower parts of the body might be slowly burned before death ensued: this was the case with Ridley. When, however, the sufferer was simply dangled over a fire, the flames blown this way and that, the agony might last for hours.

In the case of Forest, the bystanders took pity on the old man and threw the gallows into the fire, so that an end was soon made. "In what state," asked Latimer before the fire was lit, "will you die?" Whereupon the old man replied

BISHOP RIDLEY (1500(?)-1555)
From the painting in the National Portrait Gallery, London

in a loud voice: "If an angel should come down from heaven to teach men any other doctrine than what I have received and believed from my youth, I would not believe him; and if my body should be cut joint after joint, member after member, hanged, burned, or whatever pain might be done to me, yet would I never turn from my old profession." A brave old man!

After the Carthusians the principal sufferers seem to have been the Observant Friars, of whom a large number suffered for refusing to acknowledge the King's supremacy. We may read in the *Antiquities of the English Franciscans* a great many stories of these sufferings. One hopes that there is exaggeration.

For some, according to this book, were carried about the country in chains; some were racked and then strangled; some were starved to death; miracles attended the death of some: the whole prison, in one case, became filled with a heavenly and miraculous light; and an earthquake, in another case, testified to the Divine displeasure at another martyrdom.

On the 22nd day of June 1534, three days after the execution of the three Carthusians, Exmew, Middlemore, and Newdigate, was beheaded that illustrious Catholic martyr, John Fisher, Bishop of Rochester, for maintaining the Pope's supremacy; and a fortnight later, that still more illustrious martyr, Thomas More. The witty and pleasant manner of his conversation was kept up to the last. Grafton thus speaks of his last moments :—

"Besides his learning he had a great wit, and in talking verie pleasant and merie conceited, and that even to the last hower; insomuch that at hys comming to the Tower, one of the officers demanded his upper garment for his fee (meaning hys Gowne) and he aunswered, he should haue it, and toke him his cap, saying it was the uppermost garment that he had.   Likewise even going to his death at the Tower gate a pore woman called to him and besought him to declare that he had certayn evidence of hers in the time that he was in office (which after he was apprehended she could not come by) and that he would intreat she might have them agayne, or else she was undone.   He aunswered good woman have pacience a little while, for the King is so good unto me that even within this half houre he will discharge me of all businesses, and help thee himselfe.   Also when he went up the stayres on the Scaffolde, he desired one of the Shriefes officers to give him his hand to help him up, and sayde, when I come downe agayne, let me shift for myself as well as I can.   Also the hangman kneeled downe to him asking him forgivenesse of his death (as the manner is) to whome he sayde I forgive thee, but I promise thee that thou shalt never have honestie of the stryking of my head, my neck is so short.   Also even when he should lay downe his head on the block, he having a great gray beard, striked out his beard and sayde to the hangman, I pray you let me lay my beard over the block least ye should cut it." (*Chronicle of England*, Grafton, vol. ii. p. 454.)

The martyrdom of the Carthusians was the most significant, the most revengeful, the most audacious act of the new Head of the Church, the Act by which he defied, once for all, the whole power of the Pope, of Spain, and even of France.   The world trembled, people looked for some supernatural manifestation, some unmistakable sign of the Divine wrath: none came, and they understood that here was an act of open war, and that the Divine will as to the issue had not been pronounced.

Let us pass to the Marian Persecution.   I have called attention to the fact that the greater number of the martyrs belonged to the middle class and to the rank or status of craftsmen.   Thus, Christopher Wade was a linen weaver; Thomas Wats a linen draper; John Warren was an upholsterer; John Ardeley was a husbandman; Robert Bromley was a grocer; Thomas Ormond was a fuller; Williams a weaver; Margery Polley widow of a craftsman; Dirick Carver a brewer; John Laneden a rustic; John Tudson an artificer; Joan Warne a maid-servant. There were wives and widows among them, "simple women," artificers and 'prentices, maid-servants and girls.

It was the sight of their own people suffering a cruel death which made the name of Rome hateful and horrible for three hundred years and more. It was the sight of the constancy of the martyrs which laid the firm foundations of the Protestant Faith. For none of them flinched before the flames, none of them feared the pains which the Lord God in His mercy and wisdom had ordered

THOMAS CRANMER (1489-1556)
From the portrait in Jesus College, Cambridge. A. Rischgitz' Collection.

them to endure for the sake of the Cause. What was to be expected when a shoemaker such as John Noyes could die triumphant and rejoicing?

"On the next-day morning he was brought to the stake, where were ready against his coming the foresaid justice, master Thurston, one master Waller, then being under-sheriff, and master Thomas Lovel, being high-constable, as is before expressed; the which commanded men to make ready all things meet for that sinful purpose. Now the fire in most places of the street was put out, saving a smoke which was espied by the said Thomas Lovel proceeding from the top of a chimney, to which house the sheriff and Grannow his man went, and brake open the door, and thereby got fire, and brought the same to the place of execution. When John Noyes came to the place where he should be burnt, he kneeled down and said the 50th Psalm, with other prayers; and then they, making haste, bound him to the stake. And being bound, the said John Noyes said, 'Fear not them that can kill the body, but fear him that can kill both body and soul, and cast it into everlasting fire.'

When he saw his sister weeping, and making moan for him, he bade her that she should not weep for him, but weep for her sins.

Then one Nicholas Cadman, a valiant champion in the Pope's affairs, brought a faggot and set against him; and the said John Noyes took up the faggot and kissed it, and said, 'Blessed be the time that ever I was born to come to this.'

Then he delivered his Psalter to the under-sheriff, desiring him to be good to his wife and children, and to deliver to her that same book; and the sheriff promised him that he would, notwithstanding he never as yet performed his promise. Then the said John Noyes said to the people, 'They say, they can make God of a piece of bread; believe them not!'

Then said he, 'Good people, bear witness that I do believe to be saved by the merits and passion of Jesus Christ, and not by mine own deeds.' And so the fire was kindled, and burnt about him. Then he said, 'Lord have mercy upon me! Christ have mercy upon me! Son of David have mercy upon me!'

And so he yielded up his life. And when his body was burned, they made a pit to bury the coals and ashes, and amongst the same they found one of his feet that was unburnt, whole up to the ankle, with the hose on; and that they buried with the rest."

Or, to take the case of Cicely Ormes. She was a very simple woman, the wife of a worsted weaver who lived in Norwich. She was present at the martyrdom of Simon Miller and Elizabeth Cooper, and there, being affected with their constancy, she declared that she would pledge them with the same cup from which they drank :—

"She was burnt the 23d day of September, between seven and eight of the clock in the morning, the said two sheriffs being there, and of people to the number of two hundred. When she came to the stake, she kneeled down, and made her prayers to God; that being done, she rose up and said :—

'Good people! I believe in God the Father, God the Son, and God the Holy Ghost, three persons and one God. This do I not, nor will I recant; but I recant utterly from the bottom of my heart the doings of the Pope of Rome, and all his popish priests and shavelings. I utterly refuse and never will have to do with them again, by God's grace. And, good people! I would you should not report of me that I believe to be saved in that I offer myself here unto the death for the Lord's cause, but I believe to be saved by the death and passion of Christ; and this my death is and shall be a witness of my faith unto you all here present. Good people! as many of you as believe as I believe, pray for me.'

Then she came to the stake, and laid her hand on it, and said, 'Welcome the cross of Christ.' Which being done, she, looking on her hand, and seeing it blacked with the stake, wiped it upon her smock; for she was burnt at the same stake that Simon Miller and Elizabeth Cooper was burnt at. Then, after she had touched it with her hand, she came and kissed it, and said, 'Welcome the sweet cross of Christ'; and so gave herself to be bound thereto. After the tormentors had kindled the fire to her, she said, 'My soul doth magnify the Lord, and my spirit rejoiceth in God my Saviour.' And in so saying, she set her hands together right against her breast, casting her eyes and head upward; and so stood, heaving up her hands by little and little, till the very sinews of her arms did brast in sonder, and then they fell. But she yielded her life unto the Lord as quietly as if she had been in a slumber, or as one feeling no pain; so wonderfully did the Lord work with her : His name therefore be praised for evermore."

Remember that the example was not only an admonition to those who saw her death: it was related by the spectators; it was spread through the length and breadth of the land; it was written down by Foxe, in whose hands it certainly lost nothing of eloquence or of dramatic effect, and it has been read ever since by countless people. Not the martyrdom of Cranmer, Ridley, Latimer and the rest of the bishops, priests and scholars, so much as those of the "very simple" women, the plain craftsmen, built up the Protestant Faith, scattered the Spanish Fleets, and changed the Englishman of the sixteenth century, so that he of the seventeenth became possible.

The bare list of burnings in London alone, not nearly complete, as enumerated by Henry Machyn in his *Diary* (1550-1563), conveys a sense of the overwhelming horror which filled England during this reign, perhaps clearer than a laboured

The burning of M. Iohn Rogers, vicar of Saint Pulchers, and Reader of Paules in London.

treatise on the Lives and Deaths of the Martyrs. In reading the list we can see the crowds flocking to Smithfield : all their sympathies are with the sufferer ; they see him dragged on his hurdle, undressed to the shirt and tied to the stake ; they see that he flinches not nor offers to retract ; the faggots are piled about him, Heaven grant they be of dry wood ; from the flames and through the smoke they hear the voice of the martyr praising God and praying till the end comes, when his tongue swells up in his mouth and he can speak no more, or is suffocated with the smoke, or with the intensity of his agony his heart stops and merciful Death

seizes him.   Then the crowd go home again ; they dare not speak to each other ;
but they remember.

"1555.   The iiij day of Feybruary the bysshope of London went into Nugatt and odur docturs to
dysgratt (degrade) Hoper, and Rogers sumtyme vycker of sant Polkers.   The sam day was Rogers cared
be-twyn x and xj of the cloke into Smythfeld and bornyd, for aronyus opinions, with a grett compene
of the gard.

1555.   The xvj day of Marche was a veyver (weaver) bornyd in Smyth-feld dwellynge in Sordyche,
for herese, by viij of the cloke in the mornyng, ys nam was Tomkins.

1555.   The xiiij day of Aprell, the wyche was Ester day at sant Margatt parryche at Westmynster
after masse was done, one of the menysters, a prest of the abbay, dyd helpe hym that was the menyster to
the pepull who wher reseyvyng of the blessyd sacrement of the Lord Jhesus Cryst, ther cam in-to the
chyrche a man that was a monke of Elly, the wyche was marryed to a wyff : the sam day ther that sam
man saud to the menyster, What doyst thow gyff them ? and as sone as he had spokyn he druw his wod-
knyffe, and hyt the prest on the hed and struck hym on the hand, and cloyffe ys hand a grett way and after
on the harme a grett wond ; and ther was syche a cry and showtt as has not byne ; and after he was taken
and cared to presun, and after examyned wher-for he dyd ytt.   The xxiij day of Aprell was the sam man
cared to Westmynster that dyd hurt the prest, and had ys hand stryken of at the post, and after he was
bornyd aganst sant Margett chyrche with-owt the cherche-yerde.

1555.   The sam day of May was arraigned iiij men at Powlles a-for none and after-non, of Essex,
and thay wher cast for heresse and all iiij cast to be bornyd and so cared unto Nugat.

1555.   The xxv day of May were arraigned at St. Paul's for heresy, before the bishop, master
Cardmaker sometime vicar of St. Bride's in Fleet-street, and one John Warren a cloth-worker in Walbrook
and a-nodur of . . . and cast to be brent and carried back to Nugatt.

1555.   The xxx day of May was burnt in Smythfeld master Cardmaker sum-tyme veker of sant Bryd,
and master Varren clothworker, dwellyng aganst sant John in Walbroke, an hupholster, and ys wyff
behyng in [Newgate].

1555.   The x day of Juin was delevered owt of Nugatt vij men to be cared into Essex and
Suffoke to borne.

1555.   The furst day of July whent into Smythfield to borne master Bradford, a grett precher by
Kyng Edward's days, and a talow chandler's prentice dwellyng by Nugatt, by viij of the cloke in the
mornyng, with a grett compene of pepull.

1555.   The viij day of July were three more delivered out of Nugate and sent into the country
to be burned for heretics.

1555.   The xij day of July was bornyd y Canturbery iiij men for herese, ij prestes and ij laye men.

1555.   The ij day of August was a shumaker bornyd ay sant Edmundbere in Suffoke for herese.

1555.   The viij day of August, between iiij and v in the morning, was a presoner delevered into the
shreyff of Medyllsex to be cared unto Uxbryge to be bornyd ; yt was the markett day—owt of Nugatt
delevered.

1555.   The xxiij day of August was bornyd ay Stratford of bowe, in the conte of Mydyllsex, a woman,
wife of John Waren, clothworker, a huphulster over against sant Johns in Walbroke ; the whyche . . .
John her hosband was bornyd with on Cardmaker in Smythfield for herese boyth ; and the sam woman
had a sune taken at her bornyng and cared to Nugatt to his syster, for they will born boyth.

1555.   The xxxj day of August whent out of Nugatt a man of Essex unto Barnett for herese, by the
shreyff of Medyllsex, to borne ther.

1555.   The same day were burnt at Oxford for heresy doctor Latimer, late Bishop of Worcester,
and doctor Ridley, late bysshope of London ; they were some tyme grett prychers as ever was ; and at ther
bornyng dyd pryche doctur Smyth, sumtyme the master of Vetyngtun colege.

1555.   The xviij day of Dessember be-twyn 8 & 9 of the cloke in the mornyng was cared into
Smythfeld to be bornyd on master Philpot, archdeacon of Winchester, gentyllman, for herese.

The description of Doctour Cranmer, howe he was
plucked downe from the stage, by Friers and Papists,
for the true Confession of hys Faith.

Lord receaue my spirit.

Friar John.

The burning of the Archbishop of Canturbury, Doctor Thomas
Cranmer, in the Towne-ditch at Oxford, with his hand first thrust into the
fire, whetewith he subscribed before.

1556.   The xxij day of January whent into Smythfeld to berne betwyn vij and viij in the mornyng v men and ij women; on of the men was a gentyllman of the ender tempull, ys nam master Gren; and they wer all bornyd by ix at iij postes; and ther wher a commonment thrughe London over nyght that no yong folke shuld come ther, for ther the grettest number was as has byne sene at shyche a tyme.

1556.   The xxj day of Marche was bornyd at Oxford doctur Cranmer, late archebysshope of Canturbere.

1556.   The xv day of May was cared in a care from Nugatt thrug London unto Strettford-a-bow to borne ij men; the on blyne, the thodur lame; and ij tall men, the one was a penter, the thodur a cloth-worker; the penter ys nam was Huw Loveroke, dwellyng in Seythin lane; the blynd man dwellyng in sant Thomas apostylles.

1556.   The xxvij day of June rod from Nugatt unto Stretford-a-bowe in iiij cares xiij, xj men and ij women, and ther bornyd to iiij postes, and ther wher a xx M. pepull.

1557.   The iij day of April five persons out of Essex were condemned for herese, iij men and ij women (one woman with a staff in her hand), to be bornyd in Smythfeld.

1557.   The vj day of Aprell was bornyd in Smythfeld v, iij men and im women, for herese; on was a barber dwellyng in Lym-strett; and on woman was the wyff of the Crane at the Crussyd-frers be-syd the Towre-hylle, kepyng of a in ther.

1557.   The xiiij day of May was bornyd in Chepe-syd and odur places in London serten melle that was not sweet; and thay sayd that hey had putt in lyme and sand to deseyffe the pepull and he was had to the conter.

1557.   The sam mornyng was bornyd be-yond sant George's parryche iij men for heresee, a dyssyd Nuwhyngtun.

1557.   The xviij day of June was ij cared to be bornyd beyonde sant Gorgeus, almost at Nuwhyngtyn for herese and odur matters.

1557.   The xxij day of December were burned in Smyth-feld ij, one ser John Ruffe the frere and a Skott, and a woman for herese." *(Diary of Henry Machyn.)*

CHAPTER II

THE PROGRESS OF THE REFORMATION

THE question as to the proportion of Protestants to Catholics at the accession of Elizabeth, and at her death, has received various answers, depending upon the religion of the respondent. Lingard, the fairest of all the Catholic writers, estimates the number of Catholics at one-half the whole population. This was thirty years before Elizabeth's accession. Dr. Allen thought they were two-thirds (Strype, iii. 415). A great many of the better class were Catholics. Venner (1649) says that fifty years before, all physicians were Catholics. This may have been caused by study in Italian schools of medicine. A good many people in London attended mass at some Ambassador's chapel. The Spaniards when the Armada was projected relied upon the opinion that the half of England would join them. The North of England was filled with Catholics, yet they did not join the Rebellion of 1569. One-fourth of the population of Cheshire were Catholics; on the other hand, there is testimony to the effect that the number of Catholics had enormously decreased in the first thirty years of Elizabeth's reign. In 1569 there were in London twelve to fifteen places where mass was regularly said. In 1594 a Jesuit speaks of the "little sparkle of Catholic religion yet reserved amongst us" as soon to be extinguished. The common-sense view of the case seems to be this. The people of London who, as we have seen, were filled with Lollardry from the beginning of the fifteenth century; who welcomed the Dissolution of the Religious Houses; who rejoiced at such a shadow of free thought as Henry afforded them; who shuddered with horror at the flames of Smithfield;—were overjoyed at the return of the Protestant Faith. But it would be wrong to suppose that all the scholars, all who had lived among the better-class priests and friars, went over to the new Faith; they did not: a large number of gentlewomen remained steadfast; the Government showed its good sense by taking no notice, or as little as possible, of recusants. Burleigh advised against punishing these people by death; best not make martyrs; there was no true method of lessening their numbers "but by preaching and by education of the younger under good schoolmasters."

In a word, if it is intended to make any form of faith decay, there is no need of persecution : it has only to be surrounded by disabilities. If a Roman Catholic could hold no municipal office, and no State office, could not enter a grammar school or the university, could not take a degree, could not become a lawyer, could not sit in either House, could not serve in the army or the navy, then the Roman Catholic religion would fall rapidly into decay. This is exactly what happened; at the present moment, though all disabilities have been removed, the proportion of Catholics in England and Scotland is certainly not more than one in twenty. The "old" Catholics were those wealthy families which could continue in spite of all disabilities, a few noble houses and a few county people. Similar results attended the disabilities of the Nonconformists. Dissent survived its disabilities among people who cared nothing for office, people at the lower end of society, people for the most part of small trade. Among the better class, Dissent lost ground and mostly disappeared till the abolition of disabilities.

It is commonly believed that in the parish churches there was but one step from the mass to the Reformed service. This was not so (see an article by Mr. T. T. Micklethwaite on "Parish Churches in the year 1548," *Arch. Journ.* xxxv.). The Dissolution of the Religious Houses made at first very little difference in the churches. The guilds were suppressed, and therefore the lights which they kept up; the endowed lights were also suppressed; but people went on endowing new lights for the parish churches. In the year 1547 certain rules or injunctions were issued which commanded that all images which had been made the object of pilgrimage should be destroyed; that no lights should be set up before any picture except two wax tapers on the altar, and these because Christ is the Light of the World. Images which had not been abused were to remain "for remembrance only." The English Bible and the Paraphrases of Erasmus on the Gospel were to be set up in every church where the people could have access to them. Shrines, pictures of miracles, and glass depicting miracles, were to be destroyed; a pulpit was to be provided, and an alms chest to be placed by the altar.

As regards the services, changes were gradual. The High Mass continued, but the Gospel and Epistle were read in English, and a chapter from the New Testament was read after lessons at Matins and after Magnificat at Evensong. The English Litany was sung after High Mass. The Pater Noster, Creed, and Ten Commandments were sometimes publicly rehearsed in English, and Communion was refused to those who did not know them.

In the year 1548 the "Order of Communion" was put forth; in 1549 the Prayer Book appeared. Mr. Micklethwaite has drawn up an account of the parish church of 1548 before the Reformed Prayer Book, and with the alterations

made in the service up to that date.   The principal entrance was by the south
door; in the porch was a basin of holy water; the font stood sometimes in the
middle of the nave, sometimes against the west side of one of the pillars; it had
a cover which could be locked down.   Near it was a locker in which were kept
the oils, salt, etc., required for the old rite of baptism.

"At the beginning of the sixteenth century all but very poor parish churches seem to have been
furnished with pews, but the whole area was not filled with them, as at a later date.   Old pews west of the
doors are very rare, but they are found sometimes, as at Brington, Northants.   Generally all this space was
left clear, and there was a clear area of at least one bay, and often much more at the west end.   A church
with aisles had nearly always four blocks of pews, and the passages were broad alleys, that in the middle
being often more than a third of the width of the nave, and the side passages were not much less.   The
appropriation of special places to individuals seems to have been usual, and even that bugbear of modern
ecclesiastical reformers, the lock-up pew or closet, was not unknown.   These in parish churches were
generally chantry chapels, arranged for private services at their own altars and for use as pews during the
public services."

The pulpit had no fixed position: it was made movable; one of that period
still remains at Westminster.   It was ordered in 1547 that the priests and choir
should kneel in the midst of the church and sing or say the Litany; the Litany
desk came into use afterwards.   The confessional had been continued in certain
London churches: at St. Margaret Patens there was the "shrivyng pew"; at
St. Christopher le Stock the "Shriving House."   The usual custom was for the
penitent to kneel or stand before the priest, who sat in a chair.   The Bible and
the Paraphrases of Erasmus were chained to a desk somewhere in the nave.

The Rood screen, which was a music gallery, carried a loft and the organ
when there was one.   The loft contained desks for singers; it was also provided
with pricks for candles.   The great cross rose above the loft.   In the chancel
stood the high altar; when there were no aisles two smaller altars stood one on
either side.   Above the altar was a reredos of carved work; at the ends of
which hung curtains.   There was generally a super altar.   On the high altar
stood the cross, with figures, reliquaries, and images to adorn it.   Also they laid
on the altar the Textus or Book of the Gospels, with the paxbrede or tablet for
the kiss of peace.   There were generally two lights on the altar.

"It is convenient to mention here the other lights, which were kept in 1548, by the retention of the
ceremonies with which they were connected.   These were the two tapers carried by boys in processions at
High Mass, and at other services when solemnly performed; the herse light, used at Matins or Tenebres on
the last three days of Holy Week; the paschal candle, which stood in a tall candlestick, or hung in a
bason on the north side of the high altar, and was lighted with much ceremony on Easter Eve, and burned
at all the principal services throughout Paschal tide; the torches carried in the procession on Corpus
Christi Day; the lantern carried before the Sacrament when it was taken to the sick; the large standing
tapers which were placed round a corpse during the funeral service; and the candle used at baptism.
Most of the lights, which a little earlier had been common round tombs, were endowed, and as such had
been taken away, but the custom of survivors placing lights round the graves of their departed friends
would probably be continued still for a few years."

Chapels were the most usual places for tombs, but they are found in every part of the church.   The various forms of them are too familiar to require description, but the use of colour gave them much more decorative importance in an interior than they have now.   Many were painted, and others were covered with rich cloths.   Flat gravestones had often carpets laid over them, and raised tombs had palls of cloth of gold or other costly stuff.   The church of Dunstable still possesses such a pall : it is of crimson velvet, richly embroidered. Tapestries and cloths of various kinds were very much used, especially in chancels, as curtains and carpets, and as coverings for seats and desks and the like.   Every church also had special hangings for Lent, when images and pictures were covered up generally with white or blue cloths, marked with crosses and the emblems of the Passion.   The Lenten veil between the choir and the high altar seems also to have been retained in 1547, but in 1548 Cranmer and his party had partly succeeded in doing away with it.   All parts of the church were more or less adorned with imagery and pictures on walls, in windows, or on furniture.   None had been ordered to be taken away except such as had been superstitiously abused, or which were representations of "feigned miracles."

"When the priest took the Sacrament to the sick he was accompanied by clerks, who carried a cross, bell, and light.   The Sacrament itself was enclosed in a pyx, and with it was taken a cup in which the priest dipped his fingers after giving the communion.   The chrismatory was generally a little box of metal containing three little bottles for the three oils, which seem generally to have been kept together.   For use at funerals, every church had a cross, a bier, and a handbell, the last being a good-sized bell which was rung before the corpse as it was being carried to the church.   It was also used for 'crying' obits about the parish, and asking for prayers for the deceased.   Some churches had what was called the common coffin, which was used to carry bodies to the church, the most general custom being to bury without coffin.   And they had palls and torches for funerals, for the use of which a charge was made according to the quality of the pall and the 'waste' of the torches.   At weddings it was the custom to hold a large square cloth of silk or other material, called the care cloth, over the heads of the bride and bridegroom whilst they received the benediction, and it was kept for that use amongst the church goods. At St. Margaret's, Westminster, we find also a crown or circlet for brides, which appears to have been a thing of some value."

It will be seen from these quotations that the parish church contained in essentials the whole of the Catholic ritual except the parts which were ordered to be read in English.   At the same time by reading, by hearing sermons, by the newly awakened spirit of examination and discussion, the people were preparing for more drastic changes.   When they came there was no violent revolution, and though many remained faithful to the old creed, the bulk of the people in London were Protestant at heart.   The weak point of the Reformation was that as yet no one was sure that it was stable and assured.   Nor was there any such assurance till the defeat of the Spanish Armada and fifty years of the Maiden Queen had turned Protestantism into patriotism.

It is apparent (see *Archæologia*, vol. xlv.) that the ancient vestments were worn in some of the churches after the Reformation, until they fell to pieces. At the church of St. Christopher le Stock they were worn until the third year of Elizabeth, when being worn out, and no funds existing to replace them, the simple surplice was used. Twelve tables hung on the wall of the church : one containing the Ten Commandments ; eleven containing prayers to the saints. The Reformers, therefore, did not introduce a new thing when they hung up the Table of the Commandments.

It used to be a custom in many City churches to ring the bell at 5 A.M. ; not

S. B. Bolas & Co., London.

TOMB OF QUEEN ELIZABETH IN WESTMINSTER ABBEY

the "apprentice bell," but a continuation and a survival of the ancient practice to call the people to the early service. Thus, at St. Margaret's, Lothbury, in 1573, it was "resolved that after every workday we shall have morning prayer at five o'clock ; also to have a lecture every Wednesday and Friday, beginning at five o'clock and ending at six o'clock, the bell to toll half an hour after five every afternoon." The books show a good deal of whipping of men and women. They were chiefly wanderers, tramps, and their great offence was in carrying the plague about the country.

The services of the church could be made Lutheran in their character or Puritanic. The great difference was in the manner of singing. The Puritans sang in a plain tune all together; the Protestants "tossed" the Psalms from one side to the other with music of the organ. Congregational singing was one of the most important changes introduced by the Reformation. In September 1559 the new morning prayer "after Geneva fashion" was introduced at St. Antholin's, the bell ringing at 5 A.M.

There were still some processions kept up. On St. Andrew's Day a procession was conducted at St. Paul's with one priest out of every parish in the City, and on the 25th of September the boys of St. Anthony's school marched together from Mile End down Cornhill with streamers and flags, whifflers and drums.

In the church of St. Christopher le Stock we find that certain old customs were preserved: the church was decorated at Christmas with holly and ivy; at Easter with "rosemary, bay, and strawings."

The parish system seems to have been well worked; the streets were kept clean; evildoers were not allowed to harbour within the limits; taxes were collected; the sick were watched and tended.

The efforts of the more sober leaders were directed to change, it is true, but to gradual not revolutionary change. The restraint of the zealous, however, was in some churches very difficult; certain quarters of the City were far more Protestant than others: Blackfriars, for instance, became an early centre of Puritanism; at St. Martin's-in-the-Fields, on the other hand, we find the church-wardens quietly obeying every new ordinance, but keeping the old things in boxes ready for a possible return to the old order. The Dissolution of the Houses brought with it certain unexpected accompaniments. The servants of the Commissioners took away the sacred vestments and used them either for their own common wear or for saddlecloths, thus inflicting wanton insults on the faithful and bringing into contempt, with the desecration of the vestments, the very doctrines of which they were symbolical. Again, there were the relics and the images which the people had so long adored; it is true that the Church would not acknowledge the adoration of an image, but that was the practice of the common people, as it is at this day in every Roman Catholic Church. Thus sacred objects came to be treated with the utmost scorn: reliquaries were emptied and the relics thrown away; images of the Virgin were deprived of their lovely vestments, and sent about the country, shapeless lumps of wood, or brought to London to be publicly burned. In some cases an ancient and venerable fraud was discovered and pitilessly exposed. Who could resist contempt for the priests and monks who had for many generations of simple believers made the head on the Holy Rood of Boxley incline benignantly and roll its eyes upon the kneeling

POPISH PLOTS
AND
TREASONS

From the beginning of the Reign of Queen Elizabeth
Illustrated with Emblems and explain'd in Verse.

*First are describ'd the Cursed plots they
laid.
And on the side their wretched ends display'd.*

Figure 1.

THe *Pope* aloft on Armed Shoulders Rides,
And in vain Hopes the English spoils divides;
His *Leaden Bull* 'gainst good *Eliza.* roares,
And scatters dire Rebellion round our Shoars.
The Priest *Blesses* the Villians, Chears them on,
And promises Heav'ns Crown, when her Crown won.
But God doth blast their Troops, their Counsels mock
And brings bold Traitors to'th'deserved *Block.*

Figure 3.

Spains *King*, and *Romes* Triple-Crown'd Pelate Joyn,
And with them both bold *Stukely* does Combine
Ireland to conquer, And the Pope has sent,
For that Blest work , an *Holy Regiment;*
But in their way at *Barbary* they call,
Where at one Blow the *Moors* destroy them All.
See here, what such Ambitious Traitors Gain,
The shame of Christians is by *Pagans* Slain,

Figure 5.

What trusty Janizaries are Monks to *Rome,*
From their dark Cells the blackest Treasons come.
By the Popes License horrid Crimes they Act,
And Guild with piety each Treacherous Fact.
A seminary Priest, like Comets Blaze,
Doth always Blood-shed and Rebellion Raise;
But still the fatal Gibbet's ready fixt
For such, where Treason's with Religion mixt.

Figure 7.

Whilst *Spains* Embassador here Leiger lies,
Designs are laid the English to surprize;
Two Catalogues his Secretary had Got
The better two effect the Hellish Plot.
One all our Havens Names, where Foes might Land,
To'ther what Papists were to lend a hand.
For this base Trick he's forc'd to pack to *Spain*
Whilst *Tyburn* greets confederates that remain.

Figure 2.

Don John, who under Spain did with proud Hand
The then unsever'd *Neitherlands* Command,
Contrives for Englands Conquest, and does Hope
To Gain it by Donation from the Pope.
Yet to Amuse our Queen does still pretend
Perpetual peace, and needs will seem a friend;
But Heav'n looks through those Juggles and in's prime,
Grief Cuts off Him and's Hopes All at a time.

Figure 4.

The Priests, with *Crosses* Ensigne-like displaid,
Prompt bloody *Desmond* to those spoiles he made
On Irish Protestants, and from afar
Blow Triumphs to Rebellions Holy War;
But against Providence all Arts are vain,
The Crafty, in their Craft are over-tane;
Behold where *kill'd* the Stubborn *Traitor* lies,
Whilst to the *Woods* his *Ghostly Father* flies;

Figure 6.

Mad *Sommervil,* by Cruel Priests inspir'd
To do whatever mischiefe they requir'd,
Swears that he instantly will be the death
Of good and Gracious Queen *Elizabeth.*
Assaults her Guards, but Heav'ns protecting pow'r
Defeats his rage makes him a Prisoner:
Where to avoid a just, though shameful Death,
Self-strangling hands do Stop his loathsome breath.

Figure 8.

View here a Miracle—— A Priest Conveys,
In Spanish Bottom o're the path-less Seas,
Close treacherous Notes, whilst a Dutch Ship comes by
And streight Engag'd her well-known Enemy:
The Conscious Priest his Guilty Papers tears,
And over-board the scatter'd fragments bears;
But the just winds do force them back o'th' Decks,
And peice-meal all the lurking plot detects.

FOR CONTINUATION SEE BACK OF THE OTHER HALF OF THE ILLUSTRATION.

"POPISH PLOTS AND TREASONS."

For descriptions in rhyme see back.

*W. A. Mansell & Co.

Figure 9.

The Jesuites vile Doctrines do Convince
Parry, 'Tis Merit for to kill his Prince,
The fatal Dagger he prepares with Art,
And means to sheath it in her Royal Heart,
Oft he Attempts, and is as oft put by,
By the Majestick Terrors of her Eye ;
At last his Cursed Intentions he Confest
And So his welcom'd a fit Tyburn Guest ;

Figure 10.

Here *Babington* and all his desperate Band,
Ready prepar'd for Royal Murder stand,
His Motto seems to glory in the Deed,
These my Companions are whom dangers lead,
Cowardly Traitors, so many Combine
To Cut off one poor Ladies vital Twine ;
In vain,—Heaven's her Guard, and as for you ;
Behold the Hangman gives you all your due.

Figure 11.

Nor was 't with *Spain* alone, Great *Betty*'s Strife ;
Now *France* attempts upon her pretious Life ;
The Guises cause th' Ambassador to Bribe
Moody, and others of the Roman Tribe,
To Cut her off. To which they soon Consent
But watchful Heav'n does that Guilt prevent.
Stafford doth to the Councel All disclose,
And Home with shame perfidious *Mounsieur* goes.

Figure 12.

Spain's proud *Armado*, whom the Pope did Bless,
Attacques our Isle, Confident of success.
But Heav'ns just Blast doth Scatter all their force,
They fly and quite round *Scotland* take their Course ;
So many taken, burnt, and Sunk i'th' Main,
Scarce one in Ten did e're get home Again ;
Thus *England* like *Noahs* Ark, amidst the Waves
Indulgent providence from Danger saves.

Figure 13.

But now a private horrid Treason veiw
Hatcht by the Pope, the Devil, and a Jew
Lopez a Doctor must by Poison do
What all their Plots have fail'd in hitherto
What will you give me then ; the *Judas* Cries
Full *fifty thousand Crowns*, t' other replies,
Tis done — but hold, the wretch shall miss his hope,
The Treasons known, and his Reward's the Rope ;

Figure 14.

The Great *Tyrone* that did so oft embrew
Ireland with Blood, and Popish Plots Renew.
Here vanquisht Swears upon his bended Knee
To the Queens Deputy fidelity
Yet breaks that vow, and loaded with the Guilt
Of perjuries and Blood which he had spilt.
Being forc'd at last to fly his Native Land,
Carries in's Breast a sting, a Scourge in's *hand*

Figure 15.

No Sooner *James* had blest the English Throne,
But Traiterous Priests Conspire to pull him down.
Watson the poisonous Maximes does Instill,
And draws some Nobles to Join in the Ill ;
But Princes then appear the most divine,
When they with unexpected Mercy Shine.
Just as the Fatal Ax attempts the Stroke,
Pardon steps in and does the Blow Revoke

Figure 16.

In this Curs'd Powder-plot we plainly see
The Quintessence of Romish Cruelty
King Lords and Commons at one Hellish Blast
Had been destroy'd, and half our Land laid wast,
See *Faux* with his dark Lanthorn ready stands
To Light the fatal Train with desperate hands,
But Heavens All-seeing eye defeats their desire,
And saves us as a Brand snatcht from the fire ;

And now let us, with chearful Hymns of praise,
And Hearts inflam'd with love *an Altar* raise
Of Gratitude to God, who doth advance
His out-streatcht Arm in our Deliverance,
Tis only He, that doth protect his Sheep,
Tis he alone doth this poor Island keep
From Romish *Wolves*, which would us soon devour,
If not Defended by his mighty power
Tis he that doth our *Church* with freedome Crown,
And beats the Popish *Superstitions* down
Under her *feet*, and may they never rise,
Nor in vile *Darkness* Reinvolve our Eyes ;
Since Heaven whose mercies ever are most tender
Hath both restor'd our *Faith* and Faiths *Defender*

Let us to both a strict Adherence pay,
And for their *preservation* ever pray.
Since thus *Truths* happy *Bark* hath reach'd our shore
O may it *never, never* Leaves us more.

multitude? With all these aids to disbelief who can wonder if the wave of Protestant indignation mounted steadily higher; if the fiery spirit of Reform seized upon town and country, upon the sober merchant and the hot-headed 'prentice? We hear of the young men reading the Bible aloud in the churches, shouting the words they read; of girls who carried the English Primer with them to church and studied it during the singing of Matins; of men who insulted the Consecration of the Host; who attacked the priest who carried it through the streets. It is certain that London itself, almost from the beginning, was for the Reformation. (*See* Appendix V.)

A pressing difficulty, in the opening years of Elizabeth, was the illiterate and immoral condition of the clergy. So many refused the oath of supremacy that it

KNIGHT SEIZING AN ARCHBISHOP
From an illuminated MS. in British Museum.

became necessary to create lay readers. Indeed, the condition of England, including London, was calculated to fill the minds of the most ardent Protestants with dismay. During the first fifteen years of the reign, the House of Commons complained to the Queen that men were ordained who were infamous in their lives and conversation; the Bishop of London complained that even the Bishops were "sunk and lamentably disvalued by the meanest of the peoples"; the County of Essex represented that the new clergy were ignorant, riotous and drunkards; the Lords in Council represented to the Archbishop of Canterbury the evil lives of the clergy. Out of all the clergy in the City of London there were but nineteen preachers. Yet in 1559 Elizabeth ordered that there should be a sermon once a month on doctrine. And in 1586 the Bishop of London ordered the clergy to write one sermon every week. It is said that the clergy fell so low in esteem as to be treated like outcasts, incurably drunken, ignorant, and licentious.

With the general charges against the Elizabethan Clergy it appears unnecessary to bring forward specific acts which may very well be taken to be isolated cases, in no way proving general corruption. There are, however, a few which seem to show the general condition of things.

In 1562, a priest was carted through the City for saying mass.

In 1554 priests, who would not leave their wives, did penance in St. Paul's, and were beaten over the head with rods.

In 1561 the Queen, who never approved the marriage of priests, ordered those who were married not to bring their wives into Colleges.

In the same year there were found to be many conjurors in Westminster including priests, one of whom was put in pillory.

In 1557 the priest of St. Ethelburga was pilloried for sedition, and had his ears nailed to the pillory.

In 1559 there was a great burning of copes, censers, crosses, altar cloths, rood cloths, books, banners, etc.

In 1560 a priest was hanged for cutting a purse; it was his second offence.

The priest who sold his wife to a butcher, and was carried through the streets for an open shame, must hardly, one hopes, be quoted as an example. We picture him as a drunken and dissolute hog, lost to all sense of decency. The other priest who for an act of immorality was also carried about the streets may have been more common. When all the clergy married as a matter of course such scandals ceased.

As I have reproduced certain charges against the clergy and Religious of the old Faith, it is but fair to give an example of the bad character of one, at least, belonging to the clergy of the Reformation. The following letter is addressed to the Lady Bowes :—

" Right Worshipfull,

I understand that one Raphe Cleaton ys curate of the chappell at Buxton; his wages are, out of his neighbour's benevolence, about V^{li} yearely; Sir Charles Cavendishe had the tythes there this last years, ether of his owne right or my Lord's, as th' inhabitants saye. The minister aforenamed differeth little from those of the worste sorte, and hath dipt his finger both in manslaughter and p'jurie, etc. The placings or displacing of the curate there resteth in Mr. Salker, commissarie of Bakewell, of which churche Buxton is a chappell of ease.

I humbly thanke your Worship for your letter to the justices at the cessions; for Sir Peter Fretchvell, togither with Mr. Bainbrigg, were verie earnest against the badd vicar of Hope; and lykewyse Sir Jermane Poole, and all the benche, savinge Justice Bentley, who used some vaine (talk) on his behalfe, and affirmed that my Lady Bowes had been disprooved before Mr. Lord of Shrowesburie in reports touching the vicar of Hope; but such answere was made therto as his mouthe was stopped; yet the latter daie, when all the justic's but himselffe and one other were rysen, he wold have had the said vicar lycensed to sell ale in his vicaredge, althoe the whole benche had comanded the contrarye; whereof Sir Jermane Poole being adv'tised, retyrned to the benchs (contradicting his speeche) whoe, with Mr. Bainbrigge, made their warrant to bringe before them, him, or anie other person that shall, for him, or in his vicaridge, brue, or sell ale, etc. He ys not to bee punished by the Justices for the multytude of his women, untyll the basterds whereof he is the reputed father bee brought in. I am the more boulde to wryte so longe of this sorrie matter, in respect you maye take so much better knowledge of Sir Jo. Bentley, and his p'tialytie in so vile a cause; and esteeme and judge of him according to that wisdome and good discretion. Thus, humbly cravinge p'don, I comitt your good Wors. to the everlasting Lorde, who ever keepe you." This is quoted by N. Drake in *Shakespeare and his Times*, vol. i. p. 92.

And here is Ben Jonson's portrait of the City Parson—none too flattering :—

> " He is the prelate of the parish here
> And governs all the dames, appoints the cheer,
> Writes down the bills of fare, pricks all the guests,
> Makes all the matches and the marriage feasts
> Within the Ward ; draws all the parish wills,
> Designs the legacies, and strokes the gills
> Of the chief mourners ; and, whoever lacks,
> Of all the kindred, he hath first his blacks.
> Thus holds he weddings up and burials,
> As his main tithing ; with the gossips' stalls,
> Their pews ; he's top still at the public mess ;
> Comforts the widow and the fatherless,
> In funeral sack ; sits 'bove the alderman ;
> For of the wardmote quest, he better can
> The mystery than the Levitic law ;
> That piece of clerkship doth his vestry awe.
> He is as he conceives himself, a fine,
> Well furnished, and apparelled divine."

Harrison, however, speaks up for the credit of the Reformed Clergy.

The observance of Lent was maintained by law, but with difficulty, and the law was continually broken. It was a distinguishing mark of the Puritan to eat flesh on the forbidden days. Queen Elizabeth ordered that no flesh should be eaten on "fish days," namely, the forty days of Lent, Ember Days, Rogation Days, and Fridays. Licenses, however, were granted for those who either on account of bodily infirmity, or any other cause, were forbidden to fast. The license cost, for a nobleman or his wife, 26s. 8d. per annum; for a knight or his wife, 13s. 4d. per annum ; and for those of lower degree, 6s. 8d. per annum.

Thus began the evasion of the law. Butchers were licensed to kill for those privileged to eat flesh. In 1581 the House of Lords call upon the Mayor to explain why forty butchers are allowed to kill during Lent, and how it is that the eating of flesh at that season is common in the City. The Mayor replies that the facts are otherwise, and that the number of licensed butchers is only five, viz. two for either Shambles and one for Southwark.

In 1552 only three butchers are licensed. Evidently the Mayor tries strong measures. But there are more complaints from the Lords.

In 1586 the House of Lords again send representations to the Mayor.

In 1587 the Mayor, evidently wishing to shift responsibility, says that it is difficult to restrain butchers. Perhaps the House of Lords will undertake the duty of licensing. The House of Lords declines to undertake the work of the Mayor.

In 1590 the Mayor complains of butchers being licensed in privileged places. What does this mean?

In 1591 he gives licenses to six butchers. He then finds out what we have been suspecting all along, that cattle and sheep were killed outside his jurisdiction, and that flesh was brought into the City by the gates. He also proves that within the City itself a great deal more meat is killed than was wanted for Shrovetide. Here we have a proof of the Puritanic spirit. The unlicensed butchers, on the eve of Lent, kill a great deal more than is wanted for Shrovetide; the licensed butchers go on killing. Do they sell to none but persons who have paid for the privilege? And every day carcases are brought in at the gates wrapped up in some kind of cloth for disguise.

In 1615 the Mayor gives up the attempt. He says that all butchers kill and sell meat in Lent, on Fridays, and that the people buy it freely on Fridays and on the other forbidden days.

Still there is maintained the pretence of an enforced fast during Lent until the Civil War, after which there are no more attempts to make the people fast, while many of the better class, clergy and others, continue to abstain from meat on the forbidden days.

There are grave complaints, both before and after the Reformation, about the behaviour of the people in church. The complaints point to two widely different causes. The first cause, that which operated before the Reformation, was undoubtedly the formalism into which religion had fallen. To be present at Mass, merely to be present, to kneel at the right time, was the whole of religion. Sir Thomas More, a most devout Catholic, complains bitterly of the irreverence of people at church service. Outward behaviour, he says, "is a plain express mirror or image of the mind, inasmuch as by the eyes, by the cheeks, by the eyelids, by the brows, by the hands, by the feet, and finally by the gesture of the whole body, right well appeareth how madly and fondly the mind is set and disposed." He applies this observation to himself and the congregation. Sometimes "we solemnly get to and fro, and other whiles fairly and softly set us down again." "When we have to kneel we do it upon one knee, or we have one cushion to kneel upon and another to support the elbows. We never pretend to listen: we pare our nails ; we claw our head."

The second cause was the rise of the new Religion. It was inevitable that with the destruction of the old forms a period of irreverence should set in. The churches quickly began to show signs of neglect. The windows were broken, the doors were unhinged, the walls fell into decay, the very roofs were in some

A ROYAL PICNIC
From Turberville's *Book of Hunting*, 1575.

places stripped of their lead. "The Book of God," says Stubbes, "was rent ragged, and all be-torn." Some of the churches were used for stabling horses. Armed men met in the churchyard, and wrangled, or shot pigeons with hand-guns over the graves. Pedlars sold their wares in the church porches during service. Morrice-dancers excited inattention and wantonness by their presence in costume, so as to be ready for the frolics which generally followed prayers. "Many there are," said Sandys, preaching before Elizabeth even after her reforms, "that hear not a sermon in seven years, I might say in seventeen." The friends of the new doctrine expected that all the evils of the time would be instantly remedied. But the work of reform was extremely gradual.

A third reason is offered for the irreverence of the people during service, this time during the Anglican service. Many people walked about, talked and laughed. This, however, was to show their contempt for the new order; they were secretly attached to the ancient Faith; they betrayed their sympathies, not only by this intolerance, but also by crossing themselves and telling their beads in secret.

Many of the ancient customs remained. It was long before the people, in London, could be persuaded to give up their old customs. Sunday remained the weekly holiday: the people held on Sundays their wakes, ales, rush-bearings, May games, bear-baitings, dancing, piping, picnics, and gaming; they continued so to "break the Sabbath"—which was first made part of the Christian week by the Puritans—until well into the seventeenth century. After the Commonwealth I think that there were very few traces of old customs lingering in the country, and only those, such as the hanging of garlands in the chancel when a maiden died, which carried with them no doctrinal significance and could prove no occasion for drunkenness and debauchery.

Before the coming of the Puritans the funerals continued with much of the old ritual. The body was laid out in such state as the family circumstances allowed: tapers were burned round it by night and by day; the church bells still rang for the prayers of the people, though they were taught that to pray for the dead was a vain thing; the priests who visited the house of the dead repeated the Lord's Prayer; if on the way to the churchyard the procession passed a cross, they stopped and knelt, and made prayers; the body was laid in the grave wrapped in a shroud, without a coffin; it was covered by a pall, which was decorated with crosses. Those of the ancient Faith would persuade the clergymen, if they could, to omit the service; if he persisted, they left the grave and walked away. Nothing was a stronger tie to the old Religion than its burial service, and its assurance that the dead who died in the Church were assured of Heaven after due purgatory, and that the prayers of the living were of avail to shorten the pains of prison.

Machyn, the City Chronicler of this period, thus describes the simplicity of a Protestant funeral :—

"The iij day of Aprell was browth unto saint Thomas of Acurs in Chepe from lytyll sant Barthellmuw in Lothberes masteres . . . and ther was a gret compene of pepull, ij and ij together, and nodur prest nor clarke, the nuw prychers in ther gowne lyke leymen, nodur syngyng nor sayhyng tyll they came to the grave, and a-for she was pute into the grayff a collect in Englys, and then put into the grayff, and after took some heythe, and caste yt on the corse and red a thynge . . . for the sam, and contenent cast the heth into the grave, and contenent red the pystyll of sant Poll to the Stesselonyans the chapter, and after thay song pater noster in Englys, boyth prychers and odur and women of a nuw fassyon, and after on of them whent into the pulpytt and made a sermon."

The following note by Machyn presents one of the last appearances of the old Sanctuary customs :—

"The vi day of December the abbot of Westminster went a procession with his convent ; before him went all the sanctuary men with crosse keys upon their garments, and after whent iij for murder : one was the Lord Dacre's sone of the Northe was wypyd with a shett abowt him for Kyllyng of on master West, sqwyre, dwellyng besyd . . . ; and anodur theyff that dyd long to one of master comtroller . . . dyd kylle Recherd Eggyllston the comtroller's tayller, and killed him in the Lord Acurs, the bak-syd Charyng-crosse ; and a boy that kyld a byge boye that sold papers and pryntyd bokes, with horlyng of a stone and yt hym under the ere in Westmynster Hall ; the boy was one of the chylderyn that was at the sckoll ther in the abbey ; the boy was a hossear [hosier] sune a-boyff London-stone." (*Diary of Henry Machyn*, p. 121.)

The good old institution of Sanctuary died hard. Even after it was supposed to have been finished and put away it continued to linger. Abbot Feckenham made a vigorous appeal for its preservation. "All princes," he said, "and all Lawmakers, Solon in Athens, Lycurgus in Lacedemon, all have had *loca refugii*, places of succour and safe-guard for such as have transgressed laws and deserved corporal pains. Since, therefore, ye mean not to destroy all sanctuaries, and if your purpose be to maintain any, or if any be worthy to be continued, Westminster, of all others, is most worthy, and that for four causes : the first is, the antiquity and continuance of sanctuary there ; the second, the dignity of the person by whom it was ordained ; the third, the worthiness of the place itself ; the fourth, the profit and commodity that you have received thereby."

It is a common charge against the Dissolution of the Religious Houses that the old custom of open tables for all comers fell into disuse. The disuse is not without exceptions. The Houses being suppressed, of course the hospitality disappeared ; but the practice was still kept up by some of the Bishops : Archbishop Parker, for instance, fed every day a number of poor people who waited outside the gates of Lambeth for the broken meats ; while any one who chose to come in, whether at dinner or at supper, was received and entertained either at the Steward's or the Almoner's table. Order was observed ; no loud talking was permitted ; and the discourse was directed towards framing men's manners to Religion. Whether the practice of indiscriminate doles should have been kept up is another question, and one that cannot be asked of the sixteenth century. The state and dignity maintained by this Archbishop were almost worthy of Cardinal Wolsey : the Queen gave him a patent for forty retainers, but his household consisted of five times that number, all living with him and dining at his table in Lambeth Palace.

The Church House was an ecclesiastical edifice which has now entirely passed away. I know nothing about the Church House except what is found in the *Archæological Journal*, vol. xl. p. 8.

"Not a single undoubted specimen has been spared to us, though it is not improbable that the half-timbered building attached to the west end of the church at Langdon, in Essex, and now called the Priest House, is really one of these.

We have evidence from all parts of the country that they were once very common. There is, indeed, hardly an old churchwarden's account-book which goes back beyond the changes of the sixteenth century that does not contain some reference to a building of this kind. They continued in being and to be used for church purposes long after the Reformation. The example at All Saints, Derby, stood in the churchyard and was in existence in 1747." . . . "We must picture to ourselves then a long, low room with an ample fireplace, or rather a big open chimney occupying one end with a cast hearth. Here the cooking was done, and here the water boiled for brewing the church ale. There was a large oak table in the middle with benches around, and a lean-to building on one side to act as a cellar. This, I think, is not an inaccurate sketch of a building which played no unimportant part in our rural economy and rural pleasures. All the details are wanting, and we can only fill them in by drawing on the imagination. We know that almost all our churches were made beautiful by religious painting on the walls. I should not be surprised if we some day discovered that the church-house came in for its share of art, and that pictures, not religious in the narrow sense, but grotesque and humorous, sometimes covered the walls. It was in the church-house that the ales were held. They were provided for in various ways, but usually by the farmers, each of whom was wont to give his quota of malt. There was no malt tax in those days, and as a consequence there was a malt-kiln in almost every village. These ales were held at various times. There was almost always one on the Feast of the Dedication of the Church. Whitsuntide was also a very favourite time; but they seem to have been held at any convenient time when money was wanted for the church. . . . Philip Stubbes, the author of the *Anatomie of Abuses*, only knew the Church Ales in their decline. He was, Anthony Wood informs us, a most rigid Calvinist, a bitter enemy to Popery, so that his picture must be received with allowances for exaggeration. His account of them is certainly not a flattering one. He tells us that 'The Churche Wardens . . . of every parishe, with the consent of the whole parishe, provide halfe a score or twentie quarters of mault, wherof some they buye of the churche stocke, and some is given them of the parishioners themselves, everyone conferryng some-what, accordyng to his abilitie; which mault beeyng made into very strong ale or beere is sette to sale, either in the churche or some other place assigned to that purpose. Then, when this . . . is sette abroche, well is he that can gette soonest to it and spend the most at it; for he that sitteth the closest to it and spendes the moste at it, he is counted the godliest man of all the rest, and moste in God's favour, because it is spent uppon His church forsoth. But who, either for want can not, or otherwise for feare of God's wrath will not sticke to it, he is counted none destitute both of vertue and godlines. . . . In this kind of practise they continue six weekes, a quarter of a

yere, yea helfe a yeare together, swillyng and gullyng, night and daie, till they
be as dronke as rattes, and as blockishe as beastes. . . . That money . . . if all
be true which they saie . . . they repair their churches and chappels with it, they
buie bookes for service, cuppes for the celebration of the sacrements, surplesses
for Sir John, and such other necessaries.' "

The burning of St. Paul's steeple created a great sensation, and was by some
regarded as an act of God's wrath for the recent changes. Maitland[1] quotes an
original letter describing the disaster :—

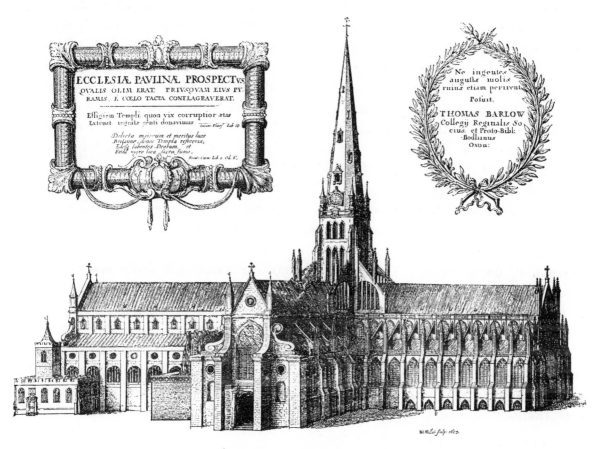

OLD ST. PAUL'S BEFORE THE DESTRUCTION OF THE STEEPLE

"A.D. 1561, on Wednesday the 4th of June, as appears by a Letter before
me from Mr. Richard Jones to Sir Nicholas Throckmorton, Ambassador from
Queen Elizabeth to the Court of France, communicated by the honourable Mr.
Yorke, it rained all the Day, and, towards Four of the Clock in the Afternoon, it
began to thunder terribly : 'When suddenly a Thunder-bolt, with a great Thunder
following, hit within a Yard of the very top of the Steeple, which forthwith
shewed his Effect, and appeared a little Fire, like unto the Light of a Torch, which,

[1] *History of London*, Book I. p. 255.

increasing towards the Weather-cock, caused the same within a quarter of an hour to fall down; whereby the Wind, which was great, and the more vehement by reason of the opening of the Steeple and Height thereof, caused the Flame so to augment, and burn the Steeple, which no Man could succour, as within an Hour the high Steeple of Paul's, which was so long in building, and so renowned, was utterly consumed to the very Battlements; which being of some Breadth and Strength, as was needful to uphold such a weight, received most part of the Timber which fell from the Spire, and began to burn with such Vehemence, as all the Timber was burnt, the Iron and Bells melted and fallen down upon the stairs within a short space. This was judged to be the end of the effect of the lightning; when forthwith the East and West roofs of the Church, partly kindled with the timber which fell from the Battlements, and with the heating of the Fire whiles it remained within the Stone Steeple, were on Fire, and ceased not to burn so extremely, as could not be provided for by no means, till that not only those ends, but the north and south ails, before one of the Clock after Midnight, were consumed, and not a piece of Timber left, nor Lead unmolten, upon any of the higher and cross Roofs and Battlements. The side Ails, tho' they were a little touched, by reason of their Crowns, remained safe, Thanks be to God. And this is all that is happened by this Misfortune, and the Church within is untouched. Your Lordship may guess what Stir and Removing there was in St. Paul's Church-yard, especially towards the North door, where divers Houses were pulled down, and much lamentation on all sides. On the East End a Pinnacle fell down and ruined a House, wherein there were seven Persons not hurt, but the good man of the House a little. Many other turmoils there were, as in like Cases it happens; which, as it grieves me to hear, so I am loth to write the same. The French here are not sorry for the Matter. All good and honest Men are sorry for it, and impute it to a terrible remembrance of God's Anger towards us for our Offences. This is enough and too much of so grievous a matter; and yet I thought I should perhaps satisfy your Lordship in writing thereof thus largely.   R. JONES.'

"LONDON, *June 5th*, 1561."

As might have been expected of a time when all the world was thinking and talking about religious doctrine, the unlearned as well as the learned, but with much more confidence and presumption, arguing entirely on the meaning of texts, passages, and detached clauses, there were fanatics in plenty. I have made a selection from the cases before me.

"William Hacket gave out that he was Jesus Christ, come to judge the World; which was soon proclaimed throughout the City of London by Edmond Coppinger and Henry Arthington, two of his Disciples; who, going from Hacket's Lodgings, at Broken-Wharf, thro' Watling-Street and the Old-Change, amidst an excessive

Multitude, to Cheapside, they mounted an empty cart near the end of Gutter Lane, and proclaimed Mercy from Heaven to all such as should repent and believe that Christ (William Hacket) was come with his Fan in his hand to judge the Earth, and to establish the Gospel in Europe, and that he was then to be seen, with his glorious Body, at one Walker's, at Broken-Wharf; and that they were Prophets, the one of Mercy, and the other of Judgment, sent by God Himself as Witnesses, and to assist in the present great Work. The first of whom incessantly proclaimed Mercy and Joys inexpressible to all such as should receive this acceptable Message; and the last denounced terrible Judgments against the Obdurate, which should not only immediately fall upon the Incredulous in this City, but that likewise all such were condemned to eternal Punishments; and, in a particular and very treasonable Manner, thundered out bitter invectives against the Queen and her Ministry; wherefore they were all apprehended, and Hacket, the pretended Messiah, soon after tried and convicted at the Old-Baily of Treason; whence he was carried to the Place of Execution in Cheapside, where, instead of shewing the least Sorrow for his Crimes, he committed the most horrid and execrable Blasphemies against God, and detestable imprecations against the Queen and her Ministers; and his associate, Coppinger, refusing all Manner of sustenance, died the next Day in Bridewell, as did Arthington, his Companion, some Time after in Wood Street Compter." Evidently three enthusiasts all equally mad and equally obstinate.

Later on, also, was the case of Anne Burnell (Sharpe, i. 552):—

"The strain which the continuation of the war and the threatened renewal of a Spanish invasion imposed upon the inhabitants of London at large was a great one, and appears to have affected the mind of a weak and hysterical woman, Anne Burnell. She gave out that she was a daughter of the King of Spain, and that the arms of England and Spain were to be seen, like stigmata, upon her back, as was vouched for by her servant, Alice Digges. After medical examination, which proved her statement to be 'false and proceedinge of some lewde and imposterouse pretence,' she and her maid were ordered to be whipt,—'ther backes only beeinge layd bare,'—at the cart's tail through the City on a market day, 'with a note in writinge uppon the hinder part of their heades shewinge the cawse of their saide punishmente.'"

Again, there was the case of William Geffery and John Moore. These two unfortunate creatures were perfectly mad, and ought to have been locked up in Bethlehem. Said William Geffery to the other lunatic, "Christ is not in Heaven, John. He is on earth and like unto us." "He is," John replied, "and thou thyself, William Geffery, art none other than Christ." "That," said William, "is perfectly correct." They therefore clapped John Moore in Bethlehem and William Geffery in the Marshalsea. This should have been enough. But it was not the fashion of the time ever to have enough of punishing. They therefore tied Geffery to the cart tail and flogged him all the way from the Marshalsea to Bethlehem, a matter of two miles. At the gate of Bethlehem the cart was stopped. Then John Moore was brought out, and Geffery was flogged again until he confessed his error and acknowledged that Christ was in Heaven and that he himself was nothing but a sinful man. They then stripped John Moore and tied him to the cart tail; at first he took the punishment smiling, but before going an arrow's shot he begged them to stop, and confessed that he was wrong. So they both went back: John Moore to Bethlehem and William Geffery to the Marshalsea, and we hear no more of them.

The Anabaptists were another perverse people who met with no mercy. On 3rd April 1575 there was found a congregation of Anabaptists in a house outside Aldgate Bars. Twenty-seven in all were arrested. On the 15th of May four of them, bearing faggots to show that they deserved death, recanted at Paul's Cross; on 22nd July two of them were burned at Smithfield, "who died in great horror, with roaring and crying." Their recantation shows the doctrines they held.

"Whereas I.I.T.R.H. being seduced by the devil, the spirit of error, and by false teachers his ministers, have fallen into certain most detestable and damnable heresies, namelie :—

1. That Christ tooke not flesh of the substance of the blessed Virgin Marie.
2. That infants of the faithful ought not be baptized.
3. That a Christian man may not be a magistrate, or beare the sword or office of authoritie.
4. That it is not lawful for a Christian to take an oth. Now by the Grace of God, and through conference with good and learned ministers of Christ His church, I doo understand and acknowledge the same to be most damnable and detestable heresies, and doo aske God here before His church mercie for my said former errors, and doo forsake them, recant and renounce them, and abjure them from the botome of my heart, professing that I certainly believe :

1. That Christ tooke flesh of the substance of the blessed Virgin Marie.
2. That infants of the faithfull ought to be baptized.
3. That a Christian man may be a magistrate, or beare the sword or office of authoritie.
4. That it is lawful for a Christian man to take an oth. And further that I confess that the whole doctrine and religion established and published in this realme of England, as also that which is received and preached in the Dutch Church, from henceforth utterlie abandoning and forsaking all and every anabaptistical error. This is my faith now, in the which I doo purpose and trust to stand firme and stedfast to the end. And that I may soo doo, I beseech you all to praie with me, and for me, to God the heavenlie father, in the name of his son our Saviour Jesus Christ."

Before this, one man and ten women were tried in the Consistory of St. Paul's and sentenced to be burned, but one woman having been converted, they resolved on banishing the rest, who were Dutch. Accordingly the nine women were led by the sheriff, and the man was tied to a cart tail and whipped all the way from Newgate to the river, where they were shipped. And there was a certain sect called the Family of Love, which gave some trouble through their obstinacy. In the year 1575 five of them recanted; in 1580 the sect were thought of sufficient importance to justify a proclamation against them. The tenets of the people do not appear, but they were accused of holding it laudable to deny their connection with their own sect, which made it impossible to convict them by their own confession.

The case of Matthew Hamont, plough-wright, may conclude these cases of strange hallucinations and the conclusions of a disordered brain. He was a common man of no education, who took to thinking and reading about doctrines which he could not understand. He finally arrived at the conclusion that the New Testament, with the Gospels, is but an invention of man, that Christ was a mere man, and so on, shrinking from nothing. This poor lunatic they gravely tried, and because he had spoken words against the Queen, they first cut off both his ears, and then, after giving him a week of pain from his wounds, they burned him for a heretic.

CHAPTER III

SUPERSTITION

AFTER Religion stalks her caricature, Superstition. Now the credulities of London in the Elizabethan age were many and wonderful.

Everybody, for instance, at that time believed in *witchcraft*. Yet there was not wanting an occasional protest.

"I saie, that there is none which acknowledgeth God to be onlie omnipotent . . . but will denie that the elements are obedient to witches, and at their commendement; or that they may at their pleasure send raine, haile, tempests, thunder, lightning. . . . Such faithlesse people are also persuaded that neither hale nor snowe, thunder nor lightening, raine nor tempestuous winds, come from the heavens at the commandement of God, but are raised by the cunning and power of witches and conjurers; inasmuch as a clap of thunder or a gale of wind is no sooner heard, but wither they run to ring bells, or crie out to burne witches, or else burne consecrated things, hoping by the smoke thereof to drive the devill out of the aire."

Witchcraft and magic were, however, recognised by the Government as real things. It was thought desirable in 1542 to pass an Act against these practices.

"It shall be felony to practise, or cause to be practised conjurations, with craft, enchantment or sorcery, to get money: or to consume any person in his body, members, or goods; or to provoke any person to unlawful love; or for the despight of Christ or lucre of money to pull down any cross; or to declare where goods stolen," etc.

This Act of Henry VIII. was repeated or confirmed by Elizabeth twenty years later, and by James I. in 1603. Cranmer, in 1549, ordered the clergy to inquire "whether you know of any that use charms, sorcery, enchantment, witchcrafts, soothsaying, or any like craft invented by the devil." And in 1558 Bishop Jewel, preaching before the Queen, said, "It may please your Grace to understand that witches and sorcerers within these last few years are marvellously increased within your Grace's realm. Your subjects pine away even to the death; their colour fadeth; their flesh rotteth; their speech is benumbed; their senses are bereft."

The precautions used against witchcraft do not belong to London, where the belief in the superstition took a less active form than in the country. A pebble with a natural hole in it, a horseshoe picked up by accident and nailed up over the door, a hare's foot in the pocket, a bit of witchwood, were simple precautions against the witch. I do not think that these superstitions were much followed in London, though there are examples that the terror of the witch prevailed in the City as well as in the country.

It is remarkable that the spread of education and the toleration of fine thoughts in religion did not destroy this horrible superstition. On the contrary it increased, and the seventeenth century, when the greatest amount of religious freedom was practised if not allowed, only made the belief in witchcraft more profound.

Who could choose but to believe when Ben Jonson himself could write of witches as follows?

> " Within a gloomy dimble she doth dwell,
> Down in a pit o'ergrown with brakes and briars,
> Close by the ruins of a shaken abbey,
> Torn with an earthquake down into the ground,
> 'Mongst graves and grots, near an old charnel-house
> Where you shall find her sitting in her form,
> As fearful and melancholie as that
> She is about : with caterpillars' kells,
> And knotty cobwebs, rounded in with spells.
> Thence she steals forth to relief in the fogs,
> And rotten mists, upon the fens and bogs,
> Down to the drowned lands of Lincolnshire :
> To make ewes cast their lambs, swine eat their farrow,
> The housewives' tun not work, nor the milk churn !
> Writhe children's wrists, and suck their breath in sleep :
> Get vials of their blood ! and where the sea
> Casts up his slimy ooze, search for a weed
> To open locks with, and to rivet charms,
> Planted about her in the wicked feat
> Of all her mischiefs, which are manifold."

We may illustrate this belief by the case of Joan Cason or Freeman (she was the wife of one Freeman). She was indicted and solemnly tried by a jury on the charge of being a witch, and of having killed by witchcraft one Jane Cooke, aged three years.

The principal evidence was Sarah Cooke, mother of the child. She kept an alehouse. She was one day drawing a pot of ale for a stranger when he remarked the languishing condition of her child, and suggested that it was bewitched. "Take," he said, "a tile from the house of the suspected person, lay it in the fire, and if she really is a witch the tile will sparkle round the cradle." Wonderful to relate, Sarah Cooke took a tile from the woman's house, laid it in the fire, and it did "sparkle round the house." At that moment Joan Cason herself looked in, gazed upon the child, and went away. Four hours after the child died. What more was wanted? There was evidence corroborative. In the lifetime of the man Freeman there was something like a rat seen about her house, something that squeaked. In the end Joan was hanged, protesting her innocence, but confessing ill conduct with one Mason, who had died of the plague.

There is also the case of Simon Penbrooke, living in St. George's Parish, Southwark. He was suspected to be a conjurer, and was summoned before a court holden in the church of St. Mary Overies either for that or for some other case. As he was talking to a proctor, presumably about his defence, he suddenly fell dead, just as the Judge entered the church. Of course the Judge remarked that it was the just judgment of God towards those that used sorcery, "and a great example to admonish others to fear the justice of God." They found upon him certain "develish" books of conjuration, with a tin man and other fearful things. And they were reminded of Leviticus xx. 6, "If anie soule turne himselfe after such as woorke with spirits and after soothsaiers, saith the Lorde, I will put my face against that soule, and will cut him off from among my people."

Another form of witchcraft was that of the professional conjurer. There was, for instance, the case of William Randoll, who was charged with conjuring to know where treasure was hid in the earth. Four others were charged with assisting at the conjuration. One has no doubt of the fact or of the means employed. Randoll used, of course, the well-known bent stick, the "verge de Jacob," which is still employed all over the world for the discovery of water, though its properties and powers in revealing the existence of metals have been of late neglected, and are now nearly forgotten. The whole of the accused were condemned to death, but in the end Randoll alone was executed. There was said at the time to be five hundred professed conjurers in the country.

The origin of touching for the King's Evil is recounted by Stow in his *Annals* in the following manner :—

"A young woman was afflicted with this disorder in a very alarming manner, and to a most disgusting degree, feeling uneasiness and pain consequent upon it in her sleep, dreamt that she should be cured by the simple operation of having the part washed by the King's hand. Application was consequently made to Edward, by her friends, who very humanely consented to perform the unpleasant request. A bason of water was brought, with which he carefully softened the tumours till they broke, and the contents discharged ; the sign of the cross wound up the charm ; and the female retired, with the assurance of his protection during the remainder of the cure, which was effected within a week."

Of talismans and amulets the sixteenth century had many. The word talisman is an Arabic corruption of the Greek, *i.e.* the influence of a planet or Zodiacal sign upon a person born under it. It was a symbolical figure drawn or engraved. It was supposed at once to procure love and to avert danger. The amulet derived from Latin *amolior*, to do away with, or baffle, averted danger of all kinds. Amber kept children from danger; a child's caul made lawyers prosper; the Evil Eye was averted by certain well-known symbols, including the locust; the closed hand, the pine cone, and other objects were amulets. The German Jew at the point of death tied his head round with knotted leather. The Turks cured apoplexy by encircling the head with a parchment strip painted with signs of the Zodiac. Spells were of all kinds.

Among the superstitions of the time must not be forgotten that favourite form of superstition known as astrology, which still flourishes, though it is not so commonly practised and believed as formerly. Many of the Fathers of the Church denounced astrology, yet astrologers continued. After the Reformation they became more open in their profession and more daring in their pretensions. The names of Nostradamus, Cornelius Agrippa, William Lilly, Robert Fludd, John Dee, and Simon Former, occur as leaders among the astrologers, some of whom were also alchemists. Some of the English professors of astrology were pupils of Cornelius Agrippa in London and at Pavia; others went to study the science at Strasburg. Judicial astrology was in great vogue in London for two hundred years after the Reformation; hundreds of people gained their livelihood by casting nativities for children in which their future was foretold. The story of Dryden and his son's nativity is well known. The astrologers picked out lucky days for the commencement of any kind of business; they told fortunes; they resolved questions; they recovered stolen goods; they predicted future events. It is, however, apparent from their own writings that they had little confidence in the stars, and that the popular part of astrology, at least, was for the most part guesswork, not without fraud. The astrologers of London in the sixteenth century formed themselves into a Society. In the year 1550 a certain Dr. Gell preached a sermon before the Society of Astrologers. Ashmole also mentions his own attendance at certain astrological banquets. But about the Society itself very little is known. Newton pointed out that the sun and stars were only other earths which could have no power over the destiny of men. But the superstition decayed very slowly.

Dr. Dee's *Diary* is a *locus classicus* for the superstitions of his time—the last quarter of the sixteenth century.

He hears knockings in his chamber, with a voice like the shrieking of an owl, but more drawn out and more soft. He is offered a sight in a crystal and he "saw"—what did he see? He does not tell us.

A friend is strangely troubled by a "spiritual creature" about midnight. Robert Gardiner reveals to him a great philosophical secret, which is received with common prayer. He hears of an alchemist who gives away "great lumps" of the philosopher's stone. He dreams that he is to be bereft of his books.

There was trouble with Anne his nurse. She was tempted by a wicked spirit who possessed her. He prayed with her; he anointed her with "holy oil" twice, the wicked spirit resisting. Despite the power of the oil Anne threw herself into the well, but was dragged out in time. Three weeks later she evaded her keeper and cut her throat.

In 1596 Dee received a message from the Queen; he was to do what he would in philosophy and alchemy; no one should hinder him. And so on to the end of the *Diary*.

In the autumn of 1899 there was found in the garden of Lincoln's Inn a thin leaden tablet about four inches square. On one side were eighty-one small squares, arranged in a large square, each with a number engraved upon it. On the other side were three names—Hasmodar, Scherchemosh, and Scharhahan, with a symbol to each. The explanation is as follows :—The square is a charm; the number eighty-one is the number of the Moon, each planet having its own number in the "science" of astrology. The arrangement of the numbers in the eighty-one squares is such that added up vertically or horizonally or diagonally the sum shall always be the same. In this case it is 369. Why 369 I cannot explain. On the other side the three names are the three spirits of the Moon, each with its hieroglyph.

The writing is an expression of an invitation or a command to the spirits to work mischief on an unfortunate man. Had the sorcerer desired good fortune he would have used a silver plate. In either case it was necessary to bury the plate in some secret place, unseen and unsuspected.

The following story is gravely told by Philip Stubbes. Perhaps he did not believe it himself; but it is certain that he meant his readers to believe it.

"This gentlewoman beeyng a very riche Merchaunte mannes daughter : upon a tyme was invited to a Bridall or Wedding, whiche was solemnized in that Toune, againste whiche daie she made great preparation, for the plumyng of herself in gorgious arraie, that as her body was moste beautifull, faire, and proper, so her attire in every respecte might bee corespondent to the same. For the accomplishment whereof, she curled her haire, she died her lockes, and laied them out after the best maner, she coloured her face with waters and Ointmentes; but in no case could she gette any (so curious and daintie she was) that could starche and sette her Ruffes and Neckerchers to her mynde; wherefore she sent for a couple of Laundresses, who did the best thei could to please her humours, but in anywise thei could not. Then fell she to sweare and teare, to cursse and banne, castyng the Ruffes under feete, and wishyng that the Devill might take her when she weare any of those Neckerchers againe. In the meane tyme (through the sufferaunce of God) the Devill, transformyng himself into the forme of a young man, as brave and proper as she in every pointe in outward appearance, came in, fainyng himself to bee a woer or suter unto her. And seyng her thus agonized, and in suche a peltyng chase, he demaunded of her the cause thereof, who straight waie tolde hym how she was abused in the settyng of her Ruffes, which thyng beeyng heard of hym, he promised to please her minde, and thereto tooke in hande the setting of her Ruffes, whiche he performed to her greate contentation, and likyng, in so muche as she lokyng her self in a glasse (as the Devill bad her) became greatly inamoured with hym. This dooen, the yong man kissed her, in the doyng whereof he writhe her necke in sunder, so she died miserably, her bodie beyng metamorphosed into blacke and blewe colours most ugglesome to behold, and her face (whiche before was so amorous) became moste deformed, and fearfull to looke upon. This being knowen, preparaunce was made for her burial, a riche coffin was provided, and her fearfull bodie was laied therein, and it covered verie sumpteously. Foure men immediatly assaied to lifte up the corps, but could not move it, then sixe attempted the like, but could not once stirre it from the place where it stoode. Whereat the standers by marveilyng, caused the Coffin to bee opened, to see the cause thereof. Where thei founde the bodie to be taken awaie, and a blacke Catte verie leane and deformed sittyng in the Coffin, setting of greate Ruffes, and frizlyng of haire, to the greate feare and wonder of all beholders. This wofull spectacle have I offered to their viewe, that by looking into it, instead of their other looking Glasses thei might see their own filthinesse, and avoyde the like offence, for feare of the same, or worser judgment : whiche God graunt thei maie doe."

ELIZABETHAN LONDON

CHAPTER I

WITH STOW

LET us climb the steps that lead to the City Wall at the Tower postern, and make a circuit by means of the Wall. We walk on the five-foot way designed for the archers. It is grass-grown between the stones. On the battlements the wall-flower grows luxuriously with the green fumitory and the red flowers of the kiss-me-quick. Looking over the Wall we perceive that the ditch is nearly filled up: all kinds of rubbish have been shot into it; there are small ponds of water here and there, and on the opposite bank are gardens in patches and what we call allotments. "Alas!" says our guide, who continually laments the past, "I remember when the ditch was full, and when the boys came to bathe in it and were sometimes drowned in it. Then fish abounded and men angled from the bank." We begin our walk. "I remember," our guide goes on, talking while he leads the way, "running along the Wall when I was a boy, nearly sixty years ago. It was a favourite pastime to run from gate to gate. That was before the suppression of the Religious." He sighed—Was he then regretting that event? "All the Houses were standing then. One thought they would stand for ever. Yet the axe was already laid to the tree: there was internal decay and external contempt, though we boys knew nothing of it. The friars in vain searched the boxes put up for them in the shops: no one would give them alms; if they went into a house, no one would give them so much as a crust of bread; there were but fifteen left in Grey Friars, and they were selling their vessels of silver and gold when they were called upon to surrender. But still their churches made a brave show. All day long the bells were ringing—'twas a city of bells. They rang from cathedral and parish church; from monastery and nunnery; from college of priests and from chapel and from spital. They rang for festivals and fasts; for pageants and ridings; for births and deaths; for marriages and funerals; for the election of City officers; for the King's birthday; for the day and the hour; they rang in the baby; they rang out the passing soul; they rang merrily in honour of the bride; they rang for work to begin and for work to cease; the streets echoed the ringing of bells all day long; for miles round London you could hear with the singing of the larks the ringing of the bells.

"A third part of the City belonged to the Houses and the Church. Why, thousands of honest people lived by working for St. Paul's and the parish churches and the monks and nuns. Look around you now." We were close to Aldgate. Stow pointed to the south-east. Near the Tower stood a venerable church in a precinct surrounded by a stone wall and containing a cloister, houses round it, a garden, a school-house, and a burial-ground. "Behold the last of them!" he said. "St. Katherine's, the smallest of all the Foundations, still exists; but changed—Ah!—changed. Where are the rest?" On the north of St. Katherine's was another precinct marked out by a wall, and within it broken walls, broken windows, and rough timber store-houses. "There was once Eastminster," said Stow. "Who is mindful of our Lady of Grace and her Cistercians? They are forgotten. Look Citywards. Yon ruins are those of the Crutched Friars. What is left to mark their abode of two hundred years and more? Their hal' was converted into a glass-house and is burned down; their church contains now a carpenter's shop and a tennis court. Turn your eyes more to the north. Those are the ruins of St. Helen's Nunnery: their chapel is part of the parish church; their hall is now the Hall of the Leathersellers' Company; their gardens also belong to that honourable Company. Or yonder, where you may behold the precinct of the Holy Trinity Priory. The Prior was also Alderman of Portsoken Ward and rode among the other Aldermen, but in habit ecclesiastical, as I myself have seen. The House kept open table for rich and poor; a noble and hospitable House it was, but in the end decayed by reason of too great hospitality. The church was pulled down and levelled with the ground—*Proh Pudor*! —the courts remain, but with other buildings; and now is that venerable and regal Foundation clean forgotten. Behold"—he pointed outside the Wall—"the place where the *Sorores Minores*, the sisters of St. Clare, lived for many years. The walls of their refectory still stand; on the site of their cloister is a fair and large store-house for armours and habiliments of war, with work-houses serving unto the same purpose. Alas! Poor Sisters! To this end has come their House of Peace and Prayer."

"Nevertheless, Master Stow, the City is more prosperous than before."

"I know not; I know not," he said impatiently. "What do I know about wealth and prosperity? Let us go on." So he left off talking about the churches and monasteries and pointed to the houses beyond the Wall. "The suburbs," he said, "have not greatly increased of late years. There has been too much plague among us. And, indeed, it would seem that we are never to be rid of plague. The Queen's Council forbade the building of new houses. As well forbid the

A True and Exact Draught of the TOWER LIBERTIES, furvey'd in the Year 1597 by *Gulielmus Haiward* and *J. Gascoyne*.

rising of the tide. There are now—as you can plainly see—a line of cottages on both sides of the road as far as Whitechapel Church. But who is to hinder? There is a line of houses along the riverside as far as Ratcliffe and even Lime-house, where once were elms so noble. But who is there to hinder? Masterless men are they, and sea-faring men and common cheats and rogues, who live beside the river, beyond the jurisdiction of the Mayor and safe from the wholesome cart tail and the penance of pillory.

"Pleasant it was, in those old days," he went on, "to overlook the quiet nuns from the Wall. There were no whispers against those holy Sisters, and no scandals. We loved to look upon them in their gardens quiet and peaceful. They prayed for the City, the nuns of St. Clare, of St. Helen's, and of Holywell. Now every man prays for himself. There were also the monks in their cloisters, walking and reading and meditating. Some there were who called the monks devourers and drones. I know not. Their prayers were asked for the dead and for the living. No one prays now for the dead, and no one asks where they lie or how they fare. Drones and devourers! They were gentlemen all by birth, —why should they work?"

It was, indeed, surprising to see the ruins of the Houses, nor had I understood, until I walked round the Wall and observed the ruins, how many there were, or how great was the destruction when the masterful King turned out the monks and nuns and gave their houses to his favourites and his courtiers. "They have taken" said Stow, "all they wanted of the stones. What are left will vanish little by little."

"But the memory will continue."

"Nay, in the minds of scholars, not of the people. Things of the past are soon forgotten. No one will teach the children about the Houses of monks and friars. If they teach them anything at all, it will be as Barnabe Googe taught his generation when he gathered into one volume all that could be alleged or invented against those holy men, if they were holy," he added, correcting himself. "Indeed a man must pay heed unto his words. I have been, myself, charged with Romish leanings because I remember things that are past and gone. What do the young folk now understand of what they have lost, because they never saw it? I am now old, and in age the mind flies back willingly to the days of youth."

Within the Wall we saw the ruins of the Crutched Friars, of St. Helen's, of the Holy Priory, of the Austin Friars, of the Papey, of Elsing Spital, of St. James's in the Wall, of the Grey Friars and of the Black Friars; without the Wall there were the ruins of Eastminster, of the Clares, of St. Mary Spital, of Holywell, of the Church House, of the Knights Hospitallers, of Clerkenwell Nunnery, of St. Bartholomew's Priory, and of the White Friars.

"The poets, doubtless," I said, "and with them the divines, meditate among these ruins."

"Alas! No. The poets write songs of love and sing them; or they go forth to the wars and sing of them. The times are brisk. It is as if the world was waking up from sleep: there are new things everywhere; we live in the present; our ships go forth to·distant lands; there is a new world, a Terra Incognita, to be explored and conquered; it is no time for meditation. When the cloister was broken down meditation fled beyond the seas. We live to fight and to get rich, and to watch against the wiles of Pope and·Spaniard."

EAST VIEW OF CLOISTERS OF COLLEGIATE CHURCH OF ST. KATHERINE
Taken down in July 1755.

"Do these ruins then inspire no regret?"

"None. The people are forgetting fast. Only old men sometimes speak of what they remember; when the last stones have been taken away, the very names will tell them nothing. Even the names are changing. Soon all will be lost and forgotten. Strange! Four hundred years those monks lived among us, and after fifty years they are already clean forgotten as much as if they had never lived."

At Bishopsgate, Stow pointed northward. "Houses," he said, "are stretching along the northern road, but slowly. Among the ruins of Holywell stands a Play house, and outside it is another. What will be the end of this passion for the theatre, I know not. Formerly, an interlude in an Inn yard, a masque in a

Company's Hall, and so enough. Now have ye every day a play set forth upon a stage, with songs and music, and boys dressed up as women."

He shook his head and led on, still following the Wall. Within the City on this north side there were many large and fair gardens, some belonging to Companies which here have their Halls, and some to merchants' houses, and some that once belonged to the Monastic Houses. They were set with fruit-trees and with beds of flowers and sweet herbs. Among the gardens stood collections of craftsmen's cottages and workshops, and the churches with their small green churchyards were almost hidden by the trees. This part of London truly had a rural look by reason of these gardens.

We passed Moorgate, the old church of the Papey close to the Wall, and further along, also close to the Wall, the church of All Hallows; we came to Cripplegate with its church outside the Wall. And passing a bend to the south, continued our walk. On the other side of the ditch was another double line of houses. "This is Aldersgate," said Stow. "The way leads to the Charter House and beyond to the village of Iseldon. You can now see the ruins of the House of the Knights Hospitallers; their noble gate yet stands, and part of their church. Beyond was the Priory of St. Bartholomew. From the Wall you may behold their cloisters; the chancel of their church is now a parish church. Close at hand is Smithfield. What things have been done at Smithfield! I was thirty years of age when Queen Mary burned her martyrs. There had been burnings before her time, but she outdid them all. Sir, she was ill-advised: she thought to make the people go back to the old Religion through fear. She might have led them back through love. I have seen the burning of those stubborn folk. Old and young, men and women, nay children, have I seen standing in the faggots, praying aloud while the flames mounted up and licked their hands and their faces. Mostly they died quickly, being smothered with the smoke; but sometimes the flames were blown away, and we saw the blackened body still in agony, and the lips that moved to the end in prayer. And we saw how the Lord answered, giving fortitude to endure or even, if we knew it, painlessness in the midst of fire. To see father, brother, neighbour, so die without fear, and as if joyously enduring torture in order to reach the gates of Heaven,—Believe me, sir, this it was that made the people what they are, and completed Henry's work."

We came to Newgate. "Behold!" he said, "the cat, emblem of Whittington, who rebuilt this gate and prison. Here is Christ's Hospital, which once was the House of the Grey Friars. It is London's chiefest glory: here shall you find boys ruled with wisdom and taught godliness, who would otherwise have joined the throngs of the masterless, and roamed about the streets and roads." And so on to Ludgate, where we left the Wall. "See," said Stow, "there are houses with many

ST. PAUL'S CHURCH
From Visscher's *Panorama of London*.

palaces of nobles all the way from Bridewell to the King's House at Westminster. And now, good sir, we leave the Wall, and we will visit the City within the Wall."

He led me by Ludgate into the precinct of St. Paul's, surrounded by a stone wall; the Cathedral looked battered and worn by the tooth of time; the spire, once the glory of the City, was gone never to be replaced; the stonework was black in parts from the smoke of the sea coal; the tracery was mouldering; about the towers of the west flew the swifts crying. "There are kites on the roof," said Stow, "which keep the City clean and devour the offal."

At Paul's Cross there was a preaching by some reverend divine: a crowd of

LATIMER PREACHING BEFORE EDWARD VI. AT WESTMINSTER
E. Gardner's Collection.

women sat on benches listening; a few men were there, but it was in working hours. The preacher argued some difficult point of doctrine, comparing texts and turning over the leaves of his small brown Geneva Bible. I observed that his hearers listened with a critical air. "For fifty years," said Stow, looking on with contempt, "they have been arguing and disputing on matters of doctrine and nothing settled yet; in the old time we were told what to believe, and we were stayed and comforted by our belief. These people prove one thing to-day and another thing to-morrow. They are pulled this way and that by the power of texts which they think they understand. Let us go into the Cathedral."

Outside, in the churchyard, everything was destroyed that formerly made the

SOUTH FRONT OF BAYNARD'S CASTLE, ABOUT 1640

place venerable and beautiful: Pardon churchyard; the "Clochard;" the cloister with the Dance of Death; Sherrington's Library; the college of the minor canons. Only Paul's Cross remained. And the Cathedral, rising up alone and gaunt, bereft of her daughters, seemed mournful and lonely. "Perhaps," said Stow, "a new church is wanted for the new Faith. St. Paul's was not built for Protestants. They know not how to treat the church. Look at yonder fellows!" He pointed to two porters who bore boxes on their heads, and entering at the North doors tramped noisily through the Cathedral, going out at the South. "They have made a right of way, a short way, through the church. Saw one ever the like? Through the church itself!"

We went in; the nave was a kind of noisy Exchange, yet not for merchants. It was full of people loudly talking of all kinds of business; ladies were there. "They make their assignations in the church," said Stow. Gallants richly dressed swaggered up and down the middle aisle; servants stood waiting to be hired; scriveners had their stools and tables, and were busy writing letters; men disputed over their affairs, yea, and quarrelled loudly. The chancel was walled off and separated from the nave and transepts. The old glory had departed from the once splendid interior: of all the chapels, shrines, altars, chantries, paintings, lights, carved marbles, work in ivory, gold and silver, nothing was left. Only bare whitewashed walls and a few plain tombs; even the painted glass, wherever it could be reached, was broken. While we looked around the organ began to play; it was accompanied by other instruments, chiefly wind instruments. With the music ascended the voices of the choir, the pure sweet voices of the boys. My old guide's eyes grew humid. "No," he said, "they have not taken all away. The music remains with us, to remind us that Heaven is left although we have whitewashed the paintings that revealed its glories."

We left the precinct by the North gate, which opens upon the back of St. Michael le Querne, and turned eastward into Chepe. The breadth of this great market had contracted since the reign of Edward the Third. The houses on the south side were much higher and better built, with timber frames and much carving and gilding. On the north side the lanes, which were formerly broad spaces for stands and sheds for the market, were now narrow, with houses on either hand: there were also houses on that side, but not continuous; here were Grocers' Hall and Mercers' Hall. Round the Standard and the Cross were stalls kept by women; the poulterers still had their shops in the Poultry, and apothecaries sold their drugs and herbs in Bucklersbury.

It was now evening, and supper time. My guide led me to the tavern called the Rose, in the Poultry. There was a goodly company assembled in the great room. Here there was music, and the drawers ran about with supper and with wine. A capon with a flask of Malmsey warmed the heart of my old guide. After supper we took tobacco and more wine, while boys sang madrigals very sweetly. The close of a summer day in the City of London brings with it a cessation of the noise of hammers and the ringing of anvils and the grinding of waggons and the shouts of those who quarrel over their work. The City became quiet; there was the tinkling of guitar and lute from the taverns and the houses; the voices of those who sang; the merry laugh of maidens, and the sober voice of age.

"Come," said Stow, "there remains the Royal Exchange. This we will see and so an end until to-morrow."

The Royal Exchange was lit up with candles. The upper walk or *pawne*[1] I found to be a collection of shops, all as light as day. Music was playing and the place was full of people; not the sober merchants, but the City madams and their daughters, the gallants, and the 'prentices. "In the summer," said Stow, "the place is open till nine of the clock, in the winter till ten. Many come here just as they go to Paul's in the morning, because they have no other place to go to and no money to spend in the tavern. Know you not the lines?

> 'Though little coin thy purseless pockets line,
> Yet with great company thou'st taken up;
> For often with Duke Humphrey thou dost dine;
> And often with Sir Thomas Gresham sup.'"

Other walks, many other walks, I have taken about London in company of good old John Stow: we have walked together along Thames Street, which is surely the very heart of the City, and in Chepe, and among the gardens of the northern part. In these walks about the streets, even then so old and so venerable, the old man waxed eloquent over the houses of the past where the great nobles had each his palace, which was also a barrack in the City of London. It was not only in and about Thames Street: all over the City he led me, prattling in his kindly garrulity. "There were kings' palaces here once," he said: "the Tower Royal where Richard's mother dwelt; and the King's Wardrobe—I can show you that; and Baynard's Castle, which is now rebuilt and remains a noble house; and Crosby Hall, where the third Richard sojourned for a while; and the Stone House in Lombard Street that they call King John's Palace, but I know not with what truth; and Cold Harbour where Prince Hal once lived; and the Savoy which was John of Gaunt's. And there were the town houses of the noblemen. What a stately house was that of the Northumberlands outside Aldgate! It is now a printing-house. And they had another house in Aldgate Ward with broad gardens, now turned into bowling-greens. And there is the house called the Erber on the east side of Dowgate. The Earl of Warwick had it, then the Duke of Clarence had it, and when it was rebuilt Francis Drake had it. There is Gresham's Mansion in Broad Street, which has become a noble college for the instruction of youths in the

---

[1] *Pawne* = a gallery.

liberal arts, so that some say that London will become like unto Oxford or Cambridge. And Whittington's house beside the church of St. Michael, now an almshouse, which was once also a college for priests. And there is the house which once belonged to Sir Robert Large, when Caxton was his 'prentice, at the corner of Old Jewry; formerly it was a Jews' Synagogue, and afterwards the House of the Brethren of the Sack. Alas! most of these houses are now in decay and inhabited by poor folk. The nobles come no more to town." Yet he showed me the house of Sir Francis Walsingham, the Queen's Secretary. It was in Seething Lane.

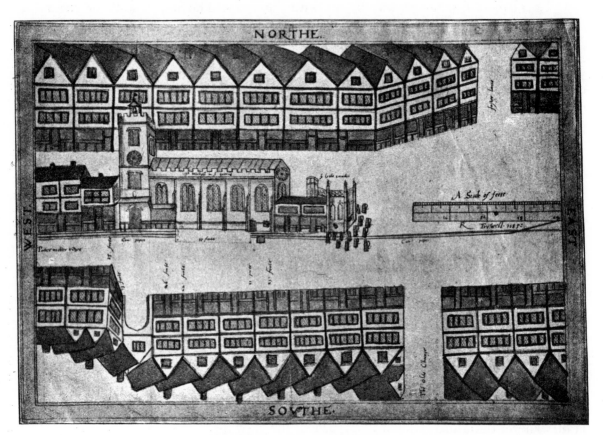

WEST CHEPE IN ELIZABETHAN LONDON

"We look for these palaces now, along the river, between Bridewell and Westminster," he said.

My old guide looked at the people as they passed with a peculiar benevolence, especially upon the young. "I have myself been a 'prentice," he said; "I know the rubs and crosses of that time; an impatient master, long hours of work, hard fare, hot blood that longs to be up and doing. Many there are who have in their latter days broken their indentures and fled to sail the seas with Oxenham or Drake; many have gone into the service of the adventurous Companies. I remember very well, very well," he sighed, "the joys of the time, the dancing on a summer evening, the wrestling, the fighting, the pageants and ridings in the streets. Life lies all before the 'prentice. What boots it to be my Lord Mayor when life is wellnigh spent?"

"Sir," my guide added, "I have shown you our City. Go now, alone, and watch the ways of the people : mark the wealth of our merchants ; look at the Port crowded with ships and the Quays cumbered with merchandise ; talk with the mariners, and observe the spirit that is in them all. Like all old men I lament the past ; but I needs must rejoice in the quickening of these latter days. And so, good sir, farewell."

A VIEW OF COLD HARBOUR IN THAMES STREET, ABOUT 1600

CHAPTER II

CONTEMPORARY EVIDENCE

LET us supplement this discourse by contemporary evidence.

There is an anonymous map of London in the sixteenth century called "Londinium Feracissimi Angliæ Regni Metropolis." It is in some respects more exact than the better known map attributed to Agas. The streets, gardens, and fields are laid down with greater precision, and there is no serious attempt to combine, as Agas does, a picture, or a panorama, with a map. At the same time, the surveyor has been unable to resist the fashion of his time to consider the map as laid down from a bird's-eye view, so that he thinks it necessary to give something of elevation.

I will take that part of the map which lies outside the walls. The precinct of St. Katherine stands beside the Tower with its chapel, court, and gardens; there are a few houses near it, apparently farmhouses; the convent of Eastminster had entirely vanished. Nothing indicates the site of the Nunnery in the Minories; yet there were ruins of these buildings standing here till the end of the last century; outside Bishopsgate houses extended past St. Mary Spital, some of whose buildings were still, apparently, standing. On the west side St. Mary of Bethlehem stood, exactly on the site of Liverpool Street Station, but not covering nearly so large an area; it appears to have occupied a single court and was probably what we should now consider a very pretty little cottage, like St. Edmund's Hall, Oxford.

Outside Cripplegate the houses begin again, leaving, between, the lower Moorfields dotted with ponds; there are houses lining the road outside Aldersgate. The courts are still standing of St. Bartholomew's Priory, Charter House, St. John's Priory, and the Clerkenwell Nunnery; Smithfield is surrounded with houses; Bridewell with its two square courts stands upon the river bank; Fleet Street is irregular in shape, the houses being nowhere in line; the courts of Whitefriars are still remaining. The Strand has all its great houses facing the river; their backs open upon a broad street with a line of mean houses on the north side.

On the south of the river there is a line of houses on the High Street; a line of houses along the river bank on either side; and another one running near Bermondsey Abbey.

Within the walls we observe that some of the Religious Houses have quite disappeared; Crutched Friars, for instance; there is a vacant space which is probably one of the courts of St. Helen's; the Priory of the Holy Trinity preserves its courts, but there is no sign of the church; there are still visible the courts and gardens of Austin Friars; there is still the great court of the Grey Friars; but the buildings of Blackfriars seem to have vanished entirely.

But Sir Thomas More has left us a description of London in his time. It is

BRIDEWELL PALACE AND THE ENTRANCE TO THE FLEET RIVER AS THEY APPEARED IN 1660
E. Gardner's Collection.

a description in terms too vague, yet interesting. He calls the City Amaurote and the Thames he calls the Anyder.

"The River Anyder riseth four and twenty miles above Amaurote, out of a little spring: but being increased by other small floods and brooks that run into it: and, among others, two somewhat bigger ones. Before the City, it is half a mile broad (hardly so much now as it was in former days being pent in and straitned to a narrower space, by the later buildings on each side): and further, broader. By all that space that lyeth between the Sea and the City, and a good sort of land also above, the water ebbs and flows six hours together, with a swift tide; when the sea flows in to the length of thirty miles, it fills all the Anyder with salt water, and drives back the fresh water of the river; and somewhat further, it hangeth

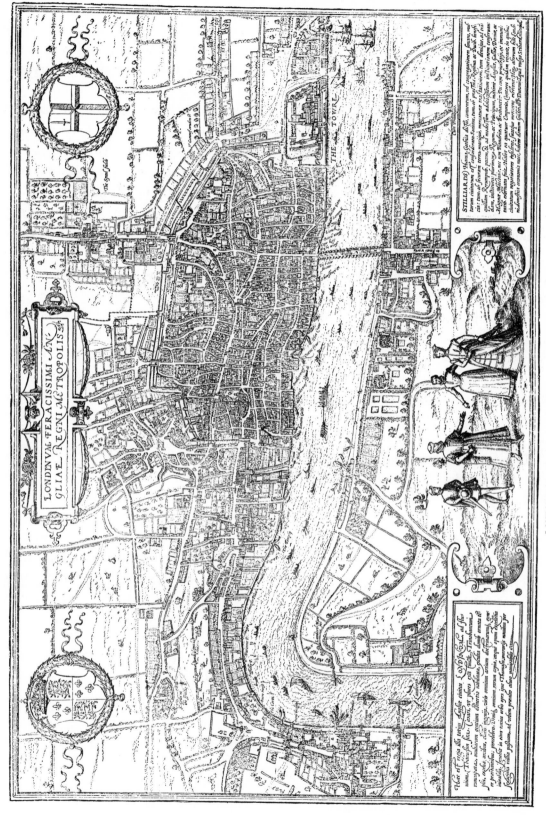

LONDINIUM FERACISSIMI ANGLIÆ REGNI METROPOLIS

the sweetness of fresh water with saltness: but a little beyond that, the river waxeth sweet, and runneth foreby the City fresh and pleasant; and when the sea ebbs and goes back again, this fresh water follows it almost to the very fall into the sea.

They have also another river, which indeed is not very great, but it runneth gently and pleasantly: for it riseth even out of the same hill that the City standeth upon, and runneth down slope through the midst of the City into Anyder." [This may be the river of the Wells; in More's time the Walbrook was probably covered over.] "And because it ariseth a little without the City, the Amaurotians have enclosed the head spring of it with strong fences and bulwarks; and so have joined it to the City: this done, to the intent that the waters should not be stopped nor turned away, nor poisoned, if their enemies should chance to come upon them. From thence the water is derived and brought down in Chanals or Brooks divers ways into the lower parts of the City. Where that cannot be done by reason that the place will not suffer it, then they gather the Rain Water in great Cisterns which doth them as good service." [This, it seems, was all the supply of Water the City had in that age, which is now much more plentifully served.] "Then next for the situation and Walls. That it stood by the side of a low Hill, in fashion almost square. The breadth of it began a little beneath the top of the Hill, and still continued by the space of two miles, until it came to the river Anyder. The length of it, which lyeth by the river-side, was somewhat more.

The City is compassed about with an high and thick wall, full of Turrets and Bulwarks. A dry Ditch, but deep and broad and overgrown with bushes, briers, and thorns, goeth about three sides or quarters of the City. To the fourth side, the River itself serveth for a Ditch.

The streets be appointed and set forth very commodious and handsome, both for carriage and also against the winds. The Streets be full twenty foot broad. The Houses be of fair and gorgeous Buildings: and in the street-side, they stand joined together in a long Row through the whole Street, without any partition or separation. On the bankside of the Houses, through the whole length of the Street, lye large Gardens which be closed in round about with the back parts of the Street. Every House hath two doors, one to the street, and a Postern Door on the backside into the Garden. These doors be made with two leaves, never locked nor bolted: so easie to be opened, that they will follow the least drawing of a finger, and shut again of themselves.

They set great store by their gardens. In these they have Vineyards and all manner of Fruits, Herbs, and Flowers, so pleasant, so well furnished, and so finely kept, that I never saw anything more fruitful, nor better trimmed in any place: and their study and diligence herein cometh not only of pleasure, but also of a certain strife and contention that is betwixt street and street, concerning the

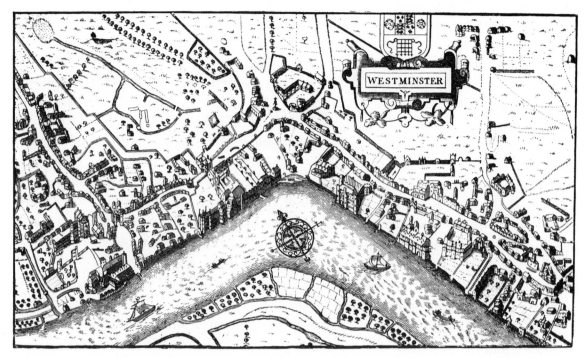

PLAN OF THE CITY OF WESTMINSTER IN THE TIME OF ELIZABETH

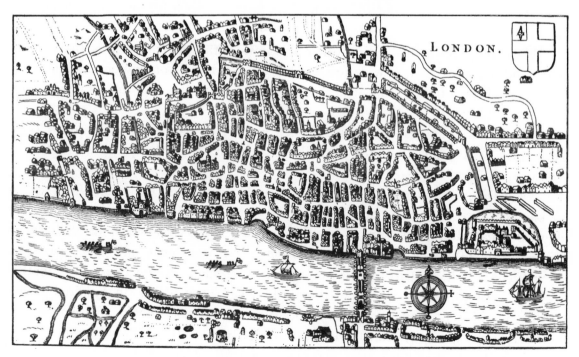

PLAN OF THE CITY OF LONDON IN THE TIME OF ELIZABETH

trimming, husbanding, and flourishing, of their Gardens, every man for his own part: and verily, you shall not lightly find in all the City anything that is more commodious, either for the Profit of the Citizens, or for pleasure. And therefore it may seem, that the first founder of the City minded nothing so much as he did these Gardens. They say, that King Utopus himself, even at his first beginning, appointed and drew forth the platform of the City into this fashion and figure that it hath now, by his gallant garnishing and the beautiful setting forth of it. Whereunto he saw that one man's age would not suffice, that he left to his posterity.

Their Chronicles, which they keep written with all diligent circumspection, containing the history of 1760 years, even from the first conquest of the Island, record and witness, that the Houses in the beginning were very low, and likely homely cottages, or poor shepherds' houses, made at all adventures of every rude piece of wood that came first to hand: with Mud-walls, and ridged Roofs thatched over with straw. But now the Houses be curiously builded after a gorgeous and gallant sort, with three stories, one over another.

The outside of the walls be made of either hard Flint, or of Plaister, or else of Brick: and the Inner-sides be well strengthened with Timber-Work.

The Roofs be plain and flat, covered with a certain kind of Plaister that is of no cost: and yet so tempered that no fire can hurt or perish it: and notwithstandeth the violence of the weather, better than any lead.

They keep the wind out of their windows with glass: for it is there much used: and some were also with fine linnen dipped in oyl or amber: and that for two commodities: for by this means more light cometh in, and the wind is better kept out." (*Utopia.*)

The following notes on England were written by one Stephen Perlin in 1558. The tract was translated for, and published in, the *Antiquarian Repertory* (vol. iv.):—

"The English in general are cheerful and great lovers of music, for there is no church, however small, but has musical service performed in it. They are likewise great drunkards; for if an Englishman would treat you, he will say in his language, *yis dring a quarta rim gasquim cim hespaignol, oim malvoysi;* that is, will you drink a quart of Gascoigne wine, another of Spanish, and another Malmsy. In drinking or eating they will say to you above an hundred times, *drind iou*, which is, I am going to drink to you; and you should answer them in their language, *iplaigiu*, which means, I pledge you. If you would thank them in their language you must say, *god tanque artelay*, which is to say, I thank you with all my heart. When they are drunk, they will swear blood and death that you shall drink all that is in your cup, and will say thus to you, *bigod sol drind iou agoud oin.* Now remember, if you please, that in this land they commonly make

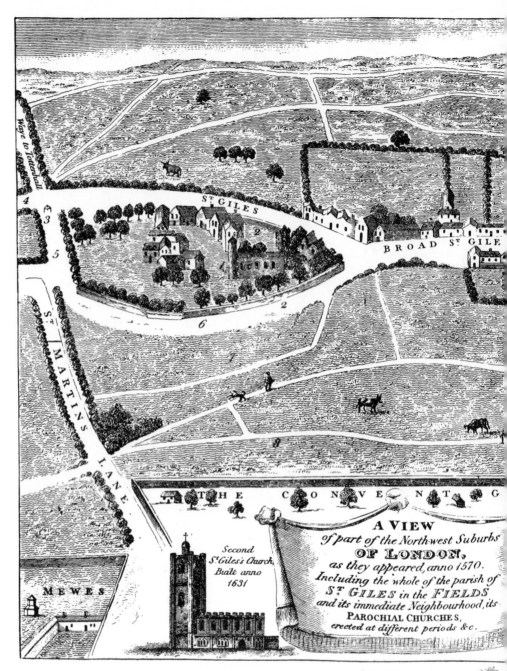

A VIEW of part of the North-west Suburbs OF LONDON, as they appeared, anno 1570. Including the whole of the parish of St GILES in the FIELDS and its immediate Neighbourhood, its PAROCHIAL CHURCHES, erected at different periods &c.

Second St Giles's Church Built anno 1631

THE PARISH OF St Giles

The part of the North West Suburbs of London, since called Saint Giles's, was about the time of habitations.——The parish derived its name if not its origin from the ancient Hospital for and dedicated to Saint Giles: before which time there had been only a small Chapel and dwellings in the flourishing times of Saint Giles's Hospital, but declined in popu- inconsiderable village till the end of the reign of Elizabeth, after which period it was The great increase of St Giles's Parish occasioned the separation of St Georges by the great Plan of London by Ralph Aggas, and partly from authorities fur-

The Seal of the A

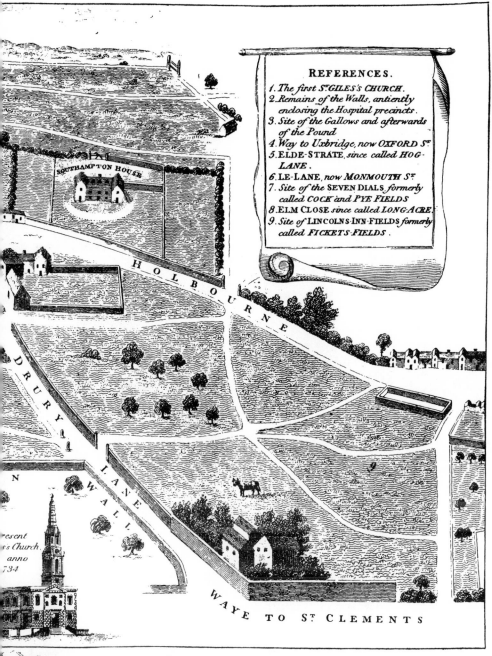

REFERENCES.

1. *The first St GILES'S CHURCH.*
2. *Remains of the Walls, antiently enclosing the Hospital precincts.*
3. *Site of the Gallows and afterwards of the Pound.*
4. *Way to Uxbridge, now OXFORD S.^t*
5. *ELDE-STRATE, since called HOG-LANE.*
6. *LE-LANE, now MONMOUTH S.^t*
7. *Site of the SEVEN DIALS, formerly called COCK and PYE FIELDS.*
8. *ELM CLOSE since called LONG ACRE.*
9. *Site of LINCOLNS-INN-FIELDS formerly called FICKETS-FIELDS.*

SOUTHAMPTON HOUSE

HOLBOURNE

DRURY LANE

WALL

WAYE TO St CLEMENTS

present s Church. anno 734

in the **Fields**, LONDON.

the Norman Conquest an un-built tract of country, or but thinly scattered with Lepers, which was built on the site of the present church, by MATILDA queen of King Henry, I. or Oratory on the Spot. — It is described in old records, as abounding with gardens lation and buildings after the suppression of that establishment, and remained but an rapidly built on, and became distinguished for the number and rank of its inhabitants. Bloomsbury Parish from it anno 1734. — The above view (which is partly supplied -nished by parochial documents) was taken anno 1570.

of St Giles

use of silver vessels when they drink wine, and they will say to you at table, *goud chere*, which is good cheer. The servants wait on their master bareheaded, and leave their caps on the buffet. It is to be noted, that in this excellent kingdom there is, as I have said, no kind of order; the people are reprobates, and thorough enemies to good manners and letters, for they don't know whether they belong to God or the Devil, which St. Paul had reprehended in so many people, saying, be not transported with divers sorts of winds, but be constant and steady to your belief.

In this country, all the shops of every trade are open, like those of the barbers in France, and have many glass windows, as well below as above in the chambers, for in the chambers there are many glazed casements, and that in all the tradesmen's houses in almost every town; and those houses are like the barbers' shops in France, as well above as below, and glazed at their openings. In the windows, as well in cities as villages, are plenty of flowers, and at the taverns plenty of hay upon their wooden floors, and many cushions of tapestry, on which travellers seat themselves. There are many bishopricks in this kingdom, as I think sixteen, and some archbishopricks, of which one is esteemed the principal, which is Cantorbie, called in English Cantorberi, where there is a very fine church, of which St. Thomas is patron. England is remarkable for all sorts of fruits, as apricots, peaches, and quantities of nuts."

In the year 1598 a German traveller, Paul Hentzner by name, visited London. This is what he says about the streets :—

"The streets in this city are very handsome and clean; but that which is named from the goldsmiths who inhabit it, surpasses all the rest: there is in it a gilt tower, with a fountain that plays. Near it on the farther side is a handsome house, built by a goldsmith, and presented by him to the city. There are besides to be seen in this street, as in all others where there are goldsmiths' shops, all sorts of gold and silver vessels exposed to sale, as well as ancient and modern medals, in such quantities as must surprise a man the first time he sees and considers them." (*See* Appendix VI.)

Stow furnishes a very clear account of the condition of the suburbs in his own time. Thus, he says that outside the Wall in the East there were no houses at all east of St. Katherine's along the river until the middle of the sixteenth century, but that during the latter half of the century there had sprung up a "continual street, or filthy strait passage, with alleys of small tenements built, inhabited by sailors; victuallers, along by the river of Thames, almost to Ratcliff, a good mile from the Tower."

He says, further, that in his time had arisen quite a new suburb between East Smithfield and Limehouse; and that good houses had been recently built between Ratcliff and Blackwall.

Outside Aldgate he mentions a "large street replenished with buildings to Hog Lane and the bars. Without the bars both sides of the street were 'pestered' with cottages and alleys, even up to Whitechapel Church and almost half a mile beyond it into the common field." Note, therefore, that close to Aldgate, just beyond Whitechapel Church, was a common which was thus encroached upon and settled on by squatters and by those who made enclosures and placed laystalls, etc., upon them. The whole of the common was thus taken up; "in some places it scarce remaineth a sufficient highway for the meeting of carriages and droves of people," a fact to be remembered and accounted for.

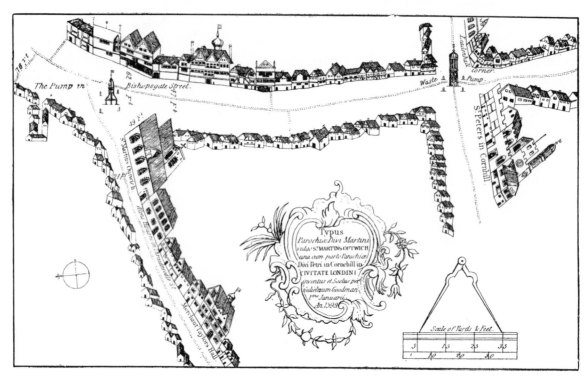

BISHOPSGATE

Going on to Bishopsgate and its highway. Outside the gate stood St. Botolph's Church; next to it the Hospital of St. Mary of Bethlehem; opposite certain houses; then, the liberty of Norton Folgate, belonging to the canons of St. Paul's; then the site of the Holywell Nunnery; all along the road to St. Leonard's, Shoreditch, except for the site of St. Mary Spital, a "continual building of small and base tenements, for the most part lately erected." Among the cottages Stow points to a certain row whose history was perhaps that of many others. The row of cottages were almshouses belonging to St. Mary Spital; the occupants were appointed by that House; they paid a yearly rent of one penny, in acknowledgment of ownership; and on Christmas Day they were feasted by the

Prior. When the Hospital was suppressed the cottages, for want of repairs, fell into decay; the new owners of the land would not take over the responsibility of the charitable endowment; they neither repaired the houses nor did they invite the tenants to a Christmas feast. On the other hand, they did not collect the rent of a penny. They were then sold, although they ought to have been continued as almhouses to one Russell, who rebuilt them and gave them his own name, and let them to tenants in the usual way.

The church of St. Leonard's contained monuments to the memory of three noble families at least: the Westmoreland Nevilles; the Blounts, Lords Mountjoy; and that of Manners, Earls of Rutland. The reason of their tombs and monuments

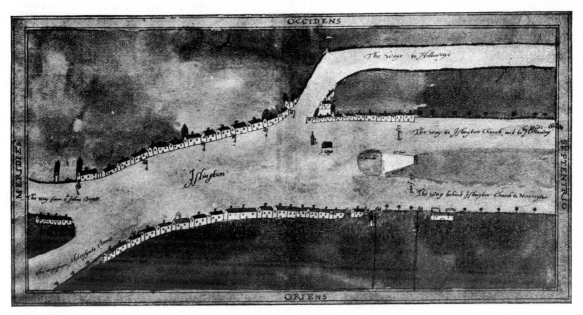

PLAN OF ISLINGTON
From a print in the British Museum. By the courtesy of the late Marquis of Salisbury.

being found in the church must be sought in the history of the manors lying north of Shoreditch.

On the north side of the City the Moor Fields continued for a long time as waste ground, seldom visited; in 1415, however, Thomas Fawconer, Mayor, broke through the City Wall and built the postern called Moorgate; he constructed causeways over the Moor; cleansed and repaired the dykes or ditches with which the Moor was intersected: so that the place was drained and made into a pleasant walk for the citizens, either on summer evenings, or on their way to Iselden and Hoxton. Sixty years later brickfields were opened in the Moor, and bricks made for the repair of the City Wall. Then citizens began to make and to enclose gardens in the Moor; in 1498 these were all taken away and an archery-field made in their place. In 1512 more dykes were made for the drainage of the Moor, and in 1527 conduits were constructed to carry the waters over the Tower Ditch into the Walbrook. The point is that in the sixteenth century the whole of the ground lying between Moorgate and Bishopsgate was unoccupied by houses. The map already referred to shows the road running north from Moorgate, and the Moor itself crossed by causeways: in the east a broad ditch crossed by bridges falls into the Tower Ditch.

The Moor formerly extended beyond Cripplegate and as far as the Fleet River; it was built upon by the Religious Houses; St. Bartholomew's Priory and Hospital; the Charter House; the Priory of St. John; and the Nunnery of Clerkenwell. Between these houses and the wall were St. Giles's Church, St. Botolph's Church, Fore Street, Whitecross Street, and other streets, making a suburb with a population in the sixteenth century of 1800 householders, or 9000 souls. The last bit of the Moor left on the north-west of the City was brickfield.

We now come to the western suburb: the earliest settled and the most thickly populated of all. Fleet Street and the streets north of it, however, belonged to the Ward of Farringdon Without.

We are now in a position to show other reasons why the extension of the City was so slow and so limited.

All round the City lay manors and estates belonging for the most part to the Church. St. Paul's Cathedral possessed a great many of these manors; the Bishop possessed many; St. Peter's, Westminster, possessed many. Finsbury, Shoreditch, Hoxton, Iselden, St. Pancras, Willesden, belonged to St. Paul's. The manor of St. Peter stretched all the way from Millbank to the Fleet River, and from the Thames to Holborn. These estates belonged to the Church; when the City received the County of Middlesex to farm, it did not receive these manors, and the owners had their rights. Foremost among these rights was that they were outside the jurisdiction of the City; the land could not be built upon without permission of the owners; what the City got was the inclusion of that part of the land outside the Wall which was bounded and defined by the Bars: that is to say, it included, without the Wall—(1) The Ward of Portsoken, formerly the lands of the Cnihten Gild; (2) The Common Land of Whitechapel; (3) The Common Land of the Moor as far as to the Fleet River, and (4) The Ward of Farringdon Without. Why did it go no farther? Because at every point beyond these limits the manors of the Church were met. At first the encroachments of the City authorities into the manors met with no opposition; perhaps the ecclesiastics felt that it was well to have the people on their lands well governed; on one occasion the City acquired rights by taking a manor on lease, as that of Mora di Halliwell in 1315. In other cases the ecclesiastics interfered and made it impossible for more houses to be built on their lands, save on their own terms, and without acknowledgment by the City Authority.

For these reasons, therefore,—the limited jurisdiction of the City ; the steady opposition of the ecclesiastical owners of the manors outside ; and the slow growth of the population,—there was little increase save in the direction of Bishopsgate Street Without, where the City had a lease of the manor, until the Dissolution of the Religious Houses and the change of owners in the manors.

CHAPTER II

THE CITIZENS

THERE was never a time when the sober citizen was more sober, more responsible, more filled with a sense of his authority and dignity. "The man," says the wise king, "who is diligent in business shall stand before princes."

EARL OF SOMERSET AND HIS WIFE
From a print in the British Museum.

They did stand before princes, these merchants of London; as their prosperity leaped up increasingly year after year, they became the creditors, at least, of princes, for Elizabeth borrowed freely and repaid unwillingly—yet in spite of this too notorious weakness, she retained to the end the deepest affection of her people.

It has been a matter of reproach to the City that it seemed at this time wholly given over to trade and the interests of trade. To reproach a city which has always been a trading city with caring chiefly for the interests of trade seems somewhat unreasonable. But is it true that London has ever been wholly devoted to trade? I cannot find such a time in the whole long history of the City: certainly not in the reign of Elizabeth, when London cheerfully raised her men and her ships for the repulse of the Armada; and cheerfully gave the Queen whatever money she asked for; at the same time, while trade became larger than before, while the individual merchants became of more importance, the City certainly lost some of its political importance and was less dreaded, while it was more caressed, by the Sovereign.

It was, moreover, with the better class, a deeply religious age; men were not afraid or ashamed of proclaiming, or of showing, their religion. When Francis Drake saw the Atlantic on one side and the Pacific on the other, he fell on his knees in the sight of the company and prayed aloud, that God would suffer him to sail upon that unknown sea: if a cutpurse was hanged, he never failed to make a moving speech, deeply religious, while on the ladder. All classes preserved as yet the Catholic practice of going often to church; they studied the Bible; they made their 'prentices attend services; they listened patiently to sermons; doctrine was considered a vital point. By the end of the sixteenth century those who favoured the old Faith were either dead or silenced; to the common people the old Faith meant a return to the flames in Smithfield; torture at the hands of the Spanish Inquisition if any should haply fall into Spanish hands; and slavery under the Spanish King should he achieve the conquest of the country; whereas the new Faith meant freedom of thought, increased wealth, advancing trade, fighting the Spaniard and capturing the Spanish galleons. Religion, therefore, was allied with prosperity.

I have spoken of the sober guise of the London merchant. That sober guise belonged to the places where the merchant was mostly found: to the Royal Exchange, for instance, or Thames Street, beside the quays and warehouses. We must not think that there was no longer brightness of colour and even splendour in the streets. The rich liveries of the great nobles were chiefly seen on the river—remember that the front of the Palace faced the river, that the back belonged to the Strand, and that the river was London's principal highway. Their varlets lolled about on the river stairs or escorted their master in his barge, but hardly belonged to the City. A Court gallant was dressed as extravagantly as he could afford, or as his estate would bear. He carried manors on his back, broad acres in his velvet cloak, with golden buckles and lace trimming, a year's rents in his fantastic doublet slashed and puffed, in his silken hose, in his splendid sword, his scabbard and the handle set with gold, in his rings, his scents, his gloves and in his chains. But the Court gallant seldom showed on Thames Street.

In Norman and Plantagenet London there were no shops, nor was there anything sold in the streets except in the market-places, and the streets set aside for retail trade. But in the Tudor time Street Cries had already begun. We find, for instance, the following pleasant verses :—

> " Who liveth so merry in all this land
> As doth the poor widow that selleth the sand ?
> And ever shee singeth as I can guesse,
> Will you buy any sand, any sand, mistress ?
>
> The broom-man maketh his living most sweet,
> With carrying of broomes from street to street ;
> Who would desire a pleasanter thing,
> Than all the day long to doe nothing but sing ?
>
> The chimney-sweeper all the long day,
> He singeth and sweepeth the soote away ;
> Yet when he comes home altho' he be weary,
> With his sweet wife he maketh full merry.
>
> The cobbler he sits cobbling till none,
> And cobbleth his shoes till they be done ;
> Yet doth he not feare, and so doth say,
> For he knows his worke will soone decay.
>
> Who liveth so merry and maketh such sport
> As those that be of the poorest sort ?
> The poorest sort wheresoever they be,
> They gather together by one, two, and three.

> Broomes for old shoes ! pouch-rings, bootes and buskings !
> Will yee buy any new broomes ?
> New oysters ! new oysters ! new new cockels !
> Cockels nye ! fresh herrings ! Will yee buy any straw ?
> Hay yee any kitchen stuffe, maides ?
> Pippins fine, cherrie ripe, ripe, ripe !
> Cherrie ripe ! etc.

> Hay any wood to cleave ?
> Give eare to the clocke !
> Beware your locke !
> Your fire and your light !
> And God give you good night !
> One o'clocke ! "

Sumptuary laws were constantly renewed and continually broken. Yet the mass of the people obeyed the unwritten law by which a man's station was shown by his dress. For more on this subject see the Chapter on Dress.

The ordering of the household was strict. Early hours were kept ; in summer servants and apprentices were up at five ; in winter at six or seven ; there were rules as to attendance at morning and evening prayers ; there was to be no quarrelling ; no striking ; no profane language.

It is said that coaches were introduced in this reign ; but there had always been coaches, *i.e.* wheeled conveyances of a kind. Such a carriage, belonging to the fourteenth century, is figured in J. J. Jusserand's *English Wayfaring Life in the Middle Ages*—a cumbrous unwieldy thing, yet still a coach. What really happened in this century was the introduction of a much more convenient kind of coach from Holland.

Stow laments the mud and the splashing in the streets. "The coachman rideth behind the horse tails, lasheth them, and looketh not behind him; the drayman sitteth and sleepeth on his dray and letteth his horse lead him home."

SHOP AND SOLAR, CLARE MARKET, NOW DEMOLISHED
From a photograph taken in 1895.

Most of the City streets, however, were so narrow and so much obstructed by houses standing out, for as yet there was no alignment except in streets like Chepe, which were highways and market streets, that no wheeled vehicle could pass at all.

There was very little more lighting at night than there had been in the preceding centuries. If a London dame ventured out of the house after dark, the 'prentice carried a link before her. Some of the old shops or sheds with "solars" over them remained in Stow's time; the last of them stood in Clare Market, and was pulled down a few years ago. See the accompanying photograph of it. Stow says that stalls had become sheds, *i.e.* roofed stalls; and then shops, *i.e.* enclosed stalls; and then "fair houses." He instances a block of houses called Goldsmiths' Row, between Bread Street and the Cross, which contained ten dwelling-houses and fourteen shops, "all in one frame, uniformly built." They were four stories high. The shops seem to have been open, but perhaps the upper part was protected with a shutter or with glass.

Inland communication was conducted by means of carts and coaches. Harrison[1] complains of the new fashion: "Our Princes and the Nobilitie have their cariage commonlie made by carts, wherby it commeth to passe that when the Queene's Majestie dooth remove from anie one place to another, there are usuallie 400 carewanes, which amount to the summe of 2400 horses, appointed out of the counties adjoining, whereby hir cariage is conveied safelie unto the appointed place. Hereby also the ancient use of sumpter horses is in maner utterlie relinquished, which causeth the traines of our princes in their progresses to shew far lesse than those of the kings of other nations."

During this long reign, in spite of plague and pestilence, the population of London increased, and the suburbs extended, as we have seen, in all directions. The increase of population was due (1) to the increase of trade in London, which required a great accession of ship-builders, boat-builders, makers of the various gear required for ships, seamen, lightermen, porters, stevedores, and the like; (2) to the large number of immigrants from France and the Low Countries; and (3) to the number of persons released from the Religious Houses. That is to say, this last is generally represented as one of the causes. To me it seems as if the influence of these people on the population of London must be regarded as quite insignificant. There were some 8000 monks, nuns, and friars who were sent into the world. Many of those who were in priests' orders obtained places in parish churches, conforming by degrees to the changes of doctrine; the monks and nuns had pensions; many of the latter went abroad; of the friars many were absorbed in the general population; a certain number, one knows not how many, refused to work, and joined the company of rogues and masterless men, but there seems nothing to show how many of them settled in London.

Here is a simple calculation of the population in 1564. There was a great plague in that year. The total number of deaths in the City for the year is stated to have been 23,660, of whom 20,136 died of plague. This leaves 3524 deaths from ordinary causes. Now, if the average mortality of the City was twenty in the thousand, we should have a population of 176,200. If, which is more likely, the average mortality was twenty-five in the thousand the population was 140,960. In the time of King James, but after much devastation by the plague, the population of London was estimated at 130,000.

It has been said that there is no street in London in which one cannot find

---

[1] William Harrison, who wrote "The Description of England" for Holinshed's *Chronicles*.

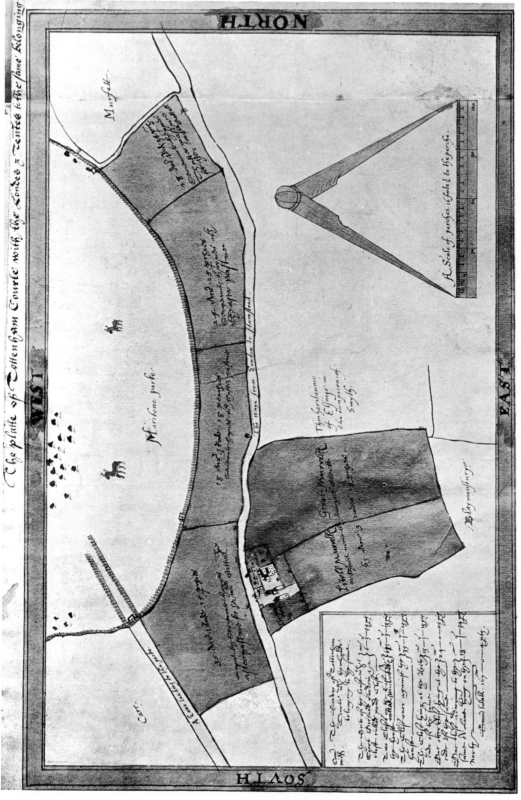

TOTTENHAM COURT

By the courtesy of the late Marquis of Salisbury.

For further particulars regarding this plan see Appendix XI.

a church and a tree. It is indeed remarkable to observe the large number of trees still existing and flourishing in the City of London, especially since the City churchyards have been converted into gardens. Of the old private gardens there are now left but few: one in St. Helen's Place; one behind the Rectory of St. Andrew's by the Wardrobe; the Drapers' Gardens, much curtailed; and the churchyards above mentioned, which have been converted into gardens. In the sixteenth century, however, London was still full of gardens, in the north part of the City much more than in the south. Every house had its garden behind; for the most part narrow, yet carefully cultivated and full of trees and flowers. If you take the part of London that has been least meddled with, the north-west corner of the City, for instance—that part bounded by London Wall on the North; by Monkwell and Noble Streets on the West; by Gresham Street on the South; and by Moorgate on the East—you will find that the blocks between the older streets are intersected everywhere by courts, alleys, narrow lanes and buildings. These were all, including the ancient churches, taken out of the gardens. Formerly, for instance, between Basinghall Street and Coleman Street there were very long gardens behind the houses; these have been used for lanes of connection, and for workmen's houses, such as Lilypot Lane and Oat Lane. Hidden away behind the houses is Sadler's Hall; here also, hidden away behind houses, is Haberdashers' Hall; here were the courtyards of inns, which formed among the gardens convenient ground for their great open courts and their stables. In this way the gardens of London gradually disappeared. In the sixteenth century, however, there were a great many still left: London presented an appearance of greenery and waving branches wherever one turned off the main roads. The chief authority on the gardens of the time is Harrison, who tells us what herbs, fruits, and roots were then grown, as well as the medicinal plants then so much cultivated.

Harrison [1] says, speaking of the flower gardens :—

"If you look into our gardens annexed to our houses, how wonderfullie is their beauty increased, not onelie with floures which Colmella calleth *Terrena sydera*, saying, 'Pingit et in varios terrestria sydera flores,' and varietie of curious and costlie workmanship, but also with rare and medicinable hearbes sought up in the land within these fortie yeares; so that in comparison of this present, the ancient gardens were but dunghills and laistowes to such as did possess them.

And even as it fareth with our gardens so dooth it with our orchards, which were never furnished with so good fruit, nor with such varietie as at this present. For beside that we have most delicate apples, plummes, peares, walnuts, filberds, etc., and those of sundrie sorts, planted within fortie yeares passed, in comparison of which most of the old trees are nothing woorth; so have we no less store of strange fruit, as abricotes, almonds, peaches, figges, corne-trees in noblemen's orchards. I have seen capers, orenges, and lemmons, and heard of wild olives growing here, beside other strange trees, brought from far, whose names I know not. So that England for these commodities was never better furnished, neither anie nation under their clime more plentifullie indued with these and other blessings from the most high God, who grant us grace withall to use the same to His honour and glorie! and not as instruments and provocations unto

---

[1] Holinshed's *Chronicles.*

further excesse and vanitie, wherewith His displeasure may be kindled, least these His benefits doo turne unto thornes and briers unto us for our annoiance and punishment which He hath bestowed upon us for our consolation and comfort."

The London garden was not only a place of recreation in the summer; it also furnished flowers for the pretty custom of decorating the rooms and strewing the floors; the gardens furnished pot herbs for the kitchen and sweet herbs for the walls and floors; branches also of fragrant woods, such as fir and pine, were hung up on the walls. I know not if this is a common custom still maintained in America; but in Hawthorne's house at Concord the rooms are still decorated and made fragrant with branches of pine such as the writer used in his lifetime. The floor of the great hall was strewn with rushes, brought chiefly from the upper reaches and low-lying grounds of the river. These rushes were of various kinds: some of them were grasses, such as that called mat-weed, of which beds were made as well as floors strewn.

The chief authorities on the London garden are Bacon in his *Essays*, and Gerard in his *Herbal*. Francis Bacon wrote his essays in Gray's Inn, whose garden he laid out and planted by request of the Benchers. His essay on the garden was written, as he says himself, for the climate of London.

"And because the breath of flowers is far sweeter in the air (where it comes and goes like the warbling of music) than in the hand, therefore nothing is more fit for that delight than to know what be the flowers and plants that do best perfume the air. Roses, damask and red, are fast flowers of their smells, so that you may walk by a whole row of them, and find nothing of their sweetness, yea, though it be in a morning's dew. Bays likewise yield no smell as they grow, rosemary little, nor sweet marjoram. That which above all others yields the sweetest smell in the air is the violet, especially the white double violet, which comes twice a year, about the middle of April and about Bartholomew-tide. Next to that is the musk-rose; then the strawberry leaves dying, which yield a most excellent cordial smell. Then the flower of the vines; it is a little dust like the dust of a bent, which grows upon the cluster in the first coming forth. Then sweetbriar, then wall-flowers, which are very delightful to be set under a parlour or lower chamber window. Then pinks and gilliflowers, especially the matted pink and clove gilliflowers. Then the flowers of the lime-tree. Then the honeysuckles, so they be somewhat afar off; of bean-flowers I speak not, because they are field-flowers. But those which perfume the air most delightfully, not passed by as the rest, but being trodden upon and crushed, are three—that is, burnet, wild thyme, and water-mints. Therefore you are to set whole alleys of them, to have the pleasure when you walk or tread."

In Ordish's *Shakespeare's London* will be found an excellent analysis of Gerard's *Herbal* as it deals with the gardens of the City and its suburbs. In it also is an enumeration of the principal gardens of the time, especially those of the Inns of Court. To these may be added the gardens belonging to those of the City Companies whose Halls were in the north part of the City, and those not yet built over which had once formed part of the monastic precincts, not to speak of the private gardens which were in many cases—such as the house of Sir Thomas Gresham in Broad Street—large and spacious. (*See* Appendix VII.)

The allusions to London and to City customs in Shakespeare are numerous, but not, as a rule, instructive. That is to say, he speaks of streets and places which we know from other sources. The Tower, the Bridge, Smithfield, Fish Street, St. Magnus Corner, the Savoy, the Tower Royal (King Richard's Palace), Westminster Hall, Eastcheap, Bankside, the Temple, Cheapside, London Stone, Baynard's Castle, Blackfriars, Paris Garden, are mentioned with the familiarity of one who lived in the City and knew all the streets intimately. It is pleasant to find them playing their parts in the immortal plays, but, as I said above, they teach us nothing.

In 1568, to escape the cruelties of Alva, a vast number of Flemings came across the sea and were received hospitably. In order to prevent their arrival proving an injury to the crafts of London, they were scattered about, finding homes in Norwich, Colchester, Maidstone, Sandwich, and Southampton, as well as in London. In the next generation they appear to have been completely merged in the English population, and the custom, common among persons of foreign descent, of anglicising their names has made it very difficult to discover the Flemish origin of a family. The earlier Flemish settlers in England were regarded with hatred. It would seem that another colony of Flemings came over before this immigration in the year 1568; they were settled in Suffolk. In 1594 a good many Portuguese came over as retainers to Don Antonio, and settled here. Among them was the Balthazar who became confectioner to King James and founded almshouses at Tottenham. There were Italians, probably connected with the Italian trade, for the " Lombardi," the Pope's men, were gone; they had a service at the Mercers' Chapel every Sunday. There were also a great many " Dutch," among whom were numbered the Flemings. Thus, in 1567, a census was taken of " foreigners " in London. There were found to be 4851 altogether, of whom 3838 were Dutch, and 720 French. A few years later the French Ambassador reports that there were 13,700 strangers in London, of whom a third were going to be turned out.

Of the hatred and suspicion entertained towards foreigners by Londoners we have many proofs. " They scoff and laugh at foreigners," says the Duke of Wurtemberg, " and, moreover, one dares not oppose them, else the street boys and apprentices collect together in immense crowds and strike to the right and left unmercifully without regard to person." Isaac Casaubon in James the First's reign complained that he had never been so badly treated as by the people of London: they threw stones at his windows; they pelted his children and himself with stones. The Venetian Ambassador of 1497 testifies to the same effect; in 1557 his successor says that it is impossible to live in London on account of the insolence with which foreigners are treated.

At the same time it must be remembered that there were quarters assigned to foreigners, and that the people must have been accustomed to see these residents

going about the streets.   Perhaps they were only insolent to foreign nobles, and
those whose dress and language were not familiar to them.   The Hanse merchants
had their house beside Dowgate, Petty Almaigne; the Flemings had theirs on the
east side of the Bridge, Petty Flanders: the French had a place in Bishopsgate

W. Knight delt.   *Jt Basire sculp.*

INTERIOR VIEW OF QUEEN ELIZABETH'S BATH
From *Archæologia*.

Ward called Petty France.   It was in Petty Flanders that certain Jews resided
under the guise of Flemings, just as in the fourteenth century they passed
themselves off as Lombards.   The Flemings built the Exchange: it was designed
after the Antwerp Bourse, by a Fleming; the workmen were specially brought
over, and appear to have been unmolested.

In February 1831 there was swept away, with all the buildings in the place called the King's Mews, where Trafalgar Square now is, a small building called Queen Elizabeth's Bath. It was a square building of fine brick. It was certainly a Bath, and had a groined roof ascribed by Mr. William Knight who sketched it to the fifteenth century. It was an interesting building of which nothing seems known. Nobody has noticed it except a writer in *Archæologia* (vol. xxv.), who gives a plan and drawing of the curious place. Like the Sanctuary at Westminster it would have been entirely forgotten but for the hand of a single antiquary, who rescued it from oblivion at the last moment.

GOVERNMENT AND TRADE OF THE CITY

CHAPTER I

THE MAYOR

IN the year 1500 a change of some importance was effected by Sir John Shaw,

MAYOR AND ALDERMEN OF THE PERIOD
From an MS. in British Museum.

Mayor of that year. Before his time the civic feasts had been held at the Hall
of the Grocers or the Taylors. Sir John Shaw built kitchens and offices at the

Guildhall and began the custom of holding the Lord Mayor's feast in that place.

The election of Sheriffs was formerly conducted by the citizens, who, by the Charter of King Henry IV., could appoint Sheriffs from their own body "according to the tenor of the Charters granted by the King's progenitors and not in any other way" (*Liber Albus*, p. 148), and in the first book of the same work the manner of the election of the Sheriff is described in greater detail (*Liber Albus*, 1861 edition, p. 39) :—

"As concerning the election of Sheriffs,—the Mayor, Recorder, Aldermen, and Commons, are to be assembled on the day of Saint Matthew the Apostle [21 September], in such manner as is ordained on the election of the Mayor; and in the first place, the Mayor shall choose, of his own free will, a reputable man, free of the City, to be one of the Sheriffs for the ensuing year; for whom he is willing to answer as to one half of the ferm [1] of the City due to the King, if he who is so elected by the Mayor shall prove not sufficient. But if the Mayor elect him by counsel and with the assent of the Aldermen, they also ought to be answerable with him. And those who are elected for the Common Council, themselves, and the others summoned by the Mayor for this purpose, as before declared, shall choose another Sheriff, for the commonalty; for whom all the commonalty is bound to be answerable as to the other half of the ferm so due to the King, in case he shall prove not sufficient."

The custom is illustrated by the following story concerning the election of William Massam as Sheriff by Sir Edward Osborne, the Mayor :—

"In this year, one day in the month of July, there were two great feasts at London, one at Grocers' Hall, another at Haberdashers' Hall (as perhaps there was in all the rest upon some public occasion). Sir Edward Osborne, Mayor, and divers of his brethren the Aldermen, with the Recorder, were at Haberdashers' Hall, where the said Mayor, after the second course was come in, toke the great standing cup, the gift of Sir William Garret, being full of hypocrase; and silence being commanded through all the tables, all men being bare-headed, my Lord openly with a convenient loud voice, used these words :—'Mr. Recorder of London, and you my good brethren the Aldermen, bear witness, that I do drink unto Mr. Alderman Massam, as Sheriff of London and Middlesex, from Michaelmas next coming, for one whole year; and I do beseech God to give him as quiet and peaceable a year, with as good and gracious favour of her Majesty, as I myself, and my brethren the Sheriffs now being, have hitherto had, and as I trust shall have.' This spoken, all men desired the same.

The Sword-bearer in haste went to the Grocers' feast, where Mr. Alderman Massam was at dinner, and did openly declare the words that my Lord Mayor had

[1] Or fee-farm rent.

used; whereunto silence made, and all being hush, the Alderman answered very modestly in this sort :—

'First, I thank God, who, through His great goodness, hath called me from a very poor and mean degree unto this worshipful state. Secondly, I thank her Majesty for her gracious goodness in allowing to us these great and ample franchises. And, thirdly, I thank my Lord Mayor for having so honourable an opinion of this my Company of Grocers, so as to make choice of me, being a poor Member of the same.' And this said, both he and all the Company pledged my Lord, and gave him thanks."

The Lord Mayor's Show in the sixteenth century, conducted partly on horseback, and partly by water, was a far finer pageant than any that our generation has been enabled to witness. The following is a contemporary account :—

"The day of St. Simon and Jude, he (the Mayor) entrethe into his estate and offyce; and the next daie following he goeth by water to Westmynster in most tryumphlyke maner. His barge beinge garnished with the armes of the citie; and nere the sayd barge goeth a shyppbote of the Queenes Majestie, beinge trymed upp, and rigged lyke a shippe of warre, with dyvers peces of ordinance, standards, penons, and targetts of the proper armes of the sayd Mayor, the armes of the Citie, of his company; and of the merchaunts adventurers, or of the staple, or of the company of the newe trades; next before hym goeth the barge of the lyvery of his owne company, decked with their owne proper armes, then the bachelers' barge, and soo all the companies in London, in order, every one havinge their owne proper barge garnished with the armes of their company. And so passinge alonge the Thamise, landeth at Westmynster, where he taketh his othe in Thexcheker, beffore the judge there (whiche is one of the chiefe judges of England), whiche done, he returneth by water as afforsayd, and landeth at powles wharfe, where he and the reste of the Aldermen take their horses, and in great pompe passe through the greate streete of the citie, called Cheapside. And fyrste of all cometh ij great estandarts, one havinge the armes of the citie, and the other the armes of the Mayor's Company; next them ij drommes and a flute, then an ensigne of the citie, and then about IXX or IXXX poore men marchinge ij and two togeather in blewe gownes, with redd sleeves and capps, every one bearinge a pyke and a target, whereon is paynted the armes of all them that have byn Mayor of the same company that this newe mayor is of. Then ij banners, one of the kynges armes, the other of the Mayor's owne proper armes. Then a sett of hautboits playinge, and after them certayne wyfflers, in velvett cotes, and chaynes of golde, with white staves in their handes, then the pageant of tryumphe rychly decked, whereuppon by certayne fygures and wrytinges, some matter touchinge justice, and the office of a maiestrate is represented. Then xvj trompeters, viij and viij in a company, havinge banners of the Mayor's company. Then certayne wyfflers in velvet cotes and chaynes, with white staves as afordsayde. Then the bachelers ij and two together, in longe gownen, with crymson hoodes on their shoulders of sattyn ; which bachelers are chosen every yeare of the same company that the Mayor is of (but not of the lyvery) and serve as gentlemen on that and other festivall daies, to wayte on the Mayor, beinge in nomber accordinge to the quantetie of the company, sometimes sixty or one hundred. After them xij trompeters more, with banners of the Mayor's company, then the dromme and flute of the citie, and an ensigne of the Mayor's company, and after, the waytes of the citie in blewe gownes, redd sleeves and cappes, every one havinge his silver coller about his neck. Then they of the liverey in their longe gownes, every one havinge his hood on his lefte shoulder, halfe black and halfe redd, the nomber of them is accordinge to the greatnes of the companye whereof they are. After them followe Sheriffes officers, and then the Mayor's officers, with other officers of the citie, as the comon sargent, and the chamberlayne ; next before the Mayore goeth the sword-bearer, having on his headd the cappe of honor, and the sworde of the citie in his right hande, in a riche skabarde, sett with pearle, and on his left hand goeth the comon cryer of the citie, with his great mace on his shoulder, all gilt. The Mayor elect in a long gowne of skarlet, and on his lefte shoulder a hood of black velvet, and a riche coller of gold of SS. about his neck, and with him rydeth the olde Mayor also, in his skarlet gowne, hood of velvet, and a chayne of golde about his neck. Then all the Aldermen ij and ij together (amongst whom is the Recorder) all in skarlet gownes ; and those that have byn Mayors, have chaynes of gold, the other have black velvett tippetts. The ij Shereffes come last of all, in their black skarlet fownes and chaynes of golde.

In this order they passe alonge through the citie, to the Guyldhall, where they dyne that daie, to the number of 1000 persons, all at the charge of the Mayor and the ij Shereffes. This feast costeth £400, whereof the Mayor payeth £200 and eche of the Shereffes £100. Immediately after dyner, they go to the churche of St. Paule, every one of the aforesaid poore men bearrynge staffe torches and targetts, whiche torches are lighted when it is late, before they come from evenynge prayer." (Drake, *Shakespeare and his Times*, vol. ii. p. 164.)

The very pretty story of Edward Osborne and the rescue of his master's daughter is narrated by Maitland as belonging to the year 1559, but the date does not matter.

Sir William Hewitt, citizen and clothworker, Mayor in 1559, lived on London Bridge. He was himself the son of a country gentleman of Yorkshire ; he had for apprentice one Edward Osborne, also son of a country gentleman, Richard Osborne, of Ashford, Kent. Hewitt had three sons and one daughter. It happened one day, the child being yet an infant, that the maid playing with her at the open window let her fall out of the window into the river below. The 'prentice Osborne,

LONDON BRIDGE

From Visscher's *Panorama of London.*

fortunately seeing the accident, boldly jumped into the river and saved the child. Years after, when the child was grown up, Hewitt, one of the richest of London merchants, refused to give her in marriage to the Earl of Shrewsbury and other noble suitors, but gave her to the man who had saved her life. Sir Edward Osborne, as he afterwards became, Mayor in 1583, was the ancestor of the Dukes of Leeds.

Until recently it was customary for the Lord Mayor to go on Sundays in state to one or other of the City churches.

On these occasions the Lord Mayor was accompanied by the sheriffs and officials of the Corporation, and escorted by the mace-bearer and sword-bearer, the latter wearing the cap of maintenance, and carrying the state sword. It was usual for the Alderman of the Ward to be present with any other alderman that pleased to come, and as many as came brought with them their ward beadles, carrying the ward maces.

Towards the latter part of the sixteenth century the practice of carrying the sword into church before the Lord Mayor became customary. It is not clear when this practice first began, but after the Fire of London and the rebuilding of the City it became the universal custom, and so continued until a comparatively recent period, when the exodus of the citizens made it not only inconvenient but an absolute tax upon the officers of the Corporation if the Lord Mayor attended church in state with his sword borne before him.

But for the time that it lasted, that is rather more than two centuries, it necessitated the introduction into the City churches of a convenient stand or case upon which the City sword was placed. The State visits of the Lord Mayor having been discontinued in the mayoralty of Sir Robert Fowler, the consequence is that the sword-stands have ceased to have any use. Those stands which had artistic merit will no doubt be preserved.

It may be taken as certain that these sword-cases or stands were not in use before the reign of Queen Elizabeth. There were many schedules of ecclesiastical furniture in existence prior to that date, but in none of them is there any mention of such an article as a sword-case, or sheath, or stand, although the list of articles is most minute. The earliest mention is in the Account Books of St. Michael's, Cornhill, published by Mr. Alfred I. Waterlow.

Under date 1574, that is, in the sixteenth year of Queen Elizabeth's reign, there is the following entry:—

"Paid for guylding of the case for my Lord Mayor's swearde . . . 9s."

Hawes was a resident in the parish, and was Lord Mayor in the year 1574-1575. He had had a new pew made for him just outside the chancel screen a year or two before, on his being appointed Alderman of Cornhill Ward, and the pew was further fitted with a gilded sword-case on his being made Lord Mayor.

The worthy Machyn has a note on a Civic hunting which reads pleasantly :—

"The xviij day of September my lord mare and my masters the althermen and mony worshephull men, and dyvers of the masturs and wardens of the xij compenys, rod to the condutt hedes for to se them, after the old coustum ; and a fore dener they hundyd and hare and kyllyd, and so to dener to the hed of the condyth, for ther was a nombur, and had good chere of the chamburlayn ; and after dener to hontyng of the fox, and ther was a goodly cry for a mylle, and after the hondys kyllyd the fox at the end of sant Gylles and theyr was a grett cry at the deth, and blohyng of hornes ; and so rod thrugh London, my lord mare Harper with all ys compene home to ys owne plase in Lumberd Street."

CHAPTER II

TRADE

THE Tudor period begins with the lowest point reached in town and country of a decline and decay that had been steadily persistent for nearly two hundred years. The prosperity of a trading city depends upon the prosperity of its

SOUTH VIEW OF THE CUSTOM-HOUSE IN THE REIGN OF ELIZABETH. BURNT IN THE GREAT FIRE, 1666
E. Gardner's Collection.

markets. There were many causes for this decay. The famines, of which there were four, in the fourteenth and fifteenth centuries; the Hundred Years' War; the Civil Wars; the weakness of the fleet and the piracies in the Channel; the growth of the power of Parliament and the consequent decay of local independence; the feeble government of Edward II. and Henry VI.; the fearful devastation of the Black Death; the changes in the manorial system;—all these things together contributed to the decay of trade over the whole country. To quote a writer on the fifteenth century. Denton, in his *England in the Fifteenth Century*, says that the decay of England commenced soon after the death of Edward I. It continued, showing an increased rate of decay, after the death of Edward II.

The country parishes everywhere, on the northern and the Welsh march, on the southern seaboard, and in the Eastern Counties, had to be exempted from payment of taxes on account of poverty; lands were untilled; there was loss of sheep and cattle; agriculture was at a standstill for fear of pirates. Or the country parishes were actually deserted: the people, ruined, had left the farms and the clearings; the churches were allowed to fall into ruin; Monastic Houses were desolate and empty because the Brethren had no longer any rents.

In the towns there were open spaces within the walls where houses had once stood. One has only to visit King's Lynn in Winchelsea for an example of this decay.

Even in London, it has been observed, for more than a hundred years after the Rebellion of Jack Straw there stood in Fleet Street the blackened ruins of two forges which that rebel's followers had burned. In all that time there was not found any who thought it worth while to rebuild the forge.

In London during the fourteenth and fifteenth centuries, although the time was one of commercial decline, there were still rich merchants. It is in a time of decay that the merchants make complaints of aliens; that they clamour for protection; that they demand the import and the export of merchandise in English ships; that they would prohibit the sending of gold and silver out of the country; let the foreign merchants be paid in kind.

The melancholy condition of the country at the beginning of the sixteenth century is described most vividly by Cunningham :—

"There is less mention made of decay in the first thirty years of the sixteenth century; but the facts were again brought forcibly forward when the Parliament of Henry VIII. began to put pressure on the owners of houses to repair their property and to remove the rubbish that endangered life in the towns. Norwich had never recovered from the fire of 1508; the empty spaces at Lynn Bishop allowed the sea to do damage in other parts of the town. Many houses were ruined and the streets were dangerous for traffic in Nottingham, Shrewsbury, Ludlow, Bridgenorth, Queenborough, Northampton and Gloucester; there were vacant spaces heaped with filth, and tottering houses in York, Lincoln, Canterbury, Coventry, Bath, Chichester, Salisbury, Winchester, Bristol, Scarborough, Hereford, Colchester, Rochester, Portsmouth, Poole, Lyme, Feversham, Worcester, Stafford, Buckingham, Pontefract, Grantham, Exeter, Ipswich, Southampton, Great Yarmouth, Oxford, Great Wycombe, Guildford, Stratford, Hull, Newcastle, Bedford,

Leicester and Berwick; as well as in Shaston, Sherborne, Bridport, Dorchester, Weymouth, Plymouth, Barnstaple, Tavistock, Dartmouth, Launceston, Lostwithiel, Liskeard, Bodmin, Truro, Helston, Bridgewater, Taunton, Somerton, Ilchester, Maldon and Warwick. There were similar dangers to the inhabitants of Great Grimsby, Cambridge, the Cinque Ports, Lewes; and even in the more remote provinces things were as bad, for Chester, Tenby, Haverfordwest, Pembroke, Caermarthen, Montgomery, Cardiff, Swansea, Cowbridge, New Radnor, Presteign, Brecknock, Abergavenny, Usk, Caerlon, Newport in Monmouthshire, Lancaster, Preston, Liverpool and Wigan, were taken in hand in 1544. In trying to interpret this evidence, however, we must remember that we are reading of attempts to repair, not of complaints of new decline; the mere fact that such attempts were made was perhaps an indication that things had reached their worst; and we are perhaps justified in inferring from the double mention of some few towns that a real improvement was effected in the others." (*The Growth of English Industry.*)

There is thus abundant evidence concerning the decay of trade. Cunningham speaks of the decay of the craft gilds and their mismanagement. This may be considered a part of the general decay and a consequence. At first, the craft gilds exercised police control over their members and so secured good order; the old authority and power of the alderman in his ward had been practically taken over by the gilds; each master had his apprentices living with him and forming part of his own household. Yet the apprentices made the riot in 1517 long remembered as Evil May Day. Another of their objects was the production of honest and good work. Yet in 1437 and again in 1503 it was enacted that no ruler of gilds or fraternities should make any ordinances which were not approved by the Chancellor of the Justices of Assize. The third object was the securing of fair conditions for those who worked in the trade. Yet consider the grievances of the journeymen in 1536 :—

"Previous Acts relating to craft abuses are recited and the statute proceeds: 'Sithen which several acts established and made, divers masters, wardens and fellowships of crafts, have by cautel and subtle means practised and compassed to defraud and delude the said good and wholesome statutes, causing divers apprentices or young men immediately after their years be expired, or that they be made free of their occupation or fellowship, to be sworn upon their holy Evangelist at their first entry, that they nor any of them after their years or term expired shall not set up, nor open any shop, house, nor cellar, nor occupy as freeman without the assent and license of the master, wardens or fellowship of their occupations, upon pain of forfeiting their freedom or other like penalty; by reason whereof the said 'prentices and journeymen be put to as much or more charges thereby than they beforetime were put unto for the obtaining and

1. The Palace of Westminster.	8. St. Margaret's Church.	15. Whitehall.	22. St. Giles's Church.	29. St.
2. St. Stephen's Chapel.	9. The King's Stairs.	16. Holbein's Gate.	23. Convent Garden.	30. St.
3. Westminster Hall.	10. Star Chamber.	17. Scotland Yard.	24. The Strand.	31. Linc
4. Westminster Abbey.	11. Lambeth Palace.	8. Charing Cross.	25. York House.	32. Linc
5. Old Palace Yard.	12. Stangate Horse Ferry.	19. King's Mews.	26. Durham House.	33. Gra
6. The Clock Tower.	13. St. James's Hospital.	20. St. Martin's Church.	27. Savoy Palace.	34. Ely
7. The Gate House.	14. St. James's.	21. St. Mary's Hospital.	28. Somerset Place.	35. Fett

From the Panorama of "London, Westminster, and Southwark, in 1543." By Anthony Van

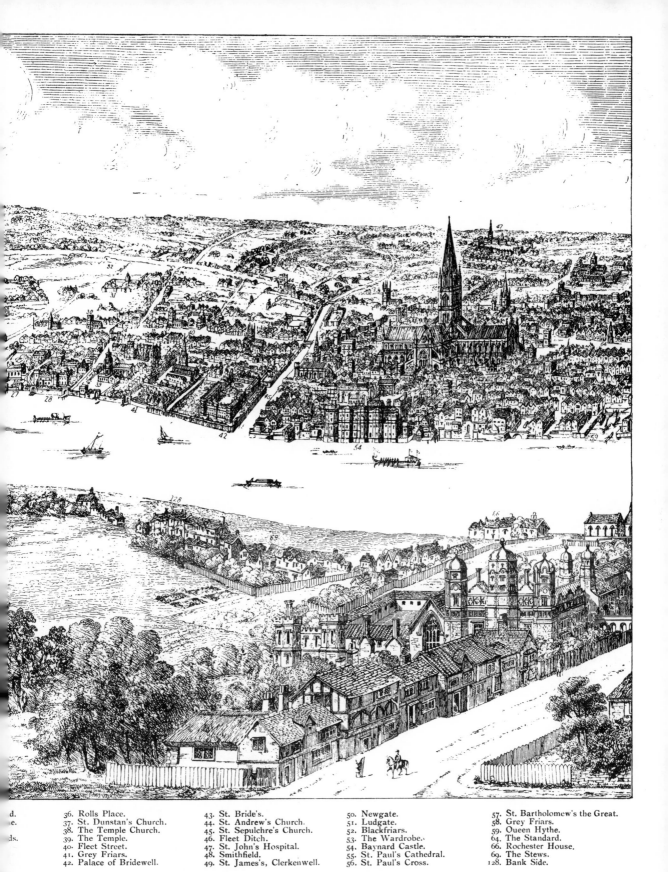

d.	36. Rolls Place.	43. St. Bride's.	50. Newgate.	57. St. Bartholomew's the Great.
e.	37. St. Dunstan's Church.	44. St. Andrew's Church.	51. Ludgate.	58. Grey Friars.
	38. The Temple Church.	45. St. Sepulchre's Church.	52. Blackfriars.	59. Queen Hythe.
ds.	39. The Temple.	46. Fleet Ditch.	53. The Wardrobe.	64. The Standard.
	40. Fleet Street.	47. St. John's Hospital.	54. Baynard Castle.	66. Rochester House.
	41. Grey Friars.	48. Smithfield.	55. St. Paul's Cathedral.	69. The Stews.
	42. Palace of Bridewell.	49. St. James's, Clerkenwell.	56. St. Paul's Cross.	128. Bank Side.

erde. (Sutherland Collection, Bodleian Library, Oxford.) *For continuation see pp.* 234 *and* 350.

entering of their freedom, to the great hurt and impoverishment of the said
'prentices and journeymen and other their friends.' Such restrictions naturally
resulted in the withdrawal of the journeymen to set up shops in suburbs or
villages where the gild had no jurisdiction; and from this they were not
precluded, in all probability, by the terms of their oath. This might often be
their only chance of getting employment, as the masters were apparently inclined
to overstock their shops with apprentices, rather than be at the expense of
retaining a full proportion of journeymen." (*The Growth of English Industry.*)

In 1545 Henry VIII. ordained the confiscation of the property of all colleges,
fraternities, brotherhoods and gilds. This measure, sweeping in its terms, was not
generally carried out. In 1547 the advisers of Edward VI. swept away all the
craft gilds in England except the Companies of London and a few gilds in
country towns. The statute provided that artisans might work where they pleased
whether they were free of the town or not.

Trade, therefore, had entered upon new conditions; this was inevitable, owing
to the many changes—the revolutionary changes which created so wide a gulf
between the fifteenth and the sixteenth centuries.

With these preliminaries we can now proceed to the revival and expansion
of trade and the development of enterprise in the sixteenth century, but more
especially during the reign of Queen Elizabeth.

The endowment of the City with a Bourse is generally attributed to the percep-
tion by Sir Thomas Gresham of the need for such a place of meeting,[1] though the
matter had been mooted and the opinion of merchants taken thirty years before.

In the year 1537, Sir Richard Gresham, the father of Sir Thomas Gresham,
whose business had taken him to Antwerp, when he saw the Bourse frequented
daily by merchants, wrote a letter to Cromwell in which he suggested the erection
of a Bourse in Lombard Street, as the place most frequented by merchants. As
nothing came of the proposal he wrote again in the following year with an
estimate of the cost, viz. £2000. If, he said, the Lord Privy Seal would induce
Alderman Sir George Monoux to part with certain property at cost price he,
Gresham, would undertake to raise £1000 towards the building before he went
out of office. Whereupon the King addressed a letter to Monoux desiring him
to dispose of certain property in Lombard Street, which was wanted for the
commonweal of the merchants. Monoux, with Gresham's consent, referred the
matter to arbitration. A yearly sum of twenty marks to be paid by the City
was offered. Monoux at first refused to take it, but afterwards, at the King's
request, consented. Then, for some unknown reason, nothing more was done.
The matter was left over for many years.

---

[1] Many of these details were published for the first time in Sharpe's *London and the Kingdom*, i. 494
et seq.

At this time Thomas Gresham (son of Sir Richard by his first wife, Audrey, daughter of William Lynne of Southwick, Northampton) was nineteen years of age, and still serving his apprenticeship to his uncle, Sir John Gresham, Mercer. He was received into the Company in 1543. In the same year he was acting for the King at Antwerp. In 1551 he was appointed Royal Agent or King's merchant, which caused him to reside at Antwerp during many months, and at frequent intervals. On the accession of Mary he was dismissed, but his services were speedily discovered to be necessary, and he was reappointed. Elizabeth continued his appointment.

In 1561 his factor, Richard Clough, wrote to him from Antwerp expressing his astonishment that London should have gone on so long without a Bourse :—

"Considering what a City London is; and that in so many years the same found not the means to make a Burse, but merchants must be contented to stand and walk in the rain, more like pedlars than Merchants. In this Country, said he (meaning Antwerp), and in all other, there is no kind of people that have occasion to meet but ye have a place for that purpose; indeed and if your business were done (here) and that I might have the leisure to go about it, and that I would be a means to Mr. Secretary to have his favour therein, I would not doubt but to make so fair a burse in London as the great burse is in Antwerp, without soliciting of any Man more than he shall be well disposed to give."

Gresham remembered the attempt made by his father in 1538 and its failure; he resolved to take up the matter again, and in some way introduced it to the Court of Aldermen, who asked him, through one of their body, what he proposed to give himself towards the undertaking. This was in 1563, two years after Clough wrote his letter. Gresham took time to consider. In 1565 he sent in the offer. He would himself erect a "comely burse" if the City would provide a suitable site.

The site was found on the north side of Cornhill. Two alleys, Swan Alley and New St. Christopher's, were purchased for £3532 : the materials of the houses sold for £478. Subscriptions were invited and came in readily. On the 7th of June 1566 Sir Thomas was able to lay the foundation stone. Every one of the aldermen laid his stone or brick, with a piece of gold for the workmen.

The architect and the design came from Flanders. The Clerk of the Work, Henryk, was a Fleming, and most of the workmen were foreigners, special permission being granted for their employment. The City gave 100,000 bricks; the stone-work came from abroad, and "to this day" (Sharpe) "the Royal Exchange is paved with small blocks of Turkish hone-stones, believed to have been imported by Sir Thomas Gresham and to have been relaid after the fires of 1666 and 1838."

Observe, therefore, that to the City belonged the site, but that the Exchange itself was the property of Gresham.

By the 22nd of December 1568 the Burse was so far complete as to allow of merchants meeting within its walls; but it was not till the 23rd of January 1571 that the Queen herself visited it in state, and gave it the name of the Royal Exchange. From the beginning a part of the Exchange was set aside for Marine Insurance, not a new thing, because it had long been the practice of the Lombard merchants in the thirteenth century to give such insurances.

The Royal Exchange became a place of recreation as well as of business. The citizens walked here on the evenings of Sundays and Holy days, where the City waits played from 7 P.M. till 8 P.M. up to the Feast of Pentecost, then they played from 8 P.M. till 9 P.M. until Michaelmas. In 1576 it was ordered that no games of football should be played within the Royal Exchange.

SIR THOMAS GRESHAM (1519(?)-1579)

The Exchange remained the property of Sir Thomas Gresham until his death, when he bequeathed the building together with his mansion in Broad Street, after the death of his wife, on certain conditions, to the City and the Mercers' Company in trust, viz. :—

"The Citizens, for their Moiety of the said Edifice, are from Time to Time to appoint four Persons duly qualified to read Lectures of Divinity, Astronomy, Musick, and Geometry, in his Mansion-house [afterwards Gresham College], and to pay annually to each of the said Lecturers a Salary or Stipend of fifty Pounds. And also to pay yearly to his eight Alms-People in *Broad-Street* (whom the Mayor and Citizens have likewise the Power of chusing) the sum of six Pounds thirteen Shillings and four Pence each. And besides, to pay annually to the Prisons of *Newgate, Ludgate, King's-Bench, Marshalsey,* and *Wood-Street Compter,* the Sum of ten Pounds each.

And the Mercers, for their Half, are, from Time to Time, to chuse three persons well accomplished, to read Lectures of Law, Physick, and Rhetorick, in the aforesaid Mansion-House called *Gresham-College,* with the same salaries to each of the Lecturers as to the above-mentioned. The said Company of Mercers are likewise obliged to pay the sum of one hundred Pounds per Ann. for four quarterly Dinners to be provided at their Hall, for the Entertainment of the whole Company; and also to pay to *Christ's, St. Bartholomew's,* the *Spital, Bethlehem,* and *St. Thomas's* Hospitals, and the *Poultry Compter,* the Sum of ten Pounds per Ann. each." (Maitland, vol. i. pp. 256-257.)

The reversion fell in on the death of Lady Gresham in 1596, when the City and the Company took steps to carry out the Trust. Gresham House became Gresham College, and so continued until the year 1767, when the Crown took over the building for an Excise office, giving the City £500 a year perpetual annuity. For some time the lectures ceased; when they were renewed they were delivered in the City of London School until the building of the present Gresham College in Basinghall Street.

We have become accustomed to consider the enterprise and restless spirit of adventure which makes the sixteenth and seventeenth centuries so full of interest, as finding their sole field in the New World and in voyages such as those of Drake and Cavendish; and in heroes such as Frobisher, Gilbert, and Raleigh. We forget the expeditions of Willoughby and Burroughs to find a north-east passage; the courage of Chancellor, who opened up trade with Russia; the travels of Jenkinson, who first crossed Russia and sailed over the Caspian Sea; the brave Captains of the Levant Company, who fought their way through the Barbary corsairs and the galleys of Spain; those faithful servants of the same Company, Newbery, Fitch, and Leedes, who discovered the long-forgotten overland route to India; the voyages of the first ships of the East India Company in seas unknown, among a people strange and suspicious; the persistent attempts to open up the African trade; we have forgotten—if we ever learned—how, all over the world, along the shores of the Baltic, in Arctic seas, round the Cape of Good Hope, in the Far East, in North-West America and in the West Indies, the sails of England carried the gallant adventurers whose very numbers make their names difficult to be remembered; across the unknown plains of Russia, across the Great Syrian desert, unvisited by Christians since the days of Bohemond and Baldwin, down the Great River, even the river Euphrates; in the Courts of the Great Mogul, in Malay land, among the Red Indians of North America,—everywhere, visible to all, were found the men of the Western Queen, as great a name to the Czar of Muscovy as to Philip of Spain.

Christs Hospital.

In Hakluyt may be found written by Anthony Jenkinson, one of the most determined and most daring of the trading travellers of this time, a list of the countries which he had visited in six years. It is as follows :—

"The names of such countries as I Anthony Jenkinson have travelled unto, from the second of October 1546, at which time I made my first voyage out of England, untill the yeere of our Lord 1572, when I returned last out of Russia.

First, I passed into Flanders, and travelled through all the base countries, and from thence from Germanie, passing over the Alpes I travelled into Italy, and from thence made my journey through Piemont into France, throughout all which realme I have thoroughly journied.

I have also travelled through the kingdomes of Spaine and Portingal, I have sailed through the Levant seas every way, and have bene in all the chiefe Islands within the same sea, as Rhodes, Malta, Sicilia, Cyprus, Candie, and divers others.

I have bene in many partes of Grecia, Morea, Achaia, and where the olde citie of Corinth stoode.

I have travelled through a great part of Turkie, Syria, and divers other countries in Asia minor.

I have passed over the mountaines of Libanus to Damasco, and travelled through Samaria, Galile, Philistine or Palestine, unto Jerusalem and so through all the Holy land.

I have been in divers places of Affrica, as Algiers, Col, Bon, Tripolis, the gollet within the Gulf of Tunis.

I have sailed farre Northward within the Mare glaciale, where we have had continuall day; and sight of the Sunne ten weekes together, and that navigation was in Norway, Lapland, Samogitia; and other very strange places.

I have travelled through all the ample dominions of the Emperour of Russia and Moscovis, which extende from the North sea, and the confines of Norway and Lapland, even to the Mare Caspium.

I have bene in divers countries neere about the Caspian sea, Gentiles, and Mahometans, as Cazan, Cremia, Rezan, Cheremisi, Mordouiti, Vachin, Nagaia, with divers others of strange customs and religions.

I have sailed over the Caspian Sea, and discovered all the regions thereabout adjacent, as Chircassi, Comul, Shascal, Shiruan, with many others.

I have travelled 40 daies journey beyond the said sea, towards the Oriental India and Cathaia, through divers deserts and wildernesses, and passed through 5 kingdomes of the Tartars, and all the land of Turkeman and Zagatay, and so to the great city of Boghar in Bactria, not without great perils and dangers sundry times.

After all this, in An. 1562 I passed againe over the Caspian sea another way, and landed in Armenia, at a citie called Derbent, built by Alexander the Great, and from thence travelled through Media, Parthia, Hircania, into Persia to the court of the great Sophie, called Shaw Tomasso, unto whom I delivered letters from the Queenes Majestie, and remained in his court 8 months, and returning homeward, passed through divers other countries. Finally, I made two voyages more after that out of England into Russia, the one in the yeere 1566, and the other in the yeere 1571. And thus being weary and growing old, I am content to take my seat in mine owne house, chiefly comforting myselfe, in that my service hath bene honourably accepted and rewarded of her majestie and the rest by whom I have beene employed."

And now it was that stories of danger from frost and from storm; of cruelties endured at the hands of savages, and pirates; of captivity among Moors; of tortures inflicted by the accursed Inquisition; of hairbreadth escapes; of wanderings over lands never before seen; of great treasures lying ready for the bold adventurer,—ran up and down the City. The 'prentice told what he had heard to fellow 'prentice; the sailors told the boys upon the wharves; the ship after her successful voyage came up to the Pool with cloth of gold for sails and dressed with flying streamers. Above all, the imagination of the youth was fired more by the splendid stories of danger and of battle and of escape from captivity than by the prospect of great riches. Do you know how John Fox escaped from Alexandria? For my own part I do not know any story better told or more certain to inspire the lads who heard it with a burning desire to be with such a company and to be doing such things. It is from Hakluyt (ii. 133), and I venture to relate it here and in his own words, to show the kind of story which quickened the pulse and fired the blood of the London youth.

"Nowe these eight being armed with such weapons as they thought well of, thinking themselves sufficient champions to encounter a stronger enemie, and comming unto the prison, Fox opened the gates and doores thereof, and called forth all the prisoners, whom he set, some to ramming up the gate, some to the dressing up of a certaine gallie, which was the best in all the roade, and was called the captaine of Alexandria, whereinto some carried mastes, sailes, oares, and other such furniture as doth belong unto a gallie.

At the prison were certaine warders, whom John Fox and his companie slew; in the killing of whom, there were eight more of the Turks, which perceived them, and got them to the toppe of the prison; unto whom John Fox, and his company, were faine to come by ladders, where they found a hot skirmish. For some of them were there slaine, some wounded, and some but scarred, and not hurt. As John Fox was thrise shot through his apparell, and not hurt, Peter Unticaro, and the other two, that had armed them with the duckats, were slaine, as not able to weild themselves, being so pestered with the weight and uneasie carying of the wicked and prophane treasure; and also divers Christians were as well hurt about that skirmish as Turkes slaine. Amongst the Turkes was one thrust thorowe, who (let us not say that it was ill fortune) fell off from the toppe of the prison wall, and made such a lowing, that the inhabitants thereabout (as heré and there scattering stoode a house or two) came and dawed him, so that they understood the case, how that the prisoners were paying their ransomes; wherewith they raised both Alexandria which lay on the west side of the roade, and a Castle which was at the Cities end, next to the roade, and also an other Fortresse which lay on the north side of the roade; so that nowe they had no way to escape, but one, which by man's reason (the two holdes lying so upon the mouth of the roade) might seeme impossible to be a way for them. So was the read sea impossible for the Israelites to passe through, the hils and rockes lay so on the one side, and their enemies compassed them on the other. So was it impossible that the wals of Jericho should fall downe, being neither undermined, nor yet rammed at with engines, nor yet any man's wisdome, pollicie, or helpe set or put thereunto. Such impossibilities can our God make possible. He that helde the Lyons jawes from rending Daniel asunder, yea, or yet from once touching him to his hurt; can not He hold the roring canons of this hellish force? He that kept the fiers rage in the hot burning oven, from the three children, that praised His name, can not He keepe the fiers flaming blastes from among His elect?

Now is the roade fraught with lustie souldiers, laborers, and mariners, who are faine to stand to their tackling, in setting to every man his hand, some to the carying in of victuals, some munitions, some oares, and some one thing, some another, but most are keeping their enemie from the wall of the road. But to be short, there was no time mispent, no man idle, nor any man's labour ill bestowed, or in vaine. So that in short time, this gally was ready trimmed up. Whereinto every man leaped in all haste, hoyssing up the sayles lustily, yeelding themselves to His mercie and grace, in whose hands are both winde and weather.

Now is this gally on flote, and out of the safetie of the roade; now have the two Castles full power upon the gally, now is there no remedy but to sinke; how can it be avoided? the Canons let flie from both sides, and the gally is even in the middest, and betweene them both. What man can devise to save it? there is no man, but would thinke it must needs be sunke.

There was not one of them that feared the shotts, which went thundering round about their eares, nor yet were once scarred or touched, with five and forty shot, which came from the Castles. Here did God hold foorth His buckler, He shieldeth now this gally, and hath tried their faith to the uttermost. Now commeth His speciall helpe; yea, even when man thinks them past all helpe, then commeth He Himselfe downe from heaven with His mightie power, then is His present remedie most readie prest. For they saile away, being not once touched with the glaunce of a shot, and are quickly out of the Turkish canons reach. Then might they see them comming downe by heapes to the water side, in companies like unto swarmes of bees, making shew to come after them with gallies, in bustling themselves to dresse up the gallies, which would be a swift peece of worke for them to doe, for that they had neither oares,

SIR FRANCIS DRAKE (1540(?)-1596)
From an engraving by Elstracke in the British Museum.

mastes, sailes, gables, nor anything else ready in any gally. But yet they are carying them unto them, some into one gally, and some into another, so that, being such a confusion amongst them, without any certaine guide, it were a thing impossible to overtake them; beside that, there was no man that would take charge of a gally, the weather was so rough, and there was such an amasedness [amazedness] amongst them."

The effect on London of the magnificent expeditions of the English was startling. Think what these things meant. The country for a long time could look back upon nothing but defeat, humiliation, civil war, and religious dissensions. There were no military achievements, no naval victories; no increase of trade;

never was the nation more depressed and humbled than at the death of Queen Mary and the accession of Elizabeth.

Then—almost suddenly—all was changed.   More than the old spirit came back to the Londoners, the descendants of the men who had followed Philpot the Mayor to the destruction of the Scottish pirate.   Not only the sea dogs of Devon, but those of Wapping, Ratcliffe, Redriff, and the Cinque Ports went forth to fight the Spaniard wherever they could find him.   Think of the career of Frobisher.   Three times he essayed the north-west passage to Cathay; he commanded one of Drake's ships in his expedition to the West Indies; he fought against the Armada; he was wounded, and died from wounds received at the siege of Crozan in Brittany.   Forty years on the sea, sword in hand, sailed this brave

DRAKE'S "GOLDEN HIND," IN WHICH HE SAILED ROUND THE WORLD, 1577-1580

captain.   London possesses his body, which lies in St. Giles's Church, Cripplegate. There was also Cavendish, the gentleman filibuster, who captured the richest prize ever known, and came home, his sails of damask, his sailors clad in silk, and his masts gleaming with cloth of gold.   Or there was the defeat, the flight after battle against overwhelming odds, which affected the imagination even more than victory.   Such was Sir John Hawkins's fight at San Juan de Ulloa, five ships against thirteen.   Even death, when death came splendidly, moved the hearts of the young men to brave deeds.   Was there ever death finer than that of Sir Humphrey Gilbert?   The last time he was seen by the people on the other ship, his companion, he was sitting on the high poop, his Bible in his hand.   "We are as near to Heaven," said the old captain, "by sea as by land."   Night fell and the men on the *Hind* saw the light of the *Squirrel* suddenly disappear.   She had gone down with all on board.   And while speaking of splendid deaths, there was that of Sir Richard Grenville. In his ship the *Revenge*, with five other vessels, he was met by a Spanish fleet of fifty-three ships; his companions fled, and the *Revenge* alone fought them all :—

> " And the sun went down, and the stars came out, far over the summer sea,
> But never a moment ceased the fight of the one and the fifty-three.
> Ship after ship, the whole night long, their high-built galleons came,
> Ship after ship, the whole night long, with her battle-thunder and flame :
> Ship after ship, the whole night long, drew back with her dead and her shame.
> For some were sunk and many were shatter'd, and so could fight us no more—
> God of battles, was ever a battle like this in the world before ? "

But at length he was captured with his crippled ship and his diminished crew.

> " But he rose upon their decks, and he cried :
> ' I have fought for Queen and Faith, like a valiant man and true :
> I have only done my duty as a man is bound to do :
> With a joyful spirit, I, Sir Richard Grenville, die !'
> And he fell upon their decks, and he died."

The ship in which Drake sailed round the world (*The Golden Hind*), when it became unfit for service, was laid up near the " Mast Dock " at Deptford, where it remained for a long series of years an object of curiosity and wonder. Hentzner, in 1598, says he saw here the ship of that noble pirate, Francis Drake. From a passage in one of Ben Jonson's plays it appears to have become a resort for holiday people, the cabin being then converted into a banqueting house. Drake's ship at Deptford is spoken of as one of the "sights" in some verses prefixed to the redoubtable Tom Coryat's *Crudities*, 1611. When the young Duke of Saxe-Weimar saw the ship in 1613, but very little remained of it. It was then lying by the river-side in shallow water, in a dock ; the lower part only was left, the upper part being all gone, for almost everybody who went there, and especially sailors, were in the habit of carrying off some portion of it. Philipott, *History of Kent*, 1659, says that in a very short time nothing was left of her. And in Moryson's *Itinerary*, 1617, it is noticed as follows—" Not farre from hence (Deptford), upon the shore, lie the broken ribs of the ship in which Sir Francis Drake sailed round the world, reserved for a monument of that great action." A chair, made out of the wood, is to be seen in the gallery of the Bodleian Library at Oxford.

Let us take a contemporary poet, to see how Drake's own generation was affected by his exploits :—

> "Awake, each Muse, awake !
> Not one I need, but all
> To sing of Francis Drake
> And his companions tall.
> One Muse may chance do well,
> Where little is to tell ;
> But nine are all too few
> To tell what he did do,
> His friends and soldiers all.

Drake was made generall
  By sea and eke by land,
And Christopher Carlisle
  Did next unto him stand.
Brave Winter too, was there,
And Captain Fourbisher,
And Knowles, and many mo,
Did all together go
  To lend a helping hand.

Three thousand Volunteers
  Were numbered with the rest,
And sailors, as appears,
  To guide them to the West,
To quell the Spaniard's pride,
Which could not be denied ;
But which could not be seene
By our most noble Queene
  And stomach'd with the best.

In more than twenty ships
  They sailed from the port.
In speed they did eclipse,
  And took St. Jago's fort :
It was a glorious day,
Before they came away,
The day of our Queen's birth,
They kept with joy and mirth
  In well beseeming sort.

Santo Domingo next
  They took and also spoiled.
The Spaniard he was vext
  To be so easy foiled.
No force could them resist ;
They did as they list.
The Spaniards bought the town,
And paid the ducats down
  For which they long had toiled.

From thence to Carthagene
  They carried victory :
Upon the Spanish main
  The city rich doth lye.
They took it by assault :
The Spaniards were in fault ;
But they could not oppose
The valour of such foes,
  And yeelded presently.

To Terra Florida
  They did direct their course,
And ever by the way
  They proved their skill and force.
With fear the Spaniards shook
While all their towne they took.
For barrels of bright gold
The towne our English sold,
  And shewed therefore remorse.

And now they have returned
  To Plymouth back once more,
And glory they have earned
  Enough to put in store.

Our Queen with great delight
Beheld the joyous sight,
And thanked them every one
For what they thus had done
By sea and on the shore.

Now, welcome all and some,
Now welcome to our isle,
For Francis Drake is come
To London with Carlisle :
And many more with him
That ventured life and limb,
And fighting side by side
Did quell the Spaniard's pride,
To cause our Queen to smile."

And if the following truly represents the spirit of the sailors, what a promising and cheerful spirit it was!

" Lustely, lustely, lustely let us saile forth,
The winde trim doth serve us, it blowes from the north.

All thinges we have ready, and nothing we want
To furnish our ship that rideth here by :
Victuals and weapons, thei be nothing skant,
Like worthie mariners ourselves we will trie.
Lustely, lustely, etc.

Her flagges be new trimmed, set flaunting alofte,
Our ship for swift swimmyng, oh, she doeth excell ;
Wee feare no enemies, we have escaped them ofte ;
Of all ships that swimmeth she beareth the bell.
Lustely, lustely, etc.

And here is a maister excelleth in skill,
And our maister's mate he is not to seeke ;
And here is a boteswaine will do his good will,
And here is a ship boye, we never had leeke.
Lustely, lustely, etc.

If fortune then faile ot, and our next vioage prove,
Wee will returne merely, and make good cheere,
And holde all together, as friends linkt in love :
The cannes shal be filled with wine, ale, and beere.
Lustely, lustely, etc."

But enough of songs, we must return to the more serious aspects of Trading England. When merchants first began to carry on foreign trade in association it is impossible to ascertain. But as we find " Men of the Emperor" and " Men of Rouen" in London in Saxon times, it is probable that foreign trade was from the beginning carried on by members of companies. These members traded each for himself; but they were associated for protection, and of necessity an " interloper" —as the private trader was afterwards called—could not carry his wares to a foreign city when he knew not the language, or the customs, nor could claim the privileges accorded to the Companies. On the other hand, behind the members stood a powerful corporation; this gave the merchants credit; this procured for them respect and protection; this provided the machinery of warehouses, markets, interpreters, and information as to laws, regulations, prices, demand, supply, privileges, and all the special points required to be mastered if trade were to be successful.

The first foreign trading Company, then, was exactly like a Trades Guild, in which only members could follow the trade, which had its own quarter, made its own laws for itself, elected its own officers, yet every member worked for himself.

The longest lived and the most important of the mediæval companies was the Hanseatic League, already mentioned at p. 82.

F. Hausstaengl

A MERCHANT OF THE STEELYARD
From the portrait by Holbein at Windsor Castle.

The earliest association of London merchants for foreign trade is that called the Staplers' Company. They claimed to have existed long before the Merchant Adventurers. There is, however, a great deal of mystery attached to their early history. Thus, if they were associated for exporting the staple wares, such as wool, lead, tin, and skins, how far did they overlap the Hanseatics? And were they all foreigners? The latter question seems answered by the law of 1253, which prohibited English merchants from exporting staple goods. Again, was this law strictly enforced? In 1362, more than a hundred years later, it was repealed.

The Merchants of the Staple are sometimes confused with the Fraternity of St. Thomas à Becket, from whom sprung a much more important body—the Merchant Adventurers. The reason of the decay of the Staplers was the growth of English industries, which forbade the exports of the most important of the staples—wool. The Staplers, however, continued their trade, having their headquarters at Antwerp, Brussels, Louvain, Calais, and Bruges, successively. It will be remembered that Edward III. established the Staple of Wool at Westminster; the name of Staple Inn preserved the fact that the merchants had houses on that site.

About the year 1358 the Fraternity of Thomas Becket received privileges from Louis, Count of Flanders, for fixing their staple of English woollen cloth at Bruges. This Fraternity gave rise to the Mercers' Company founded under Edward the Third. The Saint, son of a London mercer, was especially regarded as the protector of the Company. The Brotherhood was not at first possessed of exclusive rights, but if we suppose that they were backed by the richest traders in London, namely, the Mercers and the Drapers, and that no other London trader would compete with them, it is quite probable that they feared no competition. They got a Charter in 1406 when Henry the Fourth gave them the right of choosing their own governors; they then began to arrogate to themselves exclusive rights, which were confirmed by another Charter of 1436. So wealthy and powerful did they become that when, in 1444, they removed their headquarters from Middleburg to Antwerp, the magistrates and citizens met them outside the town, and offered them an entertainment. Their Secretary, John Wheeler (*Treatise of Commerce*, 1601), says that the "English Nation" were the real founders of Antwerp's wealth. There were troubles as to the attempts of private merchants to trade; in 1497 it was provided by Act of Parliament that every Englishman should have free entrance to foreign marts on payment of ten marks, presumably to the Fraternity. Again, in 1505, a new Charter changed their name to that of the "Merchant Adventurers of England." Under this Charter they held in their hands the export trade in woollen cloths, and were authorised to hold courts and to admit other merchants for a fee of ten marks to trade with them in Flanders, Holland, Brabant, Zeeland, and the countries adjacent under the Archduke's government. The Merchant Adventurers became a power in the land; so great a power, indeed, that when Charles the Fifth proposed to establish the Inquisition in Antwerp, he was dissuaded by the Merchant Adventurers, who threatened to leave the City if he persisted. It is said that the Company then employed 50,000 persons in the Netherlands. At this time their limits comprised all the ports from the river Somme to the German ports within the Baltic. They exported white and coloured cloths to the value of one million sterling every year, and imported, among other things, wine, copper, steel, gunpowder (could we not make

MEDALS STRUCK IN COMMEMORATION OF THE ARMADA

From medals in the British Museum.

W. A. Mansell & Co.

our own gunpowder?), silk, velvets, cloth of gold. This business was well nigh ruined by King James the First when he granted a monopoly for the sale of cloths dyed at home to Sir William Cockaine, Alderman. (See *London in the Time of the Stuarts*, p. 194.)

As the Merchant Adventurers grew richer it became necessary, according to the bad practice of the time, to bribe statesmen for a continuance of their privileges; they also increased the fees for admission. The troubles between Holland and England in the seventeenth century drove the Adventurers to Hamburg, where they remained, and were called the Hamburg Company.

The vast enlargement of trade and enterprise under Elizabeth was well begun under her father. In 1511 ships began to sail from the ports of London, Southampton, and Bristol to Sicily, Candia, Chio, Cyprus, and Tripoli; they took out woollen cloths and hides, and they brought back rhubarb, silk, corselets, malmsey, oil, cotton, carpets, and spices. An English merchant was appointed Consul at Candia; another merchant, a foreigner, was made Consul at Chio; in the year 1535 a ship took out from London a hundred persons who were settled by the English merchants as factors at the various centres of trade. Trade openings were made on the Coast of Guinea and with Morocco; ships sailed to Newfoundland and to Brazil. In the year 1583 was formed the first of the new Companies for trading purposes. This Company had an interesting but a disastrous beginning. It was started with a capital of £6000 in 240 shares of £25 each; its original idea was to find a north-east passage to China and to open trade with the Chinese. Three vessels were fitted out under the command of Sir Hugh Willoughby. Would you know how the fleet started? Hakluyt tells the story :—

"It was thought best by the opinion of them all, that by the twentieth of May, the Captaines and Mariners should take shipping, and depart from Radcliffe, upon the ebbe, if it pleased God. They having saluted their acquaiaintance, one his wife, another his children, another his kinsfolkes, and another his friends deerer then his kinsfolkes, were present and ready at the day appoynted; and having wayed ancre, they departed with the turning of the water, and sailing easily, came first to Greenewich. The greater shippes are towed downe with boates, and oares, and the mariners being all apparelled in Watchet or skie coloured cloth, rowed amaine, and made way with diligence. And being come neere to Greenewich (where the Court then lay) presently upon the newes thereof, the Courtiers came running out, and the common people flockt together, standing very thicke upon the shoare; the privie Counsel, they lookt out at the windowes of the Court, and the rest ranne up to the toppes of the towers; the shippes hereupon discharge their Ordinance, and shot off their pieces after the maner of warre, and of the sea, insomuch that the tops of the hilles sounded therewith, the valleys and waters gave an echo, and the Mariners they shouted in such sort, that the skie rang againe with the noyse thereof. One stoode in the poope of the ship, and by his gestures bid farewell to his friends in the best maner hee could. Another walkes upon the hatches, another climbes the shrowds, another stands upon the maine yard, and another in the top of the shippe. To be short, it was a very triumph (after a sort) in all respects to the beholders. But (alas) the good King Edward (in respect of whom principally all this was prepared) hee onely by reason of his sickenesse was absent from this shewe, and not long after the departure of these ships, the lamentable and most sorrowfull accident of his death followed."

Other accounts of this incident represent the King as being carried out to see this gallant spectacle, the last he was to see upon earth.

The little fleet met with bad weather off the coast of Spitzbergen; two of them, including the captain's ship, ran into a harbour of Lapland, where the whole company were frozen to death; the third got into the White Sea and so to Archangel; the captain, Richard Chancellor, procured sledges and travelled to Moscow, where he obtained from the Czar permission to trade on the northern coast of Russia. Thus was founded the Russia Company. A few years later one of the agents of the Russia Company was despatched as an Ambassador from the English Court to the Czar, who in his turn sent an Ambassador to Whitehall. On his voyage the Russian Ambassador was wrecked on the coast of Scotland. The Russia Company, hearing of the disaster, sent a deputation with a supply of everything that the Ambassador might want. On his approach to the City he was met by a company of eighty merchants on horseback, who escorted him to Highgate, where he lay that night, and on the next day was met by Lord Montague, representing the Queen, with 300 knights and esquires and 140 merchants of the Russia Company. Rooms were found for him in Gracechurch Street, where many costly gifts awaited him.

The history of this Company deserves to be written at length on account of the enterprise and intelligence of its agents. Indeed, justice has never been done to the agents and factors of the great London Companies. It was not the Directors, sitting at home at their long table, who created the Indian Empire; maintained and widened the English trade; carried the English flag over lands unknown and to peoples unheard of; it was not the Directors who opened up routes, stood before capricious despots, marked the resources of new countries and reported on their wants. These things were done by the factors and the agents, who encountered all risks, facing possibly prison, torture, disease, and sometimes a cruel death, for the enlargement of trade and the enrichment of their masters. They were the pioneers; sometimes they were the Forlorn Hope of the English trade and wealth. No Company, not even the East India Company, was better served by its agents than the Russia Company. They obtained from the Czar important privileges; they could trade in any part of Russia without safe conduct or licenses; they could not be arrested for debt; they could appoint their own officers and servants; and they had jurisdiction over all Englishmen resident in Russia. In other words, they had a monopoly of the Russian Trade.

The Company showed a clear comprehension of these advantages; they continued to attempt the north-east passage; they sent ships laden with merchandise to Archangel, whence their agents travelled over Russia; they even opened communications with Persia by means of their agent Anthony Jenkinson, who has already in his own words given us an account of his adventurous career.

7. St. John's Hospital.	58. Grey Friars.	63. Cheapside.	68. St. Mary's Overie.	74. St. Giles's, Crippleg
8. Smithfield.	59. Queen Hythe.	64. The Standard.	70. St. Thomas's Hospital.	75. Cripplegate
9. St. James's, Clerkenwell.	60. St. Martin's le Grand.	65. Cross, Cheapside.	71. St. George's Church.	76. The Barbican.
4. Baynard Castle.	61. Aldersgate.	66. Rochester House.	72. Kent Road.	77. St. Albans, Wood St
5. St. Paul's Cathedral.	62. Jew's Cemetery.	67. Winchester House.	73. Suffolk House.	78. Bow Church.

From the Panorama of "London, Westminster, and Southwark, in 1543." By Anthony Van

rde. (Sutherland Collection, Bodleian Library, Oxford.) *For continuation see pp.* 218 *and* 350.

When he sailed from the Volga to Astrakhan, he passed over the Caspian to the town of Boghaz, where he found traders from the Far East. He sent home a map of Russia, the first published in England. This way of trade, however, proved too dangerous on account of Cossack pirates who infested the Caspian Sea and robbed the Company's ships. However, the Company, anxious to secure these advantages, procured an Act of Parliament granting them the exclusive trade with the countries of Persia, Armenia, and Media, as well as Russia.

Internal troubles in Russia, such as the taking of Moscow by the Tartars, caused the Company a loss of 400,000 roubles. Pirates in the Baltic, and other misfortunes, greatly reduced the Company, but they persevered in their voyages of discovery, once more attempting the north-east passage, which was expected to do so much for them. They did not succeed, but they discovered the deep sea fisheries, and they brought home immense quantities of fish-oil and of dried salmon. They suffered from the Dutch, who followed in their wake; they obtained from the King of Denmark permission to put in at any of his seaports in Iceland or Norway; they lost their exclusive rights in Russia, but only for a time; they found themselves cut out by the Dutch, whose vessels carried more merchandise; with the authority of James the First, they sent armed vessels and seized on Spitzbergen in the King's name, calling it King James's Newland. They had to fight for their conquest, driving off Dutch, French, and Biscay sail with four English "interlopers." The Dutch, however, would not admit the pretensions of Crown or Company, sending their ships protected by men-of-war to fish, despite the protests of the English. There was fighting in the high latitudes for some years, while even the English ports refused to recognise the exclusive right of the Company. Finally, the whales became so scarce about Spitzbergen that the trade ceased to be worth fighting about.

We will continue the history of the Company in brief, though it runs far beyond the limits of our period. In the year 1620 the route by the Caspian was reopened by Hobbs, an agent to the Company, who took that way from Moscow to Ispahan. In 1623 a new treaty was concluded between James the First and the Czar, in which privileges, but not exclusive rights, were conferred upon the Company. A deadly blow was inflicted on the Company by the execution of Charles, an event naturally viewed by all sovereigns with the deepest indignation. The English merchants, who were masters of the Russian trade, were driven out and supplanted by the Dutch; and it was not until the year 1669 that the Company was allowed to trade with Russia on the same footing as the Dutch.

The real importance of the Company was decaying when it admitted any one as a member on payment of a fine of £5. The conveyance of raw silk from Persia through Russia remained their privilege until troubles broke out in Persia in 1746, which stopped the trade; they still carried on their trade with Archangel, but when the Baltic became a peaceful highway, this shorter route to Russia destroyed the Archangel trade. The Russia Company did not, it is true, acquire for the British Empire any accession of territory; but its services in exploring new routes, opening up new lines of trade, putting Great Britain into communication with foreign powers previously strangers, can hardly be exaggerated, while it fostered and encouraged and developed that spirit of enterprise, adventure, and restlessness which, since the seventeenth century, has covered half the globe with one people and one religion.

A distinction must be drawn between "regulated companies" and Joint-Stock Companies. In the former, every man traded for himself, subject to the regulations of the Company, like a Guild. In the "Russia," "Turkey," and "Eastland" Companies no one but a member could carry on that kind of trade. In the Joint-Stock Companies shareholders need not be traders and could sell or transfer their shares.

The Eastland Company was first chartered in 1579. It was privileged to enjoy the sole trade over all those parts of the Baltic shore which did not belong to the Russia Company. Now there had been carried on, from time immemorial, a trade with the Baltic ports by private adventurers who wanted no charter. Many of these, no doubt, took up their membership with the new Company, but there were some who would not, or could not. These traders, driven away from their own markets, made loud complaints, in reply to which a proclamation was issued ordering that no one outside the Company was to export to these parts the merchandise in which the Eastland Company traded; provided always that the importation of corn and grain was left free. The provision looks like a compromise, but when we ask how corn and grain were to be imported except in ships, and that, if these ships were English, they would hardly go out in ballast, one fails to see that the enemies of the Eastlanders got much by their proclamation. In 1672 the whole of Scandinavia was thrown open to all comers; and the entrance-fee to the Company was reduced to £2. The opinion of Sir Josiah Child probably settled the fate of the Company. He said that the Eastland Company had only enabled the Dutch to get ten times as much trade in the Baltic as was carried on by the English.

In the year 1581 the Turkey Company received its Charter from Queen Elizabeth. It was a Charter for a limited time, seven years, and it could be revoked at a year's notice. The Company began very well; they built large and strong ships to face the storms of the Bay, for which they received the thanks of the Council; they introduced eastern commodities at a much cheaper price; but they sometimes paid dearly for their cargoes when they had to fight the corsairs of Barbary and the galleys of Spain, and to face the fiercest animosity of the Venetians. In 1583 some of the agents of the Company, stationed at the Aleppo

House, made their way with merchandise to Bagdad, to the Persian Gulf, and thence to India and the Far East. They obtained, therefore, a new Charter giving them power to trade over India as well as the Sultan's dominions. The entrance-fee was fixed at £25 for persons under twenty-six years of age, at £50 for those over twenty-six, and at £1 for apprentices.

The Company now became extremely prosperous, carrying on a most extensive trade. This trade, by a later order under Charles II., was kept entirely in the hands of the City of London, no one, unless a resident and a freeman, being admitted into the Company. On the foundation of the East India Company there arose disputes as to the infringement of rights. This quarrel ended without any decision.

The trade of the Turkey Company declined during the seventeenth century from many causes, one of which was the rivalry of the French and their success in underselling the English goods. The Company finally closed its history in the year 1825.

The Levant Company was another trading Company established under Elizabeth. By opening up direct communication with the Levant, England procured all the productions of the East without the intervention of Venice. Only one more vessel was sent to London from Venice after the establishment of the Company, and this with a rich cargo and many passengers was wrecked and destroyed on the Isle of Wight.

For the repulse of the Spanish Armada, London contributed thirty-eight vessels, and the Society of Merchant Adventurers, ten. In 1591, or perhaps in 1589, the first voyage from London to the East Indies was undertaken. The expedition of 1591 consisted of three ships, of which one was never heard of again; and the other two lost many men from sickness. The expedition, however, led to the formation of the East India Company in A.D. 1600, with a capital of £72,000 in 1440 shares of £50 each. Their first fleet, consisting of five ships and 480 men, reached Sumatra and the Straits of Malacca, where they captured a Portuguese ship of 900 tons laden with calicoes. They settled a factory at Bantam and sailed homewards, returning to port in two years and seven months after starting.

The trade of the country was greatly advanced by the immigration of many Flemings, Dutch, Walloons, and French Huguenots, who brought over with them their own trades. They were judiciously distributed about the country, care being taken that they should neither interfere with the trade of the place nor crowd too much together. Thus at Sandwich alone there were 350 Flemish families in the year 1582; they carried on the manufactory of bags. In Norwich, Dutch and Walloons settled and made serges and silks and bombazines. Bone lace was taken to Honiton from Antwerp. In London the Flemings settled at Bermondsey, where they made felt hats and did joiners' work; at Bow, where they had dye-works; at Wandsworth, where they worked in brass; at Mortlake and Fulham, where they made tapestry. In other places workers in steel and iron, window-glass painters, cloth fullers, cloth-makers, and many other craftsmen were planted and carried on profitable industries. Among other things, sail-making was introduced into England for the first time. The pawnbroker's shop was also opened in this reign. It began with the establishment of seven banks in as many towns, to be known as "Banks for the relief of Common Necessity," which should lend money on pledges. This Bank is alluded to by Shakespeare when Sir John Falstaff urges his hostess to pawn her cups and her hangings. "Glass," he says, "glass is your only drinking: and for thy walls, a pretty slight drollery, or the story of the Prodigal or the Germans hunting in water work, is worth a thousand of these bed hangings and these fly-bitten tapestries."

The monopoly system by which the Court rewarded favourites at the expense of trade and the people was regarded by Elizabeth with favour, as an easy way of bestowing favours costing herself nothing. Many of her monopolies she withdrew as manifestly injurious to trade, yet she left many which weighed heavily upon the enterprise of the country. These monopolies were multiplied in the next two reigns, and greatly assisted to bring about the unpopularity of Charles.

Cunningham is of opinion that the borrowing of money for trading purposes was not a common practice; he bases this opinion on the very high rate of interest demanded by the usurer. There can be no doubt that usury was strictly forbidden by the Church, by the Ordinances of the City of London, and by public opinion. Yet a case quoted by him (*Growth of Trade*, p. 325) shows that men not only wanted to borrow from time to time, but that Christians, not Jews, were willing to lend on interest. In that case the lender wanted interest for a loan of £10 for three months, which amounted to 80 per cent per annum. The usurer could not get his claim allowed. Yet it is difficult to understand how business could be carried on at all except in an elementary way, if there was neither credit nor borrowing. But was the rate of interest too high for trading on borrowed money? There is every reason to believe that the profits of trade were enormous. Malyns, in his *Centre of the Circle of Commerce*, gives a table showing the profits of the trade in spices, silk, indigo, etc., early in the seventeenth century. They range from 150 to 250 per cent, *i.e.* goods bought at £100 would sell for £250 up to £350. Of course there must be set off against this apparently huge profit, losses by wrecks and pirates and the expense of the shipping. Borrowing, Cunningham thinks, was necessary to meet taxation. Since taxes were not regular, but irregular; and could not be provided for because no one knew when a tallage would be imposed or how large a percentage would be demanded, the merchant or the landowner, though perfectly solvent, might not be able to lay his hand at once on the amount demanded. A person of to-day whose estate might be worth £120,000 would find it, very possibly, difficult to meet, within a few days, the King's demand of one-fifteenth, that is £8000. If he could not realise in time he must borrow. If all the usury was confined to the lending of money to meet a sudden tax, or to a monastery for the building of a church, or for a baron to raise a force, what becomes of the popular hatred of the Jews, first as money-lenders, and of the Caursini and the Italians who were licensed by the Pope, next? And if there was no borrowing by the merchants, what was the meaning of that crowd which, after the massacre of the Jews in York Castle, rushed to the Cathedral, where they brought out the Jews' bonds—their own bonds—and burned them all? Cunningham, in a note, enumerates the demands

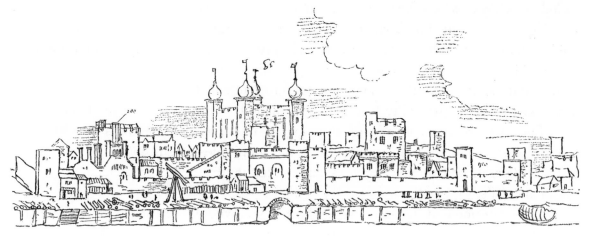

THE TOWER IN 1553
From a drawing by Wyngaerde. E. Gardner's Collection

of certain Russians against the Jews of the present day. These demands express the popular belief concerning their practice, not the truth. One would most unwillingly accept prejudice for proof, especially in the case of the race which has endured so much prejudice for so many centuries. Cunningham says, very justly, that the real objection against the Jews was that they made their money by lending it on security, which left them no risks which could be foreseen. The common people, however, did not understand the objection; they saw that the Jews practised a trade which the Church and the State would not allow to Christians; they saw that the Jews grew rich rapidly; that they were protected by the King; that they waxed insolent and sometimes insulted the Christian religion; and if they lent a Christian money they demanded an enormous, a ruinous, interest for it. Deep, indeed, must have been the popular hatred of the Jews, since Shakespeare could stir the blood of his audience by the spectacle of a Jewish usurer, three hundred years after there had been Jews in the land.

The business of the daily life, as well as that of the mercantile life, cannot, in fact, be carried on without money-lending. Works cannot be undertaken; credit cannot be secured; cargoes cannot be bought; ships cannot be laden; unless money can be obtained by advance. The banishment of the Jews; the disappearance of the Italians; took away the usurers and money-lenders by profession. There were as yet no banks to make advances on security; and money-lending was still, as it remains to this day, an occupation held in the greatest loathing. The money-lender, therefore, disguised his calling. Thus Hall (*Society in the Elizabethan Age*) furnishes a sketch of the usurer of the period. His name was George Stoddart; by trade he was ostensibly a grocer, but really a money-lender. His bargains took the form of bets. Thus he sends J. Klynt his furred nightgown for 4s. 5d., to be paid on the day of Klynt's marriage: he gives R. Leds a ring called a ryboys, which he values at £1 : 13 : 4, to be paid on the day of his marriage or else at his hour of death. For a rapier he charges 40d., to be paid at his day of marriage or else not. He gives a man £400 on the condition that during his lifetime the borrower shall pay him £80 a year. He lived for ten years, and so doubled that small capital of £400. It would be interesting to know what, if any, great City fortunes were made by this style of money-lending.

The increase of trade and of shipping in the Port of London is indicated by a passage in Camden, when he speaks of the multitudes of ships "as a very wood of trees, disbranched to make glades and to let in the light: so shaded is it with masts and sails."

The watermen of London were those who lived by the river and the port. John Taylor, the water poet, says that 40,000 people lived by the labour of the oar and scull. In 1613 there was a petition from the Company of Watermen against the erection of a theatre on the London or Middlesex side of the river, because it drew away so many people who otherwise would have been carried across the river to the theatres on the south bank. John Taylor shows us that many of these watermen had been sailors :—

"I did briefly declare part of the services that watermen had done in Queen Elizabeth's reign of famous memory, in the voyage to Portugal with the right honourable and never to be forgotten Earl of Essex; then after that, how it pleased God, in that great deliverance in the year 1588, to make watermen good serviceable instruments with their loss of lives and limbs to defend their prince and country. Moreover, many of them served with Sir Francis Drake, Sir John Hawkins, Sir Martin Frobisher, and others. Besides, in Cadiz action, the Island Voyage, in Ireland, in the Low Countries, and in the narrow seas they have been, as in duty they were bound, at continual command, so that every summer 1500 or 2000 of them were employed to the places aforesaid. . . .

Afterwards the players began to play on the Bankside, and to leave playing in London and Middlesex, for the most part, then there went such great concourse of people by water that the small number of watermen remaining at home were not able to carry them, by reason of the court, the terms, the players, and other employments, so that we were enforced and encouraged, hoping that this golden stirring world would have lasted ever, to take and entertain men and boys . . . so that the number of watermen, and those that live and are maintained by them, and by the only labour of the oar and the scull, betwixt the bridge of Windsor and Gravesend, cannot be fewer than forty thousand; the cause of the greater half of which multitude, hath been the players playing on the bankside, for I have known three companies besides the bear-baiting at once there, to wit, the Globe, the Rose, and the Swan."

Loud complaints being made by the artificers of London that foreign goods were underselling theirs, the King in 1461 prohibited the importation or sale of the following articles—the list of which shows some of the manufactures at that time established in London :—

"Any manner girdles, nor any harness wrought for girdles, points, laces of

NEAR PAUL'S WHARF
E. Gardner's Collection.

lether, purses, pouches, pins, gloves, knives, hangers, tailors' shears, scissors, andirons, cobordis, tongs, fire forksm gridirons; stocks, locks, keyes, hinges and garnets, spurs; painted papers, painted focers, paynted images, painted clothes, any between gold or between silver, wrought in papers for painters; saddles, saddle-trees, horse harness, boocis, bits, stirrups, buckles, chains, laten nails with iron shanks, terrets, standing candlesticks, hanging candlesticks, holy water stoops, chafing dishes, hanging lavers, curtain rings, cards for wool, clasps for gloves, buckles for shoes, brooches, bells (except bells for hawks), spoons of tin and lead, chains of wire as well as of laten as of iron, gratis, horns and lantern hornsm or any of these aforesaid wares, ready and wrought, pertaining to the said crafts above specified or any of them uppon payne of forfeture of all the wares." (Capper's *Port and Trade of London*.)

We have seen (p. 13) how Henry VII. passed an Act forbidding any stranger, *i.e.* foreigner, to buy or sell merchandise in the City; in his reign also was passed an Act to compel the country people to resort to the City. For it was ordered that no citizen should carry goods to any market or fair out of the City. The people of the country represented to Parliament the great hardship of being obliged to travel all the way to London in order to procure things that could only be bought in London, viz. chalices, books, vestments, and other church ornaments, victuals for Lent, linen cloths, woollen cloths, brass, pewter, bedding, iron, flax, wax, and other things. The Parliament interfered and the order was removed.

Under Henry VII. commercial treaties were concluded with the Danes and

TRADESMEN OF THE PERIOD
From a contemporary print.

with the Florentines. There was a quarrel with Burgundy and a cessation of commercial relations for three years. In 1497 (12 Hen. VII.) was passed an Act entitled "Every Englishman shall have free recourse to certain foreign marts, without exaction to be taken by any English fraternity." The meaning of the Act was this: the Merchant Adventurers' Company had arrogated to themselves the right of refusing the right of trade in any foreign port until a fine or fee of £40 should first be paid to themselves. The Act defined the extent of English foreign trade at the time. The Merchant Adventurers sent their vessels to Spain, Portugal, Brittany, Flanders, Holland, Ireland, Normandy, France, Venice, Dantzic, Eastland, Friesland, and other parts. The Parliament allowed the fine, but limited it to ten marks, or £6 : 13 : 4. We have seen the jealousy and hatred of foreigners shown by the envious outbreak of "Evil May Day" in 1517 (p. 24).

The complaints or the justification of the rioters was that there were so many foreigners employed as craftsmen that the English could get no work; that foreign merchants brought in all silk, cloth of gold, wine, etc., and that no one, almost, bought of an Englishman; that the foreign merchants exported so much wool, tin, and lead, that English adventurers could not make a living; that they forestalled the market, buying up everything all round the City, so that nothing of value came to the City markets, while some of them imported all kinds of goods that were made in this country, such as nails, locks, baskets, cupboards, stools, tables, chests, girdles, saddles, and printed cloths.

CHAPTER III

LITERATURE AND ART

THE earliest transcribers of MSS., that is to say, publishers of books, the monks, not only transcribed MSS., but they sold their copies, the sale of books forming part of the monastic revenues. These books were either plain copies for common use, as the service books and the school books, or they were illuminated, bound with decorations of gold and silver, costing very large sums. When, however, as happened in the fifteenth century, the demand for books increased, while the revenues, and therefore the numbers, of the religious in the monasteries decreased, the multiplication of books fell into the hands of laymen. In some cases the monks themselves employed laymen as transcribers. There grew up various branches of the book trade: the maker of parchment, pens, ink, colours for illumination; the writers, the binders, the illuminators, and the sellers. As regards the value of books at any time, it is impossible to estimate it, because we must first learn the purchasing power of money, which is very difficult to ascertain; *e.g.* the price of wheat, sheep, fowls, etc., is a very fallacious test, because we do not know the standards of the time. The wage test is the safest guide. For instance, six pounds a year was thought sufficient pay for the maintenance of a chantry priest—a man considered superior to the ordinary craftsman, yet not very high in the social scale. In addition we must know the whole conditions of production; the cost of materials, the time taken by transcribers for a page or a sheet, the demand, the competition, and everything else connected with the work. Some of these points have been cleared up, but most of them can never be cleared up. It must be sufficient to understand that there was a large demand for books, and that many collections of books were formed by princes and prelates and monasteries. It was a providential circumstance that the art of printing was well advanced at the time of the Dissolution of the Religious Houses. Otherwise the losses, which were great indeed, might have been very much greater, even irreparable.

The first printers in the City of London were Caxton's workmen, Wynkyn de Worde and Richard Pynson. The former set up his press in Fleet Street, "over against the Conduit," which stood at the end of Shoe Lane; the latter, outside

Temple Bar.   In the course of the century, however, the number of printers rapidly increased, and in the reign of Elizabeth the number of books published in any branch was extraordinary.   Nothing can show more conclusively the general avidity for learning and for the possession of books in every branch of knowledge.   When, indeed, we consider that the yearly output of books in Great Britain and America now amounts to some 10,000 (a large number of them new editions), which at an average of 1000 each means 10,000,000 volumes among a population of 120,000,000, who nearly all read, without counting India, which alone contains millions of readers,

OLD TEMPLE BAR IN THE TIME OF JAMES I.
E. Gardner's Collection.

and when we remember that the whole reading public of England amounted to a few thousands, it is clear that the Elizabethan output was beyond comparison greater in proportion than our own.

It could not be long before a censorship of the Press was established.   In 1526 the printing of books against the Catholic Faith was prohibited.   Later on, that of books defending the Catholic Faith was in turn prohibited.

It was in 1557 that the very singular powers were conferred upon the Company of Stationers of suppressing and prohibiting books either seditious or heretical. These powers were absolute and subject to no appeal.   Why the Company of

Stationers was entrusted with powers which belonged to the Bishop of London and the Ecclesiastical Courts does not appear. However, the Company exercised this authority for two years, when Queen Elizabeth ordered that no book should be printed without a license being first obtained. She then, illogically, granted monopolies to certain printers and booksellers for the sale of certain books specified: to one for the sale of Bibles; to another for sale of catechism; to a third for that of music-books; and so on. To the Stationers she granted the monopoly of psalters, primers, almanacks, A B C, the "little Catechism," and Nowell's English and Latin Catechism. The printer, however, was already separating from the bookseller. As yet there was no such thing recognised as the author's rights over his own property. In many cases he did not wish his name to appear; the publisher did what he pleased with the MS.

Among the early booksellers was Richard Grafton, who was printer, bookseller, and author as well. He reprinted and continued Hall's *Chronicles*. Other publishers and booksellers of the sixteenth century were Robert Redman, who quarrelled with Richard Pynson; Henry Pepwell, who died in 1539; John Day, for whom John Foxe, who wrote the *Book of Martyrs*, worked. He issued a Church music book. He also published Bibles, Sermons, and A B C's. Day had shops successively in Holborn, Aldersgate Street, and St. Paul's Churchyard. William Middleton, whose shop was in Fleet Street, near St. Dunstan's Church, was both printer and bookseller. He published Heywood's *Four P's*, and an edition of Froissart.

Henry Smyth, Redman's son-in-law, was the publisher of Littleton's *Tenures*. Richard Tottell, whose shop was within Temple Bar, published Tusser's *Hundred Good Points of Agriculture*, Grafton's *Abridgment of the Chronicles of England*, and Stow's *Summary of the Chronicles of England*. Harrison of St. Paul's Churchyard published Shakespeare's *Venus and Adonis* in 1593, but it was printed by Richard Field, a fellow-townsman of the poet. In 1594 Harrison published *The Rape of Lucrece*. The publication of the plays, however, belongs mostly to the seventeenth century. But *Romeo and Juliet, Richard II., Richard III., Henry IV.* Part I., *Love's Labour's Lost*, were published at this time, and in 1600 *Henry IV.* Part II., *Much Ado About Nothing, A Midsummer Night's Dream, The Merchant of Venice, Titus Andronicus*, and *Henry V.* all came out. In all, eleven of the plays were published in the sixteenth and the rest in the seventeenth century.

There was an astonishing number of printers and booksellers. Thus, in addition to the names mentioned above, we may note those of Middleton, Richard Field, Harrison, father and son, William Leake, Wise, Aspley, Ling, and Nathaniel Butler, Ponsonby, Edward White, Cadman, Burby, Warde, William Barley, Humphrey Hooper, John Budge, Thorpe, and Norton.

Already the bitterness of the author against the publisher has begun. Drayton speaks of the booksellers as "a company of base knaves, whom I scorn and kick at." Complaint was made concerning a book called *A Petite Palace of Petties his Pleasure* (1576), that the printer had suppressed the name of the author, and his preface, and had substituted his own name with a preface by himself. Again, the authors complained of the advertising tricks employed to increase the sale of a book. Thus, Ben Jonson addresses his bookseller :—

> "'Thou, that mak'st gaine thy end, and wisely well
> Call'st a book good, or bad, as it doth sell,
> Use mine so, too : I give thee leave. But crave
> For luck's sake it thus much favours have,
> To lie upon thy stall till it be sought ;
> Not offer'd, as it made suit to be bought :
> Nor have my title-leaf on post, or walls,
> Or in cleft-sticks, advanced to make calls
> For termers or some clerk-like serving-man,
> Who scarce can spell th' hard names : whose knight scarce can ;
> If, without these vile arts it will not sell,
> Send it to Bucklersbury, there 'twill well.'"

Unfortunately, also, the bitterness of the author against the bookseller was accompanied by bitterness against his fellow-craftsmen. Thus Barnaby Rich says :—

"'One of the diseases of this age is the multitude of books, that doth so overcharge the world that it is not able to digest the abundance of idle matter that is every day hatched and brought into the world, that are as divers in their forms as their authors be in their faces. It is but a thriftless and a thankless occupation, this writing of books : a man were better to sit singing in a cobbler's shop, for his pay is certain a penny a patch, but a book-writer, if he gets sometimes a few commendations of the judicious, he shall be sure to reap a thousand reproaches of the malicious.'" (W. Roberts, *Earlier History of English Bookselling.*)

This brief view of bookselling in the sixteenth century may be taken to include also the first twenty years of the seventeenth, after which certain changes appear in the trade and in the relations of author and publisher.

Little has been said, so far, concerning the connection of London with literature. The history of literature belongs to the nation, not to London. Yet London could even before the Elizabethan age boast of Chaucer, Gower, Skelton, Lydgate, all of whom, at some time in their lives, resided in London. And what a list, what a splendid list, is presented of the London poets in the reign of Gloriana! This list alone, without counting the poets who went before or the poets who came after, is sufficient in itself to place England in the forefront of modern literature. Consider some of the names. Shakespeare, Ben Jonson, Marlowe, Massinger, Beaumont, Fletcher, Ford, Peele, Marston, Sackvile, Sylvester, Spenser, Raleigh—one could go on till the page became a catalogue. I have counted two hundred and forty Elizabethan poets whose names, with many of their works, have survived to the present day. In the same proportion we, who can hardly number sixty poets, ought to have now 5000. But in that time expression assumed the form of poetry first and the drama afterwards; men who had a thing to say, or a theory to state, said it in poetry, just as a man who had a tale to tell presented it in the form of a drama. Not that poetry or the drama were the only things. The Elizabethan age was rich in every form and branch of literature; it had books of chivalry, as *The Seven Champions;* story books, as *The Gesta Romanorum;* jest books, as Skogan's, Tarleton's, Skelton's, Peele's;

SIR FRANCIS BACON (1561-1626)
From the painting by Paul Van Somer in the National Portrait Gallery, London.

pastoral romances, as *The Arcadia;* "picaresque" novels, as those of Nash and Dekker; histories, as those of Holinshed, Stow, Grafton; essays, as those of Bacon, Ascham, Sir Thomas Browne; satires, as those of Hall and Marston; translations from the French and the Italian. Not even in these days is there a better, larger, fresher supply of new literature. It was above all fresh; everything was new; people did not look backwards in literature; they lived in the present; at no other time in the history of the world was the present more delightful; more full of hope, more full of joy, more full of daring. There was a new religion, not yet crystallised into Puritanism: a religion in which every man, for the first time after more than a thousand years, stood up before his Maker without an interposing priest; there was a new learning, full of wonder and of delight; there were new arts; there was a new world, a larger world, full of mysteries and monsters and undiscovered marvels; there was a new pride sprung up among the people; new adventures were possible; there were new roads to riches; England held a nobler place among the nations; everything seemed possible; the wildest extravagance was permitted in talk, in song, in the drama, in enterprise. Companies could be formed to go anywhere, and to do everything. Countries there were everywhere

WILLIAM SHAKESPEARE (1564-1616)
From the Chandos portrait in the National Portrait Gallery, London.

to be conquered, or, at least, to trade with; no longer did ocean set bounds, no longer did continents stretch forth forbidding capes: the nobler spirits were arriving at a clearer grasp and understanding of what lay before them; the machinations of Spaniard, Pope, and Priest were, it seemed, finally defeated; everything was ready for the work of such men as Raleigh and Drake. Then, alas! Gloriana died, and the world of poetry sank sadly back into prose, and that for the most part of the tamest and the most creeping; an age followed when King and people were no longer in touch; when foreign politics were a betrayal and a surrender; when the whole dream of the King was not to extend and enrich his realm, but to encroach upon the people's liberties, and the whole power of the people was required to resist the encroachments of the King. How mean and miserable is the policy of Charles compared with that of Elizabeth! How paltry are the pretensions of King and Archbishop! How wretched, save for the figure of the great Protector, is the history of the seventeenth century, compared with the history of the sixteenth under the great Queen!

Harrison furnishes a contemporary opinion on "the new veine of writing":—

"This further is not to be omitted, to the singular commendation of both sorts and sexes of our courtiers here in England, that there are verie few of them, which have not the use and skill of sundrie speaches, beside an excellent veine of writing before time not regarded. Trulie it is a rare thing with us now, to hear of a courtier which hath but his owne language. And to saie how many gentlewomen and ladies there are, that beside sound knowledge of the Greeke and Latine toongs, are thereto no lesse skilful in the Spanish, Italian, and French or in some one of them, it resteth not in me; sith I am persuaded, that as the noblemen and gentlemen do surmount in this behalfe, so these come verie little or nothing at all behind them for their parts, which industrie God continue, and accomplish that which otherwise is wanting." . . . "The ladies of the court employ themselves in continuall reading either of the holie scriptures, or histories of our owne or forren nations about us, and diverse in writing volumes of their owne, or translating of other mens into our English and Latine toongs." . . . "Finallie, to avoid idlenesse, and prevent sundrie transgressions, otherwise likelie to be committed and doone, such order is taken, that everie office hath either a bible, or the booke of the acts and monuments of the church of England, or both, beside some histories and chronicles lieing therein, for the exercise of such as come into the same; whereby the stranger that entereth into the court of England upon the sudden, shall rather imagine himselve to come into some public schools of the universities, where manie give eare to one that readeth, than unto a princes palace if you conferre the same with those of other nations. Would to God all honorable personages would take example of hir graces godlie, dealing in this behalfe, and shew their conformitie unto these hir so good beginnings which if they would, then should manie grievous offenses (wherewith God is highlie displeased) be cut off and restreined, which now doo reigne exceedinglie, in most noble and gentlemen's houses, whereof they see no paterne within hur graces gates." (Holinshed's *Chronicles*.)

Leaving the great masters, let us consider a little the more popular literature of the day; the kind which has its run among the people and is forgotten; the current literature, the books of the time, the works which were bought and read by those of the citizens who read at all, probably as large a proportion as we should find at the present day, when the newspaper is the only reading of multitudes. It is not difficult to arrive at what constituted a library. There were religious books, such as Hooper's *Sermons;* there were collections of songs, such as *The Court of Venus*, against which the clergy spoke vehemently; books of chivalry and novels in great numbers, such as *Bevis of Hampton, Guy of Warwick, Arthur of the Round Table, Huon of Bordeaux, Oliver of the Castle, Four Sons of Aymon, The Witless Devices of Gargantua* and *Howleglas*. There were the English stories, *Robin Hood, Adam Bell, Friar Rushe, The Foole of Gotham*. There were satires and fables; *Æsop*, Erasmus's *Praise of Folly, The Schoolhouse of Women, The Defense of Women, Piers Plowman, Raynolde the Fox, The Palace of Pleasure*. There were translations, as *Virgil, Seneca*, and *Apulosius;* there were books of instruction, as *The Boke of Carvynge, The Boke of Cokerye, The Boke of Nurture for Men servants, The Boke of Fortune, The Boke of Curtesey, The Boke of Chesse*, and *The Hundred Points of Good Husserye*. These titles are taken from actual lists before me; the presses were extremely active and the output of books was very considerable during the whole of Elizabeth's long reign. In a word, there was as great a variety of books for the reader's choice as there is now, setting aside the modern books in science; there were poets by the hundred, dramatists, novelists of all kinds, historians, preachers, moralists, and essayists. It would take too much space and time were I to attempt an estimate or an account of the Elizabethan literature.

EDMUND SPENSER (1552(?)-1599)
From an engraving by George Vertue.

There was, however, one form of literature then playing a very important part in the education of the people which has been too much neglected by those who write of the sixteenth century. It was the ballad. In the last century, if a man had a thing to say, he wrote a pamphlet; at present if he has a thing to say and desires that the people at large should hear it, he either casts it into the form of a novel, or he sends it to the papers as a letter or as a communication. The Elizabethan, on the other hand, cast it into the form of verse; the ballad expressed the popular opinion; by means of the ballad that opinion was formed and taught; by means of the ballad events were recorded and remembered. Every event produced its own ballad. I have before me a list of a hundred ballads, taken at random from the registers of the Stationers' Company, published for the Shakespeare Society in 1849 by Payne Collier. From these registers it is evident that the ballad, as sung in private houses, in taverns, at fairs, and where people congregated ; in the streets, in the markets, and at the Carrefours where stood the Cross and the Conduit, taught and led the people as the Press now teaches and leads them.   There was a great competition in the production of new ballads ; the printers vied with each other in getting the latest or the most striking event turned into ballad form and put upon the market.   These ballads were written on every conceivable subject.   In order to illustrate their importance I have compiled the following list roughly classified.   The titles in almost all cases indicate the contents and aim of the ballad.   Some of them are very well written.

I.—RELIGIOUS

O Lord who harte in Heaven so high.
The XV. Chapter of St. Paule.
Blessed are the Dead which dye in the Lord.
King Joseas.
Lo ! here I lye a sinner.
The Just and Patient Job.
Godly, constant, wyse, Susannah.
Wisdom would I wish to have.
The Lamentation of a Damned Soul.
The Woman taken in Adultery.
Mercy's Fort.

II.—MORAL

Persuading Men from Swearing.
Against Covetousness.
Old Age and Youth.
The House of a Harlot.
Rustrius and Sapience.
Manners for Matrons.
The Cuckoo.
A Rule for Women to bring up their Daughters.
Have Pity on the Poor.
The Abuses of Wyne, Dyce, and Women.

III.—POLITICAL

Lady Jane's Lament (*i.e.* Lady Jane Grey).
Guyn the chefe of that greedy garrison.
How a Mayde should sweep your House Clean
    (the " Mayde " is Queen Elizabeth).
News out of Kent.
Lady Englonde.

IV.—TOPICAL

On the Loss of the *Greyhound*
    (with Sir T. Finch and two hundred men).

Burnyng of Paule's.

> " Lament each over the blazing fire
>   That downe from Heaven came,
> And burned S. Powles his lofty spyre
>   With lightning's furious flame.
> Lament, I say,
> Both night and day,
> Sith London's sin did cause the same."

V.—GENERAL

Tom Long the Carrier.

Come merry home, John.

Patient Grissel.

The Bachelor.

> " Hough ! For the Bachelor ! Merry doth he live,
>   All the day long he can daunce sing and playe :
> His troubles are like to water in a sieve,
>   The more it floweth in, the more it will away :
> This is the verie truth I doe declare and saye.
>   Maryed men for him may sit, sighe, and grone,
> He is well content and letteth well alone."

Give place ye Ladies.

> " Her rosial colour comes and goes
>   With such a comely grace !
> More ruddie, too, than doth the rose,
>   Within her lively face."

Cruelness of Wicked Women.

A Fairing.

The Hunt is Up.

The Ballad of Broomes.

> " New broomes, greene broomes, will you buy any ?
> Come, maidens, come quickly, let me take a penny."

The Ballad of Milkmaids.

(The Milkmaids did not like being called Malkins.   The
    name Malkin is a diminutive of Mary, and was used
    in the sense of slattern or country wench.)

> " Passe not for rybalds which mylke maydes defame,
>   And call them not Malkins, poor Malkins by name :
> Their trade is as good as anie we knowe
> And that it is so I will presently showe.
>   Downe & Downe &c."

A Merry Rhyme concerning Butchers, Graysors,
    Schole maisters and Tankard Bearers.

Ruffle, Sleeves and Hose.

The Nut Brown Mayd.

Row well ye marynors.

God send me a wyfe that will do as I say.

This list might be multiplied indefinitely.   Enough has been given to show
that the ballad was the principal medium by which the people were moved and

taught. One would not underrate the power of the sermon. At no time, not even in the seventeenth century, was the sermon more powerful than under Elizabeth; but the sermon chiefly treated of doctrine and the ballads taught morals and the conduct of life. Nay, in these cases, which were many, when a ballad secular, amatory, scandalous, or immoral, had become popular, the clergy took it in hand and moralised it: *i.e.* presented a religious parody of it, which they persuaded the people to sing instead of the first version. For example, here is part of a " moralised " ballad :—

> " To pass the place where pleasure is
>   It ought to please one fantasie,
> If that the pleasure be amis,
>   And to God's Work plaine contrarie,
> Or else we sinne, we sinne,
> And hell we winne,
> Great panic therein
>   All remedie gone.
> Except in Christ alone, alone."

We must not forget to take account in this brief review of the topical writings of the day of the difference of dialect. It is not too much to say that a Norfolk countryman would not understand a Kentish lad; and that a Yorkshire man would talk a strange tongue to a man of the Midlands. Caxton says, writing a little earlier :—

" Englishe that is spoken in one shire varyeth from another; insomuch, that in my dayes happened, that certain merchaunts were in a ship in Tamyse, for to have sailed over the see into Zelande, and for lacke of wynde they taryed att Forland, and went to land for to refresh them; and one of them, named Sheffelde, a mercer, came into a hows, and axed for mete, and specially he axed for egges; the good wyfe answerde that she could speke no French. And the merchaunt was angry, for he also could speake no French; but wolde have egges, and she understode hym not. And thenne at last another sayd, that he would have ceyren; thenne the good wyfe said, that she understode him."

In the year 1592 was published a book in prose and verse by Richard Johnson, entitled *The Nine Worthies of London*, inscribed to Sir William Webbe, Lord Mayor of London. Its wide popularity proves that it presents some, at least, of the ideas current among the people. To begin with, the "Nine Worthies" are not by any means, with one exception, those ancient citizens whom we should now consider of the greatest renown. We do not find here the names of Thomas à Becket, Whittington, Philpot, or Gresham. The things worthy to be remembered are neither enterprise in trade, nor vigilance in guarding the liberties of the City, nor the acquisition of wealth, nor charities and endowments. The only thing worthy to be remembered, even among citizens of London, is prowess of arms. The "Nine Worthies" come out, one after the other, and relate their own achievements. It is certain that Richard Johnson did not himself select these men for honourable mention, because they are clearly referred to in a passage of the *Paradise of daintie Devices :—*

> " The Worthies nine that were of might,
> By travaile wonne immortal praise ;
> If they had lived like carpet knights,
> Consuming idly all their dayes,
> Their praises had been with them dead,
> Where now abroad their fame is spread."

The work is reprinted in the *Harleian Miscellany*, vol. viii., from which I take the following extracts : first, William Walworth (p. 443) :—

> " But when I saw the rebells' pride encrease,
> And none controll and counterchecke their rage ;
> 'Twere service good (thought I) to purchase peace,
> And malice of contentious brags asswage ;
> With this conceyt, all fear had taken flight.
> And I alone prest to the traitor's sight.
>
> Their multitude could not amaze my minde,
> Their bloudie weapons did not make me shrink ;
> True valour hath his constancie assignde,
> The eagle at the sunne will never winke ;
> Amongst their troupes, incenst with mortall hate,
> I did arest Wat Tiler on the pate.
>
> The stroke was given with so good a will,
> I made the rebell coutch unto the earth ;
> His fellows that beheld ('tis strange) were still ;
> It mar'd the manner of their former mirth ;
> I left him not, but, ere I did depart,
> I stab'd my dagger to his damned heart."

Second, Henry Picard, or Pilchard, who entertained the four kings of England, Scotland, France, and Cyprus, with the Black Prince (p. 445) :—

> "When Edward triumpht for his victories,
> And held three crownes within his conquering hand,
> He brought rich trophies from his enemies,
> That were erected in this happie land ;
> We all rejoyc'd and gave our God the praise,
> That was the authour of those fortunate dayes.
>
> And as from Dover, with the prince his sonne,
> The king of Cypres, France, and Scots, did passe,
> All captive prisoners to this mightie one,
> Five thousand men and I the leader was ;
> All well prepared as to defend a fort ;
> Went forth to welcome him in martiall sort.
>
> The riches of our armour, and the cost,
> Each one bestows in honour of that day,
> Were here to be exprest but labour lost ;
> Silke coates and chaines of golde bare little sway ;
> And thus we marcht accepted of our king
> To whom our comming seem'd a gracious thing.
>
> But when the citie pearde within our sights,
> I carv'd a boune submisse upon my knee ;
> To have his grace, those kings, with earles and knights,
> A day or two to banquet it with me ;
> The king admirde, yet thankfully replide,
> ' Unto my house both I and these will ride.' "

Third, William Sevenoake, who went over to France with Henry V. as a lad just out of his apprenticeship, and there fought with the Dauphin (p. 447) :—

> " The Dolphyne then of France, a comelie knight,
>   Disguised, came by chaunce into a place,
> Where I, well wearied with the heate of fight,
>   Had layd me downe, for warre had ceast his chace ;
> And with reproachful words, as layzie swaine
>   He did salute me, ere I long had layne.
>
> I, knowing that he was mine enemie,
>   A bragging French-man (for we tearm'd them so)
> Ill brookt the proud disgrace he gave to me
>   And therefore, lent the Dolphyne such a blowe,
> As warm'd his courage well to lay about,
>   Till he was breathlesse, though he were so stout.
>
> At last the noble prince did aske my name,
>   My birth, my calling, and my fortunes past ;
> With admiration he did heare the same,
>   And so a bagge of crownes to me he cast ;
> And when he went away, he saide to mee,
>   ' Sevenoake, be prowd, the Dolphyne fought with thee.' "

Fourth, Thomas White, who founded schools and almshouses (p. 449) :—

> " I cannot sing of armes and blood-red warres,
>   Nor was my collur mixt with Mars his hew ;
> I honour those that ended countrey jarres,
>   For herein subjects shew that they are trew ;
> But privately at home I shewde my selfe,
>   To be no lover of vaine worldly pelfe.
>
> My deedes have tongues to speak, though I surcease,
>   My orators the learned strive to bee,
> Because I twined paulmes in time of peace,
>   And gave such gifts, that made faire learning free ;
> My care did build them bowers of sweet content,
>   Where many wise their golden time have spent.
>
> A noyse of gratefull thankes within mine eares,
>   Descending from their studies, glads my heart,
> That I began to wish with private teares,
>   There lived more that were of White's desert ;
> But now I looke, and spie that time is balde,
>   And Vertue comes not, being seldome calde."

Fifth, John Bonham, citizen and mercer, who went to Denmark with his merchandise, there was received at Court and distinguished himself at a tournament—the only occasion on record of a merchant fighting in a tournament—and finally led an army to victory over the Great Solyman, who made him a knight after the defeat of the Turk :—

> " Then, at a parley he admirde me so ;
>   He made me knight and let his armie go."

Sixth, Christopher Croker. Alas! the world has forgotten Christopher. He was a vintner's 'prentice. He was loved by Doll Stodie, his master's daughter ; and he burned to give her a better position ; he joined the army of the Black Prince

in France; distinguished himself there; went with him to Spain, and returned
a knight :—

> "And when Don Peter, driven out of Spaine,
> By an usurping bastard of his line,
> He craved some helpe his crowne to re-obtaine,
> That in his former glorie he might shine;
> Our king ten thousand sever'd from his host;
> My selfe was one, I speake it not in boast.
>
> With these Don Peter put the bastard downe,
> Each citie yielded at our first approch;
> It was not long ere he had got the crowne;
> And taught his wicked brother to encroch;
> In these affaires so well I shewed my might,
> That for my labour I was made a knight.
>
> Thus labour never looseth his reward;
> And he that seeks for honour sure shall speed;
> What craven mind was ever in regard?
> Or where consisteth manhood but in deed?
> I speake it, that confirm'd it by my life,
> And in the end, Doll Stodie was my wife."

Seventh, John Hawkwood, the Prince of Mercenaries. He, too, belonged to
the Black Prince and was knighted by him.

Eighth, Hugh Caverley, silk weaver, who also became a knight in France and
signalised himself afterwards by slaying a monstrous wild boar which devastated
Poland.

Ninth, and last, Henry Maleverer, grocer, Knight Crusader and Custodian
of Jacob's Well :—

> "And thus with love, with honour, and with fame,
> I did return to London whence I came."

It is a curious list, and shows what legends of former citizens had grown up
in the minds of the people. They had clean forgotten the old Patron Saints of
London, St. Erkenwald and St. Thomas à Becket; they had forgotten Philpot and
his splendid achievement over the pirates of the North Sea; they had forgotten
Waleys, Mayor of Bordeaux and of London; they had forgotten Dick Whittington;
they had even forgotten Gresham, and in place of the men who had made London
and brought wealth, prosperity, and freedom to the town, they remembered
mythical adventures and traditions of battle and of victory. One would like to
know more about the popular belief in "London Worthies."

The wholesale destruction of MSS. and mediæval libraries, at the Suppression
of the Religious Houses, though doubtless a heavy loss from an artistic point of
view, considering the loss of illuminated books, may be considered as compensated
by the increased activity of the press and the reconstruction of the library. What
was actually lost to literature? John Bale tells us, Manuscripts of the Fathers,
Schoolmen, and Commentators. Was this a loss? It is quite certain that the

17

monkish commentators regarded their text from a point of view no longer held: the Holy Scriptures, they said, were lost. The manuscript copies were very likely lost, but the press multiplied copies. I think that the greatest loss to literature was the loss of certain chronicles, of which we have so many left, which relate the history of current events as the monkish scribe heard and understood them. In any case, the destruction of so many books made it impossible, henceforward, to consider a library as made up chiefly of manuscripts; the press rapidly restored the books that were wanted; and gave the world a library filled with printed books, while the old commentators were clean forgotten.

The age of great folios and mighty scholars was the seventeenth, rather than the sixteenth, century. In the sixteenth, scholars were busy in putting forth new editions of the classics. Men like Dolet and Rabelais were not ashamed to correct for the press. The voluminous commentator came afterwards. Meantime, it is remarkable that we had no Rabelais among our writers. He, formerly a friar, came out of the cloister, his head filled with the old learning and eager for the new. His great book became at once popular, and was eagerly passed from hand to hand. The origins of his chapters have quite recently been explored and discovered in Mr. W. F. Smith's excellent translation. They are shown to be chiefly extracts from gloss and commentary, burlesqued, imitated, and held up to the ridicule and scorn of scholars. The common people understood only the bubbling mirth and laughter, coupled with the spontaneous unseemliness of the page; the scholar understood the allegory and the purpose of the writer; the ecclesiastic alone, and one of the older type, understood the true nature of the overwhelming contempt and hatred of the order that was passing away—contempt and hatred thinly veiled and concealed except for those who knew the gloss and commentary of the past. We have no Rabelais; among all our friars there was no scholar; among our ejected monks, if there were scholars, they stuck by their order; among all the priests, monks, and friars, who joined in the Reformation, there was not one who so despised the old faith as to make it the theme of such a book as that of Rabelais. Hatred there was in plenty, after the fires of Smithfield: hatred which continued to flourish in our literature and still lingers; but not the full bitterness of hatred, fear, contempt, and restlessness which fill the pages of Rabelais, Étienne Dolet, and Bonaventure des Periers.

Painting in London practically began with the Tudors, and was brought over to the City by Flemish and Dutch painters. Among these we find the names of Lucas and Gerard Horenbout, Volpe, Gerbud Flick, Johannes Corvus, Levina Terling, Susanna Horenbout, and Alice Carmillion. But the great name of Holbein towers above all the rest. This painter was born at Augsburg about 1497, went to Basle in 1516, and came to London in 1526. He continued in London, with the exception of three visits to Basle, until his death in 1543, residing first in a

lodging on London Bridge, and next in a house in the parish of St. Andrew
Undershaft, where he died.

As regards his contemporaries and successors, we are indebted to the
researches of the late John Gough Nichols for information on this point. They
are embodied in a paper published by the Society of Antiquaries (xxxix. p. 19).

The earliest Court Painter to Henry VIII. was one John Browne. He was
appointed in 1511 a Serjeant Painter with a salary of twopence a day and four ells
of cloth, valued at 6s. 8d. an ell, annually. Three pounds a year is not a large

BEN JONSON (1573(?)-1637)
From the painting in the National Portrait Gallery, London, after Gerard Honthorst.

salary, but probably he was paid in addition for any work which he might do;
thus, he was paid forty shillings for a painted tabard of sarsenet provided by him
for Nottingham Pursuivant. In 1522 he was elected Alderman for Farringdon
Without, and in 1525 he was discharged from office without having been either
Sheriff or Mayor. He gave by will to the Painter Stainers' Company his house
for their hall: the present Hall stands upon the site of Browne's bequest.

John Browne was succeeded as Serjeant Painter by Andrew Wright. This
painter received £30 for painting and decorating the King's barge. He had a
manufactory of "pink," a vegetable pigment used by painters at that time; it

was the Italian *giallo santo* and the French *stel de grain*. Wright died in 1543.

Vincent Volpe, a contemporary of the two preceding, supplied, in 1514, streamers and banners for the King's great ship, the *Henry Grace à Dieu*. He is called in 1530 the "King's Painter." It is suggested that it was Volpe who painted some of the military pictures at Hampton Court. He also received money for the decoration of the King's barge. The "King's Painter" seems to have held a higher rank than the Serjeant Painter, for Volpe's salary was £10 a year.

Two other Flemish artists, Lucas and Gerard Horenbout, were also in the receipt of salaries from the King; their father was also, perhaps, a painter and a Fleming. Their sister Susanna was a painter of miniatures. She was the wife, first, of Henry Parker the King's bowman, and, secondly, of a sculptor named Worsley.

An Italian named Antonio Toto was a native of Florence, the son of a painter and the pupil of Ridolpho. He was architect as well as painter. His principal building was the strange palace of Nonsuch (see p. 89). Toto was, like Andrew Wright, a Serjeant Painter. For the coronation of Edward VI. he provided the tabards for the heralds; he also took charge of the masques.

Another Italian attached to Henry's Court was Bartolomo Penni. The names of three women have been given above: Alice Carmillion was in Henry's service; Levina Terling in Edward's, Mary's, and Elizabeth's successively.

Holbein's most illustrious successor among his contemporaries was Guillim Streets, or Strettes. Among other paintings by this admirable artist was one of the marriage of Queen Mary. The picture, however, is lost.

Nicholas Lyzarde was Serjeant Painter to Queen Elizabeth. He died in 1571.

The names Antonio Moro and Joost van Cleef may also be added to those of the painters who lived in London during the sixteenth century.

The decay of the London schools and of learning in general, which undoubtedly began in the fifteenth century and continued until far into the following century, is difficult to understand. One can only form theories and make guesses. The fact cannot be disputed. There were forces at work which have not been recorded. The Lollardry of the late fourteenth and early fifteenth centuries seems to have been in great measure forgotten. Yet, as I have pointed out and proved, the custom of making bequests to the Religious Houses declined and decayed until it quite died away, long before the Reformation. The old spirit of revolt left behind it a steady and persistent and growing spirit of dissatisfaction. Perhaps this spirit was shown in the decay of the monastic schools. We have seen how, in 1477, four of the London clergy asked, and obtained, permission to found additional schools in four parishes. The new schools could do little; the Reformation accelerated the decay of learning partly by the abolition of the monastic schools; partly by the vast reduction in the number of ecclesiastics; partly by the loss of the endowments by which learning had been encouraged and maintained: an increased trade, with foreign enterprise, also attracted the younger men in numbers continually increasing. So few were the undergraduates of Oxford that in Queen Mary's reign only three took a degree in Divinity during the space of six years; in Civil Law only eleven; in Physic six; in Arts an average of about twenty-three. Anthony à Wood writes: "There were none that had

Spooner & Co.

HOLBEIN (1497-1543)
From the portrait by himself at Hampton Court.

any heart to put their children to any school, any farther than to learn to write— to make them Apprentices or Lawyers."

I would enumerate among the causes of the general decay in learning: (1) the unsettled nature of religious opinions; (2) the changed ideas concerning education; (3) the destruction of the Houses, which, if they turned out few scholars, offered a quiet home for the studious; (4) the advance in trade and enterprise, which attracted the youth of London far more than study; (5) the contempt into which the mass of the Protestant clergy had fallen: (6) a feeling of uneasiness about scholarship, lest it should bring one to the stake, of which there had been presented many terrifying examples.

Of music there is a much nobler record. Never before had the people been such great lovers of music, and such admirable proficients. In every barber's shop was hung a zither or a guitar; anybody played; everybody sang. Henry VIII. himself was a composer of no mean capability, and a performer equal to any. Elizabeth upon the virginals was unequalled. Many of the anthems and madrigals of the period survive to this day and are still sung. The music of the Chapel Royal was held to be better than anything of the kind in Western Europe. Would that the musical tastes and traditions of London had been preserved! They were destroyed by the Puritans. They were destroyed slowly but effectively. At the Restoration it was still the custom for gentlemen to play and sing; but not, apparently, for the trading and lower classes; during the last century, neither gentlefolk nor any other folk could play or sing; music ceased to be cultivated by the people. Nor have we yet, even, begun to be a people given to music; it is still comparatively rare to find boys who are taught to play any instrument; at no public school is it thought to be an essential part of education. Perhaps the twentieth century may witness a revival of the national love for music.

CHAPTER IV

GOG AND MAGOG

IT seems impossible to ascertain why these names were bestowed upon the City Giants. The prophet Ezekiel (chs. xxxviii. and xxxix.) prophesies against "Gog, the land of Magog, the Chief Prince of Meshech, and Tubal." In the Book of Revelation (xx. 8) Satan goes out "to deceive the nations which are in the four quarters of the earth, Gog and Magog." How were these names applied to City Giants? It was a common thing to have a City Giant who was carried in processions; there were giants at Chester, Salisbury, and Coventry; there were giants at Antwerp, Bruges, Ghent, Douai, Lille, and Brussels. The giants were in every case connected in some way with the legendary history of the City. But while every city had its own giant, who was brought out on festive occasions, this did not prevent the construction of other giants. Thus, after the victory of Agincourt, when Henry V. was received by a pageant of extraordinary splendour, a giant and a giantess stood on the Southwark end of London Bridge to greet him. The giant carried in his right hand an axe, and in the left the City keys, as if he were the porter of the town. In 1432, when Henry VI. came to England after his Coronation in France, there was another giant at London Bridge. He stood with drawn sword, and had at his side the following verses written out large :—

> "All those that be enemies to the King,
> I shall them clothe with confusion,
> Make him mighty by virtuous living,
> His mortal foes to oppress and bear them down ;
> And bid him to increase as Christ's champion.
> All mischiefs from him to abridge,
> With grace of God, at the entry of this Bridge."
>
> *Lord Mayor's Pageants.*

In 1547, when the boy-king Edward passed through the City, among the figures presented to him were two representing Valentine and Orson.

In 1554, when Philip came to London, there was a great pageant to receive him with the Queen. At the drawbridge of the Tower there were placed the two giants, Corineus and Gogmagog, holding between them a scroll inscribed with Latin verses.

In January 1559, when Queen Elizabeth rode through the City she was received with a pageant of great splendour. At Temple Bar the last show was that of the two City Giants, Corineus and Gogmagog, who had between them a recapitulation of the whole pageant. Here the singing children made a "noise," while one of them, attired like a poet, bade the Queen farewell in the name of the City.

The giants seem to have been omitted from the Royal pageants and processions of the seventeenth century.

In 1605 the Lord Mayor's Pageant was adorned by the presence of the giants.

"The first Pageant was 'The Shippe called the Royall Exchange,' in which takes place a short poetical dialogue between the master, mate and boy, who congratulate themselves on the fortunate termination of their voyage at this auspicious time, the master ending the dialogue by a punning allusion to the Mayor's name, when he declared his intention

'To make this up a cheerful *Holi-day.*'

Neptune and Amphitrite appear upon a lion and camel; and Corineus and Gogmagog, two huge giants, 'for the more grace and beauty of the show,' were fettered by chains of gold to 'Britains Mount,' the principal pageant; which they appeared to draw, and upon which children were seated, representing Britannia; 'Brute's divided kingdoms,' Leogria, Cambria, and Albania; 'Brute' himself, his sons Locrine, Camber, and Albanact; Troya Nova, or London; and the Rivers Thames, Severn, and Humber, who each declaim in short speeches, the purport of which is that as England, Wales, and Scotland were first sundered by Brutus to supply his three sons with a kingdom each, they are now again happily united in 'our second Brute,' King James the first." (Fairholt, *Lord Mayor's Pageants.*)

The giants disappeared from the Lord Mayor's Pageants soon after this. In 1633, Clod, a country-man, in Shirley's *Contention for Honour and Riches*, says :—

"When the word is given, you march to Guildhall, with every man his spoon in his pocket, where you look upon the giants, and feed like Saracens, till you have no stomach to Paul's in the afternoon." (*Ibid.*)

In the Lord Mayor's Pageant for 1673 the giants came out again. This pageant was designed by Thomas Jordan. It appears to have been their first appearance after the Fire.

"I must not omit to tell you, that marching in the van of these five pageants, are two exceeding rarities to be taken notice of; that is, there are two extreme great giants, each of them at least fifteen foot high, that do sit and are drawn by horses in two several chariots, moving, talking, and taking tobacco as they ride along, to the great admiration and delight of all the spectators; at the conclusion of the show they are to be set up in Guildhall, where they may be daily seen all the year, and I hope never to be demolished by such dismal violence as happened to their predecessors; which are raised at the peculiar and proper cost of the city." (*Ibid.*)

It would seem that in many of the pageants it was not thought necessary to set down the fact that the giants formed part, for in Henley's Orations (1730–1755) there is one on the Lord Mayor's Show which contains the following passage: "On that day, the two giants have the priviledge, if they think it proper, to walk out and keep holiday; one on each side of the great horse would aggrandize the solemnity, shew consisting often in bulk." (*Ibid.*)

In Stow's description of the setting of the watch on Midsummer's Eve, he says: "The Mayor had, beside his giants, three pageants, whereas the Sheriffs had only two, besides their giants." In Marston's *Dutch Courtezan*, acted 1605, an allusion is made to the giants: "yet all will scarce make me so high as one of the gyant's stilts that stalks before my Lord Mayor's Pageants."

George Wither (1661) calls the giants "Big-boned Colbrant and great Brandsmore."

> "The giants at Guildhall . . .
>   . . . .
> Where they have had a place to them assigned
> At public meetings, now time out of mind."

The last appearance of the giants in a procession was in 1837, when they graced the Lord Mayor's Show.

The legends of the City Giants were two in number. The first related how Brutus, one of the Trojan heroes, wandering after the Fall of Troy, like Æneas, came to Britain, which he found full of giants. He fought with these giants and destroyed them all except two, named Gog and Magog, whom he brought to his new City of London and chained to the palace gates. Another legend relates how Corineus, brother of Brutus, fought the giants Gog and Magog, and, being himself stronger than his unwieldy antagonists, threw them headlong into the sea. The two giants of Guildhall, according to this legend, were Corineus and Gogmagog. The names of Gog and Magog were certainly taken either from Ezekiel or the Book of Revelation, and were applied to the giants after Corineus had been forgotten, as the names of princes over an infidel people: they were represented, not as tutelary giants, but as conquered giants. It will be observed that one is represented as a Roman, with helmet and shield, sword, spear, and armour, while the other is apparelled, after the artist's imagination, as an ancient Briton.

They were originally made of wicker-work; after the Great Fire, which destroyed them, they were reconstructed of the same materials, but in 1707 they were made of wood, as we now see them.

SOCIAL LIFE

CHAPTER I

IN this chapter we can make a large use of contemporary literature. Thus, the first consideration in treating of the manners and customs of the people is naturally the position of the wife and the consideration shown to her. I do not think that in any country could either the position of the wife or the consideration for her surpass what was then in vogue in London. This point Emanuel van Meteren, writing in 1575, makes abundantly clear, even while he contends the exact opposite, viz. that the wife is entirely in the power of the husband. For he shows that whatever the law may be—he does not quote the law—the practice is that the wife has entire liberty; and custom, *i.e.* public opinion, against which no husband would dare to move, secures her that liberty. This is what he says :—

"Wives in England are entirely in the power of their husbands, their lives only excepted. Therefore when they marry, they give up the surname of their father and of the family from which they are descended, and take the surname of their husbands, except in the case of duchesses, countesses, and baronesses, who, when they marry gentlemen of inferior degree, retain their first name and title, which, for the ambition of the said ladies, is rather allowed than commended. But although the women are entirely in the power of their husbands except for their lives, yet they are not kept so strictly as they are in Spain, or elsewhere. Nor are they shut up, but they have the free management of the house or housekeeping, after the fashion of those of the Netherlands and others their neighbours. They go to market to buy what they like best to eat. They are well-dressed, fond of taking it easy, and commonly leave the care of household matters and drudgery to their servants. They sit before their doors, decked out in fine clothes, in order to see and be seen by the passers-by. In all banquets and feasts they are shown the greatest honour; they are placed at the upper end of the table, where they are the first served; at the lower end they help the men. All the rest of their time they employ in walking and riding, in playing at cards or otherwise, in visiting their friends and keeping company, conversing with their equals (whom they term gossips) and their neighbours, and making merry with them at child-births, christenings, churchings, and funerals; and all this with the permission and knowledge of their husbands, as such is the custom. Although the husbands often recommend to them the pains, industry, and care of the German or Dutch women, who do what the men ought to do both in the house and in the shops, for which services in England men are employed, nevertheless the women usually persist in retaining their customs. This is why England is called the Paradise of married women. The girls who are not yet married are kept much more rigorously and strictly than in the Low Countries. The women are beautiful, fair, well-dressed and modest, which is seen there more than elsewhere, as they go about the streets without any covering either of mantle, hood, veil, or the like. Married women only wear a hat both on the street and in the house; those unmarried go without a hat, although ladies of distinction have lately learnt to cover their faces with silken masks or vizards, and feathers,—for indeed they change very easily, and that every year, to the astonishment of many."

If this was the ordinary life of the London merchant's wife, the following is the contemporary ideal (Gervase Markham):—

"Next unto her sanctity and holiness of life, it is meet that our English Housewife be a woman of great modesty and temperance, as well inwardly as outwardly; inwardly, as in her behaviour and carriage towards her husband, wherein she shall shun all violence of rage, passion and humour, coveting less to direct than to be directed, appearing ever unto him pleasant, amiable and delightful; and tho' occasion of mishaps, or the mis-government of his will may induce her to contrary thoughts, yet vertuously to suppress them, and with a mild sufferance rather to call him home from his error, than with the strength of anger to abate the least spark of his evil, calling into her mind, that evil and uncomely language is deformed, though uttered even to servants; but most monstrous and ugly, when it appears before the presence of a husband; outwardly, as in her apparel, and dyet, both which she shall proportion according to the competency of her husband's estate and calling, making her circle rather strait than large; for it is a rule, if we extend to the uttermost, we take away increase; if we go a hair's breadth beyond, we enter into consumption; but if we preserve any part, we build strong forts against the adversaries of fortune, provided that such preservation be honest and conscionable; for as lavish prodigality is brutish, so miserable covetousness is hellish. Let therefore the Housewife's garments be comely and strong, made as well to preserve the health, as to adorn the person, altogether without toyish garnishes, or the gloss of bright colours, and as far from the vanity of new and fantastick fashions, as near to the comely imitation of modest matrons. Let her dyet be wholesome and cleanly, prepared at due hours, and cook'd with care and diligence, let it be rather to satisfie nature, than her affections, and apter to kill hunger than revive new appetites; let it proceed more from the provision of her own yard, than the furniture of the markets; and let it be rather esteemed for the familiar acquaintance she hath with it, than for the strangeness and rarity it bringeth from other countries.

To conclude, our English Housewife must be of chaste thoughts, stout courage, patient, untired, watchful, diligent, witty, pleasant, constant in friendship, full of good neighbourhood, wise in discourse, but not frequent therein, sharp and quick of speech, but not bitter or talkative, secret in her affairs, comfortable in her counsels, and generally skilful in the worthy knowledges which do belong to her vocation."

But to set against this is the testimony of the Elizabethan satirist Philip Stubbes.

The principal occupation of the women, he tells us—their daily life—is to lie in bed till nine or ten in the morning; to spend two hours in dressing themselves; then to go to dinner; then, "their heads pretely mizzeled with wine," they walk abroad for a time; or they sit at their open doors showing their braveries to passers-by; or they pretend business in the town and carry a basket, "under what pretence pretie concerts are practised." Or again they have those gardens in the fields outside already alluded to, whither they repair with a boy and a basket and meet their lovers.

A WOMAN'S DAY

" Daily till ten a clocke a bed she lyes,
And then againe her Lady-ship doth rise,
Her Maid must make a fire, and attend
To make her ready; then for wine sheele send,
(A morning pinte), she sayes her stomach's weake,
And counterfeits as if shee could not speake,
Vntill eleuen, or a little past,
About which time, euer she breakes her fast;
Then (very sullen) she wil pout and loure,
And sit down by the fire some halfe an houre.
At twelue a clocke her dinner time she keepes,
Then gets into her chaire, and there she sleepes
Perhaps til foure, or somewhat thereabout;
And when that lazie humour is worne out,
She cals her dog, and takes him in her lap,
Or fals a beating of her maid (perhap)
Or hath a gossip come to tell a tale,
Or else at me sheele curse, and sweare, and rale,
Or walk a turne or two about the Hall,
And so to supper and to bed: heeres all
This paines she takes; and yet I do abuse her:
But no wise man, I thinke, so kind would vse her. . . ."

STUBBES, *Anatomie of Abuses*, Part ii. p. 274.

In the streets a lady of condition was preceded by a lackey carrying a stick or wand. Gentlemen were followed by their servants carrying the master's sword. The servants were dressed in blue with the master's badge in silver on the left arm. The men kept on their hats indoors except in warm weather.

The nobles, who were mostly poor, joined with the merchant adventurers in their foreign enterprises; many of the merchants were consulted by the Sovereign and held positions of trust—for example, Gresham; yet the separation of City and Court was already beginning, as is shown by the repeated sneers of the dramatists at the vulgarity and ostentation of the City Madams. We get occasional glimpses of the lower class women and girls; they were rough in their manners and coarse in their conversation; we find them dancing in the street to the music of the tabor and the pipe; we also see them playing at ball up and down the street, like the 'prentices. They lived, like the men, on strong meat and beer; they were therefore physically strong, perhaps as strong as the young men their lovers. The richer sort of citizens had country gardens, generally small enclosures, either in or north of Moorfields, whither they resorted in the long summer evenings; their wives, it is said, used the gardens in the morning for assignations and the carrying on of intrigues.

In the morning the haunt of the gallants was St. Paul's Cathedral. (*See* Appendix VIII.) They walked up and down the middle of the nave, called then the " Mediterranean," exhibiting their new cloaks and their new feathers. After a few turns up and down, or when the clock struck eleven, they left the place and disappeared, going to some of the shops, the tobacconist's, or the bookseller's, where they took tobacco and talked about the new books. They then repaired to an ordinary and spent two or three hours over dinner, after which they went back to St. Paul's and spent there the whole afternoon.

The merchant had his Exchange; the citizen his tavern; the gallant had the apothecary's shop, where he bought and smoked his tobacco. For daily discourse and business the scholar, the divine, the poet, the wit, had the bookseller's shop. " He will sit you," said Ben Jonson, " a whole afternoon in a bookseller's shop, reading the Greek, Italian, and Spanish." He would read, and he would talk. Remember that in the year 1590 or thereabouts the art of printing had only been in use a hundred years; all the books were new books; every poet was printed or translated for the first time; the booksellers' shops contained editions, always new, of ancient classics; of living poets; of foreign writers; there was far greater interest in a new book than our age can understand: as we have seen there were in London alone at least 240 poets, known and acknowledged, whose names are still remembered, and whose poems still remain Anthologies, and there was interest among the reading world in every one of them. There may have been jealousies: poets have always been a jealous folk; but there was appreciation, and there was generosity. And the bookseller's shop was the place where all who valued new books could meet and talk of books—what talk is more delightful? What criticism more sincere than that between those who themselves belong to letters in an age when literature knows not yet the meaning of the words exhaustion or decay?

Mr. Ordish (*Shakespeare's London*, p. 233) has compiled a list of Elizabethan booksellers from the title-pages of the Shakespeare quartos. Such a list was well worth making, though it cannot be considered more than a small instalment. Indeed, the literary output was so enormous during the latter half of the sixteenth century, that the number of booksellers must have been proportionately greater than at present.

The following were some of the signs :—

I. In St. Paul's Churchyard—

> At the sign of the Angel, the Fox, the Flower de Luce and the Crown, the Greyhound, the Green Dragon, the Holy Ghost, the Gun (Edward White), the Pied Bull, the Spread Eagle.

II. By St. Dunstan's in the West—

> At the sign of the White Hart ; at the shop under the Dial.

III. In Paternoster Row—

> At the sign of the Sun.

IV. Cornhill—

> At the sign of the Cat and Parrots.

V. In Carter Lane, near the Paul Head.

Plays and masques were performed on Sunday as well as any other day ; the feeling, however, was growing rapidly in favour of a stricter attention to the Sunday, which was confused with the Sabbath. In other words, the Puritans were fast increasing in numbers and in importance.

If amusement was wanted it might also be sought in the street, where the juggler with his music and his tumbler had his regular round. He was distinguished by his thin, coloured cloak and his yellow breeches trimmed with blue. For a modest fee he performed for any who summoned him. Another form of amusement, suitable to those who could not afford to pay the itinerant juggler, and had to consider the expenditure in candles, was to sit round the fire in the evening and tell stories.

> " . . . some mery fit
> Of Mayde-Marian, or else of Robin Hood."

As for the girls :—

> " Then is it pleasure the yonge maides amonge,
> To watch by the fier the winter-nights longe ;
> And in the ashes some playes for to marke,
> And cover wardes for fault of other warke ;
> To taste white shevers, to make prophet-roles ;
> And, after talke, oft times to fille the boles."

In the private houses there was a great deal of whipping; gentlemen had their servants whipped in the porter's lodge ; to be whipped was no disgrace, but a natural part of servitude, no more to be deplored than the necessity of death ;

ladies whipped their maid-servants, their sons and their daughters; when a child had been whipped the rod was tied to her girdle, with what we should perhaps consider an excess of admonition. Children knelt before their parents until bidden to rise. On their knees, too, they asked for their father's blessing. If we may believe Caxton, who died in 1491, and therefore hardly belongs to the Tudor period, there was a great falling off in the behaviour of children in his own recollection. It is a mark of increasing years to compare things of the present with things of the past to the disparagement of the former.

> "I see that the children ben borne within the sayd cyte encrease and prouffyte· not like their faders and olders; but for mooste parte, after that they ben comeyn to theyr perfight yeres of discretion and rypnes of age, kno well that theyre faders haue lefte to them grete quantite of goodes, yet scarcely among ten two thrive. O blessed Lord! when I remember this, I am al abashed; I cannot judge the cause; but fayrer ne wyser, ne bet bespeken children in theyre youth ben no wher than ther ben in London; but at ther ful ryping, there is no carnel, ne good word found en, but chaff for the most part."

As for the boys of the household, they either went to one of the City schools or they were instructed by a tutor at home. Probably the latter was unusual when schools were ready to hand. In country places the tutor was common, and his position was anything but pleasant.

"Such is the most base and ridiculous parsimony of many of our Gentlemen (if I may so terme them) that if they can procure some poore Batchelor of Art from the Universitie to teach their children to say grace, will be content upon the promise of ten pounds a yeere at his first comming, to be pleased with five; the rest to be set off in hope of the next advouson (which perhaps was sold before the young man was born). Or if it chance to fall in his time, his lady or master tels him, 'Indeed, Sir, we are beholden unto you for your paines; such a living is lately falne, but I had before made a promise of it to my butler or bailiffe, for his true and extraordinary service.'

Is it not commonly seen, that the most Gentlemen will give better wages, and deale more bountifully with a fellow who can but a dogge, or reclaime a hawke, than upon an honest, learned, and well qualified man to bring up their children? It may be, hence it is, that dogges are able to make syllogismes in the fields, when their young masters can conclude nothing at home, if occasion of argument or discourse be offered at the table."

Did the great City merchant ever maintain the domestic chaplain? I have found no instance of such a servant in the household of a citizen. Bishop Hall assigns the domestic chaplains to the country gentleman :—

> "A gentle squire would gladly entertain
> Into his house some trencher-chappelain;
> Some willing man that might instruct his sons,
> And that would stand to good conditions.
> First, that he lie upon the truckle-bed,
> While his young maister lieth o'er his head;

Second, that he do, on no default,
Ever presume to sit above the salt ;
Third, that he never change his trencher twice ;
Fourth, that he use all common courtesies ;
Sit bare at meals, and one half rise and wait ;
Last, that he never his young master beat ;
But he must aske his mother to define,
How manie jerks she would his breech should line.
All these observ'd he could contented be,
To give five markes, and winter livery."

JOSEPH HALL, *Satires.*

As regards the 'prentices, they were considered as servants not only in the shop and warehouse, but also at home, where they waited at dinner, and followed the ladies to church and when they went abroad in the evening, carrying a lantern and a stout cudgel. For the servants, properly so called, the following regulations will show the manner of their service (Drake, ii.) :—

"Imprimis, That no servant bee absent from praier, at morning or evening, without a lawfull excuse, to be alledged within one day after, upon payne to forfeit for every tyme 2d.

2. Item, that none sweare any othe, uppon paine for every othe 1d.

3. Item, That no man leave any doore open, that he findeth shut, without there bee cause, upon payne for every time 1d.

4. Item, That none of the men be in bed, from our Lady-day to Michaelmas, after 6 of the clock, in the morning ; nor out of his bed after 10 of the clock at night ; nor, from Michaelmas till our Lady-day, in bed after 7 in the morning ; nor out after 9 at night, without reasonable cause, on paine of 2d.

5. Item, That no man's bed be unmade, nor fire or candle-box uncleane, after 8 of the clock in the morning, on paine of 1d.

. . . .

7. Item, That no man teach any of the children any unhonest speeche, or bandie word, or other, on paine of 4d.

8. Item, That no man waite at the table, without a trencher in his hand, except it be uppon some good cause, on paine of 1d.

9. Item, If any man breake a glasse, hee shal answer the price thereof out of his wages and, if it bee not known who breake it, the buttler shall pay for it on paine of 12d.

10. Item, The table must be covered halfe an hour before 11 at dinner, and 6 at supper, or before, on paine of 2d.

11. Item, That meate bee readie at 11, or before, at supper, on paine of 6d.

12. That none be absent, without leave or good cause, the whole day, or any part of it, on paine of 4d.

13. Item, that no man strike his fellow, on paine of losse of service ; nor revile or threaten, or provoke another to strike, on paine of 12d.

14. Item, That no man come to the kitchen without reasonable cause, on paine of 1d. and the cook likewyse to forfeit 1d.

15. Item, That none toy with the maids on paine of 4d.

16. Item, That no man weare foule shirt on Sunday, nor broken hose or shooes, or dublett without buttons, on paine of 1d.

17. Item, That when any strainger goeth hence, the chamber be drest up againe within 4 hours after, on paine of 1d.

18. Item, That the hall bee made cleane every day, by eight in the winter, and seaven in the sommer, on paine of him that should do it to forfet 1d.

19. That the court-gate bee shutt each meale, and not opened during dinner and supper, without just cause, on paine the porter to forfet for every time 1d.

20. Item, That all stayrs in the house, and other rooms that neede shall require, bee made cleane on Fryday after dinner, on paine of forfeyture of every one on whome it shall belong unto 3d.

All which sommes shalbe duly paide each quarter-day out of their wages, and bestowed on the poore or other godly use."

The London merchant's house in the sixteenth century steadily improved in solid comfort and even in magnificence. No one will ever be able to restore completely, or even approximately, the London of that century. We do not know the numbers of the great houses; we know only in part their constitutions, their pictures; their art; their carved work. In the streets lying off the main avenues of retail trade, especially in those streets near the riverside, a house was frequently at once a place of residence and a warehouse. One may look upon a street in Hildesheim, for instance, and be reminded of Bishopsgate Street, Aldgate, or Leadenhall Street in the time of Queen Elizabeth. That is to say, the greater number of houses were timbered with tiled roofs; the fronts all covered with carvings painted and gilded; there were scattered here and there substantial stone houses; there were still many houses whose gateway opened from some narrow city lane upon a spacious court, above which stood the hall; the lady's bower; the rooms for apprentices and servants; and, behind all, the garden. Such a house on a large scale was Gray's Inn; on a lesser scale Barnard's Inn and the smaller inns. The College of Heralds still shows the general size of the court; Doctor's Commons until fifty years ago also illustrated the old fashion of building. Bricks were coming into use, but, in the City of London, slowly. There were still many narrow and noisome courts where the hovels were of wood—making a constant danger of fire and filled with all manner of decaying abominations—a constant cause of disease.

By this time all the windows were provided with glass; many of the poorer sort, however, were furnished with the cheap glass which contained the round lumps called bull's eyes. The shops in the market-places had glass in the upper part, but the lower part still remained open, and was shut at night with a shutter. The goods were exposed outside the window, and the 'prentices stood beside them bawling, " What d'ye lack ? What d'ye lack ?"

In the more important houses the old custom of living in the great hall was still kept up. In all houses the servants and apprentices sat down with the master and his family.

The floors were still strewn with rushes, but these, on account of the cost of renewing, were seldom changed, so that underneath them, as Erasmus discovered, lay unmolested an " ancient collection of beer, grease, fragments of fish, and everything that is nasty."

The furniture of the rooms was very different from that of our own times. The following account is taken from *Archæologia* (vol. xxx. p. 2):—

"The Furniture of the different rooms is very similar, varying principally in number and quality of the articles; consisting of sets of hangings, tables with tressels, joined forms, joined stools, court-cupboards, carpets, cushions, and a few chairs; also andirons, and other fire utensils, and several pairs of virginals in different rooms, besides a pair of organs in the chapel, and 'an instrument

STAPLE INN, HOLBORN

musicall' in the chamber of presence. The carpets, which are numerous, would scarcely appear to have been used according to modern custom for the floors of the apartments, Hentzner having informed us, that the presence-chamber of Queen Elizabeth herself was strewed with hay (*i.e.* rushes) but they were principally coverings for the tables, stools, and court-cupboards; though they may have been occasionally used to cover some select part of a room, as in the presence-chamber, for instance, where a Turkey carpet is mentioned, five yards and a half long, and two yards and three-quarters broad.

The court-cupboards, which are generally considered to have been moveable closets, answering the purpose of a sideboard, were frequently much ornamented, and such an article may still be seen in old mansions, and in collections of old furniture. They were covered with carpets or cupboard cloths, and set out with cups, salvers, and plate. Some of these carpets were very handsome. In one of the inventories in that valuable authority for researches of this nature, the *History of Hengrave*, is mentioned, 'One carpet of black velvet, for the little bord, laced and fringed with silver and gould, lyned with taffita.' Some of these carpets also had cloths to lay over them, probably, when not in use, in order to protect them. In the same Inventory cushions are mentioned which in richness exceed those of the Archbishop, as 'two long cushions of plain black velvet, embroidered with roses, with gould and pearle all over, with tassels of gold and silk'; but the nature of his archi-episcopal office probably induced him to avoid too much splendour in his household. There is, however, in the chamber of presence a cushion of cloth of baudkin,[1] and in other apartments, several cushions of velvet and damask. The chair of cloth of gold and silver in the gallery was probably a State chair; and, indeed, from the paucity of these articles, they would seem to be intended only for persons of higher rank. From the 'latten andirons' in the chamber of presence being valued at forty shillings, it may be inferred that they were ornamented, and in some cases we know they were richly carved. Iachimo, describing the chamber of Imogen, says :—

> ' Her andirons—
> I had forgot them—were two winking Cupids
> Of silver, each on one foot standing, nicely
> Depending on their brands.'

The pictures are chiefly portraits of royal personages, the principal noblemen and officers of state, and the promoters of the Reformation, but the list is interesting to shew the Archbishop's selection. In some of the bed-rooms are truckle-beds (trundle-beds as they are called in some of the inventories of this age); these would seem to have been small beds generally appropriated to attendants, and placed at the foot or side of the standing or principal bed, and occasionally made to run under it during the day. The Host in the *Merry Wives of Windsor*, in answer to an inquiry after Sir John Falstaff, says, 'There's his chamber, his house, his castle, his standing-bed and truckle-bed.' Hudibras also makes the distinction :—

> If he that in the field is slain,
> Be in the bed of honour lain.
> He that is beaten may be said,
> To lie in honour's truckle-bed.'

In my Lord's chamber the bed is a field-bed, but this sort of bed may have been

---

[1] A rich and precious stuff composed of silk with threads of gold.

so called from being a folding-bed, as field-stool from fauld-stool, and not as being a camp-bed or *lit de champ*. The 'grene satten of bridgs' in the vestrye was satin of Bruges; and 'dornix,' of which there are some articles mentioned, is used for 'Tournay,' and applied to the manufacture of that place. The 'Grene saie,' in the 'Grene Galery,' and elsewhere, was probably not silk, but a species of fine cloth (sagum), one of the earliest productions of our woollen manufacture, the material of stockings, which were objected to by William Rufus, as being, from the price, too common for a king."

We may supplement this account by Harrison's description (Holinshed, i. 317):—

"The furniture of our houses also exceedeth, and is growne in maner even to passing delicacie; for herein I doo not speake of the nobilitie and gentry onlie, but likewise of the lowest sort in most places of our south countrie, that have aniething at all to take to. Certes in noblemen's houses it is not rare to see abundance of Arras, rich hangings of tapistrie, silver vessell, and so much other plate, as may furnish sundry cupbords, to the summe often times of a thousand or two thousand pounds at the least: whereby the value of this and the rest of their stuffe dooth grow to be almost inestimable. Likewise in the houses of knights, gentlemen, merchantmen, and some other wealthie citizens, it is not geson to behold generallie their great provision of tapistrie, Turkie worke, pewter, brasse, fine linen, and thereto costlie cupbords of plate, worth five or six hundred or a thousand pounds, to be deemed by estimation. But as herein all these sorts doo far exceed their elders and predecessors, and in neatnesse and curiositie the merchant all other; so in time past, the costlie furniture staied there, whereas now it is descended yet lower even unto the inferior artificers and manie farmers, who by vertue of their old and not of their new leases have for the most part learned also to garnish their cupbords with plate, their joined beds with tapestrie and silke hangings, and their tables with carpets and fine naperie, whereby the wealth of our countrie (God be praised therefore and give us grace to imploie it well) dooth infinetlie appeare. Neither doo I speak this in reprooch of anie man, God is my judge, but to showe that I do rejoise rather to see how God has blessed us with His good gifts; and whilest I behold how that in a time wherein all things are growen to most excessive prices, and what commoditie soever is to be had is daily plucked from the communaltie by such as looke into every trade, we do yet find the meanes to obtein and achive such furniture as heretofore hath beene unpossible. There are old men yet dwelling in the village where I remaine, which hath noted three things to be marvellously altered in England within their sound remembrance; and other three things too much increased. One is, the multitude of chimnies lately erected, whereas in their yoong daies there were not above two or three, of so many in most uplandish towns of the realme (the religious houses and manour places of their lordes alwaies excepted, and peradventure some great personages), but each one made his fire against a reredosse in the hall where he dined and dressed his meat.

The second is the great (although not generall) amendment of lodging, for (said they) our fathers (yea and we ourselves also) have lien full oft upon straw pallets, on rough mats covered onlie with a sheet under coverlets made of dagswain or hopharlots (I use their owne terms) and a good round log under their heads insteed of a bolster or pillow. If it were so that our fathers or the good man of the house, had within seven yeares after his marriage purchased a matteres or flockebed, and thereto a sacke of chaffe to reste his head upon, he thought himselfe to be well lodged as the lord of the towne, that peradventure laie seldom in a bed of downe or whole fethers: so well were they contented, and with such base kind of furniture: which also is not verie much amended as yet in some parts of Bedfordshire, and elsewhere further off from our southerne parts. Pillowes (said they) were thought meet onelie for women in childbed. As for servants, if they had anie sheet above them it was well, for seldom had they anie under their bodies, to keep them from the pricking straws that ran oft through the canvas of the pallet and rased their hardened hides.

The third thing they tell of, is the exchange of vessell, as of treene [1] platters into pewter, and wooden spoones into silver or tin. For so common were all sorts of treene stuffe in old time, that a man should hardlie find foure peeces of pewter (of which one was peradventure a salt) in a good farmer's house and yet for all this frugalitie (if it may so be justly called) they were scarse able to live and paie their rents at their daies without selling of a cow, or an horsse, or more, although they paid but foure pounds at the uttermost by the year. Such also was their povertie that if some one od farmer or husbandman had beene at the alehouse a thing greatlie used in those daies, amongst six or seven of his neighbours, and there in a braverie to show what store he had, did cast downe his pursse, and therein a noble or six shillings in silver unto them (for few such men then cared for gold bicause it was not so readie paiment (and they were oft inforced to give a penie for the exchange of an angell), it was verie likelie that all the rest could not laie downe so much against it; whereas in my time, although peradventure foure pounds of old rent be improved to fortie, fiftie, or an hundred pounds, yet will the farmer as another palme or date tree thinke his gaines verie small toward the end of his terme, if he have not six or seven yeares rent lieng by him, therewith to purchase a new lease, beside a faire garnish of pewter on his cupbord, with so much more in od vessel going about the house, three or foure featherbeds, so many counterlids and carpets of tapistrie, a silver salt, a bowle for wine (if not an whole neast) and a dozzen of spoones to furnish up the sute."

---

[1] Treene = wooden, especially used of plates.

Or, again, to take another contemporary authority (Hall, *Society in the Elizabethan Age*) :—

"The furniture of an Elizabethan House is illustrated by an inventory of the Household 'stuffe, goodes and cattelles' belonging to Sir Henry Parker knight (1557-60). This inventory shows two chairs only for the whole house; eight stools and forms; two square framed tables; one joined table to say mass on; a pair of 'playing tables'; twelve bedsteads; tapestry and hangings; featherbeds; blankets; bolsters; testors; curtains; counterpoints (counterpanes); seven cupboards; three carpets; andirons, fire shovels, tongs; thirteen candlesticks; certain cushions of tapestry, velvet, white satin and 'Brydges' satin; three great chests; utensils for the kitchen; the Brewhouse and the Bargehouse. The Hall was hung round with tapestry; its permanent furniture consisted of two square tables and one great chair of black velvet in which the Justice of the Peace heard cases. When the tables were spread for dinner or supper, forms were brought in. The 'Great Chamber,' formerly called the Lady's Bower, contained the forms used at meals in the Hall, one stool of black velvet for my Lady; and nothing else! In the bedrooms there were the beds and their blankets and nothing else; not a chair or a table; nothing but the bed—what does one want in a bedroom but the bed to sleep upon? For decorations one room had over the chimney a 'steyned cloth with Marie and Gabriell.' Another had curtains of sarcenet; another, of red and green say; another, 'old tapestrye worke of imagery.' In one chamber we find a bason and ewer of pewter—was this the only means of washing in the whole house? In the buttery were a dozen of fine trenchers 'cased'; six glasses; six plates for fruits; a 'garnish' of pewter vessels; two pewter plates for tarts. Nothing is said of knives—did each person still carry his own? Even then there must have been carving knives. Forks were not as yet in common use, and nothing is said about spoons."

The inventory of a farmer's goods about the same time, given in the same work, shows among the household gear, two pewter dishes, three pewter platters, two saucers, four trencher platters, six trencher dishes, two brass kettles, two candlesticks and a chafing dish, eight bowls of wood, twelve trenchers, and twelve trencher spoons; but still nothing about knives. Nor in any of the numerous inventories and accounts given in this book is any mention made of knives. We see, however, in the tables laid upon trestles, the single chair, the forms and stools, the fine tapestry of the Hall, the carpets of the Great Chamber, the testers and the curtains of the bed which stands alone in the bedroom, a compound of state and simplicity; of meanness and richness. Furniture in the modern sense had not yet appeared in the house.

To quote from Shakespeare, Gremio, in the *Taming of the Shrew*, thus speaks of his furniture ;—

> " My house within the city
> Is richly furnished with plate and gold ;
> Basins and ewers to lave her dainty hands ;
> My hangings all of Tyrian tapestry ;
> In ivory coffers I have stuff'd my crowns ;
> In cypress chests my arras counterpoints,
> Costly apparel, tents, and canopies,
> Fine linen, Turkish cushions boss'd with pearl,
> Valance of Venice gold in needlework,
> Pewter and brass and all things that belong
> To house or housekeeping."

Or take the following note of a lady's room :—

" Her bed-chamber was garnished with such diversities of sweete herbes, such varietie of fragrant flowers, such chaunge of odoriferous smelles, so perfumed with sweete odours, so stored with sweete waters, so beautified with tapestry, and decked so artificially, that I want memorie to rehearse it, and cunning to expresse it, so that it seemed her Chamber was rather some terresstriall Paradise, than a mansion for such a matelesse mystresse ; rather a tabernacle for some Goddesse, than a lodging for such a loathsome carcase."

The Tudor age was strong in small points of ceremony and etiquette, which descended even to details of housework. For instance, the ceremony to be observed in making the King's Bed, a thing which we might suppose left to a housemaid, was carefully laid down :—

" Furste a groome or a page to take a torche and to goo to the warderobe of the kynges bedd, and brynge theym of the warderobe with the kynges stuff unto the chambr for makyng of the same bedde. Where as sught to be a gentylman-usher iiij yeomen of the chambr for to make the same bedde. The groome to stande at the bedds feete with his torche. They of the warderobe opennyng the kinges stuff of hys bedde upon a fayre sheets betwen the sayde groome and the bedds fote, iij yeomen or two at the lefte in every syde of the bedde. The gentylman usher and parte commaundyng theym what they shall doo. A yoman with a dagger to searche the strawe of the kynges bedde that there be none untreuth therin. And this yoman to caste up the bedde of downe upon that, and oon of theym to tomble over yt for the serche thereof. Then they to bete and tufte the sayde bedde, and to laye oon then the bolster without touchyng of the bedd where as it aught to lye. Then they of the warderobe to delyver theym a fusty and takyng the saye thereof. All theys yomen to laye theyr hands theroon at oone, that they touch not the bedd, tyll yt be layed as it sholde be by the commaundement of the usher. And so the furste sheet in lyke wyse, and then to trusse in both sheete and fustyan rownde about the bedde of downe. The warderoper to delyver the second sheete unto two yomen, they to crosse it over theyr arme, and to stryke the bedde as the ussher shall more playnly sheweun to theym. Then every yoman layeing hande upon the sheete to laye the same sheete

THE MORE FAMILY

From a picture in the possession of Major-General F. E. Sotheby.

p. 282.

upon the bedde. And so the other fustyan upon or ij with suche coverynge as shall content the kynge. Thus doon the ij yomen next to the bedde to laye down agene the overmore fustyan, the yoman of the warderobe delverynge theym a pane sheete, the sayde yoman therewythall to cover the sayde bedde : and so then to laye down the overmost sheets from the beddes heed. And then the say ij yomen to lay all the overmost clothes of a quarter of the bedde. Then the warderoper to delyver unto theym such pyllowes as shall please the kynge. The sayd yoman to laye theym upon the bolster and the heed sheet with whych the sayde yoman shall cover the sayd pyllowes. And so to trusse the endes of the said sheete under every end of the bolster. And then the sayd warderoper to delyver unto them ij lytle small pyllowes werwythall the squyres for the bodye or gentylman usher shall give te saye to the warderoper, and to the yoman whyche have layde on hande upon the sayd bedde. And then the sayd ij yomen to lay upon the sayde bedde toward the bolster as yt was bifore. They makyng a crosse and kissynge yt where there handes were. Then ij yomen next to the feete to make the seers as the usher shall teche theym. And so then every one of them sticke up the aungel about the bedde, and to lette downe the corteyns of the sayd bedde or sparver.

Item, a squyer for the bodye or gentylman-usher aught to sett the kynges sword at hys beddes heede.

Item, a squyer for the bodye aught to charge a secret groome or page to have the kepynge of the sayde bedde with a lyght, unto the tyme the kynge be disposed to goo to yt.

Item, a groome or page aught to take a torche whyle the bedde ys yn makyng to feche a loof of brede, a pott with ale, a pott wyth wine for them that maketh the bedde, and every man.

Item, the gentylman-ussher aught to forbede that no manner of man do sett eny dysshe uppon the kinge's bedde for fere of hurtyng of the kyng's ryche counterpoynt that lyeth therupon. And that the sayd ussher take goode heede, that noon man wipe or rubbe their handes uppon none arras of the kynges, wherby they myght be hurted, in the chambr where the kyng ys specially, and in all other."

The wealth of the English was not so much illustrated, as it was proved, by their immense stores of silver and silver-gilt plate. The people bought all the plate that they could afford ; they put their savings, so to speak, in silver plate, as we put them in stocks and shares. Polydore Vergil says that there were few whose tables were not loaded with spoons, cups, and salt-cellars of silver. At the marriage feast of Prince Arthur there was in the great hall a cupboard five stages in height, set with plate valued at £1200, say £15,000 of our money ; while in the chamber where the Princess dined there was a cupboard of gold plate valued at £20,000 or £240,000 in our money. Cardinal Wolsey must have spent enormous sums upon plate. There were two banqueting rooms, in each of which was a cupboard extended along the whole length of the apartment, piled to the top with plate, and every guest chamber was provided with silver ewers, basins, and candlesticks. Of silver spoons or dishes there were none; the dishes were of pewter and the plates of wood, even in the greatest houses.

Lastly, on the subject of furniture, let me quote from another paper in *Archæologia*, vol. xxxvi. p. 284 :—

"The furniture of the hall is excessively scanty and plain, consisting of but a single table and two forms, of the total value of 4s. 6d. In the parlour, however, is a much greater abundance of furniture, as, in addition to the main table, there is the side table and another small table, a chair and six stools with embroidered cushions, besides footstools; while for the decoration of the room we find a portrait of Henry VIII. and hangings of green saye, and, for the amusement of the family and guests, a pair of virginals, a base lute, and a guitar, with chess and backgammon boards for those not musically inclined. The children's chamber, or nursery as we should call it, is comfortably provided with bedding and nursery requisites, and contains a cupboard, two coffers, and a great wicker hamper, as receptacles for the clothes, etc. The allowance of blankets appears but small, being only one pair to a bed, either in the nursery or in the bedroom of the master of the house. The latter room is provided with a walnut-tree bedstead, adorned with green fringe, and having a coverlet of tapestry, a walnut table, chairs and stools, curtains for the windows of green saye, a warming-pan, and, as a ready means of defence against thieves or intruders, a pole-axe. In an inner closet, leading out of this room, are four stills, for the use of the lady of the house.

Sir William More's own closet is so well appointed that it might almost serve as a model for the morning-room of a country squire of the present day. On the walls hang maps of the World, of France, of England, and of Scotland, and a picture of Judith, a little chronicle, and a perpetual almanac in frames. Among the accessories are a globe, a slate to write on, and a counterboard and cast of counters, with which to make calculations and cast accounts, in the manner then in vogue. On the desk are a pair of scales and a set of weights, a pair of scissors, a penknife, a whetstone, a pair of compasses, a foot-rule, a hammer, a seal of many seals, and an inkstand of pewter, with a pounce-box, and pens both of bone and steel. Around the room is a collection of about 120 volumes of books; among them are some of the best chronicles of the time, as Fabyan, Langton, Harding, Carion, etc.; translations from the classics, as well as some in their original language; for magisterial business there are the statutes of Henry VIII., Edward VI., and Mary, and all the statutes before, as well as the *New Book of Justices*, and other legal works; for medical use we find a *Book of Physic*, the *Glass of Health*, and a book against the Sweat, as well as a *Book of Medicines for*

Horses; while for lighter reading there are such books as Chaucer, Lydgate, Skelton, and others, not only in English but also in French and Italian; and for religious study, besides a Bible and Testaments in various languages, the *Scala Perfectionis, Flores Bibliae,* etc. The whole catalogue is worthy of attentive perusal by the bibliographical antiquary, and affords the titles of some English works which are not, I believe, at present known.

In the closet of the lady of the house are a few more books, principally of prayers, a large collection of trunks and boxes, a number of glass vessels of various forms and uses, and a few of enamel or china, with trenchers, knives, shears, graters, snuffers, moulds, brushes, and other miscellaneous properties of a good housewife."

Water was carried about the City from the conduits by water-carriers called "Cobbs," who carried it in large tankards, each holding about three gallons.

The palmy time of tobacco extended over the fifty years after its introduction. During this time the use of tobacco penetrated all ranks and classes of society. The grave divine, the soldier, the lawyer, the gallant about town, the merchant, the craftsman, the 'prentice, all used pipes. At the theatre the young fellow called for his pipe and for tobacco and began to smoke: presently he rose and walking over to the boxes presented his pipe to any lady of his acquaintance.

People went to bed with tobacco box and pipe and candle on a table by the bedside in case they might wake up in the night and feel inclined for tobacco. After supper in a middle-class family, all the men and women smoked together. Nay, it is even stated that the very children in school took a pipe of tobacco instead of breakfast, the master smoking with them and instructing them how to bring the smoke through the nostrils in the fashion of the day. Tobacco was bought and sold in pennyworths.

Every man carried a "tobacco box, steel, and touch." Early in the seventeenth century there are said to have been 7000 tobacconists' shops in London. This seems incredible; perhaps there were 7000 shops in which tobacco was sold. For instance, all apothecaries sold tobacco. Many of the tobacco shops were of handsome appearance. A tobacco shop had a maple block for cutting the leaf; tongs for holding the coals, and a fire of juniper at which the pipes were lighted. Tobacco was so cheap that a man might fill his pocket with it for twopence. Yet over £300,000 a year was spent in London on tobacco, while there were some—but this is impossible—who were reported to spend, habitually, £400 a year upon tobacco alone; that is, 48,000 pocketsful every year, or 130 pocketsful every day; which is absurd.

Expletives and oaths are changed with every generation. The Elizabethans had, no doubt, a great many, of which the following represent but a few. The old Catholic oaths "By'r Lady," "By the Mass," and so forth, vanished with the Reformation. We now find a lot of meaningless ejaculations, such as "God's

Wounds," "God's Fools," "God's Dines," "Cocke's Bones," "Deuce take me," "Bones a God," and "Bones a me." The now familiar "Damn" makes its appearance in literature; but indeed it had flourished in the mouths of the people for many generations. There is nothing really remarkable about the swearing of the Elizabethan period.

Every merchant formerly carried a signet-ring, on which was engraved, not his coat-of-arms, but his mark or signet. Thus, a curious signet-ring was found lying in the bed of the river while digging the foundations of London Bridge. At first it was believed to be Sir Thomas Gresham's, but that seems now to be impossible. It is engraved in *The London and Middlesex Notebook* (p. 195). The device contains the initials of the owner, with an arrangement of lines probably not intended to have any meaning except that they should be recognised as forming part of Sir Thomas Gresham's signet. Armed with this ring as an introduction, a messenger could buy and sell for the merchant—it being presumed that the ring never left its owner save to be used as a letter of recommendation and introduction. Sometimes the signet-ring was worn on the thumb. Other merchants' devices are figured in the " Notebook."

Foreigners have revealed to us some very curious and rather startling peculiarities of the custom of kissing as practised by our ancestors. Thus as early as 1466 a Bohemian nobleman named Leo von Rozmital visited England, and in the Journal of his Travel (1577) it is noted that "it is the custom there, that on the arrival of a distinguished stranger from foreign parts, maids and matrons go to the inn and welcome him with gifts. Another custom is observed there, which is that, when guests arrive at an inn, the hostess with all her family go out to meet and receive them; and the guests are required to kiss them all, and this among the English was the same as shaking hands among other nations." Erasmus, in 1499, wrote a Latin letter from England to his friend Fausto Anfrelini, an Italian poet, exhorting him in a strain of playful levity to think no more of his gout, but to betake himself to England; for (he remarks) "here are girls with angels' faces, so kind and obliging, that you would far prefer them to all your Muses. Besides, there is a custom here never to be sufficiently recommended. Wherever you come you are received with a kiss by all; when you take your leave you are dismissed with kisses; you return, kisses are repeated. They come to visit you, kisses again; they leave you, you kiss them all round. Should they meet you anywhere, kisses in abundance; in fine, wherever you move, there is nothing but kisses." In 1527 Cardinal Wolsey was appointed Ambassador Extraordinary to France. He was accompanied by George Cavendish, his gentleman usher, who wrote a Life of the Cardinal. Cavendish had gone forward to prepare his lord's lodging. He says: "And I being there (at the Sire de Créqui's Castle at Moreuil, about twelve miles from Amiens) tarrying a while, my lady Créqui issued out of her chamber into her dining chamber, where I attended her coming, who received me very gently like her noble estate, having a traine of twelve gentlewomen. And when she and her traine was come all out, she saide unto me, ' For as much,' quoth she, ' as ye be an Englishman whose custome is to kisse all ladies and gentlemen in your country without offense, although it is not soe here with us in this realme, yet I will be so bould as kisse you, and soe ye shall doe all my maids.' By meanes whereof I kissed her and all her maides." In the narrative of the visit of the Spanish nobleman, the Duke de Najera, in 1543-44, we are told that "after the dancing was finished (which lasted several hours) the Queen entred again into her chamber, having previously called one of the noblemen who spoke Spanish, to offer in her name some presents to the Duke, who again kissed her hand; and on his requesting the same favour of the Princess Mary, she would by no means permit it, but offered him her lips, and the Duke saluted her, and did the same to all the other ladies." A Greek traveller, Nicander Nucius, came to England in 1545, and remarks: "They display great simplicity and absence of jealousy in their usages towards females. For not only do those who are of the same family and household kiss them on the mouth with salutations and embraces, but even those too who have never seen them. And to themselves this appears by no means indecent." Again, when the Constable of Castile appeared at the Court of Whitehall on Saturday afternoon, 18th August 1604, after kissing Her Majesty's hands he requested permission to salute the ladies of honour (twenty in number, standing in a row, and beautiful exceedingly) according to the custom of the country, and any neglect of which is taken as an affront. Whereupon the Queen having given him leave, His Excellency complied with the custom, much to the satisfaction of the ladies.

In Shakespeare's *Henry VIII.*, at the Cardinal's banquet, the King says to Anne Bullen :—

" Sweetheart,
I were unmannerly, to take you out,
And not to kiss you."

In dancing it appears to have been the customary fee of a lady's partner. A further illustration of the custom may be seen. Foreigners of the male sex, and especially Frenchmen, are in the more frequent habit of kissing each other, and probably not the ladies. Misson, a Frenchman who travelled in England about 1697, says: "The people of England, when they meet, never salute one another, otherwise than by giving one another their hands, and shaking them heartily; they no more dream of pulling off their hats, than the women do of pulling off their headcloths."

The sin of great cities we may pass over; that of early marriage is still, as it was in Stubbes' time, a very terrible evil; the sin of drunkenness is with us still, and is present in every country. The side of charity that consists in giving doles to the poor was then neglected, and is now destroyed. We still suffer from money-lenders, though they can no longer conduct us to a life-long prison.

"Beleeue mee," says Stubbes, "it greeueth mee to heare (walking in the streats) the pitiful cryes, and miserable complaints of poore prisoners in durance for debt, and like so to continue all their life, destitute of libertie, meat, drink (though of the meanest sorte), and clothing to their backs, lying in filthie strawe, and lothsome dung, wursse than anie dogge, voide of all charitable consolation and brotherly comfort in this World, wishing and thyrsting after death to set them at libertie, and loose them from their shackles, giues, and yron bands." (Stubbes.)

As for the boys of this century, I have always thought their favourite haunt was the river, or the river-side. On the river they rowed about among the fishermen, and the swans above Bridge; the Queen's Barge swept past them with its trumpets and its hangings gorgeous to behold; the Lord Mayor and the Companies were borne along before them in state and splendour such as we have forgotten—surely nothing could have been more splendid than these barges with their long lines of flashing oars and their bows gilt and carved, and the carved work of the covered seat of state, and the servants in their green and gold. Below Bridge, in the Port, they rowed in and out among the ships as boys will about Portsmouth Harbour now; the name of each ship with her port was written on her lofty stern. The figure-head of each was bright as paint and gold would make it. If they were allowed to go on board there were sailors full of yarns, with strange things to show as well as to tell. If they went as far down as Deptford, there was Drake's ship, the ship which had gone all round the world—all round the world! If they stayed ashore, there were taverns in Wapping and St. Katherine's, where they could snatch the fearful joy of seeing the sailors drink and fight, the foreign sailors and the English sailors, and the sailors from the North Country, and those of London and the Cinque Ports. The river and the river-side were famous schools to fill the minds of London boys with an ardour for adventure; a yearning for the way of war; a burning desire to cross the seas and visit far countries; and a thirst for geography; and all the London boys of every class regularly attended the classes of this Academy.

The theatre, of course, offers a fine field for the Elizabethan satirist, Stubbes. He cannot find words strong enough to condemn the playgoer. Then there is that other source and fount of laughter, the Lord of Misrule.

"First, all the wilde-heds of the Parish, conuenting togither, chuse them a Graund Captain (of all mischeefe) whome they innoble with the title of 'my Lord of Mis-rule,' and him they crowne with great solemnitie, and adopt for their King. This king anointed chuseth forth twentie, fortie, threescore or a hundred lustie Guttes, like to himself, to waighte vppon his lordly Maiestie, and to guarde his noble person. Then, euerie one of these his men, he inuesteth with his liuerues of green, yellow, or some other light wanton colour; And as though that were not baudie (gaudie) enough, I should say, they bedecke them selues with scarfs, ribons, and laces hanged all over with golde rings, precious stones, and other jewels: this doon, they tye about either leg xx. or xl. bels, with rich handkerchiefs in their hands, and sometimes laid a crosse ouer their shoulders and necks, borrowed for the most parte of their pretie Mopsies and loouing Besses, for bussing them in the dark.   Thus al things set in order, then haue they their Hobby-horses, dragons and other antiques, togither with their baudie Pipers and thundering Drummers to strike vp the deuils daunce withall.   Then marche these heathen company towards the church and Churchyard, their pipers pipeing, their drummers thundring, their stumps dauncing, their bels iyngling, their handkerchiefs swinging about their heds like madmen, their hobbie horses and other monsters skirmishing amongst the route: and in this sorte they go to the Church (I say) and into the Church

A SHIP OF THE TIME OF HENRY VIII.

(though the Minister be at prair or preaching), dancing and swinging their handkerchiefs ouer their heds in the Church, like deuils incarnate, with such a confuse noise, that no man can hear his own voice. Then, the foolish people they looke, they stare, they laugh, they fleer, and mount vpon fourmes and pewes to see these goodly pageants solemnized in this sort.   Then, after this, about the Church they goe againe and againe, and so foorth into the churchyard, where they haue commonly their Sommer-haules, their bowers, arbors, and banqueting houses set vp, wherin they feast, banquet and daunce al that day and (peradventure) all the night too.   And thus these terrestriall furies spend the Sabaoth day." (Stubbes, *Anatomie of Abuses*, edit. by Furnivall.)

The custom of church ales is described by Stubbes with his customary vigour :—

"In certaine Townes where drunken *Bachus* beares all the sway, against a Christmas, an Easter, Whitsonday, or some other time, the Church-wardens (for so they call them) of euery parish, with the consent of the whole Parish, prouide half a score of twenty quarters of mault, wherof some they buy of the Church-stock, and some is giuen them of the Parishioners them selues, euery one conferring somewhat, according to his abilitie ; which mault, beeing made into very strong ale or beere, it is set to sale, either in the Church, or some other place assigned to that purpose.

Then, when the *Nippitatum*, this Huf-cap (as they call it) and this *nectar* of lyfe, is set abroche, wel is he that can get the soonest to it, and spend the most at it ; for he that fitteth the closest to it, and spends the moste at it, he is counted the godliest man of all the rest ; but who either cannot, for pinching pouertie, or otherwise, wil not stick to it, he is counted one destitute bothe of vertue and godlynes. In so much as you shall haue many poor men make hard shift for money to spend ther at, for it beeing put into this *Corban*, they are perswaded it is meritorious, and a good seruice to God. In this kinde of practise they continue six weeks, a quarter of a year, yea, half a year togither, swilling and gulling, night and day, till they be as drunke as Apes, and as blockish as beasts." (Stubbes, *Ibid.*)

They pretend, he says, to repair their churches with money so got :—

"But who seeth not that they bestow this money vpon nothing lesse than in building and repayring of Churches and Oratories ? For in most places lye they not like swyn coates ? their windowes rent, their dores broken, their walles fall downe, the roofe all bare, and what not out of order ? Who seeth not the booke of GOD, rent, ragged, and all betorn, couered in dust, so as this *Epitaphe* may be writ with ones finger vppon it, *ecce nunc in pu.'uere dormio ?* (Alas ;) behold I sleep in dust and oblyuion, not once scarse looked vppon, much less red vpon, and the least of all preached vppon." (Stubbes, *Ibid.*)

Of wakes and feasts and "the horrible vice of pestiferous dancing" we need say little. Nor of music, "how it allureth to vanitie" ; nor of cards, dice, tennis, and bowls, all of which we still practise ; nor of the bear-baiting which we have now discontinued. Of the reading of bad books we may still complain after the manner of Stubbes. In a word, his *Book of Lamentations* would serve with slight alterations for to-day as well as his own age.

On the exchange of English goods for foreign trifles, I find a note in Furnivall's edition of Stubbes' *Anatomy* :—

"Thou must carry beside, leather, tallow, beef, bacon, bell-metal and everything :
And for these good commodities, trifles into England thou must bring,
As bugles to make bables, coloured bones, glass beads to make bracelets withal,
For every day gentlewomen of England do ask for such trifles from stall to stall :
And you must bring more, as amber, jet, coral, crystal, and every such bable
That is slight, pretty, and pleasant : they care not to have it profitable.
And if they demand wherefore your wares and merchandise agree,
You must say 'jet will take up a straw : amber will make one fat :
Coral will look pale when you be sick, and crystal staunch blood,'
So with lying, flattering and glosing, you must utter your ware,
And you shall win me to your will, if you can deceitfully swear.

     .   .   .   .

   Lucre. Then, Signor Mercatore, I am forthwith to send ye
From hence to search for some new toys in Barbary and in Turkey ;
Such trifles as you think will please wantons best,
For you know in this country 'tis their chiefest request.
   Mercatore. Indeed, de gentlewomans here buy so much vain toys
Dat we strangers laugh-a to tink wherein dey have their joys."

The suppressing of the Religious Houses produced, for a time, a great deal of hardship and difficulty. For not only were the friars turned out into the streets, but all the people living upon the monasteries were deprived of their daily bread; many of these unfortunates took to the road and became tramps, vagabonds, masterless men and thieves; many took refuge in those parts of London which were outside the jurisdiction of the City. London, indeed, was the place which the masterless man regarded as a veritable Paradise. They flocked up to London from all quarters; they were constantly being turned out and as constantly coming back again. When Queen Elizabeth once drove out to the country cottage of Islington, she was mobbed by a gang of vagabonds who accosted her with clamours; they harboured in the brick kilns there. In some parts close to London, as Hyde Park Corner and Lincoln's Inn Fields, no one would venture after dark. Men took arms into their bedrooms at night, ready for use. Generally it seems that they hung a drawn sword at the bedside. The 'prentices, however, were the best protectors to a house. They slept in the shop, if there were a shop; or if there were no shop they slept somewhere on the ground floor, as is evident from the edifying revelations of "Meriton Latron," in which it is shown how easily the 'prentices could get out at night for these riotous and profligate meetings and drinkings. I suppose it matters nothing that this writer belongs to the next century. In such small matters the world is conservative. According to this authority, it was common for 'prentices to rob their masters, exchanging with each other or holding a kind of auction in their taverns at night. The time when the City was most free from crimes was when the men had been called out to follow the flag and fight. The worst time was after the war, when they all came back again to their old haunts, thirsting for their old amusements and more disinclined for work than ever.

CHAPTER II

FOOD AND DRINK

THE manner and times of taking food under the Tudors may be summed up as follows :—

For breakfast, those who made a meal before dinner at all, took, in the country, pottage, and, in town, "muskadel and eggs," or bread-and-butter with a draught of small ale. The Princess Mary, in 1533, used to eat so much meat for breakfast that she terrified her physicians. It does not appear, however, that the workpeople took anything at all unless it were a draught of small ale before their dinner at ten. The hour of dinner varied during the century from ten till twelve. For children there was "nuntion" or luncheon before dinner and a "bever" or slight repast between dinner and supper. Venner recommends no breakfast at all, but to wait for dinner. If, however, one cannot wait, then he advises poached eggs, with salt, pepper, a little vinegar, bread-and-butter and claret. When Cosmo, Duke of Tuscany, came to the country he visited Colonel John Nevill, and had breakfast with him, drinking Italian wine.

The dinners were plentiful and varied. A salad was served first, then the beef and mutton ; next fowls, and fish ; game followed, woodcock being the most plentiful ; and pastry and sweets came last. Honey was poured over the meat. The most important part of the meal, however, was the "banquet" or dessert which followed : at this part of the dinner an amazing quantity of sweetmeats was taken ; for this every one adjourned to another room in winter ; to the garden in summer.

In the winter fresh meat was not always to be had : most people laid in large quantities of beef in October and November, which they salted. The markets, however, made up for the absence of fresh meat by the abundance of all kinds of birds which were brought into London ; they were trapped, or shot with sling and stone, in the marshes along the lower reaches of the Thames. Pork could be had all the year round. Fresh fish was generally plentiful, but it was sometimes dear. At such times the people fell back upon stockfish, which was often bad and the cause of much disease. Herrings were brought by sea from Yarmouth in barrels, and partly salted, as they are at this day. They were a favourite form of food, and were made into pasties highly spiced.

The food of the sixteenth century was more stimulating than our own: the only drink was fermented and alcoholic, even the small beer which was the national beverage; there was no tea or coffee; vast quantities of wine were taken; there were nearly a hundred different kinds, more than half being French. Wine of Bordeaux was sold at 8d. the gallon; Spanish wine at 1s. In drinking sack, the cup was half filled with sugar. Indeed, sugar or honey was taken with everything: with roast meat, with wine, and in the form of sweetmeats; so that the teeth of most people were black in consequence.

A diet so stimulating could not fail to produce its effects in causing the people to be more easily moved to wrath, to love, to pity, to jealousy—than a diet composed of tea and coffee. There can be no doubt whatever that all classes of men and women were far readier with hand and tongue than at present; swifter to wrath; more prone to sudden outbursts; more quick with dagger or sword.

Their tables were set out on trestles for the dinner and removed after dinner. People sat on stools; the floor was strewn with rushes; the tables, not the floors, were covered with rich carpets.

A piece of the table furniture which has long since disappeared was the Roundel. It is supposed to have been used for fruit. A set of Roundels, not quite perfect, is described in *Archæologia* (vol. xxxix.). They are circular and of wood, the upper side perfectly plain; the lower side is partly covered with black paint or dye and partly white. A legend, in rhyme, runs round the outer edge, and within is a figure with a number. The figure and letters are gilt. In this example nine trenchers out of the twelve represent the Courtier, the Country gentleman, the Lawyer, and so forth—characters of the time, the verses being taken from a book called *The XII. Wonders of the World.*

It is pleasing to learn from Harrison of the reform introduced in his own time by the revival of the custom of taking vegetables of all kinds and plentifully. He says:—

"Such herbes, fruits, and roots also as grow yeerlie out of the ground, of seed, have been verie plentifull in this land, in the time of the first Edward, and after his daies; but in processe of time they grew also to be neglected, so that from Henrie the fourth till the latter end of Henrie the seventh, and beginning of Henrie the eight, there was little or no use of them in England, but they remained either unknowne, or supposed as food more meet for hogs and savage beasts to feed upon than mankind. Whereas in my time their use is not onlie resumed among the poore commons, I mean of melons, pompions, gourds, cucumbers, radishes, skirets, parsneps, carrets, cabbages, nauewes, turneps, and all kinds of salad herbs, but also fed upon as deintie dishes at the tables of delicate merchants, gentlemen, and the nobilitie, who make their provision yearlie for new seeds out of strange countries, from whence they have them aboundantlie." (Holinshed's *Chronicles*.)

The Flemings commenced the first market-gardens. Lettuce was served as a separate dish, and eaten at supper before meat. Capers were usually eaten boiled with oil and vinegar, as a salad. Eschalots were used to smear the plate before putting meat on it. Carrots had been introduced by the Flemings. Rhubarb, then called Patience, came from China about 1573. The common people ate turnip-leaves as a salad, and roasted the root in wood-ashes. Watercress was believed to restore the bloom to young ladies' cheeks.

They used mustard and horse-radish; they took anchovies with wine; they took olives with wine; they had boiled oysters; boiled radishes, artichokes raw or boiled; they poured honey or spread sugar over their beef and mutton; they served pork in many ways, but if roasted, then with green sauce of sorrel; salmon they stuck with cloves; they ate porpoises; turkeys were roasted with cloves; peacocks they roasted while they were still under a year old; pigeons they stuffed with sour grapes or unripe gooseberries; rabbits were cheap and plentiful; pies of all kinds were very popular. They made salad out of barberries in pickle or with lettuces as in modern fashion. In the ordinaries and taverns there were no wine-glasses: people drank out of green pots made of white clay. They took supper at six; this was a smaller meal than dinner, but yet a plentiful meal. In a word, the Elizabethan Englishman lived much as the modern Frenchman lives: he took two meals a day and no more. In the principal ordinaries and inns musicians attended; even in the cheaper ones a viol de gamba was kept for everybody who could play; men dined for choice at the ordinary, which was a great deal cheaper than the tavern; it was not customary for the ladies to appear at taverns. An inn was known by its painted lattice; all kinds of wine could be had at most taverns, but foreign wines were sold to the general public by apothecaries. Waiters wore aprons. In private houses, but not at ordinaries and taverns, the silver fork had been introduced.

> "The laudable use of forks,
> Brought into custom here, as they are in Italy,
> To th' sparing o' napkins."

And in Ben Jonson's *Volpone*,

> "Then must you learn the use
> And handling of your silver fork at meals."

I have found inventories of household goods as late as the end of the seventeenth century without any mention of forks. I am inclined, therefore, to believe that they came into use very slowly, and that the old fashion of eating with a knife, fingers, and bread, lasted in country houses at least until the end of the seventeenth

Tittle-Tattle; Or, the feveral Branches of Gofsipping.

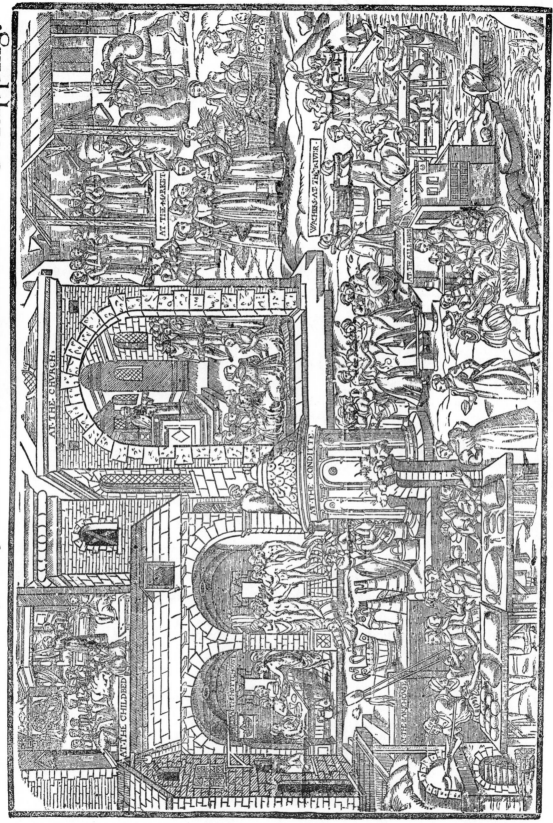

From a satirical print in the British Museum.

century. It is a survival of the old manner of eating which makes the lower class "eat with their knives." Let me add that in my own recollection the practice has almost entirely disappeared. Forty years ago one could not take dinner at a tavern or an eating-house without seeing some of the company helping themselves with their knives.

Here is the bill of a dinner given to the Lord Treasurer, the Chancellor, the Lord Chief Baron, and others not named, on 4th June 1573 :—

		s.	d.
Imprimis	Bread, ale, and beer	13	4
Item	Two sorloines of beef	10	0
,,	Four gees	7	0
,,	Four joyntes of veale	6	8
,,	Six capons	13	8
,,	Three quarters of lambe	4	0
,,	A dozen of chickens	5	0
,,	A dozen of rabbites	4	8
,,	Half a dozen quayles	6	8
,,	For butter	4	0
,,	For eggs	1	0
,,	For vinegar, vergis barberius and mustard	1	0
,,	For spices	1	0
,,	For fruite	6	0
,,	For rose water and swete water	0	8
,,	For scrill and parsley	0	6
,,	For White Wine	1	4
,,	For flowers and strong herbes	0	6
,,	For sacke	1	0
,,	For fier	5	0
,,	For cook's wages	6	0
,,	For boote hier	1	4
,,	For occupying plate, naperie and other necessaries	5	0

Unfortunately these bills never contain the whole. It is of course impossible to believe that one shilling and fourpence represents the whole of the wine consumed on this occasion.

Ben Jonson thus ridicules the care and thought expended upon feasting :—

> "A master-cook! why, he's the man of men
> For a professor! he designs, he draws,
> He paints, he carves, he builds, he fortifies,
> Makes citadels of curious fowl and fish,
> Some he dry-dishes, some moats round with broths :
> Mounts marrow-bones, cuts fifty-angled custards,
> Rears bulwark pies, and for his outer works
> He raiseth ramparts of immortal crust ;
> And teacheth all the tactics at one dinner :
> What ranks, what files, to put his dishes in :
> The whole art military. Then he knows
> The influence of the stars upon his meats,
> And all their seasons, tempers, qualities,
> And so to fit his relishes and sauces.

> He had nature in a pot, 'bove all the chymists,
> Or airy brethren of the Rosie-cross.
> He is an architect, an engineer,
> A soldier, a physician, a philosopher,
> A general mathematician."

And again in his dream of luxurious living :—

> " We will be brave, Puff, now we have the med'cine.
> My meat shall all come in, in Indian shells,
> Dishes of agate set in gold, and studded
> With emeralds, sapphires, hyacinths, and rubies.
> The tongues of carps, dormice, and camels' heels,
> Boil'd in the spirit of sol, and dissolv'd pearl,
> Apicius' diet, 'gainst the epilepsy ;
> And I will eat these broths with spoons of amber,
> Headed with diamond and carbuncle.
> My foot-boy shall eat pheasants, calver'd salmons,
> Knots, godwits, lampreys : I myself will have
> The beards of barbels served instead of salads."
>
> *The Alchemist.*

And this for a more sober supper, yet not without its points of excellence :—

> " Yet shall you have to rectify your palate,
> An olive, capers, or some better salad
> Ushering the mutton ; with a short legg'd hen,
> If we can get her full of eggs, and then,
> Limons, and wine for sauce ; to these, a coney
> Is not to be despar'd of for our money ;
> And though fowl now be scarce, yet there are clerks,
> The sky not falling, think we may have larks,
> I'll tell you of more, and lie, so you will come :
> Of partridge, pheasant, woodcock, of which some
> May yet be there ; and godwit if we can :
> Knat, rail, and ruf too, howsoe'er, my man
> Shall read a piece of Virgil, Tacitus,
> Livy, or of some better book to us,
> Of which we'll speak our minds, amidst our meat :
> And I'll profess no verses to repeat.
> To this, if aught appear, which I not know of,
> That will the pastry, not my paper, show of.
> Digestive cheese, and fruit there sure will be ;
> But that which most doth take my muse and me,
> Is a pure cup of rich Canary wine,
> Which is the Mermaid's now, but shall be mine :
> Of which had Horace or Anacreon tasted,
> Their lives, as do their lines, till now had lasted.
> Tobacco, nectar, or the Thespian spring,
> Are all but Luther's beer to this I sing."

The greatest attention was paid to the service of the table : not only, for instance, must the carving be performed in manner peculiar to each kind of creature, but each creature had its own verb signifying its carving. The terms used for carving are curious and now completely forgotten :—

" Breke that deer ; lesche that brawn ; rere that goose ; lyfte that swanne ; sauce that capon ; spoil that hen ; fruche that chekyn ; unbrace that mallard ; unlace that conye ; desmembre that heron ; display that crane ; dysfygure that pecocke ; unjoint that byterrne ; untache that curlewe ; allay that desande ; wynge that patryche ; wynge that quail ; mynce that plover ; thye that pygyon ; border that pastie ; thye that woodcocke ; thye all maner of small birds ; tymbre that fyre ; tyere that egge ; chyne that samon ; strynge that lampreye ; splatte that pyke ; sauce that plaice ; sauce that tench ; splay that breme ; syde that haddock ; tuske that berbell ; culpon that trout ; fyne that cheven ; transene that ele ; traunche that sturgeon ; under-traunch that porpus ; tayme that crabbe ; barbe that lobster. Here endeth the goodlye termes of kervynge."

The way in which the table was to be served was presented, in general terms, as follows :—

> "Slow be the servers in serving, alwaye,
>   But swift be they after, taking meate away ;
>   A special custom used is them amonge,
>   No good dishe to suffer on borde to be longe.
>   If the dishe be pleasante, whether fleshe or fishe,
>   Ten hande at once swarme in the dishe ;
>   And if it be fleshe, ten knives shalt thou see
>   Mangling the fleshe, and in the platter flee ;
>   Put there thy hands in peryl without fayle
>   Without a gauntlet or a glove of mayle."

Antiquary's Portfolio, p. 130.

And next in minute detail. Thus including the reception of a guest. Let us first remember that the plates were commonly of bread, but sometimes of wood. When they were of bread, the loaves were first carefully pared ; then the butler placed the salt-cellar before the principal guest, and in front of the salt-cellar, upon the carving knives, he was to place the bread. But before Grace this was to be removed, and replaced in thick slices one upon the other.

"Thenne the karver or sewer most asserve every disshe in his degree after order, and course of service, as folowith :—

> First, mustard and brawne, swete wine served thereto.
> Potage.
> Befe and moton, swan or geese.
> Grete pies, capon or fesaunt, leche or fretours.

Thenne if potage be chaungebill after tyme and season of the yere, as falleth, as here is rehersid : by exampel for befe and moton ye shall take

> Pestelles, or chynys of porke, or els
> Tonge of befe, or
> Tonge of the harte powdered,
> Befe stewed,
> Chekyns boylyd and bacon.

Then against the secunde cours be redy, and come into the place, the kerver must avoyde and take upp the service of the first cours, begynnynge at the lowest mete forst, and all broke cromys, bonys, and trenchours, before the secunde cours and service be served.

Thenne the secunde cours shall be served in manner and forme as ensample thereof, hereafter folowyng :—

Potage-pigge	Lamme stewed
Conye	Kidde roosted
Crane	Veneson roosted

Heronseue	Heronseue
Bitoure	Bitoure
Egrete	Pigeons
Curlewe	Rabetts
Wodecock	A bake meat
Petrigge	Stokke dovys stewed
Plover	Cony
Snytys	Mallard
Qualys	Gelys
Fretours	Wodecock
Leche	Great byrdys

After the secunde cours served, kerved, and spente, it must be sene cuppys to be filled, trenchours to be voyded, thenne by goode avysement the tabill must be take uppe in manner as folowith: first, when tyme foloweth, the panter or boteler muste gader uppe the sponys: after that done by leyser, the sewer or carver shall begyne at the lowest ende, and in order take upp the lowest messe, after the syde tabill be avoyded and take upp: and thenne to procede to the principal tabill, and there honestly and clenly avoyde and withdrawe all the service of the high tabill: therto the kerver must be redy, and redely have avoyded togeder in all the broke brede, trenchours, comys lying upon the tabill, levyng none other thyng, save the salte selar, hole brede (if any be lefte), and cuppys. After this done by good deliberacion and avysement, the kerver shall take the service of the principall messe in order and rule, begynnynge at the lowest and so procede in tule unto the laste. And thereuppon the kerver to have redy a voyder, and to avoyde all men's trenchours, broke brede in another clene disshe voyder, and cromys, which with the kervyng knyf shall be avoyded from the tabill, and thus procede untill the table be voyded. Thenne the kerver shall go into the cuppibord, and redresse and ordeyne wafers into toweyles of raynes (table-cloth) or fine napkyns, which moste be cowched fayre and honestly uppon the tabill, and thenne serve the principall messe first, and thorowe the tabill, i or ij if it so require. Therto moste be servid swete wine: and in feriall tyme, serve cheese, scraped with sugar and sauge levis, or else that it be fayre kerved hole: or frute as the season of the year geveth, strawberys, chevys, peyres, appelis: and in wynter, wardens, costardys roste, rosted on fisshe days with blanche powder, and so serve it forth.

Thenne after wafers and frute spended, all manner of thynge shall be take uppe, and avoyded, except the principall salte seler, hole brede, and kervyng knyves, the which shall be redressed in manner and fourme as they were first sette on the table: the which principall servitours of the panter or botery, havynge his towaile, shall take upp and bear it into his office, in lykewise as he first brought it unto the tabill. Thenne the principall servitours, as kerver and sewer, most have redy a longe towayle applied double to be cowched uppon the principall ende of the tabill: and that towelle must be justely drawn thorowe the tabill unto the lower ende: and if servitours to awayte thereuppon, that it be mustly cowchd and spred: after that done, there must be ordeyned basyns and ewers, with water hot or colde as tyme of the yere requireth, and to be sette upon the tabill, and to stonde unto the grace be said: and incontynent after grace saide, the servitours to be redy to awayte and attende to give water: first, to the principall messe, and after that to the seconde: incontynent after this done, the towayle and tabillclothis muste be drawen, cowched and sprad, and so by littill space taken uppe in the myddis of the tabill, and so to be delyvered to the office of the pantery or botery.

Thenne uprysing, servitours must attende to avoyde tabills, trestellis, formys, and stoolys, and to redresse bankers and quyssyons: then the butler shall avoyde the cupborde, begynnynge at the loweste, procede in rule to the hyeste, and bere it into his office. Thenne after mete, it most be awayted and well entended by servitours, if drinke be asked: and if ther be knyght or lady, or grete gentilwoman, they shall be servid upon knee with brede and wyne.

Thenne it mot be sene if strangers shall be broght to chamber, and that the chamber be clenly apparelled and dressed accordyng to the tyme of yere: as in winter tyme fyre: in sommer tyme the bedde covered with pylowes and hed shetys, in case they wolle rest: and after this done, they moste have cheer of *neweltees* in the chamber, as juncates, cherys, pepyns, and such neweltees as the tyme of yere requereth, and swete wynes, Ypocrasse, Tyre, Mustadell, bastard beruage, of the beste that may be had to the honour and laude of the principall of the house."

After the dinner was eaten what remained was taken down for the servants, and whatever was left over when these had finished was bestowed upon the poor who sat outside the doors waiting their turn. The drink was served in silver cups and bowls, or else in goblets of Venetian glass from Murano; the poorer sort had pots of earthenware bound or set in silver and perhaps pewter. As a rule not more than two or three dishes were served at a gentleman's table where there was no company. This, however, was not the case when a feast was provided, or by the merchants for themselves. Then such meat as is killed and provided by the butcher was rejected as not worthy of the occasion.

"In such cases also geliffes of all colours mixed with a varietie in the representation of sundrie floures, herbs, trees, formes of beasts, fish, foules, and fruits, and thereunto marchpaine wrought with no small curiositie, tarts of diverse hewes and sundrie denominations, conserves of old fruites forren and home bred, suckets, codinacs, marmilats, marchpaine, sugerbread, gingerbread, florentines, wild foule, venison of all sorts, and sundrie outlandish confections, altogither seasoned with suger (which Plinie calleth Mel ex arundinibus, a devise not common nor greatlie used in old time at the table, but onlie in medicine, although it grew in Arabia, India and Sicilia), doo generally beare the swaie, besides infinite devises of our owne not possible for me to remember." (Holinshed, vol. i. p. 167.)

Every kind of wine was served at these banquets, *e.g.* the fifty-six various kinds of "small wines" as Claret, White, Red, French, etc.; but also of the thirty kinds of Italian, German, Spanish, Canary, etc. And besides these here were the artificial drinks such as Hypocras and Wormwood wine, besides ale and beer.

The craftsman lived in great plenty: his diet was commonly beef, mutton, veal and pork; besides which he had brawn, bacon, pies of fruit, fowls, cheese, butter and eggs. At weddings, purifications, and so forth, the friends contributed each a dish of some kind, and the feasting that went on was incredible. At table the custom among the gentry and better sort was to observe great silence during the dinner, and on no account to show any sign of being the worse for the wine they had taken. Enough grain was grown in the country to supply it with bread; a good deal of bread was made of oats and rye; in times of dearth beans, peas, and lentils were ground up. Of home-made drinks besides ale and beer there were cider, perry, and, especially among the Welsh, mead or metheglin.

"There is a kind of swish swash made also in Essex, and diverse other places, with honicombs and water, which the homelie countrie wives, putting some pepper and a little other spice among, call mead, verie good in mine opinion for such as love to be loose bodied at large, or a little eased of the cough, otherwise it differeth so much from the true metheglin, as chalke from cheese. Truelie it is nothing else but the washing of the combes, when the honie is wroong out, and one of the best things that I know belonging thereto is, that they spend but little labour and lesse cost in making of the same, and therefore no great losse if it were never occupied." (Holinshed, vol. i. p. 170.)

An oyster feast in the morning seems unusual and unexpected in a town of working men. We may read, however, how, on 30th July 1557, a company of citizens met in the cellar of Master Smyth and Master Gytton in Amber Lane, at eight o'clock in the morning. They devoured between them half a bushel ot oysters, sitting upon hogsheads by candlelight; the oysters were accompanied by onions—was there no bread, or bread-and-butter? Only onions? And they drank with their oysters and onions copious bowls of red ale, claret, muscadel,

Walker & Cockerell.

MARRIAGE FEAST OF SIR H. UNTON
A detail from a painting in the National Portrait Gallery, London.

and malmsey. It hardly seems a good beginning of the day so far as concerns work. In these degenerate days a repast of oysters and onions, with ale and muscadel, claret and malmsey, would prove a fatal feast indeed.

Here is a note on an Elizabethan ordinary :—

"It seemed that all who came thither had clocks in their bellies, for they all strucke into the dyning-roome much at aboute the very minute of feeding. Our traveller had all the eyes (that came in) throwne upon him (as being a stranger), and he as much tooke especiall notice of them. In obseruing of whom and of the place, he found that an ordinary was the onely Rendeuouz for the most ingenious, most terse, most trauaild and most phantastick gallant : the very Exchange for newes out of all countries ; the only booke-sellers' shop for conference of the best editions, that if a woman (to be a Lady) would cast away herselfe upon a knight, there a man should heare a catalogue of most of the richest London widowes ; and last that it was a schoole where they were all fellowes of one forme, and that a country gentleman was of as great comming as the proudest justice that sat there on the bench aboue him ; for hee that had the graine of the table with his bencher payd no more then he that placed himselfe beneath the salt.

The bolder hauing cleered the table, cardes and dice are served up to the boord ; they that are full of coyne draw ; they that haue little stand by and give ayme ; the shuffle and cut on one side, the bones rattle on the other ; long have they not plaide, but oathes fly up and downe the roome like haile-shot ; if the poore dumb dice be but a little out of the square line of white, the pox and a thousand plagues breake their neckes out at a window." (*Antiquary*, vol. xv.)

The following is contemporary evidence. It is taken from the *Antiquarian Repertory* (vol. iv. p. 512), 1558 :—

"The people of London consume great quantities of beer, double and single [strong and small], and do not drink it out of glasses, but from earthen pots with silver handles and covers, and this even in houses of persons of middling fortunes ; for as to the poor, the covers of their pots are only pewter, and in some places, such as villages, their pots for beer are made only of wood.

They eat much whiter bread than that commonly made in France, altho' it was in my time as cheap as it is sold there. With their beer they have a custom of eating very soft saffron cakes, in which there are likewise raisins, which give a relish to the beer, of which there was formerly at Rye some as good as I ever drank. The houses of the people of this country are as well furnished as any in the world. Likewise, in this country you will scarcely find any nobleman, some of whose relations have not been beheaded."

A few more notes on food. They drank brewis, that is, the pot liquor with bread in it ; they were fond of pigs' faces washed and dressed by the housewife ; they bought tripe in Eastcheap, and poultry in Gracechurch Street ; they drank wines with strange names : Pedro Ximenes, Charnico, Eleatica. The clerks took their dinner at the cooks' shops by messes of so many ; the portion of the whole mess was served in a dish and one divided the food, after which they helped themselves by seniority ; a yeoman's fare was bread, beef, and beer. The poor man was served from the basket which stood in the hall and received broken meats. The Sheriffs sent such baskets and other food to the prisons. The citizens' proverbial Sunday dinner was neck of beef.

CHAPTER III

DRESS—WEDDINGS

In the Elizabethan age, the poet, satirists, and preachers are so full of the subject of feminine fashions that it becomes of great importance. The increase of wealth and the growing power of the middle class give a greater prominence to women's

Farthingale. Lady Hunsdon.

From Planché's *Cyclopædia of Costume.*

dress, while the improvement in the streets and the roads, the introduction of coaches and the development of outdoor amusements, theatres, shows, masques, gardens, and water-parties bring the wives and daughters of London more into the open.

It was a time of great expenditure upon clothes; the fashions were rich and costly; the custom was to make what we should call an ostentatious display of wealth. Ben Jonson and the dramatists are full of the extravagance of City madams. Not only did the ladies wear rich dresses; they prided themselves upon possessing a great number—as many as they could afford; in every house there was a room called the Wardrobe, in which the clothes of the household were hung up and carefully watched and kept from moth and decay.

At the beginning of her reign the Queen, who set the fashion, wore a small ruff, with a kerchief about her neck; a kind of coat of black velvet and ermine fastened at the throat only; with a waistcoat and kirtle below of white silk or silver embroidered with black; on the shoulders were humps, and the sleeves were large. Stubbes abuses the fashion because it is "proper only to a man, yet they

LADY IN THE COURT OF QUEEN ELIZABETH, 1559.   NOBLE MATRON OF ENGLAND, 1577

From *Collection of Ancient and Modern Dresses*, 1772.

blush not to wear it." The cap or coif was adorned with strings of pearls. Lawn and cambric ruffs came in shortly after Elizabeth's accession. A Flemish woman named Van der Plasse came over and set up as a starcher of ruffs. The mere mention of starch made Stubbes furiously angry; the ruff was a "master devil"; the devil himself invented starch.

The custom of wearing whalebone to imprison the figure down to the hips also began early in the reign; a long stomacher descended in front, and from the hips stood out the farthingale, horizontally; a hideous thing which was perpetuated in the hoop for two hundred years. As for the gowns they were made, to the indignation of the satirist, "of silk, of velvet, of grograin, of taffata, and of fine cloth, ten, twenty, or forty shillings a yard"; they were decorated with lace two fingers broad, or with velvet edged with lace. The petticoats were also of the finest stuff, fringed with silk, and in addition, they had a kirtle also of fine stuff and fringed with lace and silk. It appears therefore that they had first a gown which was pulled back and showed the kirtle, which itself was pulled back and disclosed the petticoat.

Their stockings were made of the finest cloth, yarn, or worsted; silk stockings

ENGLISH LADY OF QUALITY, 1588   ENGLISH NOBLEMAN, 1559

From *Collection of Ancient and Modern Dresses*, 1772.

were presented to the Queen in her third year; knitted worsted stockings were introduced from Italy; the stockings of the fine ladies were "curiously indented in every point with quicks, clocks, and open seams." They wore cork shoes made, like the petticoats and kirtle, of anything that was costly and rare and could be embroidered.

The fashions of wearing the hair were endless. It was curled in innumerable curls; it was crisped; it was built up over a cushion; it was laid out over the forehead; it was ornamented with jewels, gold, wreaths of silver and gold, and kept in place with hairpins; the women wore over their hair French hoods,

20

hats, and caps; they wore cauls made of net-wire and cloth of gold and tinsel; they wore "lattice" caps with horns; and every merchant's wife or mean gentlewoman indulged in these extravagant fashions.

> " The cappe on hyre heade
> Is lyke a sowes mawe ;
> Such another facion
> I thynke never Jewe sawe.
> Then fyne geare on the foreheade
> After the newe trycke,
> Though it coste a crowne or two,
> What then ? They may not stycke.
> If theyr heyr wyl not take colour,
> Then must they buy newe,
> And laye it out in tussocks ;
> This thynge is too true,
> At each syde a tussocke
> As bygge as a ball.
> Hyr face faire payned
> To make it shine bright
> And her bosom all bare,
> Hyr mydle braced in
> As small as a wande ;
> And some buy water of qyre
> At the paste wyf's hande."

As for the merchants' wives, their dress is described in the following lines :—

> " You wore
> Satin on solemn days, a chain of gold,
> A velvet hood, rich borders, and sometimes
> A dainty miniver cap, a silver pin,
> Headed with a pearl worth threepence."

It was a common practice to entice little children into private places and unfrequented courts there to cut off their long hair to be made up into false hair for women. Long and beautiful hair was in great request by the fashionable dames of the time. Brides especially went to the altar with flowing locks, the longer the better.

> " Come, come, my Lord, untie your folded thoughts,
> And let them dangle loose as a bride's hair."

In a word, the Elizabethan fine lady was very fine indeed; much more artificial than her grandmother, and much less beautiful therefore. She painted her face; she dyed her hair, sometimes changing the colour from time to time, a practice which explains the different colour of the hair in Queen Mary's portraits. She used perfumes copiously; she carried a large feather fan with a costly handle of silver or ivory. She also carried a mirror hanging from her girdle with which to contemplate the thing she loved best—her own face, made up, painted, and set in the frame of ruff and cap; strings of pearls were round the cap and a gold chain round the throat. And she frequented, but secretly, the wise women—there were scores of them in the city—who knew secrets ineffable—secrets that were like magic; perhaps they were magic—for the improvement and preservation of the complexion, the brightness of the eyes, the gloss of the hair, the softness and smoothness of the arm and the throat, and everything that was open to the gaze of man. Ben Jonson preserves as in a phonograph the words and voice of the wise woman.

FOR LADIES' COMPLEXIONS

" *Wit.*   They have
Water of gourds, of radish, the white beans,
Flowers of glass, of thistles, rose-marine,
Raw honey, mustard seed, and bread dough baked,
The crums of bread, goat's-milk, and whites of eggs,
Camphire, and lily-roots, the fat of swans,
Marrow of veal, white pigeons, and pine-kernals,
The seeds of nettles, purseline, and hare's-gall :
Lemons, thin-skinn'd——

Lady E.   How her ladyship has studied
All excellent things !

Wit.   But ordinary, madam :
No, the true rarities are the alvagada
And argentata of queen Isabella.

Lady T. Ay, what are their ingredients, gentle madam ?

Wit. Your allum scagliola, or pol di pedra :
And zuccarino : turpentine of Abezzo,
Wash'd in nine waters : soda dilevants,
Or your fern ashes : benjamin di gotta :
Grasso di serpe : porceletto marino :
Oils of lentisco : zucche mugia : make
The admirable varnish for the face,
Gives the right lustre : but two drops rubb'd on
With a piece of scarlet, makes a lady of sixty
Look as sixteen.   But above all, the water
Of the white hen, of the lady Estifania's.

Lady T. O, ay, that same, good madam, I have heard of :
How is it done ?

Wit.   Madam, you take your hen,
Plume it, and skin it, cleanse it o' the inwards :
Then chop it bones and all : add to four ounces :
Of carravicins, pipitas, soap of Cyprus,
Make the decoction, strain it : then distil it,
And keep it in your gallipot well gliddered :
Three drops preserves from wrinkles, warts, spots, moles,
Blemish, or sun-burnings : and keeps the skin
In decimo sexto, ever bright and smooth,
As any looking-glass : and indeed is call'd
A ceruse, neither cold or heat, oglio reale :
And mix'd with oil of myrrh and the red gilliflower,
Call'd cataputia, and flowers of rovistico,
Makes the best muta or dye of the whole world."

The stuffs worn by gentlemen were taffeta ; mockado—an inferior velvet ; grogram—a cheaper taffeta ; quellio for the ruff ; tamin ; sendall ; and many others which are now mere words.   The poorer women, not to be outdone more than was necessary, bought the same clothes, made in the same style, of the fripperer, or broker, who dealt in second-hand clothes. Now the great danger of buying second-hand clothes was that you might at the same time buy the plague.

Men were never so affected and so splendid in their dress as in the sixteenth century. They wore earrings; they wore costly brooches in their hats; the great nobles wore strings of pearls; they had thumb rings; they carried jewelled daggers; they carried a case of toothpicks with them; they carried their own napkins to the taverns; they had a favourite lock of hair, which they curled and treated tenderly, tying a rose to it or a bunch of ribbons; they wore their hair and their beards in

WEALTHY MERCHANT OF LONDON, 1588
From *Collection of Ancient and Modern Dresses*, 1772.

fantastic ways, either after the French, Italian, or Spanish manner. As for the younger men, they played the usual tricks. That is to say, they tried to make the waist small; they wore "grulled calves"; they "bleached their hands at midnight, gumming and triding their beards." Sleeves were slashed; girdles were hung with mirrors; the head was set in a ruff; high-heeled shoes raised the stature; men's cloaks were of velvet trimmed with lace; buttons, buckles, and clasps were of gold; the hats were adorned with feathers.

Tavern life in the time of the Tudors was picturesque and pleasant. The taverns were frequented not only by gallants and merchants, but by ladies. Suppers, it is true, were given to bona robas; the viol de gamba played for companies not always the most respectable; but there were rooms which the City madams used as a resort for parties of their own friends; and that without any question of offence.

The City Trained Bands were gorgeous in white doublets, with the City arms before and behind; the men-servants wore gorgeous liveries. Dress to a certain extent indicated class. Law and Divinity wore black. Furred gowns and satin sleeves marked the Sheriff or the Alderman. The plain citizen wore a cloak of

PAGE BOY, TIME OF. EDWARD VI
From *Collection of Ancient and Modern Dresses*, 1772.

brown or chocolate colour; the craftsman wore a doublet of cloth, or leather, with a leather belt, and in winter an overcoat down to the knees or the ankles. The following is the description of a runaway page :—

"One doblet of yelow million fustian, th'one halfe therof buttoned with peche-colour buttons, and th'other halfe laced downewardes; one payer of peche-colour hose, laced with smale tawnye lace; a graye hat with a copper edge rounde aboute it, with a bande p'cell of the same hatt; a payer of watchet (blue) stockings. Likewise he hath twoe clokes; th'one of vessey collor, garded with twoe gards of black clothe and twisted lace of carnacion colour, and lyned with crymsone bayes; and th'other is a red shipp russet colour, striped about th'cape, and downe the fore face, twisted with two rows of twisted lace, russet and gold buttons afore and uppon the sholdier, being of the clothe itselfe, set with the said twisted lace, and the buttons of russet silke and golde."

'Prentices wore a dress very much like that of the Blue Coat Boys, but with a flat cap. A citizen's servant wore a blue livery. Knots of ribbons were tied on the shoes. The women gathered round the conduit and the bakehouse for gossip. The tradesmen issued their own tokens which passed current. Girls who served in the shops were taken on Sundays by their sweethearts to Islington or Pimlico. Shops were furnished with cudgels for the use of 'prentices in case of a fight. The cudgels were called by various endearing names, but the favourite name was a "Plymouth Cloak." Clothes were washed at the riverside on wood or a flat stone. The love of fine dress is charged as a fault of the fair Londoners. Why they should be blamed for desiring what all men desire, viz. the appearance of bravery and splendour, is hard to understand. The sumptuary laws which were passed from time to time appear to have been intended not so much to prevent the gratification of this instinctive desire as to make different classes proclaim their rank and station by their dress. A tradesman, in fact, must not appear as a gentleman; nor a craftsman as a master. In a word, there was a constant feeling that rank should be

Sir William Russell. 1590.
From Planché's *Cyclopædia of Costume.*

indicated by outward apparel, and that every one should proclaim his station by his garments. Thus the Act of 1464 ordered

"That none below the dignity of a lord or knight of the garter, or their wives, should be allowed to wear purple, or any manner of cloth of gold, velvet or sable furs, under a penalty of 20 marks. That none below knights, bachelors, mayors, and aldermen, and their wives, should wear satin or ermine, under a penalty of 10 marks. That none but such as had possessions to the amount of 40s. per annum should be permitted to wear fustian, bustian, or scarlet cloth, and no fur, but black or white lamb, on forfeiture of 40s.

That no yeoman, nor any under that degree, should be allowed to stuff or bolster their doublets, to wear short cloaks or jackets, or shoes with pikes passing the length of eleven inches, under a penalty of 20s.

That no husbandman should use broad cloth at above 11s. a yard, nor hose above 14d. a pair: nor their wives kerchiefs whereof the price should exceed 12d. nor girdles harnessed with silver, upon pain of forfeiting at every default 40d.

And because foreign kerchiefs were brought into the country, and sold at such extravagant prices, it was ordained that any one selling lawne, nyfell, umple, or other manner of kerchief whereof the price should exceed 10s. the seller should forfeit a mark for every one that he sold above that price."

To those who take the worthy Philip Stubbes quite seriously and literally, the Elizabethan age will appear more than commonly wicked and unscrupulous; to

COURT OF WARDS AND LIVERIES IN THE TIME OF ELIZABETH

From Planché's *Cyclopædia of Costume*.

The person at the head of the table appears to be Lord Burghley ; on either side of him is a judge, who may have been there as assessors. The next on the left side is Thomas Seckford, who held the office of Surveyor from 1580 to 1589. The one opposite may be Richard Kingsmill, Attorney from 1582 to to 1589. The third on the left side may be George Goring, Receiver-General from 1583 to 1593. The opposite person with a book open may be William Tooke, Auditor 1551 to 1588. The three persons at the lower end of the table are clerks. At the left hand side next the end is the Usher with a rod. In 1578 Marmaduke Servant held this office. Opposite to him on the other side stands the Messenger, who in 1565 was Leonard Taylor. This picture was probably made about 1585.

those who are ready to make allowance for the exaggerated indignation of the satirist, the narrowness of the Puritan, and the real and genuine craving after equity, justice, and honesty, it will become manifest that the age contained, like every other age, grave abuses, great injustices, and much small meanness and trickery. Laws were passed attempting to restrain the tricks of clothiers, tanners, shoemakers, and "brokers," *i.e.* pawnbrokers and marine store-dealers. These laws failed, as all such laws must fail, because men who wish to cheat will cheat in spite of any laws that may be passed. In truth there is very little in Stubbes but does not belong to every town and every age. He laments the pride of the age. So does every satirist. Especially he laments Pride of Apparel. Take their hats for instance :—

"Sometimes they use them sharp on the crowne, pearking up like a spere, or shafte of a steeple, standing a quarter of a yard above the crowne of their heades ; some more, some lesse, as please the

Robert de Vere, Earl of Oxford.

John Clinch, Chief Justice of the Common Pleas. 1584.

Sir Edward Coke, Chief Justice of the King's Bench. 1613.

From Planché's *Cyclopædia of Costume*.

phantasies of their inconstant mindes. Othersome be flat and broad on the crowne, like the battlementes of a house. An other sort have round crownes, sometymes with one kinde of bande, sometymes with an other ; now blacke, now white, now russet, now red, now grene, now yellowe, now this, nowe that, never content with one colour or fashion two daies to an ende. . . .

And as the fashions bee rare and straunge, so is the stuffe wherof their hattes be made, divers also ; for some are of silke, some of velvet, some of taffatie, some of sarcenet, some of wooll, and, whiche is more curious, some of a certaine kind of fine haire. . . . And so common a thinge it is, that everie servingman, countrieman, and other, even all indifferently, do weare of these hattes. For he is of no account or estimation amongst men, if hee have not a velvet or a taffatie hatte, and that muste bee pincked and cunningly carved of the beste fashion. And good profitable hattes bee these, for the longer you weare them the fewer holes they haue. Besides this, of late there is a new fashion of wearyng their hattes sprung up amongst them, which they father upon the Frenchmen, namely, to weare them without bandes ; but how unseemely (I will not saie how assie) a fashion that is, let the wise judge ; notwithstanding, howe ever it be, if it please them, it shall not displease me. And an other sort (as phantasticall as the rest) are content with no kinde of hat without a greate bunche of feathers of divers and sundrie colours, peakyng on top of their heades, not unlike (I dare not saie) Cockescombes, but as sternes of pride and ensigns of vanitie." (Stubbes, 1836 edition, p. 38.)

Marriages took place at an earlier age than is now common, both for men and for women. An unmarried girl of twenty was regarded as an old maid. Thus in the *Crowne Garland of Golden Roses* the maiden laments her virginity :—

> " Twenty winters have I seen,
> And as many summers greene,
> 'Tis long enough to breed despaire
> So long a maidenhead to beare ;
> 'Tis a burden of such waight
> That I would faine be eas'd of't straight ;
> But alasse ! I am afraid
> I shall live and die a maid."

The betrothal took place forty days before the wedding :—

> " A contract of eternal bond of love,
> Confirmed by mutual joinder of your hands,
> Attested by the holy close of lips,
> Strengthened by interchangement of your rings ;
> And all the ceremony of this compact
> Seal'd in my function, by my testimony."

To make the betrothal binding there were, therefore, four points to be observed: (1) The joining of hands; (2) the exchange of kisses; (3) the exchange of rings; (4) the testimony of witnesses.

After the betrothal, the wedding :—

> " The procession accompanying a rural bride, of some consequence, or of the middle rank, to church was as follows :—The bride, being attired in a gown of sheep's russet, and a kirtle of fine worsted, her hair attired with a 'billement of gold' (decorated with long chains of gold), and her hair as yellow as gold hanging down behind her, which was curiously combed and plaited, was led to the church between two sweet boys, with bride laces and rosemary tied about their silken sleeves. There was carried before her a fair bride-cup of silver, gilt, filled with hippocras and garnished with a goodly branch of rosemary, which stands for constancy. The cup was hung about with silken ribbands of all colours. Musicians followed, then a group of maidens, some bearing bride-cakes, others garlands of wheat finely gilded ; and thus they passed on to the church."

The wedding customs were very pretty. The bride, like all unmarried women, wore a dress which exposed a portion of her bosom—you may see how far the exposure went by looking at any portrait of Queen Elizabeth ; she wore her hair flowing. Some girls married very early, even at fifteen, which was considered quite old enough to undertake the duties of a wife. On the way to and from the church, wheat was thrown on the head of the bride, just as rice is thrown now, as a symbol of fruitfulness to follow. The wedding guests wore scarves, gloves, and favours ; cake—the bride-cake—was taken to the Church and distributed after the ceremony ; brooches were also given to the young men and maidens present. Then the cup of wine was sent round : the "knitting" cup, or the "contracting" cup ; and then, carrying in her hand a piece of gilt rosemary, the bride led the way home, where, for three days, festivities, masques, mumming, music, dancing, feasting, and drinking were carried on. In some of the churches special pews were provided for newly married couples, who sat in them and listened, while the preacher discoursed on "The Bride's Bush" or "The Wedding Garment Beautified."

In 1584 the Puritans got in a Bill permitting to marry at all seasons and on every day of the year. It had been the endeavour of the Bishops to keep Lent as a season in which there was to be no marrying or giving in marriage. Meantime, the keeping of Lent remained, if only as an outward sign of revolt against the Puritans.

When there was a christening it was conducted in the mother's bedroom. After the service, the sponsors presented "Postle Spoons"; then, of course, they sat down to a solid feast, or, at least, a drink—nothing could be done without a drink; comfits were handed round with the wine, and it was not unusual for some of the guests to go away royally drunk.

THE CHRISTENING OF PRINCE ARTHUR
From a historical print in the British Museum.

An example of a marriage feast is that of one Coke, citizen, with the daughter of Mr. Nicolls, Master of London Bridge. My Lord Mayor and all the Aldermen, with many ladies and other worshipful men and women, were present at the wedding. Mr. Bacon, an eminent divine, preached the wedding sermon. After the discourse the company went home to the Bridge House to dinner, where was as good cheer as ever was known—Stow says so, and he knew very well—with all manner of music and dancing, and at night a masque till midnight. But this was only half the feast, for next day the wedding was again kept at the Bridge House with great cheer. After supper more mumming, after that more masques. One was in cloth of gold, the next consisted of friars, and the third of nuns. First the friars and the nuns danced separately, one company after the other, and then they danced together.

At a funeral the mourners first assembled at the house where lay the coffin. Here the clergyman made a speech on the virtues of the deceased. On the coffin stood a jug or pot of wine which was passed round as a loving-cup. Then every one laid branches on the coffin; money was given to the children; to the mourners ribbons, scarves, and gloves were distributed; rosemary was laid in the coffin and placed in the mourners' hats; as for what followed, we may take the funerals described by Machyn. First, the Company to which the deceased belonged, attended in their livery; the Company of Clerks attended the

¶ The order and maner of burying in the Fields such as dyed in prison, and namely, of William Wiseman.

funerals of the better class and sang over the grave; black gowns were given to as many poor men and poor women as the condition of the deceased permitted. When a great citizen died, like Master Husee, "squire and a grett marchand ventorer and of Muskovia and haberdasher," he was followed by a hundred mourners; he had five pennons of arms, and a "cotte armur," and "two heralds of arms, Master Clarenshux and Master Somerset." He was attended by the Choir of St. Paul's and by the Company of Clerks; they buried him at St. Martin's, Ludgate Hill; the church was hung with black and with escutcheons of arms; the Reader of St. Paul's preached "both days."

Master Flammock, grocer, who died in 1560, was apparently a Puritan. Many gowns were bestowed by his executors; he was taken to the church without singing or clerks, and was buried with a psalm, "after Genevay," and a sermon.

Lady Dobbes, the wife of Sir Richard Dobbes, was buried with a pennon of armes and four dozen and five escutcheons; many black gowns were given. "Master Recherdson mad the sermon, and the clarkes syngyng and a dolle of money of xx nobulles, and a grete dinner after and the compane of the Skynners in ther leverey."

Master Hulson, scrivener, was one of the Masters in Bridewell; so the Masters of Bridewell attended his funeral with green staves in their hands, and all their children, "and there was great syngyng as ever was heard." And when we have added that after most of these notes occur this passage, "And all dune to the place, fir there was a great dener," we have said all that need be said about a civic funeral.

One detail is not mentioned by Machyn. This is the custom observed till quite recently in Yorkshire, of hanging a garland or wreath of ribbons in the chancel of a church when a girl died unmarried. This custom had many forms, one or other of which was certainly observed in London. It was considered unlucky to carry away a piece of ribbon; if the wreath dropped to pieces, all the pieces were buried in the churchyard.

Persons of distinction continued to be buried within the walls of the church.

Some Companies and some parish churches still preserve funeral palls which have been presented to them at various times for the use of the members and parishioners. Thus, in May 1848, Mr. William Wansey, Prime Warden of the Fishmongers' Company, exhibited a funeral pall of most beautiful and elaborate workmanship, formed of cloth of gold richly embroidered.

"This interesting relic has been preserved in the possession of the Fishmongers' Company, having doubtless been originally used at the interments of its more distinguished members. No account of the acquisition of this fine specimen of decoration, or of the precise period when it was executed, has been preserved, and the earlier records of the Company were destroyed in the fire of London; its date may be attributed to the earlier part of the sixteenth, or the close of the previous century. The designs which decorate the head and foot of the pall are precisely similar, and the two sides likewise correspond exactly in design. On the former is presented St. Peter, the patron of fishermen, receiving from the Saviour the keys of heaven and hell; the embroideries on the two sides represent St. Peter enthroned, crowned with the tiara, with angels kneeling one on either side, throwing their censers towards him. On each side of this subject is introduced an escutcheon of the arms of the Company, with supporters. Nothing can exceed the delicacy of execution displayed in this remarkable specimen of needle-work: the countenances are full of expression, and the colours are generally remarkable for freshness and brilliancy. Another funeral pall of great beauty is in the possession of the Saddlers' Company, and has been accurately represented in Mr. Shaw's *Dresses and Decorations*." (*Archæologia*, xxxi.)

CHAPTER IV

SOLDIERS

"By an Act of Parliament, 27 Henry II., 1181, called 'An Assize of Arms,' confirmed and enlarged by 13 Edward I., 1285, every man, according to his estate and

SOLDIERS OF THE PERIOD
From Meyrick's *Inquiry into Antient Armour.*

degree, was obliged to provide a determinate quantity of such arms and armour as were then in use.[1] Constables were provided to see that their arms were correct, and proper persons, at stated periods, were appointed to *muster and train* them.

[1] See *Remembrancia*, pp. 550-551.

316

Every Freeman that had in chattels or rent to the value of sixteen marks was to have a coat of mail (*loricam*), a helmet (*cassidem*), a shield, and a lance; and so in proportion to his wealth. Another Assize of Arms was passed 36 Henry III., 1252, and in 1285 the Statute of Winchester. These made some alterations in the qualification and in the weapon. By 27 Edward I., 1298, armed horses were ordered to be provided. The Statute of 4 and 5 Philip and Mary, c. 3, 1537, changed the weapons for those of more modern construction. It also provided that all persons having an estate valued at £1000 or more should, after the 1st of May 1558, keep six horses and ten light horses, with furniture, etc. By the 33 Henry VIII., c. 5, Commissioners were appointed to see that the inhabitants of cities and boroughs were properly provided with arms, etc. Thus cities, according to their wealth or position, were obliged to have ready so many trained men. In 1335 the City of London provided twenty-five men in arms and 500 archers for the war against France. In 1360, 1400 to serve in France. Henry VIII. called upon the City to supply him with 1500 men in July 1545. The French threatening the Isle of Wight, on the 4th of August 1545, the citizens sent 1000 soldiers to Dover. In 1557 Queen Mary caused a levy to be made of 1000 horsemen, 4000 footmen, and 2000 pioneers, to assist Philip of Spain against the King of France. In 1558 another was made to protect Calais; and in 1560 another to assist the Queen's Troops against the French, who were besieging Leith, in Scotland. In 1562 a large number were sent to serve at Havre de Grace. Orders were received from the Council in 1578 to keep 2000 men in readiness. The Lord Mayor, in 1580, issued a precept assessing the Companies for providing and furnishing 1000 men. The Stationers' Company had to provide twenty men, thirteen shot, and seven pikemen. The cost of their provision, furnishing, and training was £20:10:4; and for powder and other charges, £11:3s. In 1585, 4000 men, with armour, ensigns, drums, fifes, and other furniture for the wars, the greater part being shot, mustered at Mile End, 14th April, and were reviewed by Queen Elizabeth, 18th May. In 1596 the City twice raised, in less than twelve hours, 1000 men, completely armed, for the relief of the French, besieged by the Spaniards, in Calais. In 1589, 1000 men were provided, fully equipped, to assist in placing Henry of Navarre on the French throne. In 1600, 500 men for service in Ireland. In 1624, 2000 for the Low Countries. In 1638-40, 200 men in all, for service against the Scots."

There was an ancient and time-honoured march, known as the "old English march," which fell into disuse some time before the accession of Charles the First, when Sir Edward Cecil, Lord Wimbledon, persuaded the King to issue a warrant, ordering it to be revived. The point raised is extremely interesting. The Warrant runs thus—it is dated 7th Feb. 1632:—"Whereas the ancient custome of Nations hath ever bene to use one certaine and constant forme of march in the warres, whereby to be distinguished one from another: and whereas the march of this our

English Nation, so famous in all honourable atchievements and glorious warres of this our Kingdome in forraigne parts (being, by the approbation of Strangers themselves, confessed and acknowledged the best of all Marches) was, through the negligence and carelessness of drummers, and by long discontinuance, so altered and changed from the ancient gravitie and majestie thereof, as it was in danger utterly to have bene lost and forgotten. It pleased our late deare brother prince Henry to revive and rectifie the same, by ordayning an establishment of one certaine

YEOMAN OF THE GUARD, TIME OF HENRY VIII.
E. Gardner's Collection.

Measure which was beaten in his presence at Greenwich, anno 1610. In confirmation whereof, wee are graciously pleased, at the instance and humble sute of our right trusty, etc., Edward, Viscount Wimbledon, etc., to set down and ordaine this present establishment hereunder expressed. Willing and commanding all drummers within our Kingdome of England and principalitie of Wales exactly and precisely to observe the same as well in this our Kingdome as abroad in the service of any forraigne prince or state without any addition or alteration whatsoever. To the end that so ancient, famous, and commendable a custome may be preserved as a patterne and precedent to all posteritie."

About the time of Henry the Seventh we first find mention made of coat- and conduct-money, a clothing allowance and subsistence for men on joining the army, which was sometimes advanced by the counties where the men were raised, to be afterwards repaid by the Government. These charges varied according to the times. In 1492 the conduct-money was calculated at the rate of 6d. for every twenty miles each soldier should march, to be reckoned from his residence to the place of joining the army; each soldier to swear to the number of the miles marched by him. In 1574 it was fixed at a halfpenny per mile. In 1627, coat-money to have been settled at 12s. 6d., and conduct-money at 8d. per diem, accounting twelve miles for a day's march. In 1640 it was 8d. per diem, but the day's march was not less than fifteen miles.

In dress and weapons armour had not yet disappeared, but it was much less cumbrous. The corselet, with a morion, or open head-piece, and thigh guards were still in general use; but plates of armour were frequently fastened to any ordinary tunic for the defence of the shoulders, arms, and chest. The pike-men, with their twenty-foot pikes, wore corselets, and were much disinclined to march more than five or six miles a day, owing to the weight of their dresses and weapons. The bill-men were in lighter armour, and their weapons were shorter than the pike, but very effective against cavalry. The bill was a hook-shaped blade fastened

A KNIGHT IN ARMOUR
From Meyrick's *Inquiry into Antient Armour*.

to a wooden staff, with a projecting prong at the end and back. Pike-men and bill-men were employed in protecting archers from cavalry and in covering such field-guns as were in use. Civic guards and watchmen were armed with bills. The archers wore a buff-padded jacket, with sometimes an under-shirt of light chain-armour. A jerkin, of leather or cloth, was indiscriminately worn by all ranks. The firearms were of two kinds, leaving out of view artillery. The first could be fired with a rest, and the second were practically very light artillery. The harquebus and the small petronel belonged to the first class, and the culverin, the long petronel, and the muschite (from the French mosquet, a hawk) to the second. Two men were required to handle the weapons of the second class. They had long barrels. They were fired with a match, the barrels resting on an iron fork sticking in the ground. The harquebus was originally a musket-stock with a bow fixed to it; but the term was now used to mean the long-barrelled hand-gun with a touch hole and priming pan and trigger on the right side, which was rapidly driving out other weapons and rendering armour useless.

Musters of the citizens were frequent in the reign of Henry the Eighth and Queen Elizabeth.[1] A history of the muster of the citizens on the 8th of May

PIKEMAN

From Grose's *Military Antiquities.*

1539, the 31st of Henry the Eighth, is given at length in the *Records of the Corporation*, Journal 14, folio 166. "They marched from Mile end to Whitehall, and from thence to Leadenhall, Sir Wm. Forman, Knt., Lord Mayor was in bright harness, whereof the curass, the maynsers, gaunteletts and other parts were gilt upon the crests and bordures, and with that he had a coat of black velvet with a rich cross embroidered, and a great massy chain of gold about his neck, and on his head a cap of black velvet with a rich jewel, he had a goodly jennett richly trapped, with embroidery of gold set upon crimson velvet. About him attended 4 foot men, all apparelled in white satin hose and all puffed over with white sarcenet." In 1559, July 2 and 3, according to *Stow's Chronicle*, edit. 1615, p. 639, "the Citizens mustered before Queen Elizabeth in Greenwich Park, 1400 men being present; 800 pikemen in fine corselets; 400 harquebuts in shirts of maile, with morins; and 200 halberters in Alman rivets." A large number of the citizens were also present. The price of armour at this date, as given in several records, was for "a Corslett, 30s.; Harquebus complete, 8s.; a Murrion, 6s. 8d.; Almaine rivette, 10s.; a musket, flask, touch-box and tassels, 17s. 6d.; Gunpowder, 12d. per pound."

Here, for instance (*Archæologia*, vol. xxxii. p. 32), is an account of a muster before Henry the Eighth.

"Than the sayd lorde mayor and hys brethren assemblyd thym selffs ageyn, and after longe consultac'on, they fyrst determyned, that no alyen, although he were a denyzen, shuld mustre, but onely mere Englysshmen; ffurther they thought yt not convenyent that all the hole number of Englysshmen shulde mustre and goo owte of the cytye for especyall consyderac'ons; nor that suche as had jakks, brygandynes, or cotes of fence, shulde goo yn the mustre, but onely they appoynted

1 See *Remembrancia*, p. 230.

syche whiche were hable p'sones, & hadde whyte harnes with whyte cotes, bowes, arrowes, halberds, bills or polaxes; and none other except soche as bare moryse pykes or handgonnes, whiche onely hadde plents and sculls, with whyte cotes and whyte cappes with fethers; and all thys company was comaunded to be yn whyte hose and clenly shodde. Whan yt was knowen that the Kyng hymselff wolde se the Mustre, to se howe gladly ev'y man p'pared hym, what desyre ev'y man had to do hys prince s'rvice yt was a joyfull syght to beholde of ev'y Inglysshman. Than ev'y man of substance provyded hymself a cote of sylke, & garnished theyre bassenetts with turbes of sylke sett with broches, ouches and fethers; some had theyre harnes and polaxes gylted, some had theyr breastplates cov'yd with sylvr

MUSKETEER
From Grose's *Military Antiquities.*

bullyon—ev'y man devysed to doo hys best to s've hys prynce and of thys sorte the most parte had chaynes of golde. The meaner sorte were yn cotes of white cotton, clenly hosed and shodde with the armes of the cytye before & behynde. The constables were all yn jouetts of whyte sylke over theyre harnes, with battayl axes gylt, & chaynes abowte theyre necks. The sayd lorde mayor, aldermen, recorder, shryves, & such as hadde bene shryeves, were yn whyte harnes, & o'vr that cotes of black velvet, with the armes of the cytye rychely pyrled and embroderyd upon the same, with great chaynes of golde about theyre necks, mountyd on good horsses well styrryng & rychely trapped, with battell axes yn theyre handes, & cappes of velvett yn theyre heddes; and ev'y alderman had iiij halberdars yn whyte sylke or buffe cotes attendyng on thej, with gylt halbards, and the mayer had xvj apparrellyd as you shall here hereafter; all theys were captayns of the bataylls, as you shall p'ceyve yn theyre settyng forward. The chamberlayn and councellors of the cytye, & the aldermens deputyes whiche were assigned to be wyffelers on horsebacke, were all yn cotes of whyte damask over theyr harnes, mountyd on good horsses, well trappyd, with great chaynes abowte theyre necks, and propre javilyns or battle axes yn theyre handes, with cappes of velvett on theyre heddes with ryche ouches. The wyffelers on fote were iiij C. propre lyght p'sones app'ellyd yn whyte sylke or buffe jerkyns, without harnes, or whyte hose and whyte shoes, every man havyng a slaugh sworde or a javelyn to kepe the people yn araye, with chaynes abowte theyre necks and fethers yn theyre cappes. The mynstrells also were all yn whyte, and so were the standard berers, which were the tallyst men yn ev'y warde, all app'ellyd yn sylke, for whome were made XXX newe standards with the devyses of the Cytye. . . . To see howe full of lordes, ladyes, and gentilwomen the wyndowes yn every strete were, and howe the strets of the cytye were replenysshed with people, many men wolde have thought that they that musteryd had rather byn straungers than cytezens, consydering that the stretes everywhere were so full of people, whiche was to straungers a great mervell. To reporte what good order the cytezens kept yn passing forward; what payne the wyffelers bothe on horseback & fote tooke yn keepyng the soulders yn araye; howe ryche the juells, chaynes, and app'ell were; how many goodly, talle, & comley men were there, & the nombre of the same, my wytt ys insuffycyent to exp'sse or my penne to write. Wherfore, I remytt theys poynts to theym that sawe and nombret them, and desyeryng them to remember the nombre that passed yn the muster, and not to forget yn theyr accompt theym that taryed at home or stode yn the stretes, for the one without the other sheweth not the hole puyssance of the cytye. But, whatsoever was doon and what payne so ever was takyn, all was to the cytezens a great gladness."

It will thus be seen that military array had arrived at a new and quite another kind of splendour. Armour had not gone out, but it was less cumbrous, and people believed less in its value. It availed to a certain extent against sword and pike, but not at all against bullet. The pikemen who carried pikes eighteen or twenty feet in length wore a breastplate; the billmen had lighter armour, their weapon was a hook or a staff. Both pikemen and billmen were employed in covering field-guns against cavalry. Watchmen also carried bills. The firearms were the harquebus or arquebus; the small petronel; the culverin; the long petronel and the musket. The larger kinds were fired with the barrel resting on a fork stuck in the ground. Swords and daggers were, of course, carried, and gentlemen wore expensive chain and plate armour.

Henry VIII. had a wonderful suit of armour made in Germany. It was engraved with illustrations from the lives of martyrs and saints, some of which are reproduced on p. 382, from the illustrations given in *Archæologia*.

CHAPTER V

THE 'PRENTICE

THIS chapter is inserted in the Tudor period because the 'Prentice in that century arrived at the height of his power and importance, chiefly as a disturber of the peace. The following pages sum up the regulations on the subject from the fifteenth to the eighteenth century, both inclusive.

The importance of the apprentice system caused many ordinances and regulations to be passed from time to time. Thus in 1406 no persons were allowed to put out their children as apprentices who had not land to the value of 20 shillings a year, a regulation intended, in a populous town, to keep up the *status* of trades and crafts. The Act was, however, found impossible to work, and was repealed in 1429 "to the great satisfaction of the citizens." Later on, in 1486, another attempt was made to restrict the Freedom of the City, and to keep out "mean and improper" persons by an ordinance that no apprentice should be taken nor freedom given except to such as were "gentlemen born"—this is Maitland's statement—"agreeable to the clause in the oath given to every freeman at the time he was made free, in these words, 'Ye shall take none apprentice but if he be freeborn: that is to say, no Bondman's son, nor the son of any alien.'" It does not appear, however, from the oath, that the freeman was required to be a gentleman unless every freeborn person is a gentleman. How could a blacksmith or a journeyman saddler be a gentleman?

In 1527 the Common Council passed a stringent rule as to the treatment of Apprentices :—

"'If hereafter any Freeman or Freewoman of this City take any Apprentice, and within the Term of seven Years suffer the same Apprentice to go at his large Liberty and Pleasure; and within or after the said Term agree with his said Apprentice for a certain Sum of Money, or otherwise, for his said service, and within or after the End of the said Term, the said Freeman present the said Apprentice to the Chamberlain of the City, and by good Deliberation, and upon his Oath made to the same City, the same Freeman or Freewoman assureth and affirmeth to the said Chamberlain, that the said Apprentice hath fully served his said Term as Apprentice: Or if any Freeman or Freewoman of this City take any Apprentice which at the Time of the said taking hath any Wife: Or, if any Freeman or Freewoman of this City, give any Wages to his or her Apprentice, or suffer the said Apprentices to take any Part of their own Getting of Gains: Or if any Freeman or Freewoman of this City hereafter colour any foreign Goods, or from henceforth buy or sell for any Person or Persons, or with or to any Person or Persons, being foreign or Foreigners, Cloths, Silks, Wine, Oils, or any other Goods or Merchandize, whatsoever they be, whether he take any Thing or Things for his or their Wages or Labour, or not: Or if any Person or Persons being Free of this City, by any Colour or deceitful Means, from henceforth do buy, sell, or receive of any Apprentice within this City, any Money, Goods, Merchandize, or Wares, without the Assent or Licence of his Master or Mistress; and upon Examination duly proved before the Chamberlain of the said City for the Time being, and the same reported by the Mouth of the said Chamberlain, at a Court to be holden by the Mayor and the Aldermen of the same City in their Council-Chamber: That as well the said Master, as the said Apprentice, shall for evermore be disfranchised. *God save the King!*'" (Maitland, vol. i. pp. 229-230.)

To which was added an admonition to the Apprentices:—

"'Ye shall constantly and devoutly on your Knees, every Day, serve God, Morning and Evening, and make Conscience in the due Hearing of the Word preached, and endeavour the right Practice thereof on your Life and Conversation. You shall do diligent and faithful Service to your Master for the Time of your Apprenticeship, and deal truly in what you shall be trusted. You shall often read over the Covenants of your Indenture, and see and endeavour yourself to perform the same, to the utmost of your Power. You shall avoid all evil Company, and all Occasions which may tend to draw you to the same; and make speedy Return when you shall be sent of your Masters and Mistresses Business. You shall be of fair, gentle, and lowly Speech and Behaviour towards all Men, and especially to all your Governors. And according to your Carriage, expect your Reward, for Good or Ill, from God and your Friends.'" (Maitland, vol. i. p. 230.)

The history of "Evil May Day" (p. 24) is an illustration of the growing turbulence of the 'Prentices and the relaxation of order and discipline in the City generally. The wards, in fact, had become too thickly populated for the old and simple rule of a peripatetic alderman and his sergeants: the turbulence was a sign of their weakness; yet three hundred years were to pass before an efficient night and day police could be established as the only remedy.

In the year 1582 an ordinance concerning the apparel of the 'Prentice shows still more clearly that he was getting out of hand. It was enacted by the Lord Mayor and Common Council:—

"That from henceforth no Apprentice whatsoever should presume: 1. To wear any Apparel but what he receives from his Master. 2. To wear no Hat within the City and Liberty thereof, nor any thing instead thereof, than a Woollen Cap, without any Silk in or about the same. 3. To wear no Ruffles, Cuffs, loose Collar, nor other thing than a Ruff at the Collar, and that only of a Yard and a half long. 4. To wear no Doublets but what were made of canvas, Fustian, Sackcloth, English Leather, or Woollen Cloth, and without being enriched with any manner of Gold, Silver, or Silk. 5. To wear no other coloured Cloth, or Kersey, in Hose or Stockings, than White, Blue, or Russet. 6. To wear little Breeches, of the same Stuffs as the Doublets, and without being stitched, laced or bordered. 7. To wear a plain upper Coat of Cloth or Leather, without Pinking, Stitching, Edging or Silk about it. 8. To wear no other Surtout than a Cloth Gown or Cloak, lined or faced with Cloth, Cotton or Bays, with a fixed round Collar, without Stitching, Guarding, Lace or Silk. 9. To wear no Pumps, Slippers, nor Shoes, but of English Leather, without being pinked, edged or stitched, nor Girdles nor Garters, other than of Crewel, Woollen, Thread or Leather, without being garnished. 10. To wear no Sword, Dagger, or other Weapon, but a Knife; nor a Ring, Jewel of Gold, nor Silver, nor Silk in any Part of the Apparel.

It was likewise further enacted, That every Apprentice offending against any of the above-mentioned items, was for the first offence to be punished at the discretion of his Master; for the second to be publicly whipped at the Hall of his Company; and for the third to serve six months longer than specified in his indentures. And every Master conniving at the crimes of his Apprentice committed against the tenor of the premises, should, for every such offence, forfeit to the poor of the parish wherein he dwelt six shillings and eightpence. It was also farther ordained, That no Apprentice should frequent, or go to any dancing, fencing, or musical schools; nor keep any chest, press, or other place for the keeping of apparel or goods, but in his Master's House, under the penalties aforesaid. And every such Master permitting or allowing his Apprentice to offend in any of the said cases, to forfeit as in the case of forbidden apparel." (Maitland, vol. i. p. 267.)

Maitland, after praising this wise ordinance, laments that in his time, the middle of the eighteenth century, there could not be some such good law passed to restrain the "more destructive practices of our modern Apprentices," viz. keeping mistresses, keeping horses, frequenting tavern clubs and playhouses, and "their great excesses in clothes, Linen, periwigs, gold and silver watches, etc." He does not tell us where they got the money for these expensive luxuries, but in the *Confession of Latroun Meriton* (1650) the way is fully explained: it was, namely, by robbing their masters. In the year 1595 there were more troubles caused by the 'Prentices. The Queen ordered sharp measures to be taken :—

"'And because such Assemblies and Routs were compounded of sundry Sorts of base People; some known Apprentices, such as were of base manual Occupations; some others, wandering idle Persons, of Condition, Rogues, and Vagabonds; and some colouring their wandering by the Name of Soldiers returning from the Wars, etc., therefore she had notified her Pleasure to her Council, to prescribe certain Orders to be published in and about the said City, which she would have streightly observed; and, for that Purpose, that she meant to have a Provost-Marshal, with sufficient Authority to apprehend all such as should not be readily reformed and corrected by the ordinary Officers of Justice, and them without Delay to execute upon the Gallows by Order of Martial Law. At our Manor of Greenwich, the 4th of July, 1595.'" (Maitland, vol. i. pp. 278-279.)

Sir Thomas Welford, accordingly, was appointed Provost-Marshal. He patrolled the streets with a number of horsemen armed with pistols: he arrested many of the rioters, who were tried at the Guildhall. Five of them were executed on Tower Hill, and the rioting ceased.

Of the Apprentices' riot against the Spanish Ambassador in 1641 we have heard in another place (*London in the Time of the Stuarts*, p. 38). The Lord Mayor had a good deal of trouble in appeasing the Ambassador, who said that he "hardly knew how to call that a City or even a Society of rational creatures which was seemingly divested both of Humanity and Government."

At the outbreak of Civil War the 'Prentices were on the side of the Parliament and enjoyed many opportunities of demonstrating their views and opinions, not only without reproach, but rather with the approbation of the Parliamentary party, the leaders of which encouraged the young fellows to enlist in their army, as, for example, by the following Proclamation:—

"'Whereas in Times of common Danger and Necessity the Interests of private Persons ought to give way to publick, it is ordained and declared by the Lords and Commons in Parliament, That such Apprentices as have been, or shall be listed to serve as Soldiers, for the Defence of the Religion and Liberty of the Kingdom, his Majesty's Royal Person, the Parliament, and the City of London, their Sureties, and such as stand engaged for them, shall be secured against their Masters, their Executors, and Administrators, from all Loss and Inconvenience by Forfeiture of Bonds, Covenants, Infranchisement, or other Ways: And that, after this publick Service ended, the Masters of such Apprentices shall be commanded and required to receive them again into their Service, without imposing upon them any Punishment, Loss, or Prejudice, for their Absence in the Defence of the Commonwealth.

'And the Lords and Commons do further declare, That if it shall appear, that the Masters of such Apprentices have received any considerable Loss by the Absence of their Apprentices, they will take Care that reasonable Satisfaction be made unto them out of the publick Stock of the Kingdom, according to Justice and Indifferency.'" (Maitland, vol. i. p. 361.)

In 1647 two Petitions of the "Young men and apprentices" were drawn up and presented to the House of Lords by the two factions in the City, that in the interest of the King being signed by 10,000 hands, instigated, says Maitland, by their masters.

The action and attitude of the City on this occasion belong to its general history.

The custom and practice as concerns apprentices in the eighteenth century are laid down by Strype in his account of the duties and rules of the Chamberlain's Court.

"Before him, the said Chamberlain, all Apprentices are enrolled, and made free; insomuch that none can set up Shop, or follow a Trade within the City or Liberties, if not a Freeman, and sworn before him; neither can any one turn over an Apprentice, but by his License. To him all Complaints are brought for Differences betwixt Apprentices and their Masters, who reconciles their Differences, and may punish, by Imprisonment, those that disobey his Summons, or any Apprentice that misdemeans himself to his Master or Mistress; but, upon the Apprentice's acknowledging his Fault, and begging Pardon, with Promise never to offend any more, his Fault is forgiven.

Such Apprentices as have justly served their Term of seven Years, and not broken their Indentures by Marrying, etc., are made free.

Upon the Admission of every Person into the Freedom of this City, the Chamberlain causeth an Oath to be administered unto him, to be true to the King, the Government, and observe and keep the Customs of the City; which said Oath hath been mentioned before, Chap. XXIII.

If any Master shall refuse to make his Apprentice free, when the Term of his Indenture is expired, upon Complaint made to the Chamberlain, he will cause such Master to be summoned before him, and if he cannot shew good Cause to the Contrary, will make the Apprentice free. And if an Apprentice shall be unruly or disorderly in his Master's House, or commit any notorious Fault, upon Complaint made thereof, the Chamberlain will send one of his Officers for such Apprentice, and send him to Bridewell, or otherwise punish him according to the Nature of the Offence.

If any Master shall misuse his Apprentice, by unreasonable Beating, not allowing him Necessaries, or by neglecting to instruct him, or the like, upon Complaint thereof made, the Chamberlain will send a Summons for the Master to appear before him; and upon due Hearing both Parties, will relieve the Apprentice, if his Allegations be proved to be just, or else leave the Apprentice to take his remedy against his Master in the Lord Mayor's Court. And if the

Master refuse to appear according to his Summons, the Lord Mayor and Recorder, upon Complaint thereof made unto them, will grant a Warrant to take him, and compel him to appear.

When an Apprentice, by the Consent of his Master, is to be turned over to another Master of the same trade, it must be done before the Chamberlain. And it is observed, that, if an Apprentice be turned over by the Company only of which the Master is free, it is no Obligation on the second Master to keep such an Apprentice; nor is the Apprentice compelled thereby to serve the second Master, but may depart at Pleasure, by suing out his Indentures against the first Master. Which may be done without the Privity or Knowledge of the second Master. And, therefore, it is absolutely necessary, that all Apprentices should be turned over before the Chamberlain. And thereby the first Master is discharged from him, and the second obliged to keep him; and the Apprentice will be obliged to serve the second Master, the full Term of his Indentures, although the same were made for nine Years, or more. It is the Interest of every Master and Apprentice, when any Difference happens between them, to refer the Matter to the Chamberlain; who will freely hear both Parties, and decide the Controversy, for 3s. Charge, viz. 1s. to the Officer for the Summons, and 2s. to the Clerk for the Order: Whereas, if they proceed at Law for Relief, it may probably cost both Parties six Pounds, or more, in Charges; and the Conclusion may be less satisfactory, than if decided by the Chamberlain.

THE FEES DUE TO THE CITY FOR MAKING FREE, AND THE ENROLLING APPRENTICES.

An Apprentice made free, and not enrolled, the Master pays	00 13 2
The Apprentice pays	00 02 00
If turned over before the Chamberlain, the Master or Mistress must pay extraordinary	00 02 00

And, by Virtue of the late Act for Orphans, over and above these usual Fees,

An Apprentice, when bound, must pay	00 02 06
And when admitted a Freeman	00 05 00

If an Apprentice shall omit to take his Freedom, within convenient Time after the Expiration of his Indentures, the Chamberlain may impose upon the Apprentice such a Fine, in Reason, as he shall think fit, for this Neglect, without just Cause to the Contrary.

Every Freeman ought to take particular Care not to make an Apprentice free of London, by testifying for his true Service, unless such Apprentice shall have really served him. For, if he shall privately turn his Apprentice over to a Foreigner, and let his Apprentice serve such a Foreigner, and yet testify to the Chamberlain, that the Apprentice served a Freeman; in such Case, both the Master and the Apprentice may be disfranchised, and fined at the Discretion of the Recorder, and the Chamberlain, and may cause the Freeman's Shop to be shut up." (Strype, vol. ii. pp. 475-476.)

As regards the ancient costume of an Apprentice, I again quote Stow and Strype :—

"The ancient Habit of the Apprentices of London was a flat round Cap, Hair close cut, narrow falling Bands, coarse side Coats, close Hose, Cloth Stockings, and other such severe Apparel. When this Garb had been urged by some to the Disparagement of Apprentices, as a Token of Servitude, one, many a Year ago, undertaking the Defence of these Apprentices, wrote thus, that this imported the commendable Thrift of the Citizens, and was only the Mark of an Apprentice's Vocation and Calling (and which anciently, no Question, was the ordinary Habit of a Citizen), which Point of ancient Discipline, he said, the grave common Lawyers do still retain in their Profession; for the Professors of that Learning, we see, do at this Present retain the party-coloured Coats of Serving-men at their Serjeants' Feasts; and he wished, that the Remembrance of this ancient Livery might be preserved by the grave Citizens, in setting apart a particular Time or Day for the Feast of their Apprenticeship, when they should wear their former Apprentice's Garb; making Profession in this Way, that they gloried in the Ensigns of their honest Apprenticeship.

In the Time of Queen Mary, the Beginning of Queen Elizabeth, as well as many Years before, all Apprentices wore blue Clokes in the Summer, and blue Gowns in the Winter. But it was not lawful for any Man, either Servant or other, to wear their Gowns lower than the Calves of their Legs, except they were above threescore Years of Age; but, the Length of Clokes being not limited, they made them down to their shoes. Their Breeches and Stockings were usually of white broad Cloth, viz. round Slops, and their Stockings sewed up close thereto, as if they were all but one Piece. They also wore flat Caps both then and many Years after, as well Apprentices as Journey-men and others, both at Home and Abroad; whom the Pages of the Court in Derision called Flat-Caps.

When Apprentices and Journeymen attended upon their Masters and Mistresses in the Night they went before them carrying a Lanthorn and Candle in their hands, and a great long Club on their Necks; and many well-grown sturdy Apprentices used to wear long Daggers in the Day-Time on their Backs or Sides.

Anciently it was the general Use and Custom of all Apprentices in London

(Mercers only excepted, being commonly Merchants, and of better Rank, as it seems,) to carry Water Tankards, to serve their Masters' Houses with Water, fetched either from the Thames, or the common Conduits of London.

It was a great matter, in former Times, to give 10£ to bind a youth Apprentice; but, in King James the First's Time, they gave 20, 40, 60 and sometimes 100£ with an Apprentice; but now these prices are vastly enhanced, to 500, 600, or 800£." (Strype, vol. ii.)

The question in 1628 arose, and was solemnly argued, whether an Apprentice, who is certainly bound to obedience, who must perform servile offices, who is corrected by his master, clothed by his master, and fed by his master, is or is not in a state of bondage or a bondsman. The question was resolved by Philipot, Somerset Herald, to the effect that he could not be considered a bondsman. The reason we may pass over. But Strype's remarks are interesting:—

"So that Apprenticeship in London is no Dishonour, nor Degradation; but rather an Honour, and a Degree. He is very hardy that shall embase honest Industry with disgraceful Censures, and too unjust, who shall not cherish and encourage it with Praise and Worship, as the ancient Policy of England did and doth, in constituting Corporations, and adorning the Companies with Banners of Arms, and especial Members thereof with Notes of Nobility. And, as it is an Honour, so it is a Degree, or Order of good regular Subjects; out of whose, as it were, Noviceship or Colleges, Citizens are supplied from Time to Time. We call them Colleges, according to the old Roman Law Phrase, or Fellowships of Men. For so indeed they are, comprehended within several Corporations, or Bodies of free Persons, intended to be consociated together for commerce, according to Conscience and Justice, and named Companies. So that Apprentices, according to the Esteem of our Commonwealth, when first they come to be Apprentices, first begin to be Somebody, who before were young Men without any Vocation in the World. And so by other Ascents or steps come to be Freemen of London, or Citizens; thence to be of their Companies Liveries, Governors of Companies, as Wardens and Masters; and Governors in the City, as Common-Council-Men, Aldermen's Deputies, Sheriffs, and Aldermen; and, lastly, the principal Governors, or Heads of the City, that is, Lord Mayors. And some also have been advanced, from being Citizens, to be Counsellors of State to the Prince.

It is further evident, that Apprenticeship doth not deprive of Gentry; for no Man loseth his Right to bear Arms, or to write Gentleman, unless he be attainted in Law for such a Cause; the Conviction whereof doth immediately procure Corruption in Blood; which in this Case no Man yet hath dreamt of. The Apprentice hath no more lost his Title and Right to Gentry, than he hath done to any Goods, Chattels, Lands, Royalties, or any Thing else, which, if he had never been any Apprentice, either had, might, or ought to have come unto him. The

Rights of Blood are more inherent than the Rights of Fortune, according to the Law Rule, *Jura Sanguinum nullo jure civili dirimi possunt*, i.e. The Law of Bloods cannot be destroyed by any civil Right. That Gentry is a Right of Blood, may appear by this, that no Man can truly alienate the same, or vest another in it, tho' legally he may, in Case of Adoption, which is but a human Invention, in Imitation of Nature; and, in the Truth of the Thing, no Alienation at all, but a Fiction, or an Acceptation in Law, as if it were such. Gentry is a Quality of Blood, as Virtue and Learning are of one Mind.

This is the Sum of what that learned Herald argued, in Confutation of that Opinion, that Apprenticeship extinguisheth Gentry. And he sent this his discourse to the Gentleman who desired his Judgment herein; whence, no Question, he received full Satisfaction. And the Herald took the more Pains in confuting this false Conceit, that it was a Thing unbeseeming a Gentleman to be an Apprentice to a Citizen or Burgess; because it had filled England with more Vices, and sacrificed more serviceable Bodies to odious Ends, and more Souls to sinful Lives, than perhaps any one other uncivil Opinion whatsoever. For they who held it better to rob by Land or Sea, than to beg or labour, did daily fee and feel, that out of Apprentices rose such as set upon them, standing out for lives as Malefactors; when they, a Shame and Sorrow to their Kindred, underwent a Fortune too unworthy." (Strype, vol. ii. pp. 435-436.)

Apprentices in certain cases ought to be discharged:—

"One was discharged from his Master, because his Master held no shop, and withdrew himself from the City. Another, because his Master did not teach him. Another, because his Master was in Ludgate, and entrusted him not. Another, because not enrolled within a Year. Another, because his Master was distracted in his Mind. Another, because his Master was so poor that he could not exhibit to him. Another, because his Master diverted himself to other Occupations than his own Mystery. Another, because the Master was a Leper. Another, because the Wife, after the Death of her Husband, taught him not. And lastly, another, because his Master inordinately chastised him." (Strype, vol. ii. p. 438.)

The decay of order among Apprentices may finish these notes on the class:—

"I come, in the next place, to treat of Attornies' Clerks, Apprentices, inferior Tradesmen, Coachmen, Porters, Servants, and the lowest Class of Men in this town, which are far the most numerous: And, first, of the Lawyers' Clerks and Apprentices, I find it a general Complaint, that they are under no Manner of Government; before their Times are half out, they set up for Gentlemen, they dress, they drink, they game, frequent the Playhouses, and intrigue with the Women; and it is a common Thing with Clerks to bully their Masters, and desert their service for whole Days and Nights, whenever they see fit. And indeed

People consider little else at this Day, in the Choice of Clerks or Apprentices, but the sums they are to have with them; one, two, or three Hundred Pounds are given with a Clerk or Apprentice, who may be looked upon rather as a Boarder than a Servant. He takes little Care of his Master's Business, and the Master as little to instruct him in the Mystery of his Profession." (Strype, vol. ii. p. 559.)

CHAPTER VI

THE LONDON INNS

THE town was full of inns; more especially they were established without the gates and in the Borough. A great change had come over the Inns: formerly the inn was a place of lodging; some of them, as the Inns of Court, Barnard's Inn, Gray's Inn, Staple Inn, were colleges of residence; the business of providing food and drink belonged to the tavern and the cook's shop. We have now come to the time when the inn itself provided food. Fortunately, there remain two very useful descriptions of the Inns of this time. One of them is by Harrison in Holinshed, and the other by Fynes Moryson. First, let us take that of Harrison :—

"Those townes that we call thorowfaires have great and sumptuous innes builded in them for the receiving of such travellers and strangers as passe to and fro. The manner of harbouring wherein, is not like to that as some other countries, in which the host or goodman of the house dooth chalenge a lordlie authoritie over his ghests, but clene otherwise, sith everie man may use his inne as his owne house in England, and have for his monie how great or little varietie of vittels, and what other service himselfe shall thinke expedient to call for. Our innes are also verie well furnished with naperie, bedding, and tapisserie, especiallie with naperie: for beside the linen used at the tables, which is commonlie washed dailie, is such and so much as belongeth unto the estate and calling of the ghest. Ech commer is sure to lie in cleane sheets, wherein no man hath beene lodged since they came from the landresse, or out of the water wherein they were last washed. If the traveller have an horsse, his bed doth cost him nothing, but if he go on foot he is sure to pay a penie for the same : but whether he be horseman or footman if his chamber be once appointed he may carie the kaie with him, as of his own house so long as he lodgeth there. If he loose oughts whilst he abideth in the inne, the host is bound by a generall custome to restore the damage, so that there is no greater security anie where for travellers than in the gretest ins of England. Their horses in like sort are walked, dressed, and looked unto by certeine hostelers or hired servants, appointed at the charges of the good man of the house, who in hope of extraordinary reward will deal verie diligently after outward appeerance in this their function and calling. Herein neverthelesse are manie of them blameworthie, in that they doo not onlie deceive the beast oftentimes of his allowance of sundrie meanes, except their owners look well to them; but also make such packs with slipper merchants which hunt after preie (for what place is sure from evill and wicked persons) that manie an honest man is spoiled of his goods as he travelleth to and fro, in which fear also the counsell of the tapsters or drawers of drinke, and chamberleins is not seldom behind or wanting. Certes I beleeve not that chapman or traveller in England is robbed by the waie without the knowledge of some of them, for when he commeth into the inne, and alighteth from his horse, the hostler forthwith is verie busie to take downe his budget or capcase in the yard from his sadle bow, which he peiseth slilie in his hand to feel the weight thereof: or he miss of this pitch when the ghest hath taken up his chamber, the chamberleine that looketh to the making of the beds, will be sure to remove it from the place where the owner hath set it as if it were to set it more conveniently somewhere else, whereby he getteth an inkling whether it be monie or other short wares and thereof giveth warning to such ghests as haunt the house and are of his confederacy to the utter undoing of manie an honest yeoman as he journieth by the waie. The tapster in like sort for his part dooth marke his behaviour and what plentie of money he draweth when he paieth the shot, to the like end; so that it shall be an hard matter to escape all their subtil practises. Some thinke it a gay matter to commit their budgets at their coming to the goodman of the house; but thereby they oft bewraie themselves. For albeit their monie be safe for the time that it is in his hands (for you shall not hear that a man is robbed in his inn) yet after their departure the host can make no warrantise of the same, sith his protection extendeth no further than the gate of his owne house; and there cannot be a surer token unto such as prie and watch for those booties, than to see any ghest deliver his capcase in such maner. In all our innes we have plenty of ale, beere, and sundrie kinds of wine, and such is the capacitie of some of them that they are able to lodge two hundred or three hundred persons, and their horses at ease, and thereto with a very short warning make such provision for their diet as to him that is unacquainted withall may seeme to be incredible. Howbeit of all in England there are no worse ins than in London, and yet manie are there far better than the best that I have heard of in anie forren countries, if all circumstances be duly considered. But to leave this and go in hand with my purpose. I will here set downe a table of the best thorowfaires and townes of greatest travell in England, in some of which there are twelve or sixteen such innes at the least, as I before did speak of. And it is a world to see how ech owner of them contendeth with other for goodnesse of interteinement of the ghests as about finesse and change of linen, furniture of bedding, beautie of rooms, service at the table, costlinesse of plate, strength of drinke, varietie of wines, or well using of horses. Finallie there is not much omitted among them as the gorgeousness of their verie signs at their doores wherein some doo consume thirtie or fortie pounds, a mere vanitie in mine opinion, but so vaine will they needs be and that not onelie to give some outward token of the inne keeper's welth, but also to procure good ghests to the frequenting of their houses in hope there to be well used." (Holinshed's *Chronicles*.)

Concerning the customs in English Inns, Fynes Moryson thus writes :—

"For as soon as a passenger comes to an Inne, the servants run to him, and one takes his horse and walks him till he be cold, then rubs him and gives him meate, yet I must say that they are not much to be trusted in this last point, without the eye of the Master or his servant to oversee them. Another servant gives the passenger his private chamber, and kindles his fier, the third puls of his bootes and makes them cleane. Then the Host or Hostesse visits him, and if he will eate with the Hoste, or at a common table with others, his meale will coste him six pence, or in some places but four pence (yet this course is lesse honourable and not used by Gentlemen) ; but if he will eate in his chamber, he commands what meats he will according to his appetite, and as much as he thinkes fit for him and his company, yea, the kitchen is open to him, to command the meat to be dressed as he likes best; and when he sits at Table, the Host or Hostesse will accompany him, if they have many Guests, will at least visit him, taking it for courtesie to be bid sit downe ; while he eates, if he have company especially, he shall be offerd musicke, which he may freely take or refuse, and if he be solitary the musicians will give him the good day with musicke in the morning. It is the custom and no way disgraceful to set up part of sypper for his breakfast. In the evening or in the morning after breakfast (for the common sort use not to dine, but ride from breakfast to supper time, yet comming early to the Inn for better resting of their horses) he shall have a reckoning in writing, and if it seems unreasonable the Host will satisfy him either for the due price, or by abating part, especially if the servant deceive him in any way, which one of experience will soon find. I will now only add that a Gentleman and his Man shall spend as much as if he were accompanied with another Gentleman and his Man, and if Gentlemen will in such sorte joyne together to eate at one table the expenses will be much diminished. Lastly, a Man cannot more freely command at home in his owne House than he may doe in his Inne, and at parting if he give some few pence to the Chamberlin and Ostler they wish him a happy journey."

And further :—

"In all Innes, but especially in suspected places, let him take heed of his chamber fellowes, and always have his sword by his side or by his bedside; let him lay his purse under his pillow, but always folded with his garters or something hee first useth in the morning, lest he forget to put it on before he goe out of his chamber. And to the end he may leave nothing behind him in his Innes, let the visiting of his chamber and gathering his things together be the last thing he doth before hee put his foote into the stirrup."

The list of Elizabethan taverns might be compiled at great length, but the following signs celebrated in verse will suffice :—

> "Through the Royal Exchange as I walked
>   where gallants in sattin did shine :
> At midst of the day they parted away
>   at several places to dine.
>
> The gentry went to the King's Head,
>   the nobles went unto the Crown :
> The knights unto the Golden Fleece
>   and the plowman to the Clown.
>
> The clergy will dine at the Miter,
>   the vintners at the Three Tuns :
> The usurers to the Devil will go,
>   and the fryers unto the Nuns.
>
> The ladies will dine at the Feathers,
>   the Globe no captain will scorn :
> The huntsmen will go to the Greyhound below,
>   and some townsmen to the Horn.
>
> The plummer will dine at the Fountain,
>   the cooks at the Holy Lamb :
> The drunkards at noon to the Man in the Moon
>   and the cuckolds to the Ram.
>
> The rovers will dine at the Lyon,
>   the watermen at the Old Swan :
> The bawds will to the Negro go
>   and the whores to the Naked Man.
>
> The keepers will to the White Hart,
>   the mariners unto the Ship :
> The beggars they must take their way
>   to the Eg-shell and the Whip.
>
> The farier will to the Horse,
>   the blacksmith unto the Lock,
> The butchers to the Bull will go,
>   and the carmen to Bridewell-Dock.
>
> The fishmongers unto the Dolphin,
>   the bakers to the Cheat-loaf :
> The Turners unto the Tabel will go
>   where they may merrily quaff.
>
> The taylors will dine at the Sheers,
>   the shoo-makers will to the Boot :
> The Welshmen they will take their way
>   and dine at the sign of the Goat.
>
> The hosiers will dine at the Leg,
>   and drapers at the sign of the Brush :
> The fletchers to Robin Hood will go,
>   and the spendthrift to Beggar's Bush.

The pewterers to Quart Pot,
    the coopers will dine at the Hoop :
The coblers to the Last will go,
    and the bargemen to the Scoop.

The carpenters will dine at the Axe,
    the colliers will dine at the Sack :
Your fruiterer he to the Cherry-tree
    good fellows no liquor will lack.

The goldsmiths to the Three Cups,
    their money they count as dross :
Your puritan to the Pewter Can,
    and your papist to the Cross.

The weavers will dine at the Shuttle,
    the glovers will into the Glove :
The maidens all to the Maidenhead,
    and true lovers unto the Dove.

The sadlers will dine at the Saddle,
    the painters to the Green Dragon :
The Dutchman will go to the sign of the Vrow,
    where each man may drink his flagon.

The chandlers will dine at the Scales,
    the salters at the sign of the Bag :
The porters take pain at the Labour-in-vain,
    and the horse-courser to the White Nag.

Thus every man to his humour,
    from the north unto the south :
But he that hath no money in his purse,
    may dine at the sign of the Mouth.

The swaggerers will dine at the Fencers :
    but those that have lost their wits,
With Bedlam Tom let there be their home,
    and the Drum the drummer best hits.

The cheater will dine at the Chequer,
    the pick-pocket at the Blind Ale-house :
Till taken and tride, up Holborn they ride,
    and make their end at the gallows."

In a black-letter poem called "News from Bartholomew Fayre" occurs the following short list of taverns :—

" There hath been great sale and utterance of Wine,
    Besides Beere, and Ale, and Ipocras fine,
    In every country, region, and nation,
    But chiefly in Billingsgate at the Salutation ;
    And at the Bore's Head near London Stone ;
    The Swan at Dowgate, a tavern well knowne ;
    The Miter in Cheape, and then the Bull Head ;
    And many like places that make noses red ;
    The Bore's Head in Old Fish Street ; Three Cranes in the Vintry ;
    And now, of late, St. Martin's in the Sentree ;
    The Windmill in Lothbury ; the Ship at th' Exchange ;
    King's Head in New Fish Street, where roysterers do range ;
    The Mermaid in Cornhill ; Red Lion in the Strand ;
    Three Tuns in Newgate Market ; Old Fish Street at the Swan."

22

Heywood (1608) writes :—

> "The Gentry to the King's Head,
> The Nobles to the Crown,
> The Knights unto the Golden Fleece,
> And to the Plough the Clown.
> The churchman to the Mitre
> The shepherd to the Star,
> The gardner hies him to the Rose,
> To the Drum the man of war ;
> To the Feathers, ladies you ; the Globe
> The seaman doth not scorn ;
> The usurer to the Devil, and
> The townsman to the Horn.
> The huntsman to the White Hart,
> To the ship the merchants go,
> But you who do the Muses love,
> The sign called River Po.
> The banquerout to the World's End,
> The Fool to the Fortune Pie,
> Unto the Mouth the oyster-wife,
> The fiddler to the Pie.
> The punk unto the Cockatrice,
> The Drunkard to the Vine,
> The Beggar to the Bush, then meet,
> And with Duke Humphrey dine."

It was the custom at Taverns to send presents of wine from one room to another with compliments.

The taverns were to the sixteenth century what the coffee-houses were to the eighteenth. Every man frequented his tavern : clubs were held in the taverns ; men of the same trade met in the taverns for evening discourse ; bargains and business affairs were conducted in taverns ; there were good and bad taverns ; those like the Boar's Head, East Cheap, bore a bad character ; that is to say, they were laden down by the character of Doll Tearsheet ; others, again, where Doll and her friends were not admitted, were frequented by the most respectable merchants and divines. Music was going on in most of them all day long ; and all day long the waiters, clad in blue and wearing white aprons, ran about with flasks of wine and cups, and tobacco and pipes, calling " Anon, Anon ! " and stopping to chalk a score upon the wall.

It is strange that Stow mentions neither the Boar's Head, East Cheap, which must have been a well-known tavern, or Shakespeare would not have chosen it for the haunt of the Prince and Falstaff ; nor the Mermaid, the haunt of Ben Jonson and the poets. Presumably the worthy antiquary would not have felt at home in the company of the wits.

The Boar's Head stood in that part of East Cheap now swept away. The statue of King William IV. marks the site. It was not an ancient tavern. There were no taverns formerly in East Cheap according to Stow ; the first mention of it is in the year 1537. The courtyard was large enough for the performance of plays ; at the back it looked out upon St. Michael's churchyard.

The churchyard and church of St. Michael were swept away to make the approach to new London Bridge. Between St. Michael's Lane, now Miles's Lane, and a small alley, stood four taverns in a row: the Chicken, the Boar's Head, the Plough, and the Three Kings. These taverns were thus in the midst of markets: the Grass Market in front; the Fish Market on the east; the Meat Market on the west. The tavern was rebuilt after the fire, in 1668: the new sign then made for it may be seen in the Guildhall Museum; on each side of the doorway was carved in wood a vine branch, rising three feet from the ground, loaded with leaves and clusters, and on the top of each a figure of Falstaff eight inches high. Before its demolition the house had ceased to be a tavern. Here was held a club of which Boswell was a member, in which every one assumed a Shakespearian character. It was the custom to hold convivial meetings in this house. There Falstaff and Dame Quickly and

SIGN OF THE BOAR'S HEAD IN EAST CHEAP

Doll Tearsheet and the whole merry company became real. Goldsmith wrote his essay, "A Reverie," in this tavern, and here Washington Irving gave full play to his fancy, and restored the things that never were to the place that never knew Prince Hal.

The Mermaid Tavern stood between Friday Street and Bread Street, with an entrance from Cheapside as well. The tavern has been immortalised by a poet of the seventeenth and one of the nineteenth century.

Francis Beaumont, the former, writes to Ben Jonson :—

> "What things have we seen
> Done at the Mermaid, heard words that have been
> So nimble, and so full of subtle flame,
> As if that every one from whence they came
> Had meant to put his whole wit in a jest,
> And had resolved to live a fool the rest
> Of his dull life ; then when there hath been thrown
> Wit able enough to justify the town
> For three days past ; wit that might warrant be
> For the whole city to talk foolishly
> Till that were cancelled ; and when that was gone,
> We left an air behind us, which alone
> Was able to make the two next companies
> (Right witty, though but downright fools) more wise."

And Keats, the latter, writes :—

> " Souls of poets dead and gone,
> What Elysium have ye known,
> Happy field or mossy cavern
> Choicer than the Mermaid Tavern ?
> Have ye tippled drink more fine
> Than mine host's Canary wine ? "

Or, as Fuller says of Shakespeare :—

" Many were the wit-combates betwixt him and Ben Johnson, which two I behold like a Spanish great gallion, and an English man of War ; Master Johnson (like the former) was built far higher in Learning ; Solid, but Slow in his performances. Shake-spear, with the English man-of-War, lesser in bulk, but lighter in sailing, could turn with all tides, tack about and take advantage of all winds, by the quickness of his Wit and Invention."

Lists of old taverns are, as a rule, without interest ; there are, however, a few of the London taverns of historic importance. Two have been mentioned. Thus, the Nag's Head, at the corner of Friday Street, was the pretended scene of the consecration of Parker, Archbishop of Canterbury in 1559.

At the north-west of St. Paul's Churchyard was an ancient tavern known as the Mitre. Here were given the concerts of the Society of Musicians ; and their arms, representing the lyre of Apollo, with the crest of the Swan, being put up in the front of the house, caused the original sign to be jocularly transformed into that of the Goose and Gridiron. The Swan with Three Necks, meant originally the Swan with three "nicks" or marks to denote ownership. The Belle Savage was originally the Bell, but its landlord being a man named Savage, the house was emblazoned with a bell and a savage man beside it. The Elephant and Castle became the Pig and Tinder Box ; the "Caton Fidele"—the Governor of Calais— became the Cat and Fiddle.

Fleet Street had many well-known taverns : like those in the City they were mostly approached by narrow alleys leading out of the street, as the Rainbow, Dick's, and the Mitre. Dick's stands on the site of the printing office of Richard Tottle, law stationer in the reign of Henry VIII. The Cock, later moved across the road, was one of the most famous of the Fleet Street taverns.

The "Devil" Tavern, however, was more famous even than the Mermaid. Ben Jonson drew the company from the latter tavern to the Devil ; he lived at Temple Bar in order to be near the tavern. Here he founded the Apollo Club and wrote his famous rules in Latin, which were translated into English by one of his "sons," Brome. Near the door was placed a gilt bust of Apollo with a "Welcome" in flowing lines :—

> " Welcome all who lead or follow
> To the oracle of Apollo :

Here he speaks out of his pottle,
Or the tripos, his tower bottle ;
All his answers are divine,
Truth itself doth flow in wine.
Hang up all the poor hop-drinkers,
Cries old Sim, the king of skinkers ;
He the life of life abuses
That sits watering with the Muses.
Those dull girls no good can mean us ;
Wine—it is the milk of Venus,
And the poet's horse accounted :
Ply it, and you all are mounted.
'Tis the true Phœbian liquor,
Cheers the brains, makes wit the quicker ;
Pays all debts, cures all diseases,
And at once three senses pleases.
Welcome all who lead or follow
To the oracle of Apollo ! "

The merchants conducted their business in the Royal Exchange, but the tavern was the place where the lesser traders, and the shopkeepers, and the people who came up from the country met, to arrange bargains and business of all kinds over a flask of Canary.

CHAPTER VII

THEATRES

The latter half of the sixteenth century presents a remarkable development of the Drama and of the Theatres in London. This development was like the rising tide: it advanced with a force that was irresistible. The Mayor and Aldermen did their best to drive out plays and players from their boundaries; they went, but they

THE BEAR GARDEN AND THE GLOBE THEATRE
From Visscher's *Panorama of London.*

established themselves beyond the limits of the City jurisdiction. Preachers denounced the theatre; moralists wrote pamphlets against it; yet it flourished more and more. John Stockwood, preaching at Paul's Cross, says :—

"Have we not houses of purpose, built with great charges for the maintenance of them, and that without the liberties, as who shall say, 'There, let them say what they will, we will play.' I know not how I might, with the godly-learned especially, more discommend the gorgeous playing place erected in the Fields, than term it, as they please to have it called, a Theatre." In the same sermon he asks : "Wyll not a fylthye playe wyth the blast of a trumpette sooner call thyther a thousande

than an houres tolling of a bell bring to the sermon a hundred? Nay, even heere
in the Citie, without it be at this place and some other certaine ordinarie audience,
where shall you find a reasonable company? Whereas if you resorte to the
Theatre, the Curtayne, and other places of players in the Citie, you shall on the
Lord's Day have these places, with many other that I cannot reckon, so full as
possible they can throng."

The Londoners might change their religion, but they were not going to
change their sports. They were Protestant instead of Catholic; but they kept
up their bear-baiting, their bull-baiting, their archery, their wrestlings, their
fencing, their quarter-staff play, their running at the quintain, their feats of
tumbling, their Morris dances and mummings, their plays and interludes.
But the Reformation killed the Miracle Play. The play of modern manners, or
the tragedy, or the farce, took the place of the religious play. And instead of
acting on a stage in a churchyard, the players now began to act in the broad
and ample courtyard of the inn, whose galleries afforded room for people to look
on. The authorities looked on the play from the beginning with eyes of
disfavour: the actor was considered a masterless man; he had no trade; he was
a strolling vagabond; he lived upon the largesse of those who looked on at his
performance; he was a buffoon who would assume any character at will to make
the people laugh and cry; he must be able to dance and posture like the tumblers
on the road. Again, all the idle people in the City assembled to see the play; all
the vicious people crowded to take advantage of the throng; in the theatre every
day arose disorders and brawls; young men of sober parentage were seduced into
becoming players. Witness the words of Prynne:—

"Our own experience can sufficiently inform us, that plays and playhouses are the frequent causes of
many murders, duels, quarrels, debates; occasioned sometimes by reason of some difference about a box, a
seat, a place, upon the stage; sometimes by intruding too boldly into some female's company; sometimes
by reason of some amorous, scurrilous, or disgraceful words, that are uttered of or to some female spectators;
sometimes by reason of some speeches or passages of the play, particularly applied to some persons present
or absent; sometimes by reason of some husband, or co-rival's jealousy, or affront, whose wife, or mistress,
being there in person, is perhaps solicited, abused, or jeared at in his presence; sometimes by reason of
the apprentices who resort to playhouses, especially on Shrove Tuesday; sometimes by means of other
accidents and occasions. Many have been the murders, more the quarrels, the duels, that have grown
from our stage-plays, whose large encomiums of rash valour, duels, fortitude, generosity, impatientcy,
homicides, tyranny, and revenge, do so exasperate men's raging passions, and make them so impatient of
the very smallest injury, that nothing can satisfy, can expiate, but the offender's blood. Hence it is that
some players, some play-haunters, now living, not satisfied with the murder of one, have embrued their
barbarous un-christian hands in the blood of two, of three, if not of four several men. And so far are they
from ruing the odiousness of these their bloody deeds, that they glory in the number of their murders
as the very trophies of their valour."

The Queen at the beginning of her reign issued a proclamation to prevent
players performing without license, and from handling politics or religion. In

1572 the Mayor forbade the acting of plays in London on the ground of the Plague and the danger of infection. Harrison says:—

"Plaies are banished for a time out of London, lest the resort unto them should ingender a plague, or rather disperse it, being already begonne. Would to God these comon plaies were exiled altogether, as seminaries of impiety, and their theatres pulled downe, as no better then houses of bawdrie. It is an evident token of a wicked time when plaiers waxe so riche that they can build suche houses. As moche I wish also to our comon beare-baitings used oin the sabaothe daies." (Holinshed's *Chronicles*.)

In 1574 the first steps were taken towards the regulation of players and plays. The preamble to the ordinances is set forth by Maitland, with the ordinances themselves, as follows:—

"The citizens in Common-Council observing, that the antient and innocent Recreation of Stage-Plays or Interludes, which in former Days ingenious Tradesmen and Gentlemen's Servants sometimes practised, to expose Vice, or to represent the noble Actions of their Ancestors, at certain Festival Times, or in private Houses at Weddings, and at other Splendid Entertainments, for their own Profit, was now in process of Time become an Occupation; and that many there were that followed it for a livelihood; and, which was worse, that it was become the Occasion of much Sin and Evil; great Multitudes of People, especially Youth, in Queen *Elizabeth's* Reign, resorting to these Plays; and being commonly acted on *Sundays* and *Festivals*, the Churches were forsaken, and the Playhouses thronged, and great Disorders and Inconvenience were found to ensue to the City thereby, forasmuch as it occasioned Frays and evil Practices of Incontinency; Great Inns were used for this Purpose, which had secret Chambers and Places, as well as open Stages and Galleries; where Maids, especially Orphans, and good Citizen's Children, under Age, were inveigled and allured to privy and unmeet Contracts; and where unchaste, uncomely and unshamefaced Speeches and Doings were published; where there was an unthrifty Waste of the Money of the Poor; sundry robberies, by picking and cutting Purses, uttering of popular and seditious Matter, many corruptions of Youth, and other Enormities; besides sundry Slaughters and Maimings of the Queen's Subjects, by falling of Scaffolds, Frames, and Stages, and by Engines, Weapons, and Powder, used in the Plays; and believing that, in the time of God's Visitation by the Plague, such Assemblies of the People in Throngs and Presses were very dangerous for spreading the Infection; they regulated these Plays, lest the People, upon God's gracious withdrawing of the Sickness, should, with sudden forgetting of the Visitation, without Fear of God's Wrath, and without some Respect of those good and politick Means (as the Words of the Act ran) that were ordained for the Preservation of the Commonwealth and People in Health and good Order, return to the undue Use of such Enormities. Therefore, for the lawful, honest, comely

Use of Plays, Pastimes, and Recreations in good Sort permitted by the Authority of the Common Council, it was enacted :—

'I. That no Play should be openly played within the Liberty of the City, wherein should be uttered any Words, Examples, or Doings of any Unchastity, Sedition, or such-like unfit and uncomely Matter, upon Pain of Imprisonment for the space of fourteen Days, and 5£ for every such offence. II. That no Inn-keeper, Tavernkeeper, or other Person whatsoever, within the Liberties of the City, shall shew or play, or cause to be shewed or played, within his House or Yard, any Play, which shall not first be perused and allowed by the Lord Mayor and Court of Aldermen's Order. III. No Person shall suffer any Plays to be played in his House or Yard, whereof he then shall have Rule, but only such Persons, and in such Places, as, upon good Consideration, shall be thereunto permitted and allowed by the Lord Mayor and Aldermen. IV. Nor shall take and use any such Benefit or Advantage of such Permission, until such person be bound to the Chamberlain of *London*, in certain Sums, for the Keeping of good Order, and avoiding of Discords and inconveniences. V. Neither shall use or exercise such Licence or Permission at any Time, in which the same shall be by the Lord Mayor and Aldermen restrained, or commanded to stay and cease, in any usual Time of Divine Service on the *Sunday* or Holiday, or receive any to that Purpose in Time of Service, to the same, upon Pain to forfeit for every Offence 5£. VI. And every Person to be licensed shall, during the Time of such continuance of License, pay to the Use of the Poor in Hospitals of the City, or of the Poor visited with Sickness, such Sums and Payments, as between the Mayor and Aldermen, and the Person to be licensed, shall be agreed upon ; upon Pain that, on the Want of every such Payment, such License shall be utterly void. VII. All sums and Forfeitures to be incurred for any offence against this Act, and all Forfeitures of Bonds, shall be employed to the Relief of the Poor of the Hospitals, or of the Poor infected or diseased in the City : And the Chamberlain, in his own Name, shall have and recover the same, to the Purposes aforesaid, in the Court of the outer Chamber of *Guildhall, London*, called *The Mayor's Court.*

'Provided, That this Act shall not extend to Plays shewed in private Houses, Lodgings of a Nobleman, Citizen, or Gentleman, which shall have the same then played in his Presence for the Festivity of any Marriage, Assembly of Friends, or other like Cause, without publick or common collection of Money of the Auditors or Beholders.'" (Maitland, vol. i. pp. 262-263.)

Since the players could act no more in the City, there was nothing for them but to go outside. In 1574, James Burbage and some of the Earl of Leicester's Company obtained the Queen's license to act plays in any part of England. After receiving this license Burbage proceeded to build the first theatre, the house called simply "The Theatre." This theatre was built outside the jurisdiction of the City, close to the remains of the Holywell Priory. After the Dissolution the church of this House was pulled down with most of the buildings. Houses were built upon its site, and the ruins themselves gradually disappeared. At the south-west of these ruins, on a site now marked by Dean's Mews, Holywell Lane, Burbage built his theatre at a cost of £600, the money being advanced by his father-in-law. The theatre was in shape either circular or oval, probably the former. It was built for all kind of shows and entertainments. If a large space was wanted the whole of the area could be taken by the performers; raised galleries ran round the house; for the performance of a play, a stage was erected in the middle; from the nature of the case there could be no question of any scenery. The house was built of wood and is said to have been handsomely decorated; the central area was without a roof. There were troubles and quarrels about the lease of the house, which was taken down in the year 1598-99. The wood and timber of which the house was built were removed to Bankside, where they were used for the erection of the Globe Theatre.

The second theatre of London was that called The Curtain. It is a fact which illustrates the popularity of Finsbury Fields as a place of resort that there should have been a second theatre erected so close to the first. The Curtain Theatre was built on the south side of Holywell Lane, Shoreditch. In the house, too, feats of arms, sword-play, quarter-staff, and other games took place.

The third theatre (if we count The Globe as a continuation of The Theatre) was The Fortune, built near Golden Lane, Cripplegate.

The strongest charge against the theatres was the license allowed to the clowns or jesters, who between the pieces, or between the Acts, played "jigs" or "drolls" accompanied by songs and dances, and impromptu jokes which were topical, and, as may be imagined, broad and coarse. We may easily imagine that the civic authorities, the preachers, and the pamphleteers, who were always assailing the player and driving him from place to place, were not spared when the Clown had the stage all to himself, with hundreds of grinning faces in front of him, all of whom were egging him on with laughter and applause to say or do something more outrageous still, and loved nothing so much as to see before them acted to the life some sour Puritan who could see only "filthie and beastlie" stuff in the noblest play by Shakespeare, or in any sport.

Another favourite place of resort for the citizens, especially for the more riotous sort, was Southwark, with its raised river-wall or Bankside; its numerous inns and taverns; its low-lying fields and its various amusements. There were amphitheatres for bear- and bull-baiting; in the High Street itself there was a ring for the bull; in Paris Gardens, on the east side of Blackfriars Bridge, were kept bears and dogs for the favourite, almost the national, amusement; there

The GLOBE, ROSE and BEAR-BAITING.
THEATRES;
As they appeared about the year 1612.

The BULL and BEAR BAITING.
THEATRES:
As they appeared in their first State A.D. 1560.

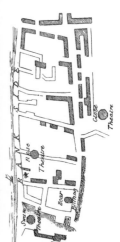

BANKSIDE, SOUTHWARK, IN 1648, WITH A VIEW OF HOLLAND'S LEAGUER, ONE OF THE
ANCIENT STEWS OR LICENSED BROTHELS SUPPRESSED DURING THE REIGN OF HENRY VIII.

p. 346.

was a kind of sanctuary in Southwark: here were allowed to reside the "Flemish Frows" still, in spite of Henry the Seventh's suppression; here were held May Day games; here was held every year the pageant of St. George's Day; and here, in the time of Henry VIII., were collected together idlers, vagabonds, and rogues in great numbers. In this place, the resort of all the young bloods and the wild element of London, the players settled down in force. The Rose, The Hope, The Globe, The Swan, all built about the same time, show the steady popularity of the Drama, in spite of the Puritanic attacks upon it, which seem to have done it no manner of harm.

At one end of Bankside stood the ruins of the Monastic House and the Clink Prison; then followed a single row of houses, at the back of which were the Bull-Baiting Ground and the Bear Garden; then the theatres already mentioned; also the Falcon Tavern, and Paris Gardens. All these places were built on a low-lying and marshy ground planted thickly with trees, intersected with ponds, ditches, and running streams—for instance, the Pudding Mill stream ran round two-thirds of Paris Gardens. For an account of the interior of a theatre and the presentation of a play I quote an imaginary account, in my own words :—

"The interior of the theatre was circular in shape. It contained three galleries, one above the other: the lowest called the 'rooms,' for seats in which we paid a shilling each, contained the better sorts. At each side of the stage there were boxes, one of which contained the music. The stage itself, a stout construction of timber, projected far into the pit, or, as Stow called it, the 'yarde.' At the back was another stage, supported on two columns, and giving the players a gallery about ten or twelve feet high, the purpose of which we were very soon to find out. On each side of the stage were seats for those who paid an additional sixpence. Here were a dozen or twenty gallants, either with pipes of tobacco, or playing cards or dice before the play began. One of them would get up quickly with a pretence of impatience, and push back his cloak so as to show the richness of his doublet below. The young men, whether at the theatre, or in Paul's Walk, or in Chepe, seemed all intent upon showing the bravery of their attire: no girls of our day could be more vain of their dress or more critical of the dress worn by others. Some of them, however, I perceived among the groundlings—that is, the people on the 'yarde'—gazing about the house upon the women in the galleries. Here there were many dressed very finely, like ladies of quality, in satin gowns, lawn aprons, taffeta petticoats, and gold threads in their hair. They seemed to rejoice in being thus observed and gazed upon. When a young man had found a girl to his taste, he went into the gallery, sat beside her, and treated her to pippins, nuts, or wine.

It was already one o'clock when we arrived. As we took our seats the music played its first sounding or flourish. There was a great hubbub in the place: hucksters went about with baskets, crying pippins, nuts, and ale; in the 'rooms' booksellers' boys hawked about new books; everybody was talking together; everywhere the people were smoking tobacco, playing cards, throwing dice, cheapening books, cracking nuts, and calling for ale. The music played a second sounding. The hubbub continued unabated. Then it played the third and last. Suddenly the tumult ceased. The piece was about to begin.

The stage was decorated with blue hangings of silk between the columns, showing that the piece was to be—in part at least—a comedy. Across the railed gallery at the back was stretched a painted canvas representing a royal palace. When the scene was changed this canvas became the wall of a city, and the actors would walk on the top of the wall; or a street with houses; or a tavern with its red lattice and its red sign; or a tented field. When night was intended, the blue hangings were drawn up and exchanged for black.

The hawkers retired and were quiet; the house settled down to listen, and the Prologue began. Prologue appeared dressed in a long black velvet cloak: he assumed a diffident and most respectful manner; he bowed to the ground.

> 'In Troy there lies the scene. From Isles of Greece
> The princes orgulous, their high blood chaf'd,
> Have to the port of Athens sent their ships.'

In this way the mind of the audience was prepared for what was to follow. We needed no play-bill. The palace before us could be no other than Priam's Palace. If there was a field with tents, it must be the battle-field and the camp of the Greeks; if there was a wall, it must be the wall of Troy. And though the scenery was rough, it was enough. One wants no more than the unmistakable suggestion; the poet and the actor find the rest. Therefore, though the intrusive gallants lay on the stage; though Troilus was dressed in the armour of Tudor time, and Pandarus wore just such a doublet as old Stow himself, we were actually at Troy. The boy who played Cressida was a lovely maiden. The narrow stage was large enough for the Council of Kings, the wooing of lovers, and the battle-field of heroes. Women unfaithful and perjured, lovers trustful, warriors fierce, the alarms of war, fighting and slaying, the sweet whispers of love were drowned by the blare of trumpets; the loss of lover forgotten in the loss of a great captain; and among the warriors and the kings and the lovers, the creeping creatures who live upon the weaknesses and the sins of their betters, played their parts upon these narrow boards before a silent and enraptured house. For three hours we were kept out of our senses. There was no need, I say, of better scenery: a quick shifting of the canvas showed a battle-field, and turned the stage into a vast plain covered with armies of Greeks and Romans. Soldiers innumerable, as thick as motes in the sun, crossed the stage fighting, shouting, challenging each other. While they fought, the trumpets blew and the drums beat, the wounded fell, and the fight continued over these prostrate bodies till they were carried off by their friends. The chiefs rushed to the front, crossed swords, and rushed off again. 'Come both you cogging Greeks!' said Troilus, while our cheeks flushed and our lips parted. If the stage had been four times as broad, if the number of men in action had been multiplied by ten, we could not have felt more vividly the rage, the joy, the madness of the battle. When the play was finished, the ale, the apples, and the nuts were passed round, and the noise began again. Then the clown came in and began to sing, and the music played—but oh, how poor it seemed after the great emotions of the play! The old man plucked me by the sleeve and we went out, and with us most of the better sort." (*London*, pp. 237-239.)

In addition to the foregoing, or as confirming and supplementing that account, I quote the following from Drake's *Shakespeare and his Times* :—

"The passion for the stage continued rapidly to increase, and before the year 1590, not less than four or five theatres were in existence. The patronage of dramatic representation made an equal progress at Court ; for though Elizabeth never, it is believed, attended a public theatre, yet had she four companies of children who frequently performed for her amusement, denominated the Children of St. Paul's, the Children of Westminster, the Children of the Chapel, and the Children of Windsor. The public actors, too, who were sometimes, in imitation of these appellations, called the Children of the Revels, were, towards the close of Her Majesty's reign especially, in consequence of a greatly acquired superiority over their younger brethren, often called upon to act before her at the royal theatre in Whitehall. Exhibitions of this kind at Court were usual at Christmas, on Twelfth Night, at Candlemas, and at Shrove-tide, throughout the reigns of Elizabeth and James, and the plays of Shakspeare were occasionally the entertainment of the night ; thus we find *Love's Labour Lost* to have been performed before our maiden Queen during the Christmas-holydays, and *King Lear* to have been exhibited before King James on St. Stephen's night. On these occasions, the representation was generally at night, that it might not interfere with the performances at the regular theatre, which took place early in the afternoon ; and we learn from the Council-books that the royal remuneration, in the age of Elizabeth, for the exhibition of a single play at Whitehall, amounted to ten pounds, of which twenty nobles, or six pounds, thirteen shillings, and fourpence, formed the customary fee ; and three pounds, six shillings, and eightpence the free gift or bounty. If, however, the performers were required to leave the capital for any of the royal palaces in its neighbourhood, the fee, in consequence of the public exhibition of the day being prevented, was augmented to twenty pounds.

The protection of the Drama by Elizabeth and her Ministers, though it did not exempt the public players, except in one instance, from the penalties of statutes against vagabonds, yet it induced during the whole of her long reign numerous instances of private patronage from the most opulent of her nobility and gentry, who, possessing the power of licensing their own domestics as comedians, and, consequently, of protecting them from the operation of the Act of Vagrancy, sheltered various companies of performers, under the denomination of their servants, or retainers—a privilege which was taken away, by Act of Parliament, on the accession of James, and, as Mr. Chalmers observes, 'put an end for ever to the scenic system of prior times.'"

There were no fewer than fourteen companies of players, under private patronage, who contributed to exhilarate the people of London and the country. Of these, Drake furnishes a chronological enumeration. "Soon after the accession of Elizabeth appeared Lord Leicester's company, the same which, in 1574, was finally incorporated by royal licence; in 1572 was formed Sir Robert Lane's company; in the same year Lord Clinton's; in 1575 companies were created by Lord Warwick, and the Lord Chamberlain, the name of Shakspeare being enrolled among the servants of the latter, who, in the first year of the subsequent reign, became entitled to the appellation of His Majesty's servants; in 1576, the Earl of Sussex brought forward a theatrical body, and in 1577, Lord Howard another, neither of which, however, attained much eminence; in 1578 the Earl of Essex mustered a company of players, and in 1579, Lord Strange, and the Earl of Derby, followed his example; in 1591 the Lord Admiral produced his set of comedians; in 1592 the Earl of Hertford effected a similar arrangement; in 1593 Lord Pembroke protected an association of actors, and at the close of Her Majesty's reign the Earl of Worcester had in pay also a company of theatrical performers."

As regards the management of his property in the play the author had the choice of two methods. He might sell the copyright to the theatre. In this case, to which authors frequently had recourse in the age of Shakespeare, the dramatist sold outright the whole rights of the piece, so that the proprietors of the theatre secured its performance exclusively to their own company. If it was a popular piece, of course, they were not anxious to publish it. If, however, the author kept the piece in his own hands, he not only had the right of publication, but he had, likewise, a claim upon the theatre for a benefit. This, towards the termination of the sixteenth century, took place on the second day, and was soon afterwards, as early indeed as 1612, postponed to the third day.

The price of a drama, when disposed of to the public players, was twenty nobles, or six pounds, thirteen shillings, and fourpence; but private companies would sometimes give more than that sum.

The price of a play when published was sixpence, and the poet received about forty shillings of an honorarium for a dedication. It has been stated, however, that Shakespeare received but five pounds for his *Hamlet*.

Hentzner, the German traveller, thus speaks of the theatres :—

"Without the City are some theatres, where English actors represent almost

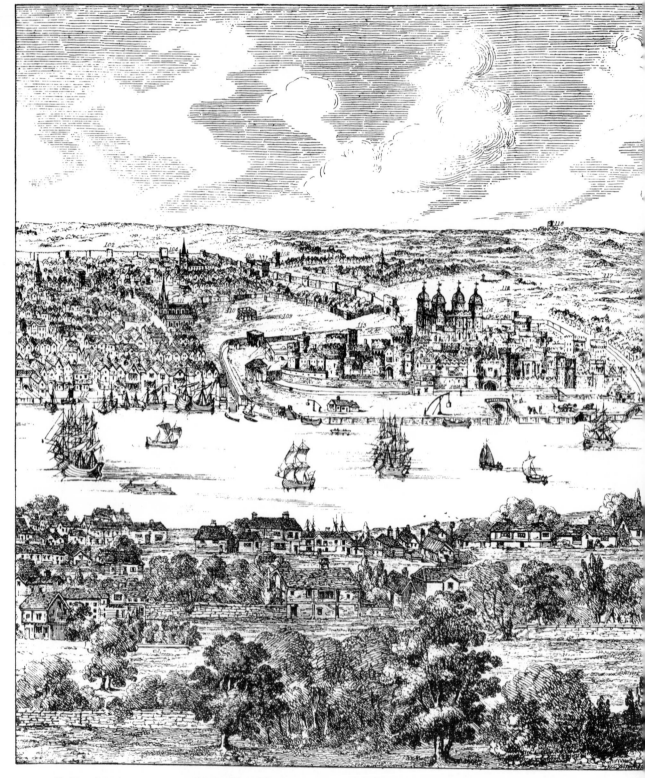

100. St. Mary Spittal.	104. Priory of Holy Trinity.	107. The Minories.	110. Place of Execution.	113. Tow
102. Houndsditch.	105. Aldgate.	108. The Postern Gate.	111. Allhallow's Church, Barking.	114. The
103. Crutched Friars.	106. St. Botolph, Aldgate.	109. Great Tower Hill.	112. The Custom House.	115. Tra

From the Panorama of "London, Westminster, and Southwark, in 1543." By Anthony Van

aerde. (Sutherland Collection, Bodleian Library, Oxford.) *For continuation see pp.* 234, 235.

every day Comedies and Tragedies to very numerous audiences; these are concluded with variety of dances, accompanied by excellent music and the excessive applause of those that are present. Not far from one of these Theatres, which are all built of wood, lies the Royal Barge, close to the river Thames; it has two splendid cabins, beautifully ornamented with glass windows, painting and carving; it is kept upon dry ground and sheltered from the weather."

The entertainment offered to the French Ambassador at the Court of Henry VIII. at Greenwich shows that acting and dressing formed part of a courtly entertainment. They began with tournaments and contests on foot and horse; they went on to an interlude in Latin, the altars being all richly dressed.

"This being ended," says the author of the *Life of Wolsey*, "there came a great company of ladies and gentlemen, the chiefest beauties in the realm of England, being as richly attired as cost could make, or art devise, to set forth their gestures, proportions, or beauties, that they seemed to the beholder rather like celestial angels than terrestrial creatures, and in my judgment worthy of admiration, with whom the gentlemen of France danced and masked; every man choosing his lady as his fancy served; that done, and the maskers departed, came in another masque of ladies and gentlewomen, so richly attired as I cannot express; these ladies maskers tooke each of them one of the Frenchmen to dance; and here note, that these noblewomen spoke all of them good French, which delighted them much to hear the ladies speak to them in their own language. Thus triumphantly did they spend the whole night from five of the clock at the night into two or three of the clock in the morning; at which time the gallants drew all to their lodgings to take their rest."

There was a kind of show called a Prolusion. This appears to have been a representation of some well-known event or legend. Thus in 1587 there was a Prolusion set forth by Hugh Offley, merchant-adventurer and leather-seller, one of the Sheriffs of the year 1588. It represented King Arthur and the Knights of the Round Table. He chose 300 good archers, personable men; and he dressed them in black satin doublets and black velvet hose; every man carried a bow of yew and a dozen waxed arrows. They marched in goodly array from Merchant Taylors to Mile End Green. Queen Elizabeth in her chariot passed them, and stopped in order to see the show. "In her whole life," she said, "she had never seen a finer company of archers." They all fell on their knees and prayed God to prosper and preserve Her Majesty. She thanked them and passed on her way, while the archers proceeded to attack the sham forts which had been set up, after which those who shot best took prizes, and Master Hugh Offley provided a banquet for all.

It is interesting to remember that the Theatre had to contend for the place of honour with the stately and courtly Masque. All that artist could do for decoration, or stage manager could devise for machinery, or that poet could imagine or invent for fable, was pressed into the service of the Masque. The dresses the players wore were most gorgeous ; the speeches were fine ; the dances and the songs were most beautiful. Real mountains contained real caves ; Dryads ran out of the woods ; Naiads lay beside running streams ; all the Gods and Goddesses of Ovid took part in the action ; there were thrones of gold and silver ; there were star-spangled skies ; sea gods and river gods appeared ; Tritons blew their shells ; mermaids swam about the sea-shell of mother-of-pearl in which sat Venus herself. And all this time the Theatre itself had no scenery and no stage management and no machinery. The Masque, however, did not assume its full development till the next century. It will be found more fully treated in the chapter on the Theatre and Art in *London in the Time of the Stuarts*. Even more popular than the theatre were the sports of bear-baiting, bull-baiting, wrestling, quarter-staff and single-stick. The favourite place for these sports was the Paris Garden beyond Bankside.

> " Yet everye Sondaye
>   They will surelye spende
> One penye or two
>   The bearwardes lyvyng to mende.
> At Paryse Garden eche Sondaye
>   A man shall not fayle
> To fynde two or three hundreds
>   For the bearwardes vaile.
> One halpenye a piece
>   They use for to give
> When some have no more
>   In their purse, I believe."

You shall read contemporary accounts of bear-baiting and bull-baiting.

"Some," says John Houghton in 1694, "keep the bull on purpose for the sport of baiting, cutting off the tips of his horns, and with pitch, tow, and such like matter, fasten upon them the great horns of oxen, with their tips cut off, and covered with leather, least they should hurt the dogs. Because these papers go into several other countries, I'll say something of the manner of baiting the bull, which is, by having a collar about his neck, fastened to a thick rope about three, four, or five yards long, hung to a hook, so fastened to a stake that it will turn round ; with this the bull circulates to watch his enemy, which is a mastiff dog (commonly used to the sport) with a short nose, that his teeth may take the better hold ; this dog, if right, will creep upon his belly, that he may, if possible, get the bull by the nose, which the bull as carefully strives to defend, by laying it close to the ground, where his horns are also ready to do what in them lies to toss the dog ; and this is the true sport.

But if more dogs than one come at once, if they are cowardly and come under his legs, he will, if he can, stamp their guts out. I believe I have seen a dog tossed by a bull thirty, if not forty foot high ; and when they are tossed either higher or lower, the men above strive to catch them on their shoulders, lest the fall might mischief the dogs.

They commonly lay sand about, that if they fall upon the ground it may be the easier. Notwithstanding this care, a great many dogs are killed, more have their limbs broke, and some hold so fast, that by the bull's swinging them their teeth are often broke out.

To perfect the history of bull-baiting, I must tell you, that the famed dogs have crosses or roses of various coloured ribbon stuck with pitch on their foreheads, and such like the ladies are very ready to bestow on dogs or bull that do valiantly; and when 'tis stuck on the bull's forehead, that dog is hollowed that fetches it off, though the true courage and art is to hold the bull by the nose 'till he roars, which a courageous bull scorns to do.

Often the men are tossed as well as the dogs; and men, bull, and dogs, seem exceedingly pleased, and as earnest at the sport as if it were for the lives or livelihoods. Many great wagers are laid on both sides, and great journeys will men and dogs go for such a diversion. I knew a gentleman that bought a bull in Hertfordshire on purpose to go a progress with him, at a great charge, into most of the great towns in the West of England.

This is a sport the English much delight in; and not only the baser sort, but the greatest lords and ladies."

And here is Laneham on the sport of bear-baiting :—

"It waz a sport very pleazaunt of theez beasts; to see the bear with hiz pink eyez leering after hiz enemiez approch, the nimbleness and wayt of the dog to take hiz avauntage, and the fors and experiens of the bear agayn to avoyd the assaults; if he were bitten in one place, hoow he woold pynch in an oother too get free; that if he wear taken onez, then what shyft with byting, with clawyng, with roring, tossing and tumbling he woold woork too wynde hymself from them; and when he waz lose, to shake his earz twyse or thryse wyth the blud and slauer aboout his fiznamy, waz a matter of a goodly releef."

We have already heard Hentzner on theatres, he has a word to say also on baiting :—

"There is still another place, built in the form of a Theatre, which serves for the baiting of bulls and bears; they are fastened behind, and then worried by those great English dogs and mastiffs, but not without great risk to the dogs from the teeth of the one and the horns of the other, and it sometimes happens they are killed on the spot; fresh ones are immediately supplied in the places of those that are wounded or tired. To this entertainment often follows that of whipping a blinded bear, which is performed by five or six men, standing in a circle with whips which they exercise upon him without any mercy; although he cannot escape from them because of his chain, he nevertheless defends himself vigorously, throwing down all who come within his reach and are not active enough to get out of it, tearing the whips out of their hands and breaking them. At these spectacles, and everywhere else, the English are constantly seen smoking the Nicotean weed, which in America is called Tobaca, and generally in this manner : they have pipes on purpose made of clay, into the farther end of which they put the herb, so dry that it may be rubbed into powder, and lighting it, they draw the smoke into their mouths, which they puff out again through their nostrils, along with plenty of phlegm and defluxion from the head. In these Theatres, fruits, such as apples, pears, and nuts, according to the season, are carried about to be sold, as well as wine and ale."

But besides these cruel forms of so-called "sport," there were more legitimate pleasures such as archery.

"During the holy days in summer," Fitz Stephen says, "the young men exercise themselves in the sports of leaping, archery, etc." The practice of archery was maintained in the City after the longbow had to give way before gun and cannon. As a pastime of the citizens only, no account of London would be complete without reference to archery. There were, as every one knows, two kinds of bow : the longbow and the crossbow. The former, for various reasons — its superiority in readiness of handling, lightness in carrying, range of flight and sureness of aim, caused it to be much more generally adopted in our armies than its rival. At Cressy, for instance, our men were armed with longbows, and the French with crossbows ; when the rain fell the longbows could be easily covered up, the crossbow could not, so that the strings were wetted and the power of the weapon greatly injured. Edward the First, who had a great opinion of the longbow as the superior weapon, ordered, on the threat of war with France, every sheriff of a county to provide 500 white bows and as many bundles of arrows. Edward the Third issued repeated proclamations ordering the practice of archery. It would seem as if the word archery in the fourteenth century included the crossbow as well as the longbow, for Edward the Second, in 1314 (Riley, *Memorials*, p. 124), commanded the City of London to furnish 300 arbalesters "more powerful for defence," and to provide them with "haketons, bacinets, collerettes, arbalests and quarels." (The haketon was a jacket of quilted leather ; the bacinet was a headpiece ; the collerette, an iron collar for the protection of the throat ; the arbalest is the crossbow ; the quarel was the bolt.)

Richard the Second ordered that every man in his household should exercise himself as occasion should permit in archery. And in 1392 an Act was passed obliging all servants to practise archery on holydays. In 1417 Henry V. ascribed his victory at Agincourt chiefly to his archers, and orders the Sheriffs of the counties to pluck from every goose six wing-feathers for the improvement of the arrow. These feathers were the second, third, and fourth of each wing. Edward IV. ordered that Englishmen in Ireland and every Irishman living with Englishmen should be provided with a bow of his own height, which was to be made of yew, wych, hazel, ash, or alder. Butts were to be erected in every township, and the inhabitants were to practise on every feast day. The same king sent a thousand archers to the Duke of Burgundy, who was to pay them sixpence a day, about five shillings of our money. Nothing can prove more conclusively the estimation in which archers were held. The same king provided for his war both guns and bows. A great deal of yew was imported at this time; it came in the Venetian ships from Dalmatia and the countries on the eastern shores of the Adriatic.

In the nineteenth year of Henry VII. the King finally decided for the long-bow against the crossbow, because "the longbow had been much used in this realm, whereby honour and victory had been gotten against outward enemies; the realm greatly defended; and much more the dread of all Christian Princes by reason of the same." Henry VII. himself shot at the butts.

There were at least five statutes issued by Henry VIII. ordering the practice of archery, but forbidding the crossbow.

The London Archers continued to hold their yearly contests in the month of September, in spite of the fact that henceforth there would be no use for the long-bow in warfare. They formed a very fine corps, had they been of any use; mean-time, the City has always loved a show, and a very fine show the Archers provided. Their captain was called the Duke of Shoreditch; the captains of the different Companies were called the Marquesses of Clerkenwell, Islington, Hoxton, and the Earl of Pancras,[1] etc.; in the year 1583 they assembled at Merchant Taylors Hall to the number of 3000 all sumptuously apparelled, "nine hundred and forty-two having chains of gold about their necks." They were escorted by whifflers and bowmen to the number of 4000, besides pages and footmen; and so marching through Broad Street, where the Duke of Shoreditch lived, they proceeded by Moorfields and Finsbury to Smithfield, where, after performing their evolutions, they shot at the target for glory.

The Finsbury Archers continued to exist and to hold their meetings till well into the eighteenth century. Mr. Daines Barrington, writing for the Society of Antiquaries in 1787, mentions that there were still living two old men who had obtained prizes in these contests as late as 1753, when they ceased. The same writer gives a map of the butts or archers' marks in Finsbury Fields as they were standing in the year 1787. The distance between the marks varies from 120 feet to 300 feet. It may be assumed that 200 feet was a fairly average distance for an arrow. The proper weight for an arrow was considered to be one ounce only; it was to be winged by three feathers: two white being plucked from the gander, and

---

[1] These titles began with Henry VII., who seeing an inhabitant of Shoreditch shoot with extraordinary skill, dubbed him Duke of Shoreditch; this being copied by others, as Marquesses, Earls, etc., drew such ridicule upon the Company as finally brought contempt on the archery itself.

one gray taken from the goose; this difference in colour showed the archer when the arrow was properly placed.

The Artillery Company or Finsbury Archers, predecessors of the present Artillery Company, enjoyed certain privileges as to dress, as to shooting at birds, and immunity from the charge of murder should any one be killed by these arrows, especially after they had cried "Fast!" as a warning.

It appears that bows and arrows were employed long after they left the field of battle for shooting rabbits and crows, partly because gunpowder was dear, but chiefly because the arrow makes no noise to frighten the game away. The London Archers continued, in spite of the fact that henceforth there would be no use of the longbow in warfare, to hold their yearly contests in the month of September.

The Honourable Artillery Company, before it received its letters patent, had been in the habit of practising archery in the fields of Islington, Hoxton, and Shoreditch. In these fields targets or butts were fixed to shoot at. Two of these butts or targets were still in existence in 1860: one at the end of Dorchester Street, Hoxton, on the east side of the New North Road near the Canal Bridge, and the other in the brickwork of the Canal Bridge above the towing-path. Two others had been destroyed about the year 1845: one in the Britannia Fields, and the other in the ground now called Wellington Square. That standing at the end of Dorchester Road was called "Whitehall." A drawing of it is given in the *L. and M. Arch. Society* (vol. ii. p. 15).

The other sports, feasts, and festivals of the City remained in the sixteenth century much as they had been before the change of Faith with certain exceptions, such as the Boy Bishop, the Feast of All Fools in the Church, and the Miracle Play with its profanity and coarseness. These vanished. There remained the Feasts of Christmas and Easter; the celebration of May Day; the Vigils of St. John, St. Peter, and St. Paul; and the Midsummer Watch. There were also Shrove Tuesday, Hocking Day, Whitsuntide, and Martinmas, with some others. The ceremonies of a Christmas banquet are preserved in Gerard Leigh's *Accidence of Armory*, and have been reproduced by Nichols. The feast was that of the year 1561. The place was the Temple. The person called Palaphilos was the Constable and Marshall, Dudley, Earl of Leicester.

"The next day I thought for my pastime to walk to this Temple, and entring in at the gates, I found the building nothing costly; but many comely Gentlemen of face and person, and thereto very courteous, saw I pass to and fro, so as it seemed a Prince's port to be at hand; and passing forward, entred into a Church of antient building, wherein were many monuments of noble personages armd in knightly habit, with their cotes depainted in ancient shields, whereat I took pleasure to behold. Thus gazing as one bereft with the rare sight, there came unto me an Hereaught, by name Palaphilos, a King of Armes, who curteously saluted me, saying, 'For that I was a stranger, and seeming by my demeanour a lover of honour, I was his guest of right': whose curtesy (as reason was) I obeyed; answering 'I was at his commandment.' 'Then,' said he, 'ye shall go to mine own lodging here within the Palace, where we will have such cheer as the time and country will yield us': where, I assure you, I was so entertained, as no where I met with better cheer or company, etc.

Thus talking we entred the Prince his Hall, where anon we heard the noise of drum and fyfe. 'What meaneth this drum?' said I. Quoth he, 'This is to warn Gentlemen of the Houshold to repair to the dresser; wherefore come on with me, and ye shall stand where ye may best see the Hall served; and so from thence brought me into a long gallery, that stretched itself along the Hall neer the Prince's table, where I saw the Prince set: a man of tall personage, a manly countenance, somewhat brown of visage, strongly featured, and thereto comely proportioned in all lineaments of body. At the nether end of the same table were placed the Embassadors of sundry Princes. Before him stood the carver, sewer, and cup-bearer, with great number of gentlemen-wayters attending his person; the ushers making place

ROBERT DUDLEY, EARL OF LEICESTER (1532(?)-1588)
From the painting by Zuccaro in the National Portrait Gallery, London.

to strangers of sundry regions that came to behold the honour of this mighty Captain. After the placing of these honourable guests, the Lord Steward, Treasurer, and Keeper of Pallas Seal, with divers honourable personages of that Nobility, were placed at a side-table neer adjoining the Prince on the right hand, and at another table on the left side were placed the Treasurer of the Household, Secretary, the Prince his Serjeant at the Law, four Masters of the Revels, the King of Arms, the Dean of the Chappel, and divers Gentlemen Pensioners to furnish the same. At another table on the other side were set the Master of the Game, and his Chief Ranger, Masters of Houshold, Clerks of the Green Cloth and Check, with divers other strangers to furnish the same. On the other side against them, began the table, the Lieutenant of the Tower, accompanied with divers Captains of foot-bands and shot. At the nether end of the Hall began the table, the High Butler, the Panter, Clerks of the Kitchin, Master Cook of the Privy Kitchin, furnished throughout with the souldiers and guard of the Prince; all which, with number of inferior officers placed and served in the Hall, besides the great resort of strangers I spare to write.

The Prince so served with tender meats, sweet fruits, and dainty delicates confectioned with curious cookery, as it seemed wonder a world to observe the provision ; and at every course the trumpetters blew the couragious blast of deadly war, with noise of drum and fyfe, with the sweet harmony of violins, sackbutts, recorders, and cornetts, with other instruments of music, as it seemed Apollo's harp had turned their stroke. Thus the Hall was served after the most ancient order of the Island ; in commendation whereof I say, I have also seen the service of great Princes, in solemn seasons and times of triumph, yet the order hereof was not inferior to any. But to proceed, this Hereaught Palaphilos, even before the second course came in, standing at the high table said in this manner : 'The mighty Palaphilos, Prince of Sophie, High Constable Marshall of the Knights Templars, Patron of the Honourable Order of Pegasus'; and therewith cryeth 'A Largess.' The Prince, praysing the Hereaught, bountifully rewarded him with a chain to the value of an hundred talents.

I assure you, I languish for want of cunning, ripely to utter that I saw so orderly handled appertaining to service ; wherefore I cease, and return to my purpose.

The supper ended, and tables taken up, the High Constable rose, and a while stood under the place of honour, where his atchievement was beautifully embroidered and devised of sundry matters, with the Ambassadors of foreign nations, as he thought good, till Palaphilos, King of Armes, came in, his Hereaught Marshal, and Pursivant before him ; and after followed his messenger and Caligate Knight ; who putting off his coronal, made his humble obeysance to the Prince, by whom he was commanded to draw neer, and understand his pleasure ; saying to him, in few words, to this effect : 'Palaphilos, seeing it hath pleased the high Pallas to think me to demerit the office of this place ; and thereto this night past vouchsafed to descend from heavens to increase my further honour, by creating me Knight of her Order of Pegasus ; as also commanded me to join in the same Society such valiant Gentlemen throughout her province whose living honour hath best deserved the same, the choice whereof most aptly belongeth to your skill, being the watchman of their doings and register of their deserts ; I will ye choose as well throughout our whole armyes, as elsewhere, of such special gentlemen, as the gods hath appointed, the number of twenty-four, and the names of them present us : commanding also those chosen persons to appear in our presence in knightly habit, that with conveniency we may proceed in our purpose. This done Palaphilos obeying his Prince's commandement, with twenty-four knights, all apparelled in long white vestures, with each man a scarf of Pallas colours, and them presented, with their names, to the Prince ; who allowed well his choice, and commanded him to do his office. Who, after his duty to the Prince, bowed towards these worthy personages, standing every man to his antiety, as he had born armes in the field, and began to shew his Prince's pleasure ; with the honour of the Order."

And here is a note from Stow on Christmas Customs :—

"Against the feast of Christmas, every man's house, as also their parish churches, were decked with holm, ivie, bayes, and whatsoever the season of the yeere aforded to be greene ; the conduits and standards in the streets were likewise garnished. Amongst the which, I read, that in the yeere 1444, by tempest of thunder and lightning, on the first of February at night, Paul's steeple was fired, but with great labour quenched, and toward the morning of Candlemas day, at the Leaden Hall in Cornhill, a standard of tree, beeing set up in the midst of the pavement fast in the ground, nayled full of holme and ivy, for disport of Christmas to the people, was torne up and cast downe by the malignant spirit (as was thought), and the stones of the pavement all about were cast in the streetes, and into divers houses, so that the people were wore agast at the great tempests."

Let us pass on to the great Festival of May Day.

" Forth goeth all the court both most and lest,
    To Fetch the floures fresh, and braunch and blome—
    And namely hauthorn brought both page and grome
    And than rejoysen in their great delite ;
    Eke ech at other throw the floures bright,
    The primerose, the violete, and the gold.
    With freshe garlants party blew and white."

Philip Stubbes says :—" Against Maie, Whitsondaie, or some other tyme of the yeare, every parishe, towne, and village assemble themselves together, bothe men, women, and children ; and either goyng all together, or deviding themselves into companies, they goe some to the woodes and groves, some to the hilles and mountaines, some to one place, some to another, where they spend all the night in pleasant pastymes, and in the mornyng they returne bringing with them, birch, bouwes, and braunches of trees to deck their assemblies withal. But their chiefest jewel they bring from thence is their Maie poole, which they bring home with greate veneration, as thus :—They have twentie or fortie yoke of oxen, every oxe havyng a swete nosegaie of flowers tyed on the tippe of his hornes, and these oxen drawe home the Maie poole (this stinckyng idoll rather), which is covered all over with flowers and hearbes, bounde rounde aboute with stringes from the top to the bottome, and sometyme painted with variable colours, with two or three hundred men, women, and children followyng it with greate devotion.   And thus being reared up, with handkerchiefes and flagges streamyng on the toppe, they strawe the grounde aboute, binde greene boughs about it, sett up sommer halles, bowers, and arbours hard by it ; and then fall they to banquet and feast, to leape and daunce aboute it, as the heathen people did at the dedication of their idolles. . . . I have heard it credibly reported," he sarcastically adds, " by men of great gravity, credite, and reputation, that of fourtie, three score, or a hundred maides goyng to the wood over night, there have scarcely the third parte of them returned home againe as they went." (*The Anatomie of Abuses,* 1836 edition, p. 171.)

Herrick says :—

" Get up . . . and see
    The dew bespangling herbe and tree ;
Each flower has wept, and bow'd toward the east,
Above an hour since ; . . . it is sin,
        Nay profanation, to keep in ;
When as a thousand virgins on this day,
Spring sooner than the larks to fetch in May !
        Come, my Corinna, come ; and comming marke
        How each field turns a street, each street a parke
            Made green and trimmed with trees ; see how
            Devotion gives each house a bough,
            Or branch ; each porch, each doore ere this,
            An arke or tabernacle is,
        Made up of white-thorn neatly interwove,
    As if here were those cooler shades of love.

> Can such delights be in the street,
> And open fields, and we not see't ?
> Come, we'll abroad ; and let's obey
> The Proclamation made for May,
> And sin no more, as we have done, by staying.
>
> There's not a budding boy, or girle, this day
> But is got up, and gone to bring in May ;
>   A deale of youth, ere this, is come
>   Back, and with white-thorn laden home.
>   Some have dispatcht their cakes and creame,
>   Before that we have left to dreame ;
> And some have wept, and woo'd, and plighted troth,
> And chose their priest, ere we can cast off sloth ;
>   Many a green gown has been given ;
>   Many a kisse, both odde and even ;
>   Many a glance too has been sent
>   From out the eye, Love's firmament ;
> Many a jest told of the keyes betraying
> This night, and locks pickt, ye w'are not a Maying !"

Of the festive appearance of the streets in summer, and the hospitality of the citizens, and the setting of the Midsummer Watch, Stow speaks at length (Thoms's edition, p. 39) :—

"In the months of June and July, on the vigils of festival days, and on the same festival days in the evenings after the sun setting, there were usually made bonfires in the streets, every man bestowing wood or labour towards them ; the wealthier sort also, before their doors, near to the said bonfires, would set out tables on the vigils, furnished with sweet bread and good drink, and on the festival days with meats and drinks plentifully, whereunto they would invite their neighbours and passengers also to sit and be merry with them in great familiarity, praising God for His benefits bestowed on them. These were called bonfires as well of good amity amongst neighbours that being before at controversy were there, by the labour of others, reconciled, and made of bitter enemies loving friends ; and also for the virtue that a great fire hath to purge the infection of the air. On the vigil of St. John the Baptist, and on St. Peter and Paul the apostles, every man's door being shadowed with green birch, long fennel, St. John's wort, orpin, white lilies, and such like, garnished upon with garlands of beautiful flowers, had also lamps of glass, with oil burning in them all the night ; some hung out branches of iron curiously wrought, containing hundreds of lamps alight at once, which made a goodly show, namely in New Fish Street, Thames Street, etc."

At Whitsuntide 1900 I was at Treves. It is the custom on Whit Sunday to hold a great procession in which, apparently, the whole population takes part through the principal streets to the Cathedral. The girls are dressed in white with white flowers in their hair ; the younger girls carry baskets filled with white flowers ; men, women, and children are all chanting as they go ; groups of

A FÊTE AT HORSELYDOWN IN 1590

From a picture by G. Hoffnagle at Hatfield House.

Drawn by Ingram, photographed by D. Diamond

priests, boys in scarlet, beadles and other ecclesiastical selections, adorn the procession. If that were all I should not notice it in this place. But in addition every street through which the procession passed was decorated with branches. And here for the first time I understood the lines already quoted, how

> " Each field turns a street, each street a parke
> Made green and trimmed with trees ; see how
> Devotion gives each house a bough,
> Or branch ; each porch, each doore, ere this,
> An arke or tabernacle is,
> Made up of white-thorn neatly interwove."

For the decking of the house did not consist of a branch or a bunch over a porch or a window, but the whole ground-floor of every house was covered with great boughs closely placed side by side so as to look like a lane of trees. Herrick did not exaggerate.

Stow goes on to speak of the Marching Watch :—

" Besides the standing Watches all in bright Harness, in every Ward and Street in this city and Suburbs, there was also a Marching Watch, that passed through the principal Streets thereof, to wit, from the little conduit by Paul's Gate to West Cheap, by the Stocks through Cornhill, by Leaden Hall to Aldgate, then back down Fenchurch Street, by Grasse church, about Grasse church conduit, and up Grasse church street into Cornhill, and through it into West Cheap again, and so broke up. The whole way ordered for this marching watch extendeth to three thousand two hundred Taylor's Yards of Assize ; for the furniture whereof with Lights, there were appointed seven hundred cressets, five hundred of them being found by the Companies, the other two hundred by the Chamber of London. Besides the which Lights every Constable in London, in number more than two hundred and forty, had his Cresset ; the charge of every Cresset was in Light two shillings and four-pence, and every cresset had two men, one to bear or hold it, another to bear a Bag with Light, and to serve it, so that the Poor Men pertaining to the Cressets, taking Wages, besides that every one had a strawen Hat, with a Badge painted, and his breakfast, amounted in number to almost two thousand. The marching Watch contained in number about two thousand men, part of them being old Soldiers, of skill to be Captains, Lieutenants, Serjeants, Corporals, etc., Wiflers, Drummers, and Fifes, Standard and Ensign Bearers, Demilances on great Horses, Gunners with hand guns, or half Hakes, Archers in coats of white Fustian, signed on the breast and back with the Arms of the City, their Bows bent in their Hands, with Sheafs of Arrows by their Sides ; Pikemen in bright Corslets, Burganets, etc., Halbards, the like the Billmen in Almain Rivets, and Aprons of Mail in great Number. There were also divers Pageants, Morris Dancers, Constables, the one-half, which was one hundred and twenty on St.

John's Eve, the other half on St. Peter's Eve, in bright harness, some over Gilt, and every one a jornet of Scarlet thereupon, and a Chain of Gold, his henchman following him, his Minstrels before him, and his Cresset Light passing by him, the Waits of the City, the Mayor's officers for his Guard before him, all in a livery of woosted, or Sea Jackets party-coloured, the Mayor himself well mounted on Horseback, the Swordbearer before him in fair Armour well mounted also, the Mayor's Footmen, and the like Torch Bearers about him, Henchmen twain upon great stirring Horses, following him. The Sheriffs' Watches came one after the other in like Order, but not so large in Number as the Mayor's; for where the Mayor had, besides his Giant, three Pageants, each of the Sheriffs had, besides their Giants, but two Pageants; each their Morris Dance, and one Henchman, their Officers in jackets of woosted or Sea, party-coloured, differing from the Mayor's and each from other, but having harnessed Men a great many.

This Midsummer Watch was thus accustomed yearly, time out of Mind, until the year 1539, the 31st of Henry VIII., in which year, on the 8th of May, a great Muster was made by the Citizens at the Mile's End, all in bright Harness, with Coats of White Silk, or Cloth and Chains of Gold, in three great Battels, to the number of fifteen thousand, which passed through London to Westminster, and so through the Sanctuary, and round about the Park of St. James, and returned home through Oldborne. King Henry, then considering the great Charges of the Citizens for the Furniture of this unusual Muster, forbad the Marching Watch provided for at Midsummer for that Year; which being once laid down, was not raised again till the year 1548, the 2nd of Edward VI., Sir John Gresham then being Mayor, who caused the Marching Watch, both on the eve of St. John Baptist and of St. Peter the Apostle, to be revived and set forth in as comely order as it hath been accustomed, which Watch was also beautified by the number of more than three hundred Demilances and light Horsemen, prepared by the citizens to be sent into Scotland for the rescue of the town of Haddington, and others kept by the Englishmen." (Stow, vol. i.)

As for dancing, never was there a time when it was more popular. Everybody danced: the Queen at Whitehall danced the brawl; the kitchen-maid in the street danced the ney. They danced the solemn *pavane*, the *Cassamezzo galliard*, the *canary* dance, the *Coranto*, the *Cavolta*, the *jig*, the *galliard*, the *fancy*, and the *Ney*, and perhaps many more. They played cards: they played at primiero, trumpe, gleek, gresso, new cut, knave out of doors, ruff, noddy, most and pace; they got through the long winter evenings mainly with the help of cards. Bowling was a summer amusement; tournaments belonged to the Court; hunting was an amusement for the richer sort; the people also fought cocks, wrestled, practised archery, and played quarter-staff. The old

Catholic feasts and sports—such as the Feast of Fools, the Boy Bishop, the Mysteries in the Churches, were abolished; but in their own houses they had mumming and mummers; for the ladies there was embroidery; there was also fine work of all kinds. And there was a great demand for monsters: a pig with eight legs; strange fishes caught in the river; a mermaid quite fresh, unfortu-

THE DANCING PICTURE
By Holbein and Janet, in the possession of Major-General F. E. Sotheby.

nately dead, caught off the Yarmouth Roads; a calf with two backs; a lobster with six claws; these things were always on exhibition, for the most part, in Fleet Street. Their Morris dances, their Maypoles, Whitsun Ales, their fairs and wakes, and, in fact, every occasion for meeting together, singing, feasting, and dancing, this Protestant city kept up.

Among the amusements of the people must not be forgotten the common custom of telling stories. The long evenings when the family gathered round the fire, the only light in the room, were tedious: they could hardly go to bed much before eight, though they rose long before daybreak. Story-telling was an amusement which had long ago pleased the Saxons and the Danes, who recounted the great deeds of their ancestors to wile away the winter evening. Perhaps many of the stories which found their way into books during the sixteenth century served this purpose, while the merry jests of Skogan, and Peele, and the rest, certainly formed part of the story-teller's *répertoire*.

Another amusement was that of reading. We have already seen what an immense field was opened up for those who loved books, by the shoals which during Elizabeth's reign were issued from the press.

The first Lottery was set on foot in the year 1559. The drawing took place at the west door of St. Paul's, and continued daily from the 11th of January to the 6th of May following. The Lottery did not gain its full power until the eighteenth century. It is sufficient here to record the first appearance of this baleful institution, fruitful mother of crime.

CHAPTER VIII

THE POOR

HARRISON says that there are "four kinds of poor: the poor by impotence, as the fatherless child, the blind man, and the incurably sick man; the poor by casualty, as the wounded soldier; the thriftless poor, as the rioter that hath consumed all; the vagabond that will abide nowhere; and, finally, the rogues and strumpet which are not possible to be divided in sunder."

As regards the last sort. Harrison's description tells everything that is wanted.

"Such as are idle beggars through their owne default are of two sorts, and continue their estates either by casuall or meere voluntarie meanes: those that are such by casuall means, are in the beginning justlie to be referred either to the first or second sort of poore afore mentioned; but degenerating into the thriftlesse sort, they doo what they can to continue their miserie, and with such impediments as they have to straie and wander about, as creatures abhorring all labour and every honest exercise. Certes I call these casuall meanes, not in respect of the originall of their povertie, but of the continuance of the same, from whence they will not be delivered, such is their owne ungratious lewdnesse and froward disposition. The voluntarie meanes proceed from outward causes, as by making of corosives, and applieng the same to the more fleshie parts of their bodies; and also laieng of ratsbane, sperewort, crowfoot, and such like unto their whole members, thereby to raise pitifull and odious sores and moove the harts of the goers by such places where they lie, to yerne at their miserie and bestow large almesse upon them. How artificiallie they beg, what forcible speech, and how they select and choose out words of vehemencie, whereby they doo in maner conjure or adjure the goer by to pitie their cases, I passe over to remember, as judging the name of God and Christ to be more conversant in the mouths of none; and yet the presence of· the heavenlie majestie further off from no men than from this ungracious companie. Which maketh me to think that punishment is farre meeter for them than liberalitie or almesse, and sith Christ willeth us cheeflie to have a regard to Himselfe and His poore members.

Unto this nest is another sort to be referred, more sturdie than the rest, which having sound and perfect limbs, doo yet, notwithstanding, sometime counterfeit the possession of all sorts of diseases. Divers times in their apparell also they will be like serving-men or laborers; oftentimes they can plaie the mariners, and seeke for ships which they never lost. But in fine, they are thieves and caterpillars in the common-wealth, and by the word of God not permitted to eat, sith they doo but lick the sweat from the true labourers' browes, and beereve the godly poore of that whiche is due unto them, to mainteine their excesse, consuming the charitie of well-disposed people bestowed upon them, after a most wicked and detestable manner.

It is not yet full threescore yeares since this trade began; but how it hath prospered since that time, it is easie to judge, for they are now supposed, of one sex and another, to amount unto about 10,000 persons; as I have heard reported. Moreover, in counterfeiting the Egyptian rogues, they have devised a language among themselves, which they name Canting, but other pedlers French, a speech compact thirtie years since of English, and a great number of od words of their own devising, without all order or reason; and yet such is it as none but themselves are able to understand. The first deviser thereof was hanged by the necke, a just reward no doubt for his deserts, and a common end to all of that profession. . . .

The punishment that is ordeined for this kind of people is verie sharpe and yet it can not restreine them from their gadding; wherefore the end must needs be martiall law, to be exercised upon them, as upon theeves, robbers, despisers of all lawes, and enimies to the common-wealth and welfare of the land. What notable roberies, pilferies, murders, rapes, and stealings of yoong children, burning, breaking and disfiguring their lims to make them pitifull in the sight of the people, I need not to rehearse; but for their idle roging about the countrie, the law ordeineth this manner of correction. The roge being apprehended, committed to prison, and tried in the next assises (whether they be of gaole diliverie or sessions of the peace), if he happen to be convicted for a vagabond either by inquest of office, or the testimonie of two honest and credible witnesses upon their oths, he is then immediately adjudged to be greeviously whipped and burned through the gristle of the right eare, with a hot iron of the compasse of an inch about, as a manifestation of his wicked life, and due punishment received for the same. And this judgment is to be excuted upon him, except some honest person woorth five pounds in the queenes books in goods, or twentie shillings in lands, or some rich housholder to be allowed by the justices will be bound in recognisance to reteine him in his service for one whole yeare. If he be taken the second time, and proved to have forsaken his said service, he shall then be whipped againe, bored likewise through the other eare and set to service; from when if he depart before a yeare be expired, and happen afterwards to be attached againe, he is condemned to suffer paines of death as a fellon (except before excepted), without benefit of clergy or sanctuarie, as by the statute doth appeare. Among roges and idle persons finallie, we find to be comprised all proctors that go up and down with conterfeit licenses, coosiners, and such as gad about the countrie, using unlawfull games, practisers of physiognomie and palmestrie, tellers of fortunes, fensers, plaiers, minstrels, jugglers, pedlers, tinkers, pretensed scholars, shipmen, prisoners gathering for fees, and others so oft as they be taken without sufficient licence. From among which companie our bearewards are not excepted and just cause; for I have read that they have either voluntarilie, or for want of power to master their savege beasts, beene occasion of the death and devoration of manie children in sundrie countries by which they have passed, whose parents never knew what was become of them." (Holinshed, vol. i.)

The great increase of rogues and vagabonds of all kinds led in the year 1561 to a proposition for a House of Correction. The plan or scheme of which was drawn out at full length, is published in *Archæologia* (vol. xxi. p. 451).

The House was to be strong and in two divisions: one for the men and the other for the women. It was to be built and furnished by the alms of the people where it was put up—in this case Westminster was proposed. In furnishing, care must be taken that everything should be simple, because "it is to be considered beforehand that ye shall have to do with the most desperatest people of the earth, geven to all spoyle and robbery and soch as will break from you and steale."

For work, it must be of a kind that they cannot steal or destroy. A Mill, therefore, for the men, or a Lime Kiln; and for the women a Wheel for cotton wool or woollen yarn. Of officers there must be six Masters: a clerk; a porter and keeper; two beadles, and a miller.

The rations for the inmates were to be as follows:—To every four women, at every meal, one pound of beef, potage, bread and drink. To every two men working in the mill, double this allowance. The allowance of bread was to be sixteen ounces a day. The allowance of beer was to every four women one "pottell" of single beer a day, but to the men double that quantity. On fast days an equivalent of butter, cheese, herrings, "pescodes," and such like.

There were to be two pairs of stocks and shackles for the refractory. The Matron was to be a strong woman—the Elizabethan female of the baser kind did not weaken her muscles and her nerves with tea; and, which is very significant, it is added, "ye must be careful of fyer, for the people are desperate and care not what mischief they do."

I do not know whether this proposed House of Correction was erected or not.

The present seems the best place and time to speak of systematic attempts at Poor Relief.

The relief of the poor was a duty enjoined on all men. Almsgiving was considered especially a virtue becoming to kings and princes. Alfred gave alms continually. The Monastic Houses never turned away a beggar without a meal to speed him on his way. Rich and noble persons kept open house at Christmas, Easter, and Whitsuntide. Already the custom was commenced of leaving lands or money to the church or to the monastery saddled with the condition of alms to be bestowed on the anniversary of the donor. By the laws of Ethelred, which probably only confirmed a custom, the third part of the tithe due to the Church was to be set aside for the use of the poor. In the Canons of Ælfric the same proportion is enjoined to be so reserved. And in all the Monastic Houses a certain part of the revenues was expended on the Almonry or the Infirmary.

The custom of giving indiscriminately to any vagrant who demanded alms, created a class of "masterless" men who would do no work and wandered about the country. It took some centuries of this growing evil before men could be brought to connect vagrancy with indiscriminate almsgiving. At first the efforts made to repress vagrancy were directed towards compulsory work. No one dared to maintain, perhaps no one dared to think, that it was wrong to give alms to a beggar merely because he was a beggar; but every one understood that the labourer must somehow be made to work. Had the Clergy and the Monastic Houses perceived the truth, vagrancy might have been reduced to a few companies of outlaws and marauders. But we cannot blame the clergy of the thirteenth century for failing to understand what the clergy of the present century are still unable to understand. When the law interfered, the situation was wellnigh desperate. The Black Death of 1348-50 had made labour scarce and wages high. The necessity of suppressing able-bodied begging and of sending the able-bodied beggar back to his native place and his proper work was forced upon the Government. The Labour Statutes endeavoured to force men to work and to keep down wages. In the fourteenth century, just as to-day, there was a natural limit imposed upon wages by the price of grain and food. The rustic who understood nothing about this limit, naturally desired higher and still higher wages; if he could not get this increase in his own parish, he went elsewhere: he begged his way; he found food at the monastery; he tasted the joys of food which was got without any work for it; he therefore easily dropped into the condition of the masterless man and the able-bodied beggar.

In 1349 the law stepped in. No one must give alms, money, or food to the able-bodied, so that for lack of bread they might be compelled to work. The rustics, in order to escape the terrors of this law, ran about the country from place to place. They pretended to be lame, blind, dumb, paralysed; in this disguise they wandered about begging with impunity unless they were detected. They pretended (case of impostor—Riley) to go on pilgrimage: they joined companies of pilgrims, begging by the way, and so got along for a time without

24

working. Therefore in 1388 other laws were framed. Nobody was allowed to beg at all without a letter granting him a license; nobody was allowed to go on pilgrimage without a license; nobody was to go anywhere outside his own part of the country without a license. If any were found without such warrant or permission they were clapped into the stocks. The Act endeavoured to put a stop not only to able-bodied vagrancy, but also to beggars who were crippled or afflicted, for they, too, were forbidden to roam.

The citizens of London were especially severe on masterless men.

The law, at the same time, recognised the duty of relieving the impotent, and the deserving poor, and the right of these to demand relief. Wherever they were found they were compelled to go back to the place to which they belonged by birth.

Nothing could be better or more effectual than these laws if they could have been enforced. But how were they to be enforced? Where were the police who might patrol the roads? How were the villagers disposed towards laws which made them accept whatever wages the Lord of the Manor chose to give them? In the City of London what were the opinions of the working class, of the craftsmen? And how could the Alderman in his ward ascertain that every man was following his own craft? No doubt the power of arresting, punishing, and sending to their own villages the wandering rustic, had the effect of keeping down the number of the beggars. In a short time, too, the natural increase of the population relieved the scarcity of labour. Moreover the relief of the poor by each parish was ordered by the setting aside of a portion of the tithe for their benefit (a revival of the Saxon law); and in those cases where the tithes went to a monastic house, the same portion should be payable by the monks or nuns. The jealousy with which the religious Orders were already regarded is shown by the enactment of this provision by Richard II. and its confirmation by Henry IV.

If the laws against grants of the fourteenth century had been enforced there would have been an end of the evil. Unfortunately, they could not be enforced. In the country there was no kind of Police; in London the City had outgrown the old government by Aldermen and Ward, and the people were overflowing the City boundaries and were beyond the jurisdiction of the Mayor. Now the control of the county would not be very effective, say, at Wapping or at Bermondsey, when the people began to settle there. During the whole of the fifteenth century the demand for able-bodied men for the war in France first, and the Civil wars next, was so great that there seem to have been few vagrants in the country. Indications, however, are by no means wanting of a "masterless" element in London.

The cessation of the wars threw a large number of men out of employment;

worse than this, it found them unwilling or unable to settle down again to steady work. Other causes also operated to produce the same result. The English nobles had ceased to maintain their large retinues: no longer did an Earl of Warwick ride into London with seven hundred gentlemen and men-at-arms; Sir Thomas More says expressly that the men who formerly had been in this kind of service either starved or became thieves. Again, the changes in the industrial condition of the country threw many people out of work: lands formerly arable were turned into pasture; sheep runs took the place of cornfields; one shepherd was wanted instead of half-a-dozen labourers. There was again a great rise in prices, owing to the influx of silver. In fifty years provisions of all kinds were doubled in price while wages rose only thirty per cent. Add to these causes the continuance of indiscriminate almsgiving.

The evil grew continually during the whole of the sixteenth century.

Early in the sixteenth century the City of London began to pass regulations against vagrants. They forbade able-bodied vagrants to beg and citizens to give money to unlicensed beggars: in other words, they revived and enforced the old laws. Great strictness was ordered. Vagrants had the letter V fastened on their breasts, and were driven through Cheapside to the music of a basin ringing before them. Four surveyors were appointed to carry out these instructions. There was also an officer appointed, called "Master and Chief Avoyder and Keeper out of this City and the liberties of the same all the mighty vagabonds and beggars and all other suspected persons, except such as wear upon them the badge of the City." The vagrants, when apprehended, were whipped at the cart's tail; they also had to wear collars of iron about their necks. Those who were allowed to beg had tokens of tin given to them by the Aldermen. As for the relief of the deserving poor, there were the "Companies' stores," granaries of wheat provided for emergencies; alms were asked for every Sunday at the church doors; the old hospitals were suppressed at the Reformation until St. Bartholomew's and St. Mary of Bethlehem were granted to the City by Henry VIII. and reopened as hospitals. The City did not show to advantage in giving money to the poor; we must remember that for many centuries charity had been understood as indiscriminate alms given by the Church and by rich men. What private persons gave was for the advantage of their souls. Latimer and Lever thundered in vain. Latimer says:—

"Now what shall we say of these rich citizens of London? What shall I say of them? Shall I call them proud men of London, malicious men of London, merciless men of London? No, no, I may not say so; they will be offended with me then. Yet must I speak. For is there not reigning in London as much pride, as much covetousness, as much cruelty, as much oppression and as much superstition as was in Nebo? Yes I think, and much more too. . . . But London was never so ill as it is now. In times past men were full of pity and compassion, but now there is no pity; for in London their brother shall die in the streets for cold, he shall lie sick at the door between stock and stock . . . and perish there for hunger: was there ever more unmercifulness in Nebo? I think not. In times past, when any rich man died in London they were wont to help the poor scholars of the Universities with exhibitions. When any man died, they would bequeath great sums of money towards the relief of the poor. When I was a scholar in Cambridge myself I heard very good report of London, and knew many that had relief of the rich men of London; but now I can hear no such good report, and yet I inquire of it, and hearken for it; but now charity is waxen cold, none helpeth the scholar, nor yet the poor."

Lever said :—

"Nowe speakynge in the behalfe of these vile beggars, . . . I wyl tell the(e) that art a noble man, a worshipful man, an honest welthye man, especially if thou be Maire, Sherif, Alderman, baily, constable or any such officer, it is to thy great shame afore the worlde, and to thy utter damnation afore God, to se these begging as thei use to do in the streates. For there is never a one of these but he lacketh eyther thy charitable almes to relieve his neede, or els thy due correction to punysh his faute. . . . These sely sols have been neglected throughout al England and especially in London and Westminster: But now I trust that a good overseer, a godly Byshop I meane, wyl see that they in these two cyties shall have their neede releeved, and their faultes corrected, to the good ensample of al other tounes and cities."

Then St. Thomas's Hospital and Bridewell were obtained from the King. The latter was designed as a House of Instruction and Correction. It was to receive the child "unapt for learning"; the "sore and sick when they be cured"; and persons who have lost their character and either cannot work or cannot find any who will employ them. The children were to be made to work; the others were to be taught certain trades. They were to be such as would not interfere with the crafts carried on in the City.

The treatment of the poor began by being the work of the towns, each town working out its own experimental methods. This was followed by legislation in Parliament.

The Act of 1573, of which we have read Harrison's account, enjoined boring through the ear and whipping, and at the third offence death. The Middlesex Sessions Rolls show that these sentences were actually carried out. Between 6th October and 14th December 1591, 71 vagrants were sentenced at the Sessions to be branded and whipped.

Who were vagrants? They were defined as proctors or procurators; persons pretending to knowledge in "Phisnomye, Palmestrye, and other abused Scyences," masterless men; "fencers, bearewardes, players, minstrels,"—not belonging to some noble lord; jugglers, pedlars, tinkers, chapmen; labourers refusing customary wages; counterfeiters of passes; scholars of Oxford and Cambridge who beg without license; sailors not licensed; discharged prisoners without license; impotent poor. But of these, players, bearwards, and pedlars were allowed to carry on their calling subject to license.

In every parish the Justices of the Peace were to make a register of the names of the poor. Every month they were to search for strange poor.

Justices in the country and Mayors in London were to assess and tax the people for the relief of the poor; and those who refused to pay were to be imprisoned. Three years later it was ordered that "stock" of wool, flax, hemp, iron, or other stuff, should be provided for the work of the poor. Between 1575 and 1597 other statutes were passed for the prevention of increased settlement of poor families. No more houses to be built within three miles of London westward except for people assessed at £5 in goods or £3 in land. No tenement houses to be built, and no inmates to be received.

In 1597 there was great discussion in the House of Commons on the whole subject of poor relief. Finally an Act was passed by which the relief of the poor was placed in the hands of church-wardens and four overseers of Poor elected every Easter. They had to teach children and bind them apprentice; they provided work for the adult; they relieved the impotent; they built hospitals; they levied rates; they made Houses of Correction; they resorted to more whipping and to banishment, with death for return.

Next there is the interference of the Privy Council ordering the Justices of the Peace to look after the vagrants and to report. Here is a brief summary.

1573. Mayor has received a second letter from the Privy Council on subject of vagrants.

1579. Common Council considered the work of the poor at Bridewell and referred to Lords of the Council.

1583. Privy Council recommenced prevention of Irish beggars.

1594. City meets Justices of Middlesex on subject.

London—1572. Mayor issued precept to Aldermen to inquire about poor of every parish. Another precept to use the church-wardens—thus to assess the whole ward—to make them pay who had given nothing, and to make them pay more who had given too little.

In 1573. Assessments proving too little, collections were made in churches.

1576. Each parish was to elect a surveyor who every night for a week should help the constable, beadle, and church-wardens in visiting the houses and sending away vagrants.

Then followed a double method—relief and repression undertaken by the parish and municipal authorities together. The vagrants were taken to Bridewell, where the sick were picked out and sent to St. Thomas's and St. Bartholomew's —thence returned to Bridewell—and made to work for their diet. The parish looked after the rest of the poor. The children were sent to Christ's Hospital. The impotent were relieved.

It seems as if so strict a system must have been successful. But it was not.

In 1601 the Act of 1579 was reconsidered and slightly altered.

1610. An Act for building one or more Houses of Correction in every county was brought in.

The supply of corn for the markets occupied Parliament a great deal between 1610 and 1630. There were bad harvests, and general distress. The Privy Council tried to prevent scarcity, to find work for the poor, and to regulate trade in the interests of the working classes. Against times of scarcity of fuel, a coalyard was established in London for the poor. Watchmen were provided in time of plague. More almshouses existed then than now for the old and impotent.

It is customary to speak of the time immediately following the Reformation as especially hard-hearted and uncharitable. For instance, here is a certain passage, one of many, in Stubbes's *Anatomie*, which is certainly strong evidence of a lack of charity. It is as follows :—

"There is a certayne citie in Ailgna (Anglia) called Munidnol (Londinum) where as the poore lye in the streetes, upon pallets of strawe, and wel if they have that too, or els in the mire and dirt, as commonly it is seene, having neither house to put in their heades, covering to keepe them from the colde, nor yet to hyde their shame withall, nor a pennie to by them sustenaunce, nor any thing els, but are suffered to dye in the streetes like dogges or beastes, without any mercy or compassion shewed to them at all. And if any be sicke of the plague (as they call it) or any other mortall disease, their maisters and mistresses are so impudent (having made, it shoulde seeme, a league with Sathan, a covenant with hell, and an obligation with the devil, never to have to doe with the workes of mercie) as straight way they throwe them out of their doores : and so being caried forth, either in cartes or otherwise, or laied downe eyther in the streetes, or els conveiyed to some olde house in the fields or gardens, where for want of due sustentation, they ende their lives most miserably. Truely, brother, if I had not seene it, I would scarsly have thought that the like Turkishe crueltie had bene used in all the world."[1]

I would again call attention, however, to a point which has already been mentioned in these pages. Before the suppression of the Religious Houses these places had taken over and held in their own hands the whole management of the poor, the sick, and the disabled, save those whom the City Companies took under their own care. For centuries, therefore, the people had been taught to regard the care of the sick and old, and in a great manner the feeding of the poor, as belonging especially to the Religious. It is part of the mediæval mind that the poor do so belong to the monastic orders and not to the laity. When, therefore, the Houses were suppressed, the modern spirit of Charity had to be actually created in the hearts of the people. It was then that the education in philanthropy began which has been going on ever since.

[1] *The Anatomie of Abuses*, Turnbull's edition 1836, p. 50.

This outburst of Stubbes is a first lesson in brotherly love. Another part of the same lesson is his tirade against hard-hearted creditors, which is quoted here, because it applies especially to the citizens of London, tender and compassionate in some respects, but flinty-hearted as regards the poor prisoners who cannot pay their debts :—

"Believe me, it greeveth me to heare (walking in the streetes) the pitifull cryes and miserable complayntes of poore prisoners in durance for debte, and like so to continue all their life, destitute of libertie, meate, drink (though of the meanest sort), and clothing to their backes, lying in filthie straw and lothsome dung, worse than anie dogge, voyde of all charitable consolation and brotherly comfort in this world, wishing and thirsting after deathe to set them at libertie, and loose them from their shackles, gives, and iron bandes. Notwithstanding, these merciless tygers (the usurers) are grown to such barbarous crueltie that they blush not to say 'tush, he shall eyther pay me the whole, or else lye there till his heeles rotte from his buttocks; and, before I will release him, I will make dice of his bones.' But, take heed, thou devil (for I dare not call thee Christian), least the Lord say to thee, as hee sayd to that wicked servant (who, having great summes forgiven him, would not forgive his brother his small debt, but, catching him by the throate, sayd Paie that thou owest), Binde him handes and feete, and cast him into utter darknesse, where shall bee weeping and gnashing of teeth."

The charities of London consisted of Hospitals for the sick, almshouses, schools, and doles for the poor. It was customary for great men, ecclesiastics, and Religious Houses, to give every day large quantities of food to the poor, whereby they were encouraged to remain poor. Stow records many instances of this mischievous and promiscuous charity. Henry II., for instance, to show his repentance for the death of the Archbishop, fed every day 10,000 persons from the first of April till the harvest, a time of year when food is dearest and scarcest.

Let me follow Stow's list of Foundations in chronological order.

1. In very ancient times the Hospital of St. James for leprous women.

2. In 1197 Domus Dei, or St. Mary Spital, outside Billingsgate.

3. In 1247 the Hospital of St. Mary Bethlehem turned afterwards into a lunatic asylum.

4. 1322 Elsing Spital for 100 poor men.

5. 1337 The College of St. Laurence Poultney.

6. 1358 The Almshouses of Stodies Lane.

7. 1367 John Lofken's Hospital at Kingston-on-Thames.

8. 1384 John Philpot's Almshouses for 13 poor people.

9. 1400 Thomas Knoles bequeathed his house as an almshouse.

10. Whittington's College (1421), an almshouse for 13 poor men.

11. John Carpenter, almshouse for 4 poor men.

12. Robert Chicheley money for a dinner to 2400 poor men and twopence each on his " minde day."

13. Philip Malpas, numerous benefactions to prisoners, poor folk, girls' marriage portions, etc.

14. Richard Rawson, girls' marriage portions.
15. Henry Keble, girls' marriage portions and seven almshouses.
16. John Colet, St. Paul's School, 353 poor men's children.
17. John Tate enlarged and increased St. Anthony's House and Almshouses.
18. George Monox, almshouses for 13 poor people at Walthamstow.
19. John Milbourne, almshouses for 14 poor people.
20. John Allen left rents for the use of the poor.
21. Andrew Judd, almshouses.
22. Richard Hills, the Merchant Taylors' School.
23. Sir Thomas Gresham, almshouses.
24. Sir Thomas Rowe, almshouses.
25. Ambrose Nicolas, almshouses.
26. John Fuller, almshouses.
27. Dame Agnes Foster, enlargement of Ludgate Hill Prison.
28. Avice Gibson, almshouses.
29. Margaret Danne, money to be lent to young men beginning as ironmongers.
30. Dame Mary Ramsay, endowment of Christ's Hospital.

The following are later endowments. Thus Sir Thomas White, citizen and Merchant Taylor, Mayor, purchased Gloucester Hall at Oxford; he founded St. John's College there; he erected schools at Bristol and Reading; to Bristol he gave £2000 for the purchase of lands. This would produce £120 a year, which was to be administered by the Mayor of Bristol. He gave £800 to be lent to 16 poor Clothiers at £50 apiece as security for ten years, and after that the money to pass to other towns, *i.e.*

1579 Reading	1589 Winchester
1580 The Merchant Taylors' Company	1590 Oxford
	1591 Hereford
1581 Gloucester	1592 Cambridge
1582 Worcester	1593 Shrewsbury
1583 Exeter	1594 Lynn
1584 Salisbury	1595 Bath
1585 Westchester	1596 Derby
1586 Norwich	1597 Ipswich
1587 Southampton	1598 Colchester
1588 Lincoln	1599 Newcastle.

He gave to the City of Coventry £1400 with which to purchase lands to the annual value of £70. Twelve poor men to have 40s. each free alms; then four young men were to have loans of £10 for nine years. He did the same thing for Northampton, for Leicester, and for Warwick. A worthy benefactor, indeed!

In 1560 Richard Hills gave £500 towards the purchase of a house called the

Manor of the Rose, where the Merchant Taylors founded their school. At the same time William Lambert, Draper, Justice of the Peace in Kent, founded an almshouse for the poor in East Greenwich called Queen Elizabeth's Almshouses.

In 1568 Sir Thomas Rowe gave the City a new burial-ground by Bethlehem Hospital; he also endowed a sermon every Whit Monday; gave £100 to be lent to eight poor men; and founded an endowment for the support of ten poor men, giving them four pounds a year.

William Lambe was a benefactor to the City in the sixteenth century. He was a clothworker by trade. In the year 1543, on the suppression of the Religious Houses, he obtained possession by purchase of the smallest of them all, the Chapel or Hermitage standing at the corner of the wall at the end of Monkwell Street. It was called St. James's in the Wall, and was endowed by Henry the Third. Lambe repaired or rebuilt the Chapel, and placed in the former garden or in the ancient buildings certain almshouses for bedesmen. In 1577 he died, leaving this foundation and other sums of money to the Clothworkers. The Great Fire spared a part of Lambe's Chapel and Almshouses.

Lambe also drew together several springs of water near the present Foundling Hospital to a head, called after him Lamb's Conduit, though the name is now spelt without the "e." He then conveyed the water by leaden pipes to Snow Hill, where he rebuilt a ruinous conduit and laid in the water.

"He also founded a Free Grammar School at *Sutton Valens*, the Place of his Nativity, in *Kent*, with a master at £20, and an Usher at £10 per Ann. and an Alms-house for six poor people, endowed with £10 yearly. He gave £10 per Ann. to the Free School at *Maidstone* in *Kent*, for the Education of needy Men's Children; three hundred pounds to the poor Clothiers in *Suffolk*, *Bridgnorth* and *Ludlow* in *Shropshire*. He left to the Clothworkers' Company his Dwelling-House, a little to the South-West of *Cripplegate*, with Lands and Tenements to the value of £30 per Ann. for paying a Minister to read Divine Service on *Sundays*, *Wednesdays*, and *Fridays*, every week, in the Chapel adjoining to his House, called St. *James*, in the Wall by *Cripplegate*; and for Clothing twelve Men with a Frize Gown, one Lockram Shirt, and a good strong pair of Winter Shoes; and twelve Women with a Frize Gown, a Lockram Smock, and a good pair of Winter Shoes, all ready made for wearing; to be given to such as are poor and honest, on the first of October. He also gave £15 towards the Bells and Chimes of St. Giles's Without *Cripplegate*; £6:13:4 yearly to the Company of Stationers, for the relief of twelve poor People of the Parish of St. *Faith*, under *Paul's*, at the rate of 12d. in Money, and 12d. in Bread, to each of them, on every Friday through the year; £6 per Ann. and £100 to purchase Land, for the Relief of Children in *Christ's* Hospital; £4 to

St. *Thomas's* Hospital in *Southwark*; besides some other Charities to the Prisons, and for portioning poor Maids." (Maitland, vol. i. p. 264.)

It will be seen that the building of almshouses was the favourite method of charitable endowment. Schools were occasionally endowed but not so commonly as almshouses. The sight of an old man broken down, unable to earn his bread, is one which appeals to the most hard-hearted. The necessity of educating the young was less understood, for the simple reason that the children of the working class were regarded as simply growing machines for labour, just as their fathers were regarded as machines in active working order whose opinions or wishes were never so much as asked, while any effort on their part to express an opinion was put down at once. This view of the working classes, which lasted till the middle of the nineteenth century, explains a great deal of what we now consider apathy on the part of those who should have known better; it explains among other things the opposition to reform, and the jealousy and dread of the working class; and it explains why so few schools were endowed in comparison with the number of almshouses.

CHAPTER IX

CRIME AND PUNISHMENT

THE divers kinds of punishment and the laws are set forth by Harrison (Holinshed, vol. i.):—

"The greatest and most greevous punishment used in England, for such as offend against the state, is drawing from the prison to the place of execution upon an hurdle or sled, where they are hanged till they be halfe dead, and then taken downe and quartered alive, after that their members and bowels are cut from their bodies and throwne into a fire provided neere hand and within their one sight even for the same purpose. Sometimes if the trespasse be not the more hainous, they are suffered to hang till they be quite dead. And whensoever any of the nobilitie are convicted of high treason by their peeres, that is to saie, equals (for an inquest of yeomen passeth not upon them, but onlie of the lords of the parliament) this maner of their death is converted into the losse of their heads onlie, notwithstanding that the sentence doo run after the former order. In triall of cases concerning treason, fellonie, or anie other greevous crime not confessed, the partie accused doth yeeld, if he be a nobleman, to be tried by an inquest (as I have said) and his peeres; if a gentleman, by gentlemen; and an inferiour by God and by the countrie, to wit the yeomanrie (so combat or battle is not greatlie in use) and being condemned of fellonie, manslaughter, etc., he is eftsoons hanged by the necke till he be dead, and then cut downe and buried. But if he is convicted of wilful murder, doone either upon pretended malice, or in anie notable robberie, he is either hanged alive in chains neere the place where the fact was committed (or else upon compassion taken first strangled with a rope) and so continueth till his bonds consume to nothing. We have use neither of the wheele nor of the barre, as in other countries, but when wilful manslaughter is perpetrated, beside hanging, the offender hath his right hand commonlie striken off before or neere unto the place where the act was doone, after which he is led forth to the place of execution, and there put to death according to the law." (*See* Appendix X.)

Felony was involved in various kinds of crime: such as breach of prison; disfiguring the person; robbery in disguise; rape; conspiracy against the prince;

embezzlement of the master's money ; carrying horses into Scotland ; stealing hawks' eggs ; unnatural offences ; witchcraft, conjuring, sorcery, and digging up of crosses ; prophesying upon arms, cognizances, names and badges ; casting of slanderous bills ; poisoning ; desertion ; clipping of coin ; taking goods from dead men ; highway robbery ; stealing of deer ; forging documents, etc., these were all, with some others, felony.

"If a woman poison her husband she is burned alive, if the servant kill his master he is to be executed for petie treason, he that poisoneth a man is to be boiled to death either in water or lead, although the partie die not of the practise ; in cases of murther all the accessories are to suffer paines of death accordingly. Perjury is punished by the pillorie burning in the forehead with the letter P, the rewalting[1] of the trees growing upon the grounds of the offendors and losse of all his moveables. Manie trespasses also are punished by the cutting of one or both eares from the head of the offendor, as the utterance of seditious words against the magistrates, grainmakers, petie robbers, etc. Roges are burned through the eares, carriers of sheep out of the land by the loss of their hands, such as kill by poison are either boiled or skalded to death in lead or seething water. Heretikes are burned quicke, harlots and their mates by carting, ducking, and dooing of open penance in sheets, in churches and market steeds are often put to rebuke. . . . Roges and vagabonds are often stocked and whipped, scolds are ducked upon cucking stooles in the water. Such fellons as stand mute and speak not at their arraignement are pressed to death by huge weights laid upon a boord, that lieth over their brest, and a sharpe stone under their backs, and these commonlie hold their peace, thereby to save their goods unto their wives and children, which if they were condemned should be confiscated to the prince. Theeves that are saved by their bookes and cleargie, for the first offense, if they have stolen nothing else but oxen, sheepe, monie, or such like, which be no open robberies, as by the high waie side or assailing of any man's house in the night, without putting him in fear of his life, or breaking up of his wals or doores, are burned in the left hand, upon the brawne of the thumb with an hot iron, so that if they be apprehended againe, that marke bewraieth them to have been arraigned of fellonie before, whereby they are sure at that time to have no mercie. I doo not read that this custom of saving by the book is used anywhere else than in England, neither doo I find (after much diligent enquirie) what Saxon prince ordained that law. . . . Our third annoiers of the common-wealth are roges, which doo verie great mischief in all places where they doo become. For whereas the rich onlie suffer injurie by the first two, these spare neither riche nor poore ; but whether it be great gaine or small, all is fish that commeth to net with them, and yet I saie that both they and the rest are trussed up apace. For there is not one yeare commonlie, wherein three hundred or four hundred of them are not devoured

---

[1] Rewalt = to give up or surrender (*Century Dictionary*).

and eaten up by the gallowes in one place and other. It appearth by Cardane (who writeth it upon the report of the bishop of Lexouia) in the geniture of King Edward the sixt, how Henrie the eight, executing his laws verie severelie against such idle persons, I meane great theeves, pettie theeves and roges, did hang up threescore and twelve thousand of them in his time. He seemed for a while greatlie to have terrified the rest; but since his death the number of them is so increased, yea although we have had no warres, which are a great occasion of their breed (for it is the custom of the more idel sort, having but once served or seen the other side of the sea under colour of service to shake hand with labour, for ever, thinking it a disgrace for himself to return unto his former trade) that except some better order

THE PILLORY
From a historical print in the British Museum.

be taken, or the lawes be better made to be executed, such as dwell in uplandish towns and little villages shall live but in small safety and rest. For the better apprehension also of theeves and mankillers, there is an old law in England very well provided, whereby it is ordered, that if he that is robbed, or any man complaine and give warning of slaughter or murder committed, the constable of the village whereunto he cometh and crieth for succour, is to raise the parish about him, and to search woods, groves, and all suspected houses and places, where the trespasser may be, or is supposed to lurke; and not finding him there, he is to give warning unto the next constable, and so one constable after serch made to advertise another from parish to parish, till they come to the same where the offender is harbored and found. It is also provided, that if anie parish in this business doo not his dutie, but suffereth the theefe (for the avoiding of trouble sake) in carrieng him to the gaile, if he should be apprehended, or other letting of their worke, to escape the same parish, is not onlie to make fine to the king, but also the same with the whole hundred wherein it standeth, to repaie the partie robbed his damages, and leave his estate harmlesse. Certes this is a good law, howbeit I have knowne by mine owne experience, fellons being taken to have escaped out of the stocks, being rescued by other for want of watch and ward, that theeves have been let passe, bicause the covetous and greedie parishoners would neither take the paines, nor be at the charge to carrie them to prison, if it were far off, that when hue and crie have beene made even to the faces of some constables, they have said : ' God restore your losse, I have other business at this time !' And by such meanes the meaning of manie a good law is left unexecuted, malefactors imboldened, and manie a poore man turned out of that which he hath swet and taken great paines for, toward the maintenance of himself and his poore children and familie." (Holinshed, vol. i.)

Among the punishments mentioned above was that of boiling alive. One unfortunate, named Rose, a cook in the house of the Bishop of Rochester, poisoned eighteen persons, of whom two died. He seems to have done this wilfully. He was boiled to death. This fearful punishment was inflicted by lowering the criminal slowly, inch by inch, affixed to a post into a deep caldron full of boiling water. How long the torture lasted before the heart stopped is not recorded.

The penalty for bloodshed in the King's Court was the loss of the right hand. The ceremony observed for such a punishment made a ritual of a remarkable and imposing ceremony.

The offender, to quote Pike (*History of Crime*, vol. ii. p. 83), "was brought in by the Marshal, and every stage of the proceedings was under the direction of some member of the royal household. The first whose services were required was the Serjeant of the Woodyard, who brought in a block and cords, and bound the condemned hand in a convenient position. The Master Cook was there with a dressing knife, which he handed to the Serjeant of the Larder, who adjusted it, and held it 'till the execution was done.' The Serjeant of the Poultry was close by with a cock, which was to have its head cut off on the block by the knife used for the amputation of the hand, and the body of which was afterwards to be used to 'wrap about the stump.' The Yeoman of the Scullery stood near, watching a fire of coals, and the Serjeant Farrier at his elbow to deliver the searing-irons to the surgeon. The chief Surgeon seared the stump, and the Groom of the Salcery held vinegar and cold water, to be used, perhaps, if the patient should faint. The Serjeant of the Ewry and the Yeoman of the Chandry attended with basin, cloths, and towels for the surgeon's use. After the hand had been struck off and the stump seared, the Serjeant of

On the off hip of the Croupière.

EXECUTION OF A SAINT

On the near side of the Croupière.

MARTYRDOM OF A SAINT

On the off side of the Croupière.

THE STORY OF ST. AGATHA

On the off side of the Croupière.

FURTHER PUNISHMENT OF ST. AGATHA

On the near side of the Croupière.

TORTURE OF ST. GEORGE

On the near hip of the Croupière.

BEHEADING OF A FEMALE SAINT

From the engravings upon Henry VIII.'s Armour in the Tower of London.

the Pantry offered bread, and the Serjeant of the Cellar offered a pot of red wine, of which the sufferer was to partake with what appetite he might."

Pickpockets, still called cutpurses, abounded. They formed a distinct profession; there was even a school for them. This educational establishment was carried on by a certain man named Wotton, at a house near Billingsgate, in the year 1585. Purses were worn at the girdle, attached by a chain or by a leathern string, and the pickpocket could be known by the horn thimble worn on the right thumb to protect it from the knife with which he cut the purse. Maitland says (p. 269) :—

> "Amongest our travells this one matter tumbled owt by the waye, that one Wotton, a gentilman borne, kepte an Alehowse att Smarts Keye neere Byllingsgate, and reared upp a newe trade of lyffe, and in the same howse he procured all the Cuttpurses abowt this Cittie to repair to his said howse. There was a Schole Howse sett upp to learne younge boyes to cutt purses. There were hunge up two devices, the one was a pockett, the other was a purse. The pocket had in yt certen cownters, and was hunge abowte with hawkes bells, and over the toppe did hannge a little sacringe bell; the purse had silver in it; and he that could take owt a cownter without any noyse was allowed to be a publique ffoyster, and he that could take a peece of sylver owt of the purse without the noyse of any of the bells, he was adjudged a judiciall Nypper. Note that a ffoyster is a Pickpocte and a Nypper is termed a Pickepurse or a Cutpurse."

Among the many additions to Literature made during the Elizabethan age we have as detailed a description of the rogues, vagabonds, and the criminal class in London as we can desire. Their tricks and cheats; their way of living; their language or slang, can all be read in books of the time. Harrison, already quoted, furnishes a great deal; more may be read in Awdeley, Harman and Rowlands, Dekker, etc. To spare the curious reader a great deal of trouble, he is referred to Furnivall's *Rogues and Vagabonds of Shakspere's Youth.*

Harman's account of these cheats and rogues is full of entertaining anecdotes. For instance, there is the story of the robbery of his cauldron by the "Upryght men," and how he recovered it :—

> "I lately had standinge in my well house, which standeth on the backeside of my house, a great cawdron of copper, beinge then full of water, havinge in the same halfe a doson of pewter dishes, well marked, and stamped with the connizance of my armes, whiche being well noted when they were taken out, were set aside, the water powred out, and my caudren taken awaye, being of such bygnes that one man, unlesse he were of great strength, was not able far to cary the same. Notwithstandynge, the same was one night within this two yeares convayed more than half a myle from my house into a commen or heth, and ther bestowed in a great firbushe. I then immediatly the next day sent one of my men to London, and there gave warning in Sothwarke, kent strete, and Barmesey streete, to all the Tynckars there dwelling. That if any such Caudron came thether to be sold, the bringar therof should be stayed, and promised twenty shyllings for a reward. I gave also intelligence to the water men that kept the ferres, that no such vessel should be ether convayed to London or into essex, promysing the like reward, to have understanding therof. This my doing was well understand in many places about, and that the feare of espyinge so troubled the conscience of the stealer, that my caudoren laye untouched in the thicke firbushe more than halfe a yeare after, which, by a great chaunce, was found by hunters for conneys; for one chaunced to runne into the same bushe where my caudren was, and being perceaved, one thrust his staffe into the same bushe,

and hyt my caudren a great blowe, the sound whereof dyd cause the man to thinke and hope that there was some great treasure hidden, wherby he thought to be the better whyle he lyved. And in farther searching he found my caudren; so had I the same agayne unloked for."

The Hooker or Angler was one who by day walked about the streets, observing the windows and what was kept in them. At night he carried a stick fitted with a hook. He opened the window from the outside, and by means of his hook got out what he wanted. Once, says Harman, the Hookers dragged from a bed, in which lay asleep a man and two boys, the blankets and upper sheets, leaving them in their shirts.

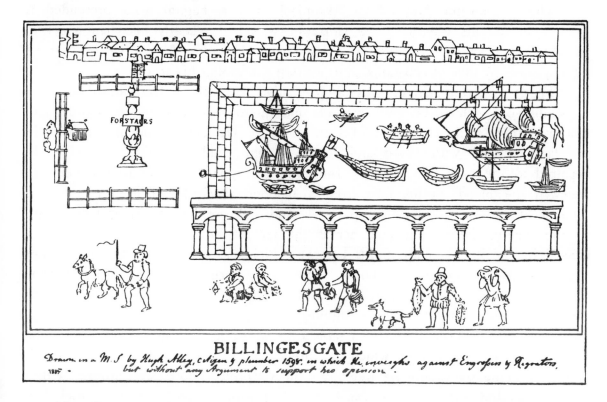

BILLINGESGATE

Drawn in a M.S by Hugh Alley, citizen & plumber 1598. in which he inveighs against Engrosers & Regrators, 1598. but without any Argument to support his opinion.

The Rogue professed a part and dressed up to it. Harman tells a story of two rogues who wanted to break into a house but could not, because it was of stone, with the mullions of the windows too close for them to creep in. They had, however, a "horse-lock." They woke up the tenant, who had with him only an old woman, and begged for alms. He opened the window and held out his hand with a penny in it. They seized his hand: he naturally thrust out the other to succour the first; they seized that as well, and clasped the two into the horse-lock, so that he was a prisoner until he gave up all the money in the house.

The "wild" Rogue is a variety distinguished by greater courage. Harman quotes one as a beggar by inheritance. "His grandfather was a beggar; his father was one; and he must needs be one by good reason."

The "Prygger of Prauncers" was a horse-stealer; the Pallyard of Clapper-dogen was one of the counterfeit sick men; he knew how to raise blisters, and to create a sore place by means of spearwort or ratsbane. The former raises a blister which passes away in a night; the latter a sore place that is incurable.

The Frater—in the name we seem to catch a memory of the extinct Friar—carried at his girdle a black box, in which there was a licence (forged) to beg.

The Abram man was one who feigned to have been mad, and to have been kept in Bedlam for a term of years.

The Freshwater Mariner or Whipjack was a beggar who pretended to be a sailor on his way to get a ship; or who had recently been shipwrecked; or who had been robbed by pirates; and who showed a forged writing signed, as it seemed, by men of substance and position confirming his story.

The Counterfeit Crank was a pretended epileptic. He carried a piece of white soap, which he put into his mouth to represent the epileptic foam. Harman draws a lively picture of such a man. He begged about the Temple, his face covered with blood and his rags with mud and dirt. At noon he repaired to the back of Clement's Inn, where in a lane leading to the fields he renewed the blood on his face from a bladder which he had with him, and daubed his jerkin and hose again with mud. A certain printer watched him: in the evening he took a boat across the river; the printer followed him and caused him to be taken up in St. George's Fields as a common beggar. They took him to the Constable's house, where they stripped off his rags, showing him to be a healthy and comely man with no sign of any disease; in his pockets they found the sum of thirteen shillings, three pence, and a halfpenny; they gave him an old cloak of the Constable's, in which he sat by the fire and drank three quarts of beer; after which he threw off the cloak and ran away naked. But they found out where he lived, viz. in a "pretty house, well stuffed, with a fair joined table, and a fair cupboard garnished with pewter." So they took him to Bridewell, where they painted him, first in his disguise, and next in his proper attire. Then they whipped him through London and brought him back to Bridewell, where he stayed till they thought fit to let him go.

The Dommerar pretended to be dumb: he carried a forged licence, and generally pretended to have lost his tongue. One of them was, unluckily for himself, caught by a surgeon, who proved that he had a tongue though he had neatly folded it away somewhere; and as the fellow still would not speak, the surgeon tortured him till he did. This done, they haled him before the magistrate, who administered the usual medicine.

The Drunken Tinker's career may be dismissed; so may that of the Pedlar; the Jackman made false writings and forgeries.

The "Demander for Glymmar" was a woman who pretended to have been burned out, and carried a begging licence.

The Basket women carried laces, pins, needles and girdles for sale. They bought coney skins and they stole linen from the hedges.

The "Autem Morte" and the "Walking Morte" were also pedlars, and of evil repute.

The Doxy was the companion and the confederate of the Upright Man.

The Dell, the Kynchen Morte, and the Kynchen Cove were boys and girls in training for the life of the vagabond.

Queen Elizabeth was fond of driving into the country as well as going upon the river. One summer evening she rode out from Aldersgate, along the road now called Goswell Road, towards the village of Iseldon or Islington. Just outside the town she was surrounded and beset by a number of beggars, to her great annoyance. Wherefore she sent her running footman, Stone, to the Mayor and to the Recorder complaining of this nuisance. The Recorder sent out warrants that same night to the quarters complained of, and into Westminster, with the result that seventy-four beggars were apprehended and sent to Bridewell, where they were "punished" (*i.e.* soundly flogged). Some of them were found to be very rich and usurers.

The mob under Elizabeth did not venture in assemblies on acts of violence. One or two exceptions must be made. Once an armed company, headed by gentlemen, attacked Bridewell. Seeing that their object was the release of certain unrepentant women whose profession concerned the gentlemen only, it is probable that the whole of the rioters were gentlemen. On another occasion the 'prentices rose against foreigners. Instances of hatred between Spanish residents and citizens of London are common in the pages of Machyn. Thus on October 15, 1554, a Spaniard killed a servant of Sir George Gifford without Temple Bar. The cause of the quarrel is not stated. Ten days afterwards the unfortunate foreigner was hanged at Charing Cross. On the 4th of November following there was a great fray at Charing Cross between Spaniards and English. Not many were hurt, and those who began it were arrested, especially a blackamoor. In January another Englishman was murdered by three Spaniards, two of whom held him while the other ran him through. In April was hanged a certain person, servant to a poulterer. He robbed a Spaniard in Westminster Abbey, and for the offence was condemned to be hanged for three days, and then to be buried under the gallows. He was hanged in a gown of tawny frieze, and a doublet of tawny taffeta, with hose lined with sarcenet. Before being turned off he railed at the Pope and the Mass.

Of street violence there was still a great deal, but not so much as formerly. The following letter speaks for itself.

"On Thursday laste (Feb. 13th 1587) as my Lorde Rytche was rydynge in the streates, there was one Wyndam that stode in a dore, and shotte a dagge at him, thynkynge to have slayne him ; but God provyded so for my L. Rytche that this Wyndam apoyntynge his servant that mornynge to charge his dagge with 11 bulletts, the fellow, doubtinge he mente to doe sum myschefe with it, charged it only with powder and paper, and no bullett ; and so this L.'s lyfe was thereby saved, for otherwyse he had beene slayne. Wyndam was presently taken by my Lord Rytche's men, and, beynge broughte before the Counsell, confessed his intende, but the cause of his quarrell I knowne not ; but he is commyted to the Towre. The same daye also, as Sir John Conway was goynge in the streetes, Mr. Lodovyke Grevell came sodenly uppon him, and stroke him on the hedd with a sworde, and but for one of Sir John Conwaye's men, who warded the blow, he had cutt off his legges ; yet did he hurte him sumwhat on bothe his shynns ; the Councelor sente for Lodovyke Grevell and have commytted him to the Marchallcye." (Drake, *Shakespeare and his Times*, vol. ii.)

The cucking-stool, trebucket, or tumbril, for the ducking of a scold, was commonly found in every village. There were several kinds of it. One was a chair set at the end of a braser which acted on a see-saw principle ; one a stump put into the ground at the edge of the water. Another was a "standard" fixed at the entrance of a pond. To this was attached a long pole, at the extremity of which was fastened the chair. Such an one stood almost within the memory of man at the great reservoir in the Green Park. Another kind was a sort of cart on four wheels, with a braser, at the end of which was the chair. All over Oxford these things are found, also at Wootton Bassett, Broad Water Worthing, Leominster, Marlborough, Newbury, Scarborough, Warwick, Ipswich. In 1777 a woman was ducked at Whitchurch.

The trial of Ben Jonson, an account of which has been recovered by Mr. John Cordy Jeafferson for the Middlesex County Record Society, began with the inquest on the body of one James Feake, held in Holywell Street, St. Leonard's Shoreditch, in the thirty-ninth year of Queen Elizabeth, and on the 10th day of December. The said James Feake was killed in a brawl by one Gabriel Spencer, who struck him with his sword in its scabbard in the right eye, so that he fell down, and after languishing for three days, died of the wound. What was done to Gabriel Spencer does not appear. Perhaps the case was treated as one of self-defence. However, Gabriel Spencer presently met with his reward. For in the month of September following, viz. in 1598, the said Gabriel fell to quarrelling with a young man named Ben Jonson, in Shoreditch, or Hoxton Fields ; from words they quickly came to blows, and Gabriel was pierced by Ben Jonson's sword through the right side, so that he died immediately. Jonson was thrown into prison and was tried for manslaughter, not for murder. He pleaded guilty ; he also pleaded his clergy, read his "neck-verse," and was released in accordance with the statute 18 Eliz. c. 7, after being branded in the hand with what the London people called the Tyburn T.

I have found one instance, the earliest, of a kind of transportation. Among Frobisher's Company were six men condemned to death. Their sentence was commuted into banishment. They were sent on board Frobisher's ship, to be landed on the shores of "Freezeland," that is Greenland or Labrador, with weapons and provisions. They were instructed to win the good-will and friendship of the natives and to inquire into their "estate." In other words, to find out all that could be learned concerning them. It is unfortunate that history makes no further mention of these pioneers.

The story of Thomas Appletree : his terrible accident ; his deadly peril ; his repentance ; and his pardon, is pathetic. I suffer Stow to tell it in his own words :—

"The seventeenth day of July, the Queenes moste excellent Maiestie, being in ye river of Thamis, betwixt hir Highnesse Mannour of Greenewiche and Detteforde, in hur privie Barge, accompanyed with Monsier Schemere the French Embassadour, the Earle of Lincolne, and Maister Vizchamberlaine, etc., with whim she entred discourse about waightie affaires ; it chanced that one Thomas

THE CUCKING-STOOL
From an old print in the British Museum.

Appletree, a yong man and servant to Maister Henrie Carie, with two or three children of hir Maiesties Chappell, and one other named Barnard Acton, being in a Boate on the Thamis, rowing up and downe betwixte the places above named, the foresaide Thomas Appletree hadde a Caliver or Harquebuze, whych he hadde three or foure times discharged with Bullet, shooting at randone very rashly, who by greate misfortune shot one of the Watermen, being the seconde man nexte unto the Bales of the saide Barge, labouring with hys Oare (whyche sate wythin five feete of hir Highnesse), cleane through bothe hys armes ; the blowe was so greate and greevous, that it moved him out of his place, and forced hym to crye and scritche oute piteouslye, supposing hymselfe to be slain, and saying, he was shot through the body. The man bleeding abundantly, as though he had had 100 Daggers thrust into hym, the Queenes Maiestie showed such noble courage as is moste wonderfull to be heard and spoken of, for beholding hym so maimed, and bleeding in such force, she never bashed thereat, but shewed effectually a prudent and magnanimous heart, and moste courteously comforting the pore man, she bad hym be of good cheere, and saide hee should want nothing that might bee for his ease, commaunding hym to be covered till such time as hee came to the shoare, till which time hee lay bathing in his owne bloud, which might have been an occasion to have terrified the eyes of the beholders. But such and so great was the courage and magnanimitie of our dread and soveraigne Ladie, that it never quailed. To be short, Thomas Appletree and the rest were apprehended and brought before her honorable Counsell, who with great gravitie and wisedome employed their times verie carefully, and with greate diligence examined the saide Appletree and his companions, and finding the case moste hainous and wicked, justly pronounced againste him the sentence of death, and commit him to the Marshalsea in Southwarke, from whence ye Tuisday following hee was brought through the Citie with the Knight Marshalles men, ledde up to the Tower Hill, and so to Radcliffe upp to Blackwall, and so downe to the waterside, where was a Gibet sett upp, directly placed betwixte Detforde and Greenewiche, for the execution of this malefactour, who in deed verie pitifully bewayled the offence hee had committed, and as well in prison as by the waie prepared himselfe verie penitently and willingly to offer his body to the death.

Thus verie godly hee purposed to finish his miserable and wretched life, and so prepared himselfe to ascend and goe upp the Ladder, and being on the same, he turned himselfe, and spake to the people as followeth : Good people, I am come hither to die, but God is my Judge, I never in my life intended hurt to the Queenes Most excellent Maiestie, nor meant the harme of any creature, but I pray to God with all my heart long to prosper and keepe her Highnes in health, who blesse and defende her from all perilles and daungers, who prosper her in all her affaires, and blesse her moste Honorable Counsell, giving them grace to doe all things to the glorie of God, and the benefit of this realme ; but of all things I am moste sorie for my offence, and wofully bewaile the same ; and more, I am penitent and sorie for my good Maister, Maister Henrie Carie, who hath been so grieved for my fault, suffering rebuke for the same : I would to God I had never been borne that have so grievously offended him. And with that the teares gusht oute of his eyes verie faste. This saide, hee persuaded all men to serve God, and to take an example by him, and every night and morning moved them devoutly to say the Lord's Prayer. And as the executioner had put the rope about his necke, the people cried stay, stay, stay, and with that came the right Honorable sir Christopher Hatton, Vizchamberlaine to her highnes, who enquired what hee had confessed, and being certified, as is before expressed, hee bailed his bonet, and declared, that the Queenes Maiestie had sent him thither both to make the cause open to them how hainous and greevous the offence of ye said Thomas Appletree was, and further to signifie to him her gracious pleasure ; and so continued his message, as ye may reade it printed by itself, and annexed to this discourse. Which, when he had declared, the hangman was commanded to take the roape from his necke. Appletree being come downe from the Ladder, received his pardon, and gave God and the Prince praise for so great a benefite as he had by her moste gracious bountie received. This done, Maister Vizchamberlaine saide : Good people pray for the Queenes Maiestie, and then was this prayer saide, which is usually reade (for the preservation of her Maiestie) in the Church : O Almighty and everlasting God, the Lord of Lords, and King of Kings, which dost fro' thy throne behold all the dwellers of the earth, most heartily we beseech thee with thy favour to behold our moste gracious soveraigne lady Queen Elizabeth, etc. Whereunto all the people joyfully accorded to saye Amen, crying, God save the Queen : casting up their Cappes." (Stow's *Chronicles of England.*)

One of the last cases of ordeal by battle belongs to the year 1571.

"The eighteenth of June, in Trinitie terme, there was a combat appointed to have been fought for a certeine manour and demaine lands belonging thereunto in the Ile of Hartie, adjoining to the Ile of Shepie in Kent. Simon Low and John Kime were plaintifs, and had brought a writ of right against Thomas Paramore, who offered to defend his right by battell. Whereupon the plaintiffs aforesaid accepted to answer his challenge, offering likewise to defend their right to the same manour and lands, and to prove by battell, that Paramore had no right nor good title to have the same manour and lands. Hereupon the said Thomas Paramore brought before the judges of the common plees of Westminster, one George Thorne, a big, broad, strong set fellow ; and the plaintifs Henrie Nailer, maister of defense, and servant to the right honourable the earle of Leicester, a proper slender man, and not so tall as the other. Thorne cast downe a gantlet, which Nailer tooke up, upon the sundaie before the battell should be tried. On the next morow, the matter was staied, and the parties agreed, that Paramore being in possession should have the land, and was bound in five hundred pounds to consider the plaintifs, as upon hearing the matter the judges should award. The queens majestie abhorring bloodshed, and (as the poet very well saith)

" Tristia sanguinei deuitans praelia campi "

was the taker up of the matter, in this wise. It was thought good, that for Paramore's assurance, the order should be kept touching the combat, and that the plaintifs Low and Kime should make default of appearance ; but that yet such as were sureties for Nailer their champions appearance, should bring him in ; and likewise those that were sureties for Thorne, should bring in the same Thorne, in discharge of their band ; and that the court should sit in Tuthill Fields where was prepared one plot of ground of one and twentie yards square, double railed for the combat. Without the west square a stage being set up for the judges, representing the court of the common plees.

All the compasse without the lists was set with scaffolds one above another, for people to stand and behold. There were behind the square where the judges sat, two tents, the one for Nailer, the other for Thorne. Thorne was there in the morning timelie, Nailer about seven of the clock came through London, apparelled in a doublet, and gallie gascoine breeches all of crimsin satin, cut and rased, a hat of blacke velvet, with a red feather and band, before him drums and fifes plaieng. The gantlet cast downe by George Thorne was borne before the said Nailer upon a sword's point, and his baston (a staffe of an ell long, made taper wise, tipt with horne) with his shield of hard leather was borne after him, as Askam a yeoman of the queenes gard. He came into the place at Westminster and staieng not long before the hall door, came back into the king's street, and so along thorough the Sanctuarie and Tuthill street into the field, where he staied till past nine of the clocke, and then Sir Jerome Bowes brought him to his tent: Thorne being in the tent with Sir Henrie Cheinie long before.

About ten of the clocke, the court of common plees remooved, and came to the place prepared. When the Lord chief Justice, with two other his associates were set, then Low was called solemnlie to come in, or else to lose his writ of right. Then after a certeine time, the suerties of Henrie Nailer were called to bring in the said Nailer, champion for Simon Low. And shortlie thereupon, Sir Jerome Bowes, leading Nailer by the hand, entred with him the lists, bringing him downe that square by which he entred, being on the left hand of the judges, and so about till he came to the next square, just against the judges, and there making courtesie, first with one leg and then with the other, passed foorth till he came to the middle of the place, and then made the like obeisance and so passing till they came to the barre, there he made the like courtesie, and his shield was held up aloft over his head. Nailer put off his netherstocks, and so barefoot and barelegged, save his silke scauilones to the ankles, and his dublet sleeves tied up above the elbow, and bareheaded, came in, as is aforesaid. Then were the suerties of George Thorne called to bring in the same Thorne; and immediately Sir Henry Cheinie entering at the upper end on the right hand of the judges, used the like order in comming about by his side, as Nailer had before on that other side; and so comming to the barre with like obeisance, held up his shield. Proclamation was made that none should touch the barres, nor presume to come within the same, except such as were appointed.

After all this solemne order was finished, the lord chiefe justice rehearsing

the maner of bringing the writ of right by Simon Low, of the answer made
thereunto by Paramore, of the proceeding therein, and how Paramore had
challenged to defend his right to the land by battell, by his champion Thomas
Thorne, and of the accepting the triall that was by Low with his champion
Henrie Nailer; and then for default of appearance in Low he adjudged the land
to Paramore, and dismissed the champion, acquiting the suerties of their bands.
He also willed Henrie Nailer to render againe to George Thorne his gantlet.
Whereto the said Nailer answered, that his lordship might command him anie
thing, but willingly he would not render the said gantlet to Thorne except he
could win it. And further he challenged the said Thorne to play with him
half a score blowes, to shew some pastime to the lord chiefe justice and to the
other there assembled. But Thorne answered, that he came to fight, and would
not plaie. Then the lord chiefe justice commending Nailer for his valiant
courage, commanded them both quietlie to depart the field, etc." (Stow's *Chronicles
of England.*)

APPENDICES

APPENDIX I

THAMES WATER

"Peter Morice, a Dutchman, in 1580 explained before the Lord Mayor and Aldermen his invention for raising the Thames water high enough to supply the upper parts of the City, and threw a jet of water over the steeple of St. Magnus Church. Before this time no such thing had been known in England. Whereupon the City granted him a lease for 500 years of the Thames water, and the places where his mills stood, and of one of the arches of old London Bridge, at 10s. yearly. Two years afterwards they granted him another arch on the same terms. He received large grants from the City to help him to complete this curious system of hydraulic mechanism. In the Act for rebuilding the City after the Great Fire it was provided that Thomas Morris should have power to rebuild with timber his water-house for supplying the City (18 & 19 Charles II. c. 8). The works continued in the family till 1701, when they were sold for £36,000 to Richard Soames, and afterwards became the property of a Company. On June 23rd, 1767, the fifth arch was granted for the use of the Company. By Act of Parliament, 3 Geo. IV. cap. 109, July 26th, 1822, the Acts relating to the Company were repealed. The Company were to be paid £10,000, and their works to be removed by, or at the expense of, the New River Company." (*Remembrancia.*)

This invention and the subsequent supply of the whole City with water laid on, killed the Company of Water-bearers.

"The 'Rules, Ordinances, and Statutes made by the Rulers, Wardens, and Fellowship of the Brotherhood of Saint Cristofer of the Water-bearers of London,' are dated October 20th, 1496 (*Transactions of the London and Middlesex Archæological Society*, vol. vi. p. 55). Their hall was situated in Bishopsgate Street, near Sun Street, now numbered 143 and 144, Bishopsgate Street Without:—'Robert Donkin, Citizen and Merchant Taylor of London, left by his will, dated December 1st, 1570, that messuage or howse which he purchased of the Company of Water-bearers on the 9th of October, 1568.'"

APPENDIX II

SIR HUMPHREY GILBERT'S ACADEMY

IN 1570 Sir Humphrey Gilbert laid before the Queen a plan for an Academy or University of London.

His plan was as follows :—

"Seeing that young gentlemen resort most freely to London there should be an Academy, viz. :—

1. A master for G. and L., £40.
2. Four Ushers at £20.
3. One Hebrew at £50.
4. One Logic and Rhetoric, £40.
   Exercise and instruction in English.
5. One Reader of Moral Phil., £100.
6.   ,,   ,,   ,, Natural Phil., £40.
7. Two mathematicians ea. at £100 $\begin{cases} \text{1. Arith., Geom., Fort.} \\ \text{2. Cosmog., Astronomy, Navigation.} \end{cases}$
8. Two Ushers at £40.
9. Riding Master.
10. Drill Master, £66 : 13 : 4.
11. Physician £100, with a garden.
12. Reader of Civil Law, £100.
13. Reader of Divinity, £100.
14.   ,, ,, Law, £100.
15. Teacher of French, £26 ; Spanish, £26 ; Italian, £26 ; Dutch, £26 ;
    with Ushers at £10.
16. Master of Defence, £36.
17. Dancing and Vaulting School, £26.
18. Music, £26.
19. Steward, Cooks, Butlers, etc., £600.
20. Minister and Clerks, £66 : 13 : 4.
21. Teacher of Heraldry, £26.
22. Librarian, £26.
23. Treasurer, £100.
24. Rector.
    Amounting in all to £2966 : 13 : 4 a year.

"By erecting this academie, there shall be hereafter an effect, no gentleman within the Realm but good for something ; whereas now the most parts of them are good for nothing. Your Majesty and your successive Courtes shall be for ever, instead of a nurserie of idlenes, become a most noble Academy of Chevallrie, Policy, and Philosophie."

APPENDIX III

PETITION AGAINST ALIENS

"In most pitious and lamentable wise shewing and complaining unto your most excellent highness, your humble, true and faithful subjects, and contynualle orators, that is to sey, mercers, grocers, drapers, goldsmythes, skynners, haberdassers, Taylers, ledyrsellers, pursers, poyntmakers, glovers, powchemakers, Sadlers, Cutlers, pewterers, Cowpers, gyrdlers, founders, Cordeners; vyntners, sporyars, joyners, and all other Chapmen, retailers, occupiers of every craft, mystery, and occupation, in all and every your Cities, ports, towns, and boroughs within this noble realm of England. That where your said realm and land is so inhabited with a great multitude, needy people, strangers of divers nations, as Frenchmen, galymen, pycardis, flemings, keteryckis, Spaynyars, Scottis, Lombards, and divers other nations, that your liege people, Englishmen, cannot imagine nor tell wherto nor to what occupation that they shalle use or put their children to lerne or occupy within your said cities, boroughs, ports and towns of this your said realm, with many other Chappmen and poor commons using the said crafts, mysteries, and occupation in all and every shire of this your said realm! . . . now it is so, most redoubted Sovereign lord, that innumerable needy people of galymen, Frenchmen and other great multitudes of alien strangers, do circuit, wander, go to and fro, in every your Cities, ports, towns, and boroughs in all places, as well within franchises, privileges, and liberties, as without, to every man door, taking up standing, and there make their shows, markets and sales of divers wares and merchandise to their own singular profits, advantage, and advails, to the great disturbance, empoverishing, hurt, loss, and utter undoing of your natural subjects and liege people in all and every city, port, borough, town, and places of your said realm : and also of more convenience for their advancement, the said Aliens strangers use to hire them servants of their own nation, or other strangers, or go about wander, and retail in all cities, ports, towns and boroughs, and all other places to bye, sell, retail, and occupy seats and merchandise at their pleasure, without lawful authority or license, contrary to the said acts and statutes afore provided, and contrary to the Charters, liberties, constitutions, and confirmations made, given, and granted by your said noble predecessor, afore rehearsed : by means of which unlawful retailing so customably haunted, used, and occupied, your liege people and natural subjects, their wives, children, and servants, be utterly decayed, empoverished, and undone, in this world, unless your excellent and benign grace of your tender pity be unto your said subjects gracious at this time showing in this behalf. And without a short remedy be had herein, your said subjects be not able, nor shall not be of power to pay their rents nor also to maintain their poor households and to bear lot and scot and all other priests' benevolences, and charges in time of need and war for the defence of your grace and of this your said realm, for the repressing, subduing, and vanquishing of your ancient enemies Frenchmen, and all other their adherents and banished men outwards." (*Furnivall.*)

APPENDIX IV

THE ORDER OF PROCESSIONS

" Messengers of the Court.
Gentlemen of lesse note.
Esquiers.
Esquiers of the Body.
Clarkes of the Chancery.
Clarkes of the Signet.
Clarkes of the Privy Seale.
Clarkes of the Counsell.
Masters of the Chancery.
Knights Batchlers.
Knights Banneretts.
              Trumpets soundinge.
Serjeants at Law.
Queenes Serjeants.
The Queen's Attorney and the Queen's Solicitor together.
The Baron of the Exchequer.
The Judges of the Common Pleas.
The Judges of the King's Bench.
The Lorde Chiefe Justice of the Common Pleas, and the Lord
    Chiefe Justice of the Exchequer.
The Lord Chief Justice of England, and the Master of the
    Rolls.
The Younger Sonnes of Nobility.
Knight of the Privy Counsell.
Knights of the Garter.
The Principall Secretary.
The Treasurer of the Queen's House, and Controller of the
    Queen's House.
The Queen's Clarke and Hat-bearer.
Two Heralds.
The Barons two and two.
Two Heralds.
The Bishops.
The Vicounts.
Two Heralds.
The Earls.

An Herald or King of Armes.

The Marques, etc.

Places for Dukes.

The Lord Chancelor of England.

The Lord Treasurer of England.

The Archbishop of Canterbury.

Clarenciaux King of Armes.

The Sergeants at Armes with Staves.

Bearer of the Capp Royal, and the Carrier of the Marshall Rod of England.

The Sword bearer on either side him.

The Great Chamberleine of England.

The Steward of the Queenes House on the left side.

Then the Queene in her Chariotte.

The Four Querryes of the Stable come next, with the Queen's footmen: and without them all in a ranckc wayted the Pentioners with their Partisans.

Then the Master of the Horse.

Then the Chamberleine of the Queenes House.

Then the Vice-chamberleine with many Noblewomen, Ladyes and others.

In this order passing to St. Peter's Church, in Westminster: was there met with the Queen's Almoner, the Dean of Westminster with the Prebends and all the Quier in their Copes."

APPENDIX V

THE CHANGES OF RITUAL

On 28th July 1900 was published in the *Athenæum* of that date a paper by the late Rev. Prebendary Kitto, Vicar of St. Martin's in the Fields, on the changes effected in the rites and ceremonies of that church during the years 1537-1560 or thereabouts. This instructive document was compiled from the accounts and papers preserved in the archives of the church.

Thus the ritual remained much the same during the reign of Henry VIII. as it had been before the commencement of the Reformation. They provided, as of old, candles, palms, incense; they hallowed sacred coals for Easter Eve; they provided lights for the font, for the rood loft, and for the altars; they set up the Easter sepulchre; they used the great Paschal Candle, the tabernacle, and the pyx; they maintained the side altars, and they not only repaired the vestments but they received gifts of new vestments. They had obits and "minds," celebrated mass and kept up the images.

In 1538 lights before images were forbidden; but a perpetual light was maintained at the high altar.

In 1539 the Parish sold the iron and latten candlesticks which had been used for the images.

In the same year a Bible was bought for the church. It cost 12s. 8d.

In 1540 Henry is described under the title of "Defender of the Faith and Supreme Head, under God, of the Church of England and Ireland."

In 1547 they sold all the wax they had in stock, according to the injunction.

In 1548 no more lights were allowed. The Parish sold the rest of their candlesticks, and bought a Paraphrase of the Gospel and a Communion Cup; they also whitewashed the church, in order, I suppose, to obliterate the pictures.

In 1549 the altars were stripped: there were to be no more flowers or garlands, no incense and no lights.

In 1550 they set up a box for the poor; sold their vestments; bought white surplices, and put a green cloth over the "Communion Table."

In 1553 they sold the "old broken stuff of the Rood Loft" and made "Communion Pews."

In the same year they were made to feel the mutability of things religious, because everything had to be restored at great expense. Their candlesticks, however, were of tin. They bought a cross for processions; a mass-book, a holy water stoup with a sprinkle; a basket for the holy bread; a pyx and all the other old vessels. Also, because under Edward they had written texts on the walls, they were now ordered to wipe them all out.

In 1559 they began to go back again to the Edwardian time, but not immediately. In 1560 the Bible was restored.

It is worthy of note that the parish officers were a little uncertain, after their melancholy experience, of the stability of things. They therefore kept the vessels bought in the time of Queen Mary until 1569, when, feeling somewhat reassured, they sold them all.

APPENDIX VI

GOLDSMITHS' ROW

"OPPOSITE to the Cross in Cheapside, on the south side of the street, there stood a superb pile of buildings, called Goldsmiths' Row, extending from the west to Bread Street. This Row was erected in 1491, by Thomas Wood, Goldsmith, Sheriff of London. Stow describes it in 1598 as 'the most beautiful frame of fair houses and shops that be within the walls of London, or elsewhere in England. It containeth in number ten fair dwelling-houses and fourteen shops, all in one frame, uniformly builded four stories high, beautified toward the street with the Goldsmith arms and the likeness of Woodmen (in memory of the founder's name) riding on monstrous beasts, all of which is cast in lead, richly painted over and gilt.' 'This said front was again new painted and gilt over in the year 1594, Sir Richard Martin being then Mayor, and keeping the Mayoralty in one of them' (Stow, edition 1633). 'At this time the City greatly abounded in riches and splendour, such as former ages were unacquainted with. Then it was beautiful to behold the glorious appearance of Goldsmiths' shops in the South Row of Cheapside, which, in a continued course, reached from the Old Change to Bucklersbury, exclusive of four shops only of other trades in all that space' (Maitland's *History of London*, edition 1760, vol. i. p. 301). King Charles the First in 1629 issued a Proclamation ordering the Goldsmiths to plant themselves, for the use of their trade, in Cheapside or Lombard Street. The Lords of the Council, in 1637, sent a letter to the Lord Mayor and Aldermen (*vide* vii. 197), ordering them to close every shop in Cheapside and Lombard Street that did not carry on the trade of a Goldsmith, about twenty-four in all, Grove and one Widow Hill, Stationers; Dover, a Milliner; Brown, a Bandseller; Sanders, a Drugster; Medcalfe, a Cook; Edwards, a Girdler, etc.— Rushworth's 'State Papers.'" (*Remembrancia*, p. 106, n. 1.)

APPENDIX VII

LONDON PLANTS

In the *Archæologia* may be found the following enumeration of plants grown in an Elizabethan garden :—

Adderstong—Ophioglossum.
Affodyll—Narcissus Pseudo-narcissus.   Affodyll Daffadilly.
Appyl—Apple—Pyrus Malus ; and garden varieties.
Asche tre—Ash—Fraxinus excelsior.
Auans—Geum urbanum, Avance or Avens.
Betony—Saachys Betonica.
Borage—Borrago officinalis.
Bryswort—Bruisewort, Brusewort or Brisewort—Bellis perenni.
Bugull—Bugle—Ajuga reptans.
Bygull—Bigold—Chrysanthemom segetum.
Calamynte—Calamintha officinalis.   "The garden mynt."
Camemyl—Chamomile—Anthemis nobilis.   "Camamyll."
Carsyndylls? "Cars or Carses—cress."
Centory—Great Centuary.
Clarey—Clary—Salvia sclarea.
Comfery—Comfrey—Symphytum officinale.
Coryawnder—Coriander.
Cowslippe—Cowslip.
Dytawnder—Dittander and Dittany.
Egrimoyne—Egremoyne.
Elysauwder—Smyrnium Olusatrum.
Feldwort—Felwort and Fieldwort.
Floscampi? Campion?
Foxglove—Digitalis purpurea.
Fynel—Fennel.
Garleke—Garlick.
Gladyn—Iris foetidissima or Iris Pseudacorus.
Gromel—Gromwell.
Growdyswyly—Growndyswyly—Groundswyll.
Hasel tre—Hazel tree.
Haw thorn—Hawthorn.
Henbane—Hyoscyamus niger.
Herbe Ion.
Herbe Robert—Geranium Robertianum.
Herbe Water—Herb Walter.

Hertystonge—Hartystonge—Hart's-tongue.

Holyhocke—Althaea rosea, or Malva sylvestris or Althaea officinalis.

Honysoke—Honeysuckle.

Horehound—Marrubium vulgare.

Horsel—Horselle—Horsehele.

Hyndesall ?—Hind-heal.

Langbefe, generally supposed to be Helminthia echioides.

Lavyndull—Lavandula vera.

Leke—Leek.

Letows—Lettuce.

Lyly—Lily.

Lyverwort.

Merege.　Cannot identify.

Moderwort—Motherwort.

Mouseer—Mouse ear.

Myntys—Mint.

Nepte—Nep or Neppe or Nept.

Oculus Christi—Salvia verbanaca.

Orage—Atriplex hortensis.

Orpy—Orpies.

Ownyns and Oynet.

Parrow ?　Cannot identify　? mistake for Yarrow.

Pelyter—Pellitory.

Percely—Perselye—Parsley.

Pere—Pear.

Peruynke—Periwinkle.

Primrole—Primrose.

Polypody—Polypodium vulgare.

Pympernold—Pimpernel.

Radysche—Radish.

Redenay.　Cannot identify.

Rewe—Rue.

Rose—Rosa, red and white.

Rybwort—Ribwort.

Saferowne—Saffron.

Sage—Salvia officinalis.

Sanycle—Sanicle.

Sauerey—Savory.

Scabyas—Scabious.

Seueny—Seniue.　Common mustard or field senive.

Sowthrynwode—Southernwood.

Sperewort—Spearwort.

Spynage—Spinach.

Strowberys—Strawberries.

Stychewort—Stichewort.

Tansay—Tansy.

Totesayne—Tutsan—Hypericum Androsæmum.

Tuncarse—Town cress.

Tyme—Thyme.

Valeryan—a general name for Valeriana.

Verveyn—Vervain—Verbena officinalis.

Violet—Viola.   Generally V. odorata.

Vynys and Vyne tre—Vine.

Walwort—Walwort or Danewort of Dwarf elder.

Warmot—Wormwood.

Waterlyly—Water lily.

Weybrede—Plantago major.

Woderofe—Woodruffe.

Wodesour—Woodsour.

Wurtys—Wortys.

Wyldtesyl—Teazel.

Ysope—Hyssop.   "Ysopus is ysope."

(Archæologia, vol. l. p. 167.)

APPENDIX VIII

THE GALLANTS' WALK IN ST. PAUL'S

"Your mediterranean isle is then the only gallery, wherein the pictures of all your true fashionate and complemental Gulls are, and ought to be hung up. Into that gallery carry your neat body: but take heed you pick out such an hour, when the main shoal of islanders are swimming up and down. And first observe your doors of entrance, and your exit: not much unlike the players at the theatres: keeping your decorums, even in phantasticality. As for example: if you prove to be a northern gentleman, I would wish you to pass through the north door, more often especially than any of the other: and so, according to your countries take note of your entrances.

Now for your venturing into the walk. Be circumspect, and wary what pillar you come in at: and take heed in any case, as you love the reputation of your honour, that you avoid the serving-man's log, and approach not within five fathom of that pillar: but bend your course directly in the middle line, that the whole body of the church may appear to be yours: where, in view of all, you may publish your suit in what manner you affect most, either with the slide of your cloak from the one shoulder: and then you must, as 'twere in anger, suddenly snatch at the middle of the inside, if it be taffeta at the least: and so by that means your costly lining is betrayed, or else by the pretty advantage of compliment. But one note by the way I do especially woo you to, the neglect of which makes many of our gallants cheap and ordinary, that by no means you be seen above four turns: but in the fifth make yourself away, either in some of the semsters' shops, the new tobacco-office, or amongst the booksellers, where, if you cannot read, exercise your smoke, and inquire who has writ against this divine weed, etc. For this withdrawing yourself a little will much benefit your suit, which else, by too long walking, would be stale to the whole spectators: but howsoever if Paul's jacks be once up with their elbows, and quarrelling to strike eleven: as soon as ever the clock has parted them, and ended the fray with his hammer, let not the Duke's gallery contain you any longer, but pass away apace in open view: in which departure, if by chance you either encounter, or aloof off throw your inquisitive eye upon any knight or squire, being your familiar, salute him not by his name of Sir such a one, or so: but call him Ned, or Jack, etc. This will set off your estimation with great men: and if, though there be a dozen companies between you, 'tis the better, he call aloud to you, for that is most genteel, to know where he shall find you at two o'clock: tell him at such an ordinary or such: and be sure to name those that are dearest, and whither none but gallants resort. After dinner you may appear again, having translated yourself out of your English cloth cloak into a light Turkey grogram, if you have that happiness of shifting: and then be seen, for a turn or two, to correct your teeth with some quill or silver instrument, and to cleanse your gums with a wrought handkerchief: it skills not whether you dined, or no: that is best known to your stomach: or in what place you dined: though it were with cheese, of your mother's own making, in your chamber, or study.

Now if you chance to be a gallant not much crost among citizens: that is, a gallant in the mercer's books, exalted for satins and velvets: if you be not so much blest to be crost (as I hold it the greatest blessing in the world to be great in no man's books): your Paul's walk is your only refuge: the Duke's tomb is a sanctuary: and will keep you alive from worms, and land-rats, that long to be feeding on your carcass: there you may spend your legs in winter a whole afternoon: converse, plot, and talk any thing:

jest at your creditor, even to his face: and in the evening, even by lamp-light, steal out: and so cozen a whole covey of abominable catchpolls.. Never be seen to mount the steps into the quire, but upon a high festival day, to prefer the fashion of your doublet: and especially if the singing-boys seem to take note of you: for they are able to buzz your praises above their anthems, if their voices have not lost their maiden-heads: but be sure your silver spurs dog your heels, and then the boys will swarm about you like so many white butterflies: when you in the open quire shall draw forth a perfumed embroidered purse, the glorious sight of which will entice many countrymen from their devotion to wondering: and quoit silver into the boys' hands, that it may be heard above the first lesson, although it be read in a voice as big as one of the great organs.

This noble and notable act being performed, you are to vanish presently out of the quire, and to appear again in the walk: but in any wise be not observed to tread there long alone: for fear you be suspected to be a gallant cashiered from the society of captains, and fighters." (*The Gull's Horn Book.*)

APPENDIX IX

MONTHLY PROVISION TABLE THROUGH THE YEAR 1605

		Jan.	Feb.	Mar.	April.	May.	June.	July.	August.	Sept.	Oct.	Nov.	Dec.
M E A T	Rooe	...	...	...	...	...	—	—	—	—	—	—	—
	Bucke	...	...	...	...	—	—	—	—	—	...	...	...
	Braune	—	—	...	...	...	...	...	...	...	...	...	...
	Muttone	—	—	—	—	—	—	—	—	—	—	—	—
	Pigge	—	—	—	—	...	—	—	—	—	—	—	—
	Hare	—	—	—	...	—	—	—	—	—	—	—	—
	Beefe	—	—	—	—	—	—	—	—	—	—	—	—
	Veale	—	—	—	—	—	—	—	—	—	—	—	—
	Lambe	—	...	—	—	—	—	—	—	...	...	—	—
	Dowe	—	—	...	...	...	...	...	...	...	—	—	—
	Baconn	—	—	—	—	—	—	—	—	—	—	—	—
	Porcke	—	—	—	—	—	—	...	...	...	—	—	—
	Rabbetts	—	—	...	—	—	—	—	—	—	—	—	—
	Hinde	—	—	...	—	...	...	...	...	...	—	—	—
	Kidde	...	—	—	—	—	—	—	—	—	—	—	—
	Stagges	...	...	...	...	—	—	—	—	—	...	...	...
	Gote	...	...	...	...	...	...	...	—	—	...		
F O W L	Bustarde	—	—	—	—	—	...	...	...	...	—	—	—
	Goose	—	—	—	...	...	...	...	...	—	—	—	—
	Green Goose	...	...	...	...	...	—	—	—	...	...	...	...
	Heron	—	...	—	...	...	—	—	—	...	—	—	...
	Egrett	—	...	...	—	—	...	...	...	...	...	...	...
	Widgeon	—	—	—	...	...	...	...	...	...	—	—	—
	Curlewiake	—	...	...	...	...	...	...	...	...	...	—	—
	Turkie	—	—	—	—	—	—	—	—	—	—	—	—
	Phesaunte	—	—	—	—	—	—	—	...	...	...	—	—
	Pullett	—	—	...	—	—	...	...	...	...	...	—	—
	Bayninge	—	—	—	—	—	...	...	...	...	...	—	—
	Ruffe	—	—	—	—	—	...	...	...	...	—	—	—
	Plover	—	—	...	...	...	...	...	...	...	—	—	—
	Snipe	—	—	—	...	...	...	...	...	...	—	—	—
	Partreges	—	—	—	—	—	—	—	—	—	—	—	—
	Larckes	—	—	—	—	—	—	—	...	...	—	—	—
	Crayne	—	—	—	...	...	...	...	...	...	—	—	—
	Storcke	—	—	—	—	...	...	...	...	...	...	—	—
	Shoveller	—	...	...	...	...	...	...	—	—	—	—	—
	Brue	—	...	...	—	—	...	...	...	...	...	...	...
	Curlewe	—	—	—	—	...	...	...	...	...	...	—	—
	Gull	—	...	...	...	...	—	—	—	—	—	...	—

MONTHLY PROVISION TABLE—*continued*

	Jan.	Feb.	Mar.	April.	May.	June.	July.	August.	Sept.	Oct.	Nov.	Dec.
F O W L Peacocke	—	—	—	—	—	—	—	—	—	...	—	—
Henne	—	—	—	...	...	...	...	...	...	...	...	—
Redshanke	—	—	—	...	...	...	...	...	...	...	—	—
Knotte	—	—	—	...	...	...	—	—	—	...	—	—
Blankett	—	...	...	...	...	—	...	...	...	...	...	...
Stockdoves	—	—	—	...	...	...	...	...	...	...	...	...
Indecocke	—	...	—	...	...	...	...	...	...	...	...	...
Quales	—	...	—	...	...	...	...	...	...	...	—	—
Thrush	...	—	—	...	...	—	...	...	...	—	—	—
Pidgeons	...	—	—	...	—	—	—	—	...	—	—	—
Stennts	...	—	—	...	...	—	...	...	...	...	—	—
Turtells	...	—	—	...	...	...	...	...	...	...	—	—
Goldnye	...	—	—	...	...	...	...	...	...	...	...	—
Jedcokes	...	—	—	...	...	...	...	...	...	...	...	...
Pevetts	...	...	...	...	...	—	—	...	...	...	...	...
Sea Pie	...	...	...	...	...	—	...	...	...	...	...	...
Pea Chicks	...	...	...	...	...	—	...	...	...	...	...	...
Petterells	...	...	...	...	...	—	—	...	...	...	...	...
Stares	...	...	...	...	...	—	...	...	...	...	...	...
Churre	...	...	...	...	—	...	...	...	...	...	...	...
Sparrows	—	...	...	...	...	...	...	...	...	...	...	...
Swanne	—	—	—	...	...	...	...	...	...	...	...	—
Hernne	—	...	...	...	...	...	...	...	...	—	..	...
Bitter	—	—	—	...	...	—	—	...	...	—	...	—
Mallarde	—	—	—	...	...	...	...	...	...	—	—	...
Cudberduce	—	...	...	...	...	...	...	...	...	...	—	—
Cullver	—	—	—	...	...	...	...	...	...	—	—	—
Caponne	—	...	...	—	—	—	—	...	...	...	—	—
Godwite	—	—	—	—	—	...	—	—	...	...	—	—
Ree	—	—	—	...	...	—	...	...	...	...	—	—
Dotterell	—	...	...	—	—	—	...	...	...	...	—	...
Teale	—	—	—	...	...	...	...	...	...	...	—	—
Woodcocke	—	...	—	...	...	...	...	...	...	...	—	—
Plover	—	...	...	...	...	...	...	...	...	...	...	...
Fellfaire	—	—	...	...	...	...	...	...	—	...	...	...
Finshes	—	—	—	...	...	...	...	...	—	...	...	...
Smalebirds	...	—	—	...	...	...	...	...	...	...	...	...
Chickens	...	...	...	—	—	—	—	—	...	...	...	...
Chitt	...	...	...	...	—	—	—	—	...	...	...	...
Kennecis	...	...	...	...	—	—	—	—	...	...	...	...
Mewe	...	...	...	...	...	—	—	—	...	...	...	...
Tearne	...	...	...	...	...	—	—	...	...	...	...	...
Blackbirds	...	...	...	...	...	—	...	...	...	—	—	—
Young Turkies	...	...	...	...	...	—	—	—	...	...	...	...
Auk	...	...	...	...	...	...	—	—	...	...	...	...
Martines	...	...	...	...	...	...	—	—	...	...	...	...
Crouces	...	...	...	...	...	...	—	—	...	...	...	...
Dunlings	...	...	...	...	...	...	...	...	—	...	...	...
Railes	...	...	...	...	...	...	...	...	—	—	...	...
Lapwine	...	...	...	...	...	...	...	...	...	—	—	...
Golne	...	...	...	...	...	...	...	...	...	...	—	...

MONTHLY PROVISION TABLE—*continued*

		Jan.	Feb.	Mar.	April.	May.	June.	July.	August.	Sept	Oct.	Nov.	Dec.
F I S H	Kennecis	...	...	...	...	...	...	...	...	...	...	...	...
	Pearches	...	—	—	...	...	—	—	—	—	—	—	—
	Linge	—	—	—	—	—	—	—	—	—	—	—	—
	Tunny	—	—	—	—	—	...	...	...	...	...	—	—
	Turbutt	—	...	...	—	—	—	—	—	—	—	—	—
	Whitinge	—	—	—	—	—	—	—	—	—	—	—	—
	Soles	—	—	—	—	—	—	—	—	—	—	...	—
	Lamprons	—	—	—	—	—	...	...	...	...	—	—	—
	Carpe	—	...	...	...	...	—	...	...	—	—	—	—
	Tench	—	...	...	—	—	—	—	—	—	—	—	—
	Oysters	—	—	—	—	—	...	...	...	—	—	—	—
	Cockells	—	...	...	—	—	...	...	...	—	—	—	—
	Codde	—	—	—	—	—	—	—	—	—	—	—	—
	Porposse	—	—	—	—	—	...	...	...	...	...	—	—
	Haddocke	—	—	—	—	—	...	—	—	...	...	—	—
	Sealumpe	—	—	—	—	—	—	—	—	...	...	—	—
	Place	—	—	—	—	—	—	—	—	—	—	...	...
	Chevine	—	—	—	—	—	—	—	—	—	—	...	...
	Pike	—	—	—	—	—	—	—	—	—	—	...	...
	Eles	—	—	—	—	—	—	—	—	...	...	—	—
	Crabbs	—	—	—	—	—	—	—	—	—	—	—	—
	Crevices	—	...	...	—	—	—	—	—	—	—	—	—
	Styrgeon	—	—	—	—	—	—	—	—	—	—	—	—
	Seals	—	—	—	—	...	—	—	—	...	—	—	—
	Thornebacke	—	—	—	—	—	—	...	...	...	...	—	—
	Salmon	—	—	—	—	—	—	...	...	...	...	—	—
	Dace	...	—	—	—	—	—	—	—	—	—	—	—
	Habberdine	...	—	—	—	—	—	—	—	—	—	—	—
	Roche	...	—	—	—	—	—	—	—	—	—	—	—
	Mussels	...	—	—	—	...	...	...	...	—	—	—	—
	Crefishes	...	—	—	...	...	...	...	...	...	...	...	...
	Smeltes	—	—	—	—	—	—	—	...	...	...	...	...
	Barbell	—	—	—	—	—	—	—	—	—	—	...	...
	Breame	—	—	—	—	—	—	—	—	—	—	...	...
	Rudds	—	...	...	—	—	—	—	—	—	—	...	...
	Lobsters	—	—	—	—	—	—	—	—	—	—	—	—
	Praunes	—	—	—	...	...	...	...	...	—	...	...	...
	Herings White	...	...	...	—	...	...	...	...	...	...	...	...
	Herings Red	...	...	...	—	...	...	...	...	...	...	...	...
	Herringes	...	...	...	...	...	...	...	...	...	...	...	...
	Britt	...	...	...	—	...	—	—	—	...	...	...	...
	Conger	...	...	...	—	...	—	...	...	...	...	...	...
	Cunninge	...	...	...	—	...	—	...	...	...	...	...	...
	Goodgions	...	...	...	—	...	—	—	—	—	—	...	...
	Rochetts	...	...	...	—	—	—	—	—	—	—	...	...
	River Trout	...	...	...	—	—	...	...	—	—	...	...	...
	Trout	...	...	...	—	—	—	—	—	—	...	...	...
	Flounders	...	...	...	—	—	—	—	...	—	—	—	...
	Lamprais	...	...	...	—	—	...	...	...	...	...	...	—
	Mades	...	...	...	—	—	—	—	—	—	—	...	...
	Loche	...	...	...	—	...	...	...	...	...	...	...	—

MONTHLY PROVISION TABLE—*continued*

	Jan.	Feb.	Mar.	April.	May.	June.	July.	August.	Sept.	Oct.	Nov.	Dec.
Gurnard	...	...	...	—	—	—	—	—	—	—	...	...
Sprates	...	...	...	—	...	...	...	...	...	...	...	...
Dabes	...	...	...	—	—	—	...	—	—	—	...	—
Dory	...	...	...	—	—	—	—	—	—	—	...	...
Millett	...	...	...	—	—	—	—	—	...	...	...	...
Perches	...	...	...	—	—	...	...	...	...	...	...	...
Burbott	...	...	...	—	—	—	...	...	...	...	...	...
Menewes	...	...	...	—	...	...	...	...	...	...	...	...
Mackarell	...	...	...	...	—	—	—	—	...	...	...	...
Shads	...	...	...	...	—	...	—	...	...	...	...	...
Mopps	...	...	...	...	...	—	—	...	...	...	...	...
Breate	...	...	...	...	...	...	—	—	—	—	—	...
Smalcod	...	...	...	...	...	...	...	...	...	...	—	—
Shrimps	...	...	...	...	...	...	...	...	...	...	...	—
Perrewinkell	...	...	...	...	...	...	...	...	...	...	...	—

(FISH)

Maitland gives a Table of Prices for the years 1274, 1302, 1314, 1531, and 1550. Note that in the years 1314 and 1550 provisions were excessively dear.

	1274.	1300 or 1302.	1314.	1531.	1550.
A Fat Cock	...	1½d.	...	¾d.	...
The best Hen	3½d.	...	1½d.	...	9d.
,, Pullet	1¾d.	¾d.	...	...	6d.
,, Capon	2d.	2½d.	2½d.	1s.	1s. 4d. to 1s. 8d.
,, Goose (according to season)	5d. or 4d.	4d.	3d.	...	6d. to 9d.
,, Wild Goose	4d.	...	...	...	...
,, Pigeon	3 for 1d.	...	3 for 1d.	12 for 10d.	12 for 1s. 2d.
,, Mallard	3½d.	1½d.	...	...	...
,, Wild Duck	1¾d.	...	...	...	...
,, Partridge	3½d.	1½d.	...	...	...
,, Larks (per dozen)	12 for 1d.	...	...	12 for 5d.	12 for 8d.
,, Pheasant	4d.	...	...	...	...
,, Heron	6d.	6d.	...	...	2s. 6d.
,, Plover	1d.	1d.	...	...	4d.
,, Swan	3s.	3s.	...	...	6s. 8d.
,, Crane	3s.	1s.	...	...	6s.
,, Peacock	1d.	...	...	...	...
,, Coney	4d.	...	...	...	...
,, Hare	3½d.	...	...	...	...
,, Kid (according to season)	10d. or 6d.	...	...	...	...
,, Lamb	6d. or 4d.	1s. 4d. or 4d.	...	...	...
,, Plaice	1½d.	...	...	...	...
,, Soles (per dozen)	3d.	...	...	...	...

PROVISION TABLE—*continued.*

	1274.	1300 or 1302.	1314.	1531.	1550.
The best Mullet	2d.	...	...	...	...
„ Haddock	2d.	...	...	...	...
„ Conger	1s.	...	...	...	...
„ Turbot	6d.	...	...	...	...
„ Mackerel	1d.	...	...	...	...
„ Gurnard	1d.	...	...	...	...
„ Herring (according to season)	6 for 1d. or 12 for 1d.	...	...	...	...
„ Lamprey	4d.	...	...	...	...
„ Oysters	2d. a gallon	...	...	...	...
„ Salmon (according to season)	5s. or 3s.	...	...	...	...
„ Eels	25 for 2d.	...	...	...	...
„ Smelts	100 for 1d.	...	...	...	...
A Quarter of Wheat	...	4s.	...	...	8s. to 13s.
„ Pease	...	2s. 6d.	...	...	3s. to 5s.
„ Oats	...	2s.	...	...	4s.
A Bull	...	7s. 6d.	...	...	...
A Cow	...	6s.	12s.	...	...
A Fat Sheep	...	1s.	...	2s. 10d.	2s. 4d. to 4s. 4d.
An Ewe	...	8d.	...	...	1s. 8d. to 2s. 6d.
An Ox	...	...	£1:4s. or 16s.	£1 : 6 : 8	£2:5s. to £1:8s.
A Hog	...	...	3s. 4d.	3s. 8d.	...
Eggs	...	...	20 a 1d.	...	...

APPENDIX X

EXECUTIONS

THE following is a list of executions which took place in the thirty years ending 1586. It shows the various crimes which were then considered capital :—

1563. A soldier executed at Newhaven for drawing his weapon without orders.
1563. A sergeant and soldier executed for drawing their weapons against their captain.
1569. Philip Mestrell a Frenchman, and two Englishmen, hanged for counterfeiting money.
1569. Sixty rebels executed at Durham.
1569. A 'prentice hanged for murdering his master.
1569. Five rebels executed at York.
1570. Thomas and Christopher Norton executed for treason.
1570. John Throckmorton and five others executed for treason.
1570. John Felton hanged for nailing the Pope's Bull to the Bishop of London's Palace.
1570. Two young men hanged for debasing coin.
1570. Dr. John Storie hanged for high treason.
1571. Rebecca Chamber burnt for poisoning her husband.
1572. Barneie, Mather, and Rolfe, hanged for treason.
1572. Martin Bullocke hanged for robbery and murder.
1572. Duke of Norfolk beheaded for treason.
1573. Percy, Earl of Northumberland, beheaded as a conspirator.
1573. John Hall and Oswald Wilkinson hanged for treason.
1573. A man hanged for murder.
1573. George Browne hanged for murder.
1573. Anne Sanders, Anne Drurie, and trustie Roger hanged as accessories to murder.
1573. Anthonie Browne hanged for felony.
1574. Peter Burchet hanged for murder.
1575. Two Dutch Anabaptists burnt at Smithfield.
1575. Twenty-two pirates executed.
1575. Thomas Greene, goldsmith, hanged for clipping coin.
1576. A woman burnt at Tunbridge for poisoning her husband.
1576. A man hanged at Maidstone as an accessory to poisoning.
1577. Cuthbert Maine hanged as a Romanist.
1577. John Nelson and Thomas Sherewood hanged for denying the Queen's supremacy.
1577. John de Loy and five Englishmen executed at Norwich for counterfeiting coin.
1577. Seven pirates hanged at Wapping.
1577. An Irishman hanged on Mile End Green for murder.
1580. A man named Glover hanged for murder.
1580. Richard Dod hanged for murder.

1580. William Randall hanged for conjuring.

1581. A man hanged at St. Thomas Waterings for begging by a licence signed by the Queen's own hand counterfeited.

1581. Edward Hance a seminary priest hanged.

1581. Edmund Campion, Ralfe Sherwin, Alexander Briars, hanged for high treason.

1581. John Paine executed at Chelmsford for high treason.

1581. Thomas Foord, John Shert, Robert Johnson, priests, hanged for designs against Elizabeth.

1582. Laurence Richardson and Thomas Catcham executed for Romanism.

1582. Philip Prise hanged in Fleet Street for killing a Sheriff.

1583. Thomas Worth and Alice Shepheard hanged in Shoolane for killing a 'prentice.

1583. Elias Shackar hanged at Bury St. Edmunds for spreading seditious literature.

1583. Ten priests hanged.

1583. John Lewes burnt at Norwich for heresy.

1583. John Slade and John Bodie hanged for high treason.

1583. Ten horsedealers hanged at Smithfield for robbery.

1583. Edward Arden hanged for treason.

1583. William Carter hanged for high treason.

1584. Francis Throckemorton hanged for treason.

1584. William Parrie hanged for treason.

1585. Thomas Awfeld and Thomas Weblie hanged for publishing seditious matter.

1586. Two seminary priests hanged at Tyburn.

1586. A witch burnt at Smithfield.

1586. A woman executed at Tyburn for adultery.

1586. Two priests hanged at Tyburn for treason.

1586. Jone Cason hanged for witchcraft.

1586. A man named Foule hanged for robbing his wife.

1586. Henry Elks hanged for counterfeiting the Queen's signature.

1586. Seven persons condemned for treason.

1586. John Ballard, a priest, executed for conspiring with Anthony Babington against Elizabeth. With him were executed John Savage, Barnewell, Tichborne, Tilneie, Edward Abingdon, Anthony Babington.

1586. Thomas Salisbury executed for treason. With him suffered Henry Dun, Edward Jones, Charnocke, Robert Gage, Jerom Bellamie.

1586. Three seminary priests hanged at Tyburn.

1563-1586—76 Executed for high treason.

       71 Rebels.

       17 Murder.

        3 Military offences.

       12 Counterfeiting and clipping coin.

        2 Counterfeiting Queen's signature.

       29 Pirates.

        2 Witchcraft and conjuring.

        3 Heresy.

       12 Robbery.

        1 Adultery.

APPENDIX XI

PLAN OF TOTTENHAM COURT

(Marquis of Salisbury's Collection, Hatfield House)

(Endorsed 1) The plot of Toten'am Coorte.

(Endorsed 2) Ap. 1591 Totenham Cort.

Below the plan is written :—

" M^d. [memorandum] there doth belonge to the said Scite of Tottenham Court two other Closes over and above the pastures mentioned in this plotte; And not here mentioned by reason they lye so farr distaunt from the said londes mentioned in this plott : Viz the one of the said Closes doth lye in Kentishe Towne in the said Countie, distaunt one Mile and more from the farthest part Northward of the ground mentioned in the said plott, late in the Tenure of Widowe Glover : And the other Close contayning 4. Acres by estimacõn doth lye in the parishe of St Pancrasse in the said Countie now or late in the Tenure of Willm̃ Bunche, distaunt from the South part of the saied landes mentioned in the said plott one quarter of A myle : wch saied two Closes wth two Tenem^ts there (As I am enfourmed) are demised unto Serieaunt [Serjeant] Haynes for certaine yeares yet enduring, by the right Honourable Henry late Earle of Arundell, And Robert late Earle of Leyester ; yeelding yearley to the Cofferer of hir Ma^ts [Majesty's] housholde— lxvi^s viii^d. The charge of the new building of one of the Tenem^ts, And the continuall Repairing thereof, hath (As I am enfourmed) cost Serieaunt Haynes—xxxiii^li vi^s viii^d. And the new building of the other, wth the repairing thereof did coste Alexander Glover late Hearde there—xx^li or thereabouts.

Also I am enfourmed, that Serieaunt Haynes doth hold the said ffowre Closes, lying next the said Parke pale, wth thafter pasture of two of the same Closes, beyng the middle Closes ; yeelding yearlie ffiftie loades of hay, to be delivered at the Muse, ffor and twords her Ma^ts [Majesty's] provision there, cleere above all charges ; every loade to contayne 18. hundred weight. And thafter pasture of the other two Closes are to be used for the feede of her Ma^ts Cattell untill the feaste of the Purification of o^r Lady following.

Also I finde one Danyell Clerke one of her Ma^ts servaunts doth now dwell in the Scite of the said howse, wch is A very slender building of Timber and Bricke And hath beene of a larger building, then now it is : ffor some little parte hath been pulled downe of late, to amend some part of the howses now standing ; wch has beene repaired of late, by the said Alexander Glover Heard there : And other some part being two Roomes, whereof the one Roome contayneth in breadth w^thin the wall 15 foote ; And in lengthe 24 foote ; And thother Roome is 15 foote broade, and in length 34 foote very greatlie decaied, wch will coste to be repaired—lx^li at the least. And the said cheife howse, one Stable, and two barnes, And A little Close called Ponde Close, wth the Ortcyard, And the two Closes called Murrells mentioned in the platt are used to be fedd wth her Ma^ts Cattell, At the discretion of her Ma^ts Officers.

6^t Aprilis 1.5.9.1

p̃. me Willm̃ Nector."

NOTE ON AGAS'S MAP AT THE END OF THE VOLUME

RALPH AGAS was born about 1540. He was a land-surveyor, and his chief claim to notice lies in the three maps or plans he made of London, Oxford, and Cambridge. Of these the one reproduced in this volume, entitled "A Survey of the Cities of London and Westminster, the Borough of Southwark and parts adjacent," was engraved by Edward J. Francis, and edited by W. H. Overall, F.S.A. Mr. Overall made a careful examination of all the facts, and believes that the original map of Agas was not made earlier than the year 1591, though it has been commonly supposed to have been made about 1560. Of the original, two copies are extant —one in the Guildhall, and the other in the Pepysian Collection at Magdalen College, Oxford.

In 1737 G. Vertue published a copy of Agas's map, altering the original in many important particulars, which are enumerated by Mr. Overall in his account of the map. Among these may be mentioned the water-bearers seen off Tower Stairs and the Steelyard, filling their casks, which are slung across the backs of horses, by the aid of a long-handled ladle. In Vertue's map this interesting detail is turned into a meaningless one, namely, a man driving cows into the water with a whip. In Agas the figures seen in the fields are in Elizabethan costume; in Vertue's map they are in the costume of William III.'s reign. Other particulars omitted in Vertue are the royal barge in mid-stream off Baynard's Castle; the Martello Tower at the mouth of the Fleet; the Chapter House and the Church of St. Gregory on the south side of St. Paul; and various other points. By noting these details, Vertue's spurious reproduction can be at once distinguished from the genuine map of Agas.

INDEX

INDEX

THE END

Printed by R. & R. CLARK, LIMITED, *Edinburgh.*